MW00975200

Exchange & Outlook: Constructing Collaborative Solutions

Duncan Mackenzie
Joel Semeniuk

MACMILLAN
TECHNICAL
PUBLISHING
U·S·A

Exchange & Outlook: Constructing Collaborative Solutions

Copyright © 2000 by MTP

FIRST EDITION: *June 2000*

All rights reserved. No part of this book may be reproduced or transmitted in any form or by any means, electronic or mechanical, including photocopying, recording, or by any information storage and retrieval system, without written permission from the publisher, except for the inclusion of brief quotations in a review.

International Standard Book Number: 1-57870-252-6

Library of Congress Catalog Card Number: 00-100496

04 03 02 01 00   7 6 5 4 3 2 1

Interpretation of the printing code: The rightmost double-digit number is the year of the book's printing; the rightmost single-digit number is the number of the book's printing. For example, the printing code 00-1 shows that the first printing of the book occurred in 2000.

Composed in Quark and MCPdigital by MTP

Printed in the United States of America

Trademarks

All terms mentioned in this book that are known to be trademarks or service marks have been appropriately capitalized. New Riders Publishing cannot attest to the accuracy of this information. Use of a term in this book should not be regarded as affecting the validity of any trademark or service mark. Windows, Exchange, and Outlook are all registered trademarks of Microsoft Corporation.

Warning and Disclaimer

This book is designed to provide information about Microsoft Exchange and Microsoft Outlook. Every effort has been made to make this book as complete and as accurate as possible, but no warranty or fitness is implied.

The information is provided on an as-is basis. The authors and MTP shall have neither liability nor responsibility to any person or entity with respect to any loss or damages arising from the information contained in this book or from the use of the discs or programs that may accompany it.

Publisher
David Dwyer

Executive Editor
Al Valvano

Managing Editor
Gina Brown

Product Marketing Manager
Stephanie Layton

Acquisitions Editor
Leah Williams

Development Editor
Katherine Pendergast

Project Editor
Elise Walter

Copy Editor
Kelli Brooks

Indexers
Cheryl Lenser
Miriam Lowe
Lisa Stumpf

Manufacturing Coordinator
Chris Moos

Book Designer
Louisa Klucznik

Cover Designer
Aren Howell

Composition
SCAN Communications Group, Inc.

Contents

About the Authors

Duncan Mackenzie works for Microsoft Consulting Services, where he spends most of his time helping build the line of business applications based on the Microsoft platform and toolset. Duncan is a Microsoft Certified Solution Developer, System Engineer, and Trainer, but is focused on developing systems with Visual Basic, COM, and the Microsoft Back Office products.

Joel Semeniuk is one of the cofounders of ImagiNET Resources Corp., a Microsoft Development Partner located in Winnipeg, Manitoba. Joel has a degree in computer science from the University of Manitoba and has worked as a Microsoft Certified Trainer across North America, as a System Architect and Developer for large international firms, and as a Project Manager for IBM and ImagiNET Resources. Joel has had the opportunity to work with Microsoft Exchange Server since its early Alpha stages. He is dedicated to working with organizations to help them realize the potential collaborative possibilities with the power set of integrated products that Microsoft provides.

About the Technical Reviewers

Todd O. Klindt has been working with Exchange since version 4.0 and received the MCSE certification in August of 1997. He currently works at Engineering Animation, Inc., as a PC systems and Exchange administrator. He can be reached at todd@klindt.org.

Wesley H. Peace is an MCSE and senior consultant in the Transaction Services Practice for NCR Corporation. As a consultant, he specializes in the delivery of Microsoft services to a wide client base. He specializes in Exchange Server, Windows 2000, System Integration and Architecture, as well as other advanced Microsoft applications. He is also a contributing author to *Exchange Server Survival Guide* and *Exchange Server 5.5 Unleashed*, published by SAMS.

Dedication

This book is for the two most important people in my life. My wife Candice, whose patience and understanding is unmatched by anyone I know. Candice, I'm actually coming to bed now. And to my son Joshua, who will someday look at this book and understand why daddy was so very tired for such a long time.

I thank you both for giving my life more fulfillment than I ever thought possible.

Joel Semeniuk

To my wife Laura, whose support and patience have allowed me to continue my writing.

Duncan Mackenzie

Acknowledgments

I would first like to thank Duncan for introducing me to the world of writing books. I would also like to thank everyone at MTP who has worked so hard to help keep us focused, on track, and accurate. You are all perfect examples of true professionalism in this industry.

Joel Semeniuk

I would like to thank my friend Joel who asked me to work with him on this project. I would also like to extend my gratitude to everyone at the various branches of MTP with whom I have worked over the last two years.

Duncan Mackenzie

Introduction

This book is divided into three sections that build upon one another. The first section establishes a base (Why build collaborative solutions?), and is followed by a section on the tools that can be used to build collaborative solutions. The third section demonstrates how you should plan and design effective collaborative solutions. It also presents the appropriate amount of implementation detail to help any collaborative development process. The goal of this book is to provide a concise set of ideas, strategies, tools, and insight on how to build advanced collaborative solutions for companies and information technologists who want to extract the most functionality out of their Microsoft infrastructure. This book assumes that all underlying technology is from Microsoft.

Part I: What Kind of Puzzles Can We Build— Collaborative Possibilities

This section describes the reasons most corporations have to create advanced collaborative solutions. Instead of jumping into technology and implementation detail, this section first outlines some common collaborative solutions that can be built using the tools and technologies described in the remainder of the book. In essence, this section establishes the business case for developing collaborative solutions while bringing forth a vision of the growing collaborative potential for business.

Part II: Pieces of the Puzzle—The Components of Collaboration

Part II of this book describes the specific technologies that can be used together to build and extend the workflow/collaborative functionality of Microsoft Exchange Server. Generally, this section explains all the tools you can use and provides a general description of how those tools and products can work together to create the final solution.

Additionally, this section focuses on all of the products that can be utilized to create advanced collaborative solutions. This section describes the collaborative functionality provided by Outlook 2000, Office 2000, Microsoft Exchange 5.5, Visual Studio 6.0, and of course, the World Wide Web.

Part III: Laying Out the Pieces—Designing and Developing Collaborative Solutions

After all of the pieces have been identified, you need to address how the pieces fit together to build particular types of collaborative solutions. This section identifies the types of collaborative solutions you can create and how you can use each tool to construct them. Also, this section recognizes any design and implementation constraints you need to consider and address.

Intended Audience

This book is intended for a fairly broad audience. It touches many areas that other collaborative solution books do not. First, we justify collaborative development, which should appeal to most business managers and higher end IT managers. Next, we lay out what is needed to construct a comprehensive collaborative solution, which should appeal directly to IT managers as well as architects, project managers and technical leads. Then, we describe how the tools work. Finally, we provide enough low-level technical information to provide a strong basis for any developer destined to implement a final solution.

Overview of Collaborative Development

This chapter will discuss the following topics:

- **Why You Should Collaborate**
  In this section, we will explore some of the reasons that corporations should invest time and money into an advanced collaborative environment.

- **Examples of Collaboration**
  This section provides some examples of both effective and ineffective collaborative solutions you can build in the workplace.

- **Defining Aspects of Collaboration**
  Here, we will define aspects of successful collaborative solutions.

- **The Future of Collaboration**
  The future of computing, let alone collaboration, is an extremely vast and unpredictable place; however, there seem to be trends that you can successfully rely upon to help forecast this future. This section describes some of those trends to help build a picture of a collaborative tomorrow.

Why You Should Collaborate

Is it just me or is the amount of information the modern working professional needs to manage and absorb on a daily basis reaching a critical mass? What happens when this critical mass is reached? Simple—our brains explode! Not a nice picture, is it? However, I believe that most organizations today are faced with the ever-increasing demands placed on information management.

Consider the following. There once was a time when a simple pulp and paper mill merely produced paper. Some type of process was designed to take logs into one end of the mill and spew processed paper out of the other side. The day-to-day activities of the mill focused on keeping it running to maintain standard production throughput. Typically, it was established that the mill would be able to produce X amount of paper over a given time period with slight variances produced by maintenance activities. Well, times have changed considerably in this regard. Now, mills are highly automated, recording gigabytes of process data at every step of the production process. Every recordable detail is gathered and relayed to some very sophisticated hardware and software whose sole purpose is to make the paper production process more efficient over time.

What does the previous example have to do with this book? If you read carefully, you might notice that I wrote "gigabytes of information." Somehow, the modern-day paper mill is capable of using all this information to make complex decisions regarding adjustments its production processes to ensure that optimal manufacturing levels are met and maintained over time. In a way, this is exactly what this book is attempting to shed light on—absorbing and managing information in the work place to streamline and enhance your business processes.

In fact, your day-to-day activities are much like the processes of the production mill. You can consider yourselves like the massive and complex computers managing gigabytes of data collected during the mill's production process. However, instead of getting your information from little devices that collect raw data off of the production line, you typically gather information from your peers. After the mill's computer systems assimilate the data, they can then analyze it and modify the mill's processes to ensure efficiency. Just like the mill's computers, you are also expected to provide feedback to those who provide you with information to ensure that you complete the required aspects of your job.

Managing and disseminating information is the entire heart of collaboration. The *Webster's Encyclopedic Dictionary* states that the definition of collaboration is "to work together, especially on work of an intellectual nature." Collaboration is not a new concept. What is new are the methods of collaboration and the demands placed on the efficiency of collaborating in the modern work force. Why should you collaborate? Because you need to! If you don't, you will meet one of two possible destinies. The first: Your organization will continue its survival, but at a heavy management and organizational cost, which might mean losing an extremely important competitive edge. The second: Your brains explode!

Managing Information Correctly

Computers are here to help us, right? You might think that this is the case; however, in my experience I have observed the opposite. Many organizations do not use the typical desktop computer to its fullest extent, or even for the services it was intended to provide. In fact, many organizations seem to use computers as glorified typewriters. I am always astonished at the number of organizations that still have policies requiring printed copies of all correspondence, including faxes, documents, and even email! Can you believe a technology that can execute millions of instructions per second is used as a glorified word processor? This is like using the heat generated from a nuclear power plant to make toast. Let me try to clarify my point with an example. The following is a day in the life of a typical consultant working for a fictional networking consulting company called Pro-to-Call.

Bill, a senior project·manager for the company Pro-to-Call, arrives at work at 8:00 a.m. sharp every day. Bill is the project manager for many ongoing projects with various clients throughout the metropolitan area. To effectively manage his time, Bill has decided to equip himself with the latest and greatest technologies, such as a hand held Windows CE device, a powerful laptop computer, and a desktop computer connected to the corporate network for use when he is actually in the office. In addition to the work Bill needs to perform for his clients on an ongoing basis, he also needs to ensure that Pro-to-Call can invoice appropriately for his time. This typically means that Bill will spend approximately 15 minutes per week filling out a Microsoft Excel-based time sheet used for project tracking and invoicing. Because Bill is extremely diligent at recording all his meetings and appointments in his CE Calendar, Bill uses this information to help him construct his weekly time sheet. He simply scrolls through his CE Outlook Calendar a day at a time and manually tallies the time he spent at each client.

Additionally, Bill manages nine technical resources. He gathers his team's hours via email once per week and consolidates them into a Microsoft Excel spreadsheet that he submits to the billing department for invoicing. This process typically takes approximately one hour of Bill's time per week. In addition to recording the hours each member of his team has spent on a given project, status and update information is included with each email he receives from them.

Weekly status reports are required by Pro-to-Call from all of their consultants to record the client activity for that week. Bill spends an additional two hours per week filling out client status reports and submitting them via email to the project control office. Status reports are typically created from Bill's memory, saved emails, and scratch notes he has made during meetings in his notebook.

Bill's clients also require status reports. Bill spends an additional one hour per client per week creating Weekly Client Reports that are printed and delivered to the client in hard copy. Weekly client reports are typically assembled by cutting information from existing client status reports, which were previously created for internal purposes, and pasting the contents into the weekly client reports, which are given to the client.

Additionally, month end status reports must be submitted on the third Thursday of every month. Month end status reports are executive summaries of what has been accomplished during the previous month and what is to be expected in the coming month. Diligently, Bill pores over old weekly status reports to assimilate monthly status information. He then creates a Microsoft Word document from a customized corporate template to enter the data and submits the document via email to the project control office. Typically, monthly status reports take approximately three hours to complete.

After time sheets have been submitted by all the employees, the recorded hours are reentered into an off-the-shelf time and billing package used to generate time report summaries and invoices. The job of reentering all the time sheet information into the time and billing package takes approximately three hours per week for a data entry clerk. The process of generating invoices from the entered hours takes an additional four hours every two weeks.

Status reports are gathered on a weekly basis by the project control office and assimilated into one large Microsoft Word file that is saved on the corporate e-file system. Typically, the process of consolidating status reports takes an average of three hours of time and is performed by a data entry clerk.

In addition to status reports and time sheets, Bill must also take time to attend mandatory biweekly project manager meetings. The purpose of project manager meetings is to allow project managers within Pro-to-Call to share information and insight on issues they have addressed. Typically, project manager meetings are three hours long.

Upon first glance, it seems that this company has its act together. Bill seems to be using the technology that he possesses efficiently. Email is the primary source of communication between employees, and most of the flow of information is electronic—which is good for trees. Pro-to-Call also seems to have a very well established process of recording and reporting information, which shows that they have placed a great deal of thought into their business process. Or does it? If we examine this process a bit closer, we will see that the flow of information from technical resource to the project manager to the client and project control office is still very much paper based, minus the paper.

What is a paper process minus the paper? Take a close look at the methods that Pro-to-Call employees use to transfer information between each other. When Bill receives emails from consultants he manually tallies their hours and reenters them into a second email. The process of submitting hours is really no different than a written note placed on Bill's desk. I know, the electronic version is faster, more efficient, and easier to organize. However, the information, which in this case is the number of hours each technical resource has spent on Bill's project, is not immediately usable. This means that the information needs to be reentered into another format to be used in a consolidated fashion.

What is the flaw in the preceding example? After we observe the entire flow of information, we begin to realize that it is modeled on a paper-based flow of information. Pro-to-Call probably had some pre-established method of transferring information between employees that was based on paper—such as weekly time sheets and project status reports. When Pro-to-Call decided to use computers more efficiently, they simply used them to model an existing paper-based business process; and this, as you have seen, leads to an extremely inefficient way of transferring information.

Now, don't get me wrong. I am not saying that all paper-based processes are bad. What I am stating is that there are always other ways of looking at information management. We need to utilize and construct new ways of entering, transferring, and using the hoards of data that we manage daily using the technology at hand. If we don't, our computers are nothing more than an overpriced typewriter and in-basket.

The Signal-to-Noise Ratio of Information

Not only is there a lot of information in our lives, but there are bags of informational garbage we must sift through to find the personally relevant information. You're probably thinking, "Much like reading this book!" An excellent example of this is trying to find information on the Internet. One day, I searched for my last name (which is not very common as you might have already observed) in one of the more popular search engines of the day. Interestingly, the search engine reported over 200 results, none of which had any relationship to my last name. Not very useful is it? The stuff you don't want to get back in a search result is *noise*. All the stuff you want returned from the search query is *signal*. The higher the signal and the lower the noise means that you don't have to waste your precious time sifting through useless information to get what you want. When the opposite is true, you might experience a situation similar to the one I had when searching for my name on the Internet—you might get a whole lot of useless information.

What we really need is a set of tools that we can use to automatically sift through heaps of information to pull out and organize the data that we need. This is a key concept of advanced collaboration. Well built collaborative solutions help minimize the noise that we manually filter through and maximize the signal we need to do our jobs. Additionally, a thoughtful collaborative solution helps to organize our information into manageable and meaningful collections allowing us to extract the most meaning out of the least amount of information.

Defining Collaboration

It is time to define what I mean by *advanced collaboration*. After our previous discussion, we can safely say that advanced collaborative solutions should satisfy the following criteria:

- The collaborative solution should be based on the actual requirements placed on the management of information, not on an existing paper-based business processes.

- Information should be introduced into the collaborative solution only once. Additionally, the information entered should be maintained in a structured format so that it can be utilized at additional data management points.

- Emphasis should always be given to gathering and circulating only required information to reduce the demands placed on managing information that is not needed.

- All data should be entered, stored, and manipulated electronically as much as possible.

- Inserting new data into the collaborative environment should be performed as seamlessly as possible to reduce data entry tasks that are mundane and error prone.

- The collaborative solution should always be robust enough to handle changing business practices without extensive rework of the fundamental architectures and technologies that define the solution.

Obviously, not every collaborative solution will fit the preceding criteria. However, you should always try to keep in mind the overall goals of the processes that you are trying to improve. Additionally, you might not have the ability to reach all the preceding criteria with one solution because typically the development of complex collaborative solutions are performed iteratively and rolled out over time. This means that there is a great deal of overlap with existing business processes until the entire solution is created.

Collaborative Possibilities

After discussing what collaboration should be, let's take a look at some collaborative possibilities that are well within your reach and are easier to implement than you might think.

Let's visit Bill from Pro-to-Call again. However, in this scenario, Pro-to-Call has taken the time to analyze how it can better use technology to streamline its business.

Bill, a senior project manager at a high-tech computer consulting firm called Pro-to-Call, begins work at 8:00 a.m. sharp every day. Bill is the project manager for many ongoing projects with various clients throughout the metropolitan area. To effectively manage his time, Bill has decided to equip himself with the latest and greatest technologies, such as a hand held Windows CE device, a powerful laptop computer, and a desktop computer connected to corporate network when he is actually in the office. In addition to servicing his clients, Bill also ensures that the appropriate time is billed against his projects. Bill is in charge of nine technical resources and must manage and approve the time each resource has spent on his project. To help ease this burden, each of Bill's technical resources is also equipped with a hand held Windows CE device, and each resource is responsible for recording all client activity performed during the day into his CE Calendar while assigning standard project and work codes for each of his tasks. Once per day, each of the technical resources is required to synchronize the data contained on his hand held CE device with his desktop computer connected to the corporate LAN. Every Monday morning, Bill receives an automatically generated email that summarizes the hours and tasks performed by each of his nine resources on his project over the previous week. Bill has the opportunity to approve or disapprove the submitted hours. After the submitted hours and tasks have been approved, the hourly information is automatically entered into the corporate accounting package and is used to generate invoices to the client. Bill's hours are also included in this process.

When recording client activity data into the hand held Windows CE device, status information is also gathered. This status information is automatically assembled and used when project managers generate status reports for the client or for internal review processes.

In addition to his many client-focused activities, Bill must also take time to attend mandatory biweekly project manager meetings. The purpose of project manager meetings is to allow project managers within Pro-to-Call to share information and insight on issues they have addressed over the past two weeks. The information that is shared between project managers is based on client status reports and billing reports that have been automatically generated and emailed to each of the project managers the day before the meeting to encourage early review. The process of reviewing the reports prior to the meeting allows the meetings to be as short and to the point as possible.

So, what makes the second example so much better than the first? First of all, a lot less time is taken to manage the flow of information. Data is entered once and is instantly distributed for approvals, invoices, and reporting. Comparing this example with the first, you can see that this saves approximately 12 to 15 hours a month of Bill's time. Bill can spend that extra time being a project manager instead of a very expensive and highly educated typist.

Secondly, there is a great deal less error in the data. The first example discussed a process where employees email their hours to Bill. Bill then correlates and retypes the team's hours into an Excel spreadsheet. Additionally, before an invoice can be generated, the hours need to be typed in again into an off-the-shelf time and billing package. Here, there are three possibilities for the introduction of errors into the data. The second example eliminates these points of errors by ensuring that data is entered only once. Of course, entering the correct data into the overall process is in the hands of the employee, but it was to begin with. Additionally, you might notice that Bill is responsible for viewing a report of all hours and status information before the data is sent to the invoicing department. This acts as a data validity checkpoint that helps minimize errors and omissions in data.

Let's look at Table 1.1, which reflects the time and money savings the second example provides over the first, looking only at Bill and his technical resources.

Table 1.1   Collaborative Time Savings

Description	Time Required (Scenario 1)	Time Required (Scenario 2)	Time Savings (per month)
Tracking Daily Activities	15 min per day per person.	15 min per day per person.	0
Submission of Hours and Status	1 hour per week per person.	None, hours are submitted automatically.	40 hours (1 hour per person - 10 people over a month)
Generating Weekly Status Reports	2 hours per week.	None, status information can be gathered automatically.	8 hours

Description	Time Required (Scenario 1)	Time Required (Scenario 2)	Time Savings (per month)
Generating Client Status Reports	1 hour per week.	None, status information can be gathered automatically.	4 hours
Generating Month End Status Reports	3 hours per month.	None, status information can be gathered automatically.	3 hours
Total savings per month			55 hours

Of course, this example is completely fictitious. However, it does serve to make a point: By managing information differently and exploiting the functionality that technology provides, you can greatly enhance the way you do business in addition to reducing your day-to-day paper chase burden. I'm not sure about you, but by reducing the amount of time I need to spend writing and rewriting mundane information, my outlook of the day is greatly affected in a positive way. And that is good for everyone.

Instant Routing and Approval

What we haven't talked about yet is the ability to electronically route and approve information. This ability is key to most advanced collaborative solutions. Think of the approval processes as a checkpoint. Not only do you use approval processes to say "yes" to expenses or vacations, but you can also use approvals as a data validation technique.

In any case, routing and approvals seem to go hand-in-hand. Think of a legal document that needs to be drawn up and signed between parties in two different cities. First, the contract is drawn up by one of the parties and faxed to the second party. If the receiving party simply signs and files the contract without informing the first party, the contract is not legally binding. Generally, when you approve something, you usually tell someone about the approval as well as forward any required or relevant information. In an advanced collaborative solution, the approval process is typically one stop of information in the routing process as it continues its journey.

In the simple case, routing and approvals can be accomplished using basic email. For example, Bill, from our previous example, can send a quick email to his supervisor asking: "Can I book holidays from December 23, 1999 to January 4, 2000?" Bill's supervisor can simply reply stating "NO." Or, in another scenario, reply "Yes," forwarding Bill's request to someone in the human resource department of Pro-to-Call for formal processing.

This simple case would seem to work more often than not. However, what if your organization has a more complex approval process? Additionally, what if you want to ensure that *only* the destined approver(s) actually approved the request? For example, think of some form of war time military organization. Just pretend that this organization uses some collaborative system to select and approve bombing targets. This collaborative solution must ensure that appropriate approvals and processes have been met before the actual bombing takes place. Additionally, you want to make darn sure that the people doing the approving are who they are supposed to be and not just someone who casually walked by a logged on PC. In this example, the advanced collaborative solution would employ predetermined routing tables and digital certificates to ensure that the appropriate approval routes are always taken and impersonation of the approver never occurs.

Even the most complex routing/approval solutions are extremely easy to implement using the technologies and techniques provided in this book. We will come back to implementation details of such a solution in Chapter 14, "Designing and Building Workflow Solutions."

Entering Data Once

The second narrative regarding Bill from Pro-to-Call touches on a very important point. Data should be entered into the system only once. Why should data need to be entered, re-entered, and then re-entered again to be useful? Email, even though it does define the very heart of modern electronic collaboration, is simply not enough to effectively transfer data between two people in a useful and reusable manner. Finding better ways of acquiring and entering new information into your collaborative world is required. These new ways should not place any unnecessary burden upon those who are gathering the information. Additionally, the information that is gathered should be inserted into your collaborative solution in such a manner that you do not have to manually manipulate it for it to be available or useful to others.

If you look at our second scenario, Bill and his technical resources never actually fill out a time sheet. Hours that they spend working on Bill's project are automatically assimilated into centralized corporate data. How is this accomplished? In our example, each consultant uses a Windows CE device to track all of her appointments and tasks using the CE Calendar. Pro-to-Call modified the appointment entry form to prompt for corporate work code and project code information. This means that every appointment and task can be tracked by project and work codes. When the consultants synchronize their calendars with data on the corporate network, automatic events are fired that assimilate this information into a corporate database. The only real requirements placed on the consultants are to accurately record their time and then to synchronize the CE Calendar with their MS Outlook Calendar at least once a day. This doesn't become much of a problem because Pro-to-Call also has developed friendly reminders that prompt consultants to enter calendar information just before lunch and at the end of the day.

Of course, Pro-to-Call is a completely fictitious company; however, the solutions presented in this scenario are completely possible to implement with just a bit of know-how. In fact, by the end of this book, you should have no problem designing and implementing such a system.

Getting at Data—Fast!

Bill did not need to wait for all of his team members to finish sending emails to generate a client activity report. Because all of the information was already entered somewhere in the collaborative solution, it was instantly available for Bill's review and approval.

You shouldn't have to wait to gain access to information that is already available somewhere else. I think I remember reading a phrase or two that talks about "information at your fingertips." This is exactly what I am getting at. If the data has already been recorded, you should be able to generate a report on it. This is not an issue when all of the data is systematically entered and maintained in a central location. Retrieving data instantly in situations that are not as centralized seems to cause a bit more of a problem. Thankfully, with some thought and some powerful tools, you can simplify this process to ensure that the most current and correct data is always accessed.

I touch on an important point in the previous paragraph: The most correct data should be accessed. How do you verify that data is correct? Checkpoints, obviously. In the "Instant Routing and Approval" section of this chapter, we discuss the fact that approvals can be used as data verification checkpoints in a routing process. In fact, approvals are among your strongest strategies to help minimize erroneous data inserted into your ever precious data warehouse.

In our Pro-to-Call example, it is not a good idea for the accounting department to send out invoices to clients based on submitted hours *before* the project manager, Bill, has a chance to carefully check for omissions, errors, or malicious activity. Therefore, you must be sure to base your invoices on "approved" hours to guarantee that no billing issues arise.

The flaw in most workgroup solutions is that it is still the responsibility of individuals to react to and use data that arrives via basic email. For example, I receive about 20 to 30 emails a day and spend approximately five to six seconds reading each email, depending on the size and importance of each message. If I don't see anything too important, I delete the email. If I see something that requires attention, I usually flag the message for follow-up because I am usually in the middle of something when I receive the email. Of course, I set a reminder for the follow-up for about two hours. Basically, even if the email is important, I usually deal with it at some future time. This delay usually negates the instant responses you expect when collaborating electronically with others.

What you need to keep sight of is that a properly designed collaborative solution does not create additional work but, in fact, reduces the amount of work that individuals need to perform a particular task. For example, if I receive an email from one of my employees asking for vacation time approval, I probably have to take the time to check and see how many days the individual has accrued over the year, how many days of holidays the individual has already taken this year, and if any conflicts would arise if the individual were to take his holidays over the requested period. If researching this information takes a considerable amount of time, I will probably put this task off until I have the appropriate amount of time to dedicate to it. However, if much of this work has already been performed for me, my decision could become much more instantaneous and my employee could obtain his approval very close to instantly. For example, there is no reason that the system could not automatically check to see if the individual has accrued enough vacation time for the request. Additionally, my collaborative solution could also check to see if any conflicts would arise from the vacation leave. After all checkpoints have been passed, the system could generate a vacation request email containing summary information, and all I would have to do is say "I approve" or "I do not approve." This would only take seconds, and I could address it as soon as the email arrives in my inbox, instead of putting it off.

So, in essence, email is great. However, because of email, we typically receive a heck of a lot more messages in a day requesting and providing information than someone might have received 20 years ago, thus placing higher demands on our time. We must try to create better collaborative solutions to effectively filter out noise and increase the amount of signal to ensure that we manage information better and at a higher rate.

Future of Collaboration

So what does the future hold for collaborative computing? I believe that we have only started realizing the importance of changing the way we manage information.

I believe that natural interaction between computers and humans will change the face of collaboration. Full audio/visual interaction between humans and computers is desperately required to help bring down the tremendous learning curve many are still faced with when using computers effectively. However, until we have the hardware and software in place to effectively implement such interfaces, we must make due with what we have: computers that are excellent at gathering and manipulating textual information. We are on the verge of having mainstream desktop computers powerful enough to effectively recognize speech at an extremely fast and accurate rate. Additionally, new database technologies, such as SQL Server 7.0, are making it easier for organizations to store and manipulate data types that were much more difficult to manage in the past, such as images and large amounts of textual and binary information.

I also believe that corporations will need to re-evaluate their technology investment. Businesses will require technology that will enhance their entire business, not a specific business process. Computers should not simply be used to create fancy letters and presentations or even to manipulate small to large amounts of information in a proprietary database format. Complete industry unification regarding how we should store and manipulate data is also required to break away the proprietary walls that prevent our precious information from being utilized in endless other ways.

Currently, we are viewing the birth of such realities. We are observing corporations, such as Microsoft, changing the way we manage our information. The products that Microsoft creates are geared at managing and disseminating information in ways that help break these barriers by ensuring that the storage and retrieval of such information is performed using industry standards, such as HTML, LDAP, SMTP, POP, IMAP, NNTP, and TCP/IP. Microsoft is also working on enhancing and developing new standards that will augment our current spectrum of data management possibilities. It is obvious that after we all talk the same language, we can begin to communicate in ways we can only imagine.

Obviously, Microsoft is not the only entity that is determined to make the management of information easier and more effective. In fact, the general premise of the Internet is the driving force behind all movements to standardize and disseminate data. However, Microsoft's products are the topic of this book, so we will focus all of our attention to its cause.

In the technological future, watch for the following advancements to come to reality:

- The demand for portability will drive the development of smaller devices that are much more robust. Such devices will be permanently connected to an information backbone, and data will literally be at your fingertips and provide a complete natural interface.

- More robust standards will be developed to help transfer information in a more unified and secure way. This will ensure that we will be able to retrieve and cross reference all relevant data, anywhere, regardless of the medium of storage or the products used to manage that storage.

- Bandwidth will need to be addressed in all aspects of computing—from large corporate needs to small companies with only one or two computers to the home user. Currently, bandwidth costs are one of the primary reasons that smaller corporations and organizations fail to effectively collaborate. Greater bandwidth at extremely low costs must be realized.

Our Next Steps

Now that we have taken some time to discuss advanced collaboration, our next step is to learn more about the different classifications of advanced collaborative solutions. We will also take some time to explore these different classifications by creating and discussing various examples that will highlight and further explain the concepts behind the solution as well as provide some explanation as to which classification of collaborative solutions should be used in given environments.

Author's Note

I recommend that everyone reading this book should pick up a copy of Business @ The Speed of Thought, *by Bill Gates. The book is one of the best compilations of technical insight and direction I have ever read. Mr. Gates is an amazing visionary and, I'm quite proud to say, shares my vision of the future.*

Chapter Summary

In this chapter, we discussed the following:

- The reasons that we have to implement advanced collaborative solutions in our business

- Definitions and aspects of advanced collaborative solutions

- The author's look into the future of collaboration

2
Typical Collaborative Development Examples

In the previous chapter, we looked at some of the problems that exist with managing the extreme amounts of information that you deal with on a daily basis. We concluded that there must be some better alternative to brute force and hard work. That alternative is the construction of advanced collaborative solutions in the workplace. In this chapter, we will focus on the various types of collaborative solutions that can be built to help you cope with your information management burden.

Microsoft breaks collaborative development into five categories. In fact, Thomas Rizzo, author of *Programming Microsoft Outlook and Microsoft Exchange* (Microsoft Press, 1999, 0735605092), was the first author I have read who formally uses these categories to classify collaborative development. These classifications seem to work in almost all cases, so I will continue to reference them throughout this book.

The following is a list of the categories that can be used to classify the collaborative applications that can be built using the products and knowledge offered in this book:

- Email-based solutions
- Tracking solutions
- Workflow solutions
- Real-time solutions
- Knowledge management

Of course, not all collaborative applications fit nicely into just one of these categories. In fact, you can think of these categories as non mutually exclusive, because it is conceivable to have more than one of these categories applied to most collaborative solutions that you can build.

Our next task is to dive deeper into the meaning of each of these categories to help you understand what collaborative functionality each presents.

Email-Based Solutions

Let's start with email-based solutions. Although this is the first category in the list, it is not the simplest or most functionally restricted. In fact, quite the opposite is true. Email-based solutions are among the most common type of electronic collaboration that exists anywhere. In fact, there is not much that you need to do to implement effective email-based solutions when you use Microsoft Outlook and Microsoft Exchange, because this form of collaboration is the entire heart of these products.

The root of all email-based solutions is, of course, email. But it doesn't need to stop there. In fact, email-based solutions are those that can be built on the messaging infrastructure and functionality of the underlying email and client services. What does this mean? Basically, email solutions are bound by the functionality of the products they are implemented on. The more functionality that the underlying software and infrastructure can provide, the more sophisticated the email-based solution.

In our case, the underlying messaging infrastructure is Microsoft Exchange, and the messaging client is Microsoft Outlook 2000 (or, you might be so bold as to include the entire suite of products that make up Microsoft Office 2000). Here, you can use Exchange to deliver the messages and Outlook to manage the messages using rules, views, custom programming, and a strong integration into the rest of the Microsoft Office family of products.

Typically, as soon as you install Exchange and Outlook, you have the ability to create enhanced email-based collaborative solutions with little to no effort. With a little more effort, you can easily extend these products to encompass the functionality that is not native to them.

Note

As you can see, Figure 2.1 depicts messages being sent from one user to the next through some messaging infrastructure. I intentionally depicted the messaging infrastructure as a cloud because it really doesn't make a difference at this point and I like clouds.

You might have also noted that your everyday email isn't the only form of message being sent between two people. Email-based solutions can consist of tasks and contact and appointment information. This functionality is usually left in the hands of the email client. For example, Eudora does not have the capability to send and interpret Outlook Task assignment messages. ◆

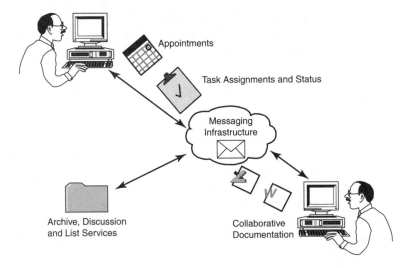

Figure 2.1   *Email-based collaborative solutions.*

What kind of email-based solutions can you build? This really depends on your underlying messaging platform. For example, years ago I used basic POP3 and SMTP mail to collaborate quite effectively using my Eudora mail program. However, I was bound by the type of content that my messages could contain, which back then was an ASCII message body with UUEN-CODED attachments. Today, using suites of products such as Office 2000 and Exchange Server, we have the ability to communicate in an almost unbounded way. We can seamlessly pass contact information, assign tasks, and route Office documents to our peers at the click of a button. Even more interestingly, we can still use POP3 and SMTP as the underlying messaging protocols if we want to; however, the combination of Exchange Server and Outlook provide a more robust messaging platform. This proves that as the functionality of the product increases, so do the bounds of what we can accomplish with email-based solutions.

Here are some examples of collaborative solutions that can be created with email-based technologies. Take note that the following examples require little to no effort when Outlook and Exchange create the base of your messaging infrastructure:

- **Group calendaring.** Group calendaring is very popular in most organizations. Using Group calendaring functionality, you can email meeting invitations to others you want to attend the meeting. When the others receive the invitation, they have the ability to accept or decline the offer. If they accept the offer, a meeting is automatically created in their calendar application and appropriate reminders are set. Group calendaring can also expand to resource scheduling, such as for conference rooms, projectors, and other items that can be booked for periods of time. This allows people to electronically check the schedule of these items, as well as place an immediate booking without anyone else getting involved.

- **Task management.** More and more organizations are using task management features to delegate and track tasks performed in the workplace. In its simplest form, task management allows users to request another to perform some action, such as creating a marketing survey by the end of the week. The delegated task is sent via email and arrives in the destination inbox as a Task Request. Similar to meeting requests discussed previously, the receiving user has the ability to accept or decline the task. If he accepts the task, it is automatically assimilated into his personal task list, and all appropriate reminders are set. In addition, the user who accepts the task can send regular status reports, sent as email messages, to the original sender to keep them updated on progress.

- **Help desk.** A great way to submit non-critical help desk requests is via email. I'm sure that most would use the telephone in more extreme cases. However, non-critical help desk matters can be submitted via an email message. To ensure that all the appropriate data is gathered for the help desk workers, a customized data entry form can be created to uniformly gather all the important information. After this information is gathered, it can be sent via email to a general help desk inbox to await processing. We will discuss more help desk scenarios as we progress in this book.

- **Document libraries.** Document libraries are a great way to organize and store various types of documents you create or receive in the work place. If document libraries simply store the documents in your messaging infrastructure, they provide no more functionality than a simple file system. However, with advanced document libraries, you not only store the document, you also maintain extra Meta information that is used to describe and classify the contents of the data. You can use this Meta information to sort, group, and find related documents much more quickly than you can with a traditional file system. Using email, you can easily submit documents and required Meta data to a central repository where it can be maintained.

- **Discussion forums.** Discussion forums provide a way for a large number of people to communicate with one another using email. However, instead of emailing questions and responses to everyone all at once, all content is mailed to a centralized location: the Discussion Forum. Here, all the content is maintained in conversation threads. Users of discussion forums have the ability to simply read the messages in the forum or add content to the forum by submitting to the forum. Advanced discussion forums are not limited to simple textual discussions. They can have complex and graphical interfaces that allows for enhanced forms of communication.

- **List services.** List services are much like the discussion forum discussed in the preceding paragraph, with a few major exceptions. Instead of having users go to the content, all new content comes to the users. This means that there is typically only one contributor to the content of a list service. When new content is published, subscribed users are presented with the content in the form of an email message. These email messages can take on many forms, ranging from simple ASCII text to more advanced HTML pages with embedded active content.

- **Anonymous suggestion.** Anonymous suggestion solutions allow people to submit suggestions or criticism regarding some issue in the form of email messages. After the email message is received by the anonymous suggestion solution, it is stripped of all header information that could be used for identification, thus preventing the receiver of the message from knowing who might have sent the message. Anonymous suggestions solutions are used by many organizations to allow its members to speak freely about business processes, corporate policies, and personnel without the threat of consequence.

- **Mail management agents.** Mail agents are advanced email management tools that sort and manipulate email as it is being received based on message content and/or sender. Corporations can deploy corporate mail agents to unify how mail is organized in their collaborative environment. Mail management agents can be very simple, such as agents that automatically delete mail older than a given number of days, or advanced, such as mail management agents that automatically respond to incoming email in ways that are based on message content.

The preceding list does not encompass all the ways that you can use email to collaborate. In fact, I'm sure that you can probably devise a dozen other solutions that can be developed using basic email communication.

Tracking Solutions

The second group of collaborative applications is tracking solutions. Tracking solutions provide the functionality that you might expect—they track stuff. Business has always required the capability to record events, documentation, conversations, and actions for future reference. Tracking solutions, as shown in Figure 2.2, help to accomplish these goals.

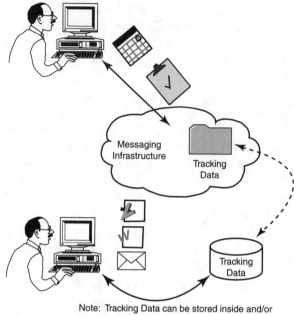

Note: Tracking Data can be stored inside and/or
outside of the Messaging Infrastructure

Figure 2.2   *Tracking solutions.*

Note

The tracking solution diagram might need a little explanation. As we have already stated, tracking solutions provide you with the ability to record various actions or events regarding objects represented in your environment. Figure 2.2 demonstrates that you are not restricted to where you can store your data. In fact, you might want to store the tracking data within your messaging infrastructure, such as Outlook Journaling (a topic we will discuss in Chapter 5), or outside your messaging infrastructure, such as in Microsoft SQL Server.

Additionally, with some further effort, you can integrate many platforms together to form one unified tracking solution. This allows you to exploit the appropriate functionality that each of your products provides. ◆

Tracking solutions can stand alone or be part of a much larger workflow collaborative solution. Examples of stand-alone tracking solutions include the following:

- **Contact activity tracking**. Contact activity tracking provides businesses with the capability to record the various forms of interaction that transpire between people inside or outside of an organization. For example, sales people might want to record all the messages, phone calls, email, or documents regarding particular people in a corporate contact list.

This activity allows the sales people to keep accurate track of all sales activity, which helps them to become better sales people. Effective contact activity tracking makes it very easy for users to record the transpired activity to the point that it can be completely automatic. For example, an effective contact activity tracking solution should automatically record all emails sent to and from contacts in a contact list. This lifts the burden of entering this form of activity information from the user.

- **Help desk tracking.** Help desk employees need to meticulously maintain status information on open help desk tickets. This means that there should be some way of recording when the ticket was submitted, when and who worked on the ticket, as well as what was done to resolve the problem. This information can also be used for long-term statistical analysis. An effective tracking solution helps make these tasks as seamless as possible.

- **Project status reports.** Weekly status reports are typically gathered over time. A project status report tracking solution would allow team members to submit status information electronically. The tracking solution automatically records the time and date of the submission, the status reporting period, and the individual who submitted the status data.

- **Service activity.** You might want to record all service activity performed on equipment, such as computers or vehicles. Such a tracking solution records information, such as the reason for service, the date and time of service, and the cost of servicing every time the item is serviced. This allows you to maintain a service history for any given asset.

- **Employee evaluations.** Every time an employee is evaluated, the results of the evaluation can be stored electronically in a tracking solution. Every evaluation for every employee can be recorded and maintained over time. This information can then be compiled and used to generate concise performance reports for annual reviews.

An example of a tracking solution that is part of a much larger collaborative environment might be a task and project management solution. An advanced task and project management application employs many forms of tracking, but it also requires some controlled flow of information between users who are expected to interact on the project. For example, it is simply not enough for a project manager to track the hours of each of her team members who works on a given project. The project manager must also consolidate and approve such information to submit to the billing department for invoicing. The obvious requirement for including some form of workflow control leads us into our next section.

Workflow Solutions

It is my personal opinion that we have only begun addressing the benefits of introducing complete workflow solutions in business. So many modern corporations have begun to realize that if they want to maintain any competitive advantage they must be able to adjust to the new information management demands placed on them. Complete workflow solutions solve many issues. For example, developing workflow solutions forces corporations to analyze how and why data is managed, and this form of analysis can provide very useful insight into their complex business processes. In fact, many corporations find that when attempting to improve business processes, workflow solutions are an extremely important tool in increasing efficiency and cutting processing costs.

What are workflow solutions? Some argue that sending simple email is workflow. However, this isn't the case. Workflow solutions are typically built on top of an existing email infrastructure, but they constitute much more than simple email messages. Workflow is the result of merging business rules and processes with the electronic flow and storage of information. Instead of leaving the responsibility of controlling the flow of information to the individual employee, business rules are defined and enforced by the collaborative solution. In fact, the workflow application enforces all business rules all the time, ensuring complete unification of business processes in the entire organization. This allows individuals to be less concerned with the overall business process and more focused on their jobs.

Note

As you can see in Figure 2.3, workflow solutions are the most fun to implement. In the diagram, you can see that A sends a request to B. B has the opportunity to accept or deny the request. If denied, the result is forwarded back to A. If accepted, the request is passed along to C.

Also note that our messaging infrastructure is now a smart messenger. This means that all the corporate business logic is integrated into the core-messaging environment. When A sends a request, it is the job of the messaging infrastructure to determine who receives the request. This means that to implement such solutions, you need a method of representing organizational structure in your collaborative solution you need to define business logic that is responsible for controlling the flow of information between the organizational units. ◆

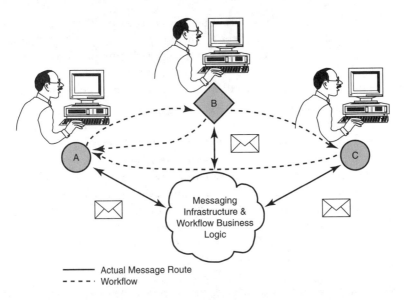

Figure 2.3   *Workflow solutions.*

Here are some general examples of common workflow solutions that are typically implemented to help fulfill one or more specific business requirements:

- **Vacation requests.** A workflow-based vacation request solution allows employees to simply request vacation time. Every vacation request is forwarded to the employee's manager. If the manager approves the vacation, the request is forwarded to the human resource department for final approval and processing. If the manager rejects the vacation request, a message is sent back to the employee. The collaborative solution maintains the employee/manager hierarchy and it assists the person in the human resource department responsible for final processing.

- **Time sheet submissions.** Workflow can also be applied to time sheet submissions. For example, when time sheet information is submitted, the data is typically passed to someone within the organization whose responsibility is to correlate and consolidate the information. After this process is performed, the results can be forwarded to others for additional processing or review. The employees do not need to know who requires the time sheet information because the components that make up the workflow solution maintain all routes and processes.

- **Help desk.** Help desk solutions not only require adequate tracking, as described in the previous section, they also require forms of workflow.

Here, you can conceptualize a help desk scenario where end users submit help desk requests. After the help desk request is received, it is categorized and passed to one or more help desk employees where they employ some technique to resolve the problem. If the problem cannot be resolved, it is escalated and routed to the next level of support staff.

- **Document collaboration.** In many organizations, the process of writing business plans, project summaries, or other corporate material is not left to one person. Document collaboration allows many people to work on the same content, providing feedback and revisions to one another as the content grows. This allows one person to begin composing the documentation. When complete, the document can be automatically forwarded to the next individual or group of individuals for additions or revisions. The process can be completed when the original author is emailed the final version or when the document reaches the appropriate end points.

When defining workflow solutions, the workflow process becomes difficult to determine. All workflow solutions share a clear division between the business rules, the routes that information must take, and particular roles within the organization that act upon the routed information. If you look very closely at all of these examples, you will find that each of them talks about some predefined route between people who fill certain roles. Additionally, the routes seem conditional based on decisions that individuals make during the routing process. In fact, to clarify the matter, you can define workflow solutions as those that clearly define and maintain the following:

- **Roles.** To allow your workflow solution to adapt, you must use roles, such as Manager and CEO, to define the endpoints of routed information. This allows you to apply a more general business rule to control the route that information must follow. For example, if you say that Jim must send a vacation request to Rod, you are defining one specific business rule that only applies to Jim and Rod. However, if you state that all mill operators must forward all vacation requests to their shift manager, you are defining a more generic rule that can be applied to a much wider body of people.

- **Routes and rules.** Routes and rules are nearly inseparable in a workflow environment. Rules define the guts of a particular business process. If the business process that the rule defines includes the flow of information between two or more entities, you've created a route. Hence, rules can define routes. You cannot completely use these two terms interchangeably because not all rules define routes, as you will see when we define more complex collaborative solutions.

- **Data.** Data is, of course, what is traveling between two endpoints in a particular leg of a route. Not only do you define what the data is, but also its format. Some examples of data that might travel a route are project status report data, marketing reports created during document collaboration, or even a simple help desk request. The type of workflow solution being created determines the type and form of the data.

In addition, workflow solutions are not just about routing information from point A to point B. They are also about centralizing and streamlining business processes. This means that you might take the opportunity to implement additional processing at each stop in the route of a workflow solution that will check or manipulate the data in some way (see Figure 2.4).

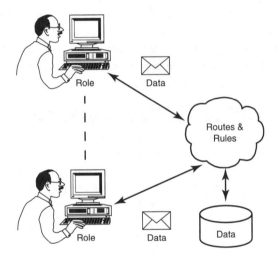

Figure 2.4   *Workflow components solutions.*

Tip

Remember: To effectively design workflow solutions, you must always begin with the business process. ◆

Let's look at the vacation request example. You can add a great deal of checks and bounds to help streamline the process. For example, when a user submits a vacation request, the workflow solution can first check to see if the employee who made the submission has enough vacation time remaining to fulfill the request. This means that the system must first consolidate all the time already taken that year and compare it against the annual vacation time the employee has accrued plus any banked time. If the employee has no vacation time left, the request doesn't need to be forwarded to the employee's manager. This additional processing also saves the employee's manager time because he knows for certain that if he received the vacation request, the employee must have enough vacation time remaining.

I will talk more about designing advanced workflow solutions in Chapter 15, "Designing and Building Knowledge Management Solutions."

Real-Time Solutions

Here is where the real fun begins. Real-time solutions are those that allow users to share information with one another instantly, or as instantly as bandwidth allows. The biggest problem with workflow and email solutions is that they require users to be responsible enough to check their email on a very regular basis. In fact, not only do the users need to check their email, but they also have to respond to that email; and as you know, depending on the number of emails that you receive each day, instant responses are rare. Real-time solutions require instant interaction in real time. They allow interaction between one or more people without delay, similar to conversing over the phone or interacting in a face-to-face discussion.

Note

As you can see from Figure 2.5, real-time solutions are not necessarily tied into a messaging infrastructure, but they do rely on some form of communication system, such as the Internet. I might also point out that even though your messaging infrastructure is not a requirement, it still can be used to support real-time collaboration for reasons, such as maintaining a directory of people you can collaborate with. ◆

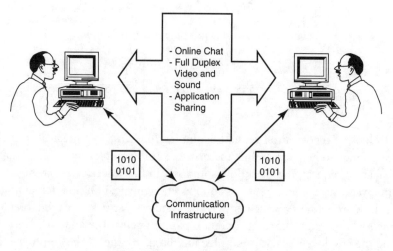

Figure 2.5 *Real-time collaborative solutions.*

Before we go any further, let me provide some examples of some commonly used real-time solutions:

- **Help desk desktop takeover.** Picture the following. You are working on the corporate help desk when you get a support call from a frantic user who thinks he has lost all his work. Instead of talking him through possible scenarios over the phone, you can simply say, "Just let me take a look," and take control of his computer, displaying exactly what he sees on your monitor. This allows you to assess and fix the associated problem without having to step the user through a complicated and confusing process over the phone. This form of collaboration is becoming an extremely important aspect of all help desk centers.

- **Writing this book.** Writing this book has very much been a collaborative effort. When more than one author is responsible for the content, it is extremely important that they communicate as much as possible, and in many cases, communication can include real-time collaboration. Real-time collaboration allows two or more people to review one document at the same time. Additionally, the authors and reviewers can discuss various issues interactively even though none of them are in the same room. This form of interactive brain sharing is essential when meeting timelines and when budgets are constrained.

- **GUI design.** When writing business applications, it is tremendously important that the Graphical User Interface (GUI) is designed to user specifications. In many cases, the process of GUI approval can take extreme amounts of time and can include a large amount of travel if the business client is spread geographically. Using real-time solutions, you can present and discuss a potential GUI to all related parties at the same time. During the real-time presentation, you can walk through graphical elements of your application and make minor modifications as you go. Any real-time collaboration that you can introduce during the development process typically cuts costs and increases customer satisfaction.

- **Virtual meetings.** How many times have you traveled for 45 minutes to attend a meeting only to hop in your car 20 minutes later and make the 45-minute return trip? Real-time collaboration allows you to attend meetings without actually attending the meeting. The first and simplest form of virtual meetings is online chat sessions. The disadvantage with chatting is that someone actually needs to type something before she can be heard, which doesn't always work in some meetings. You can also attend a virtual meeting using full duplex audio and video software that opens the door to a greatly expanded method of interaction.

You might have noticed that I didn't focus on some of the plain old fun stuff you can do with real-time solutions, such as using video phones to call someone for lunch or mounting a camera on the coffee machine so that everyone in the office can see if there is enough for one more cup before making the long walk to the lunch room. These are also very simple to accomplish if you possess the technology and the know-how.

Knowledge Management

It might be difficult to grasp what knowledge management collaboration is because everything we have been trying to accomplish in this book relates to some form of knowledge management. In this case, knowledge management can be explained as knowledge acquisition, dissemination, and reference. When individuals in a corporation obtain or devise specific expertise in a particular area, knowledge management solutions help make this expertise available to others.

> ## Note
>
> *Knowledge management. The biggest catch phrase since intranet. Figure 2.6 depicts users in an organization benefiting from expert knowledge inserted into our knowledge management infrastructure.*
>
> *As in previous discussions, our knowledge management solution is represented using a cloud. This indicates that the implementation detail is quite open for variance. Knowledge can be maintained inside or outside of a messaging infrastructure. In many cases, you need to use the best functionality of many products to represent and access knowledge maintained by your knowledge management solution.* ◆

Our help desk is a great place to use as an example. One of the long-term goals of a help desk is to decrease the time required to solve specific problems. To accomplish this, help desks need to decrease the time their employees spend performing research on new or repetitive problems. It makes sense that if someone else has already solved the problem, the solution should be readily available. Knowledge management solutions help this process by providing two very important features. The first is to allow help desk employees to record all the information gathered during the processing of a help desk ticket. This probably includes information such as the category of problem (hardware, software), the description of the problem (such as error messages), and the eventual solution to the problem. The second knowledge management feature allows help desk employees to perform searches on existing information contained within the knowledge base.

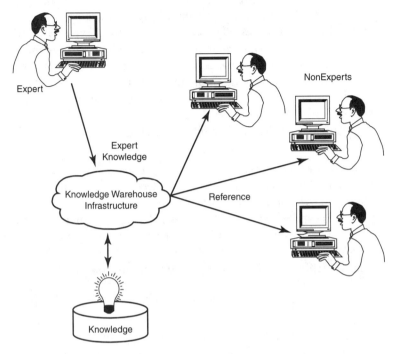

Expert

NonExperts

Expert
Knowledge

Knowledge Warehouse
Infrastructure

Reference

Knowledge

Figure 2.6   *Knowledge management collaborative solutions.*

In essence, knowledge management solutions require the ability to effectively gather and classify knowledge of some form. In addition, knowledge management solutions must provide the means of efficiently allowing users to search the ever-growing knowledge base using key words and categories. This process allows the entire organization to benefit from the discoveries and expertise gathered in the workplace instead of relying on a very small handful of people to solve very specific problems time and time again. This helps the organization leverage the expertise it possesses across its entire environment.

Here are some examples of knowledge management solutions that can be built using the topics described in this book:

- **Help desk knowledge base.** As we have already discussed, help desks require some means of recording the solutions found to the problems that are called in by users. Help desk employees can then employ this information to help solve the same or similar problems much quicker. You can take this a little further by stating that this information could be published across the entire organization providing end users with the ability to search for solutions to common problems directly. This effectively allows users to solve some of their own problems.

- **Vendor-supplied technical knowledge bases.** An example of a vendor-supplied technical knowledge base is Microsoft's TechNet. TechNet is a collection of white paper articles, product documentation, and knowledge base articles regarding discovered support issues. People whose jobs are to support Microsoft operating systems and products can use TechNet to search for solutions to problems or issues they discover. This leverages the support and technical expertise gathered by Microsoft to help technical support people solve problems quicker and cheaper.

- **Medical knowledge bases.** We can easily extend knowledge management solutions to medicine. Very few of us are experienced doctors who diagnose symptoms of serious illness with ease. The non-doctors among us can benefit from this knowledge by categorizing and publishing symptoms and diagnosis information gathered by medical science over the years. Such knowledge bases might someday replace the Family Medical Guide most of us have on our bookshelf.

I could continue with countless examples of knowledge bases that you can build in your environment. What you need to understand is that knowledge bases represent and store information much differently than a typical database, and you should not use the terms interchangeably or get them confused. This does not mean that you cannot use database technology to represent knowledge in a knowledge base, however.

Making the Decision

So what kind of solution will you build for your organization? The problem isn't as complex as it may seem. To help you understand which solution might fit well into your needs, I have created the Collaborative Solution Matrix, illustrated in Table 2.1. This matrix helps define what type of collaborative solution or combination of collaborative solutions you can employ to help design and build advanced solutions in your workplace.

Table 2.1   The Collaborative Solution Matrix

Properties of Collaboration	Email Based	Tracking	Workflow	Real-Time	Knowledge
Data is unstructured.	X*				
Communication is rare.	X*				
Simple send/ response interaction.	X				

Properties of Collaboration	Email Based	Tracking	Workflow	Real-Time	Knowledge
Structure data.					
Static route.	X		X		
Dynamic route based on business rules.			X		
Requires instant response or interaction.				X	
History maintenance.		X			
Provides reference material to others in organization.	X				X
Integrates decision making processes.			X		
Need to capture knowledge, organize, and publish information gathered by people in the organization.	X	X			X

* *Refers to solutions that can be created using text-based email messages.*

Collaboration as a Concept

You might have noticed while reading this chapter that I don't spend any time talking about design and implementation techniques or even about products that could be used to create such solutions. I want you to understand that collaboration isn't about a specific product. Collaboration isn't Lotus Notes. Collaboration isn't Outlook. And collaboration isn't Exchange. When I talk about advanced corporate electronic collaboration, I am referring to the functionality you gain by creating such solutions—and as you have already seen, the solutions seem limited only to your imagination.

Additionally, I want to stress that organizations need to take this approach more often. Many organizations question, "What can I do with Exchange Server?" and mistakenly use the answer to help model their internal processes. This is, of course, the incorrect way of designing and enhancing a business process. Remember that all of this technology is geared to extending and enhancing business and commerce, not the other way around. You should always try to understand how you can first better your business processes, then look to technology to help make those ideas possible.

I'm going to end this chapter with a quote from an amazingly informative book called *Reengineering the Corporation: A Manifesto for Business Revolution*, written by Michael Hammer and James Champy, published by Harperbusiness; ISBN: 088730687X. The quote provides an excellent example of the idea that you must always begin with your business processes.

Extended Quote

Our first case concerns IBM Credit Corporation, a wholly owned subsidiary of IBM, which, if it were independent, would rank among the Fortune 100 service companies. IBM Credit is in the business of financing the computers, software and services that the IBM Corporation sells. It is a business of which IBM is fond, since financing customer's purchases is an extremely profitable business.

In its early years, IBM Credit's operation was positively Dickensian. When an IBM field salesperson called in with a request for financing, he or she reached one of fourteen people sitting around a conference room table in Old Greenwich, Connecticut. The person taking the call logged the request for a deal on a piece of paper. That was step one.

In step two, someone carted that piece of paper upstairs to the credit department, where a specialist entered the information into a computer system and checked the potential borrower's creditworthiness. The specialist wrote the results of the credit check on the piece of paper and dispatched it to the next link in the chain, which was the business practices department.

The business practices department, step three, was in charge of modifying the standard load covenant in response to customer request. Business practices had its own computer system. When done, a person in that department would attach the special terms to the request form.

Next, the request went to a pricer, step four, who keyed the data into a personal computer spreadsheet to determine the appropriate interest rate to charge the customer. The pricer wrote the rate on a piece of paper, which, with the other papers, was delivered to a clerical group, step five.

There, an administrator turned all this information into a quote letter that could be delivered to the field sales representative by Federal Express.

The entire process consumed six days on average, although it sometimes took as long as two weeks. From the sales reps point of view, this turnaround was too long, since it gave the customer six days to find another source of financing, to be seduced by another computer vendor, or simply to call the whole deal off.

...

Eventually, two senior managers at IBM Credit had a brainstorm. They took a financing request and walked it themselves through all five steps, asking personnel in each office to put aside whatever they were doing and to process this request as they normally would, only without the delay of having it sit in a pile on someone's desk. They learned from their experiments that performing the actual work took in total only ninety minutes—one and one half hours. The remainder—now more than seven days on the average—was consumed by handing the form off from one department to the next. Management had begun to look at the heart of the issue, which was the overall credit issuance process.

...

In the end, IBM Credit replaced its specialists—the credit checkers, pricers, and so on—with a generalist. Now, instead of sending an application from office to office, one person called a deal structurer processes the entire application from beginning to end: No handoffs.

How could one generalist replace four specialists? The old process design was, in fact, founded on a deeply held (but deeply hidden) assumption: that every bid request was unique and difficult to process, thereby requiring the intervention of four highly trained specialists. In fact, this assumption is false; most requests were simple and straightforward. The old process had been over designed to handle the most difficult applications that management could imagine. When IBM Credit's senior managers closely examined the work the specialists did, they found that most of it was little more than clerical: finding a credit rating in a database, plugging the numbers into a standard model, pulling boilerplate clauses from a file. These tasks fall well within the capability of a single individual when he or she is supported by an easy-to-use computer system that provides access to all the data and tools the specialists would use.

IBM Credit also developed a new, sophisticated computer system to support the deal structurers. In most situations, the system provides the deal structurer with the guidance needed to proceed. In really tough situations, he or she can get help from a small pool of real specialists—experts in credit checking, pricing, and so forth. Even here handoffs have disappeared because the deal structurer and the specialists he or she calls in work together as a team.

The performance improvement achieved by the redesign is extraordinary. IBM Credit slashed its seven-day turnaround to four hours. It did so without an increase in head-count—in fact, it has achieved a small head-count reduction. At the same time, the number of deals that it handles has increased a hundredfold. Not 100 percent, but one hundred times.

I think you get the point.

Chapter Summary

In this chapter, we discussed the following:

- The different categories that can be used to define collaborative solutions. We also stated that many collaborative solutions could fit into many of these categories at the same time.

- Many examples of collaborative solutions for each of the defined categories. The examples make it easier to understand the meaning and functionality that each of the categories dictate.

- A narrative example written to prove that we should always begin our collaborative solution with business processes.

Part **II**

Pieces of the Puzzle–The Components of Collaboration

3

Overview of Collaborative Tools and Techniques

In the previous chapter, we discussed the different types of collaborative solutions you can create in the work place. Additionally, I boldly stated that the design of an effective collaborative solution must always begin with the business process in a top down approach. Before we discuss how you can design and build advanced collaborative solutions, we must first define the tools and the platforms you can utilize for your construction. In this chapter, I will describe the technological foundations of advanced collaborative solutions that will help lay the canvas for the big picture.

Note

Some readers might find this chapter very "light" because the topics focus on the overall functionality of many different products, as well as how each product fits into the construction of collaborative solutions. Feel free to skim over the areas you are already familiar with, because the sections of this chapter do not entirely depend on one another for continuity. ♦

The big picture is simply the understanding that a successful collaborative solution is a product of *all* the technologies used to create it. You must realize that collaboration is *not* one single product. For example, if you look at a house, what do you look for to determine if it is well constructed? Do you simply look at the type of nails used? Do you look at the quality of the wood? Do you consider the house well built if the concrete that the house is built upon has no cracks? Or, can you simply look to the construction company's reputation to determine whether the house is well built? You cannot simply look at one particular aspect of a house to determine how well it is constructed. This would be similar to a house inspector saying that a house is well constructed by simply looking at the type of shingles used for the roof. In this discussion, you cannot assess the effectiveness of a collaborative solution without looking at the entire set of technologies used to design and construct the solution; hence, in this chapter, I will explore all the products we typically bring together to form a unified collaborative solution.

The Base Products

Every great structure is always set upon an appropriately supportive foundation. Let's take a closer look at the pieces you can use to build a collaborative foundation. We will observe each component at a very high level so that you have a basic understanding of the functionality each component provides, as well as how each technology fits into an overall collaborative solution. Please note that I am not going to cover every aspect of every product. In fact, I will simply define the functionality that you, as collaborative architects and developers, can call upon to design and implement your solution.

Table 3.1 is a summary of the products and technologies that will be covered in this chapter.

Table 3.1   Products and Technologies Covered in This Chapter

Software Products	Development Tools and Technologies
Microsoft Exchange	COM, DCOM, COM+
Microsoft SQL Server 7.0	CDO and MAPI
Windows 2000	Visual Basic, VBA, and Visual Script
Internet Information Server	
Outlook and Office 2000	
Windows CE	

Microsoft Exchange

A few years ago, I conducted a technical seminar in Montreal, Canada. While traveling from Montreal's International Airport, I was amazed at the speed the vehicles traveled, even during rush hour times. I thought to myself, "Why can't we travel at this speed in other cities?" Was it simply because Montreal had better, faster cars with better and faster drivers? As this may well be the case, the conclusion is fairly straightforward. Montreal has a transportation infrastructure that can meet the demands placed on it. You're probably flipping back to the cover asking yourself if you've picked up the correct book. However, this discussion leads to the reason I chose Microsoft Exchange Server as the primary topic of this book. Every efficient transportation system requires an effective transportation infrastructure.

Thus, every successful attempt at building advanced collaborative solutions must also be built on superior infrastructure and messaging technology, and I believe that these requirements are met by Microsoft Exchange Server. Let's take a closer look at the functionality that Microsoft Exchange provides to the collaboration effort. Because this is *not* a book dedicated to Microsoft Exchange in its entire form (which would include administration, performance tuning, deploying, and designing), we will only look at the functionality the product provides as it relates to collaborative development. As with everything else, I'm going to classify each functionality into one of three different categories:

- Messaging infrastructure
- Collaborative storage
- Business modeling

Tip

A great place to get additional information on Exchange Server administration is Exchange System Administration *by Janice Rice Howd, New Riders Publishing (ISBN: 0-7357-0868-1).*

If you need information on implementation specifics, a great reference is another New Riders book, Implementing Exchange Server *by Doug Hauger, Marywynne Leon, and William C. Wade III (ISBN: 1-5620-5955-6).* ◆

Messaging Infrastructure

Let's begin looking at the different functionality that fits into the messaging infrastructure category. Because most collaborative solutions deal with communication in some form, this is the obvious place to start. When designing and building collaborative solutions, you must have an effective messaging transport, and in short, Microsoft Exchange provides a superior messaging infrastructure in almost every aspect.

When defining a good messaging infrastructure, you need to take a look at specific aspects, such as reliability, extensibility, flexibility, and maintainability. The remainder of this section will be devoted to the discussion of these aspects of Microsoft Exchange that make it the perfect collaborative messaging backbone.

Note

Please note that our discussion is concerned with Microsoft Exchange version 5.5 with Service Pack 3, unless otherwise specified. Platinum, version 6 of Exchange Server, additionally provides all of the primary functionality and more; however, we will spend a little more time discussing Exchange 2000 later in this chapter. ◆

Robust Messaging

Using a messaging server, such as Microsoft Exchange, to simply send and receive basic email is one thing. However, using Microsoft Exchange as the core messaging transport for your collaborative applications is a completely different issue that must be addressed separately. Typically, in your collaborative environment, you will require a messaging server that can maintain normal message delivery for an ever increasing number of users, as well as manage all the messages generated by collaboration. These additional messages can be generated from activities, such as workflow and routing, knowledge postings and searches, calendaring and tasking events, and other activities, such as automatic contact activity journaling. Developers of collaborative solutions must rely on their messaging infrastructure to provide superior performance and reliability leaving you to focus on the actual collaborative solution.

Microsoft Exchange was built with these activities in mind. The following aspects of Microsoft Exchange make it one of the world's best and robust messaging platforms:

- **Unlimited message store.** You must ensure that your messaging backbone has enough storage capacity for the load that you will place on it from your collaborative solution. Microsoft Exchange does not limit the amount of messages you can store. In fact, the only limitation is the hardware.

- **Single-instance messaging.** Just because Exchange has an unlimited message store doesn't mean that you should store message content inefficiently. Microsoft Exchange ensures that messages are only stored once in a messaging store. This means that if someone sends 10 people a message on a server, the server only maintains one copy of the message in the message store. This is an important aspect of collaborative computing because some of the messages your solutions might generate can be quite large.

- **SMP capabilities.** Microsoft Exchange was built to use all the hardware that the underlying operating system utilizes. Thus, if Windows NT was installed on a computer with eight processors, Microsoft Exchange has the capability to use all eight processors. There is nothing magical in this capability because Microsoft Exchange conforms to a multi-threaded application model, and each thread can run independently from one another on separate processors. Hence, the greater the number of processors, the greater number of Exchange threads that can run simultaneously.

- **Hot and fast backups.** When implementing collaborative solutions, it is extremely important that developers assume that the infrastructure that supports the solution is up and running all the time. This means that all types of downtime must be minimized. Microsoft Exchange helps reduce downtime by providing the ability to perform hot backups. Hot backups provide the capability for Microsoft Exchange to back up messages without the temporary pause in normal services.

- **Scalability.** What happens when your collaborative backbone cannot handle the load placed on it? Simple: You add new servers. As time goes on, you might need to dedicate certain collaborative services to specific Microsoft Exchange servers, such as dedicated public folder servers. Microsoft Exchange provides for this capability by allowing administrators to simply add a server to an Exchange site. The site automatically recognizes the new server and begins integrating it into the messaging environment by beginning data and directory replication. Client computers do not need to be reconfigured in any way for them to effectively use the services provided by the new server.

- **Advanced message delivery and routing.** When implementing advanced collaborative solutions, you shouldn't need to worry about whether or not a message is successfully sent across a particular link. You can rely on Microsoft Exchange's capability to automatically reroute messages through the messaging infrastructure without any administrative intervention. Microsoft Exchange also attempts to send a message across the least cost route (which is the most efficient route in most cases). If the least cost route is unavailable, the next lowest cost route is chosen.

Robust Content

We just discussed how Microsoft Exchange provides a rich messaging platform for any collaborative application you can conceive. I will now talk a little about the types of messages that can be sent through the messaging infrastructure and how this relates to collaboration.

The format of a message is typically determined by the type of client you are using. For example, if you are using POP3 across a VT100 terminal interface (I still do this once in a while to remind myself how good we have it nowadays), your message content will be limited to straight ASCII text. Most of you probably use extremely robust messaging clients, such as Microsoft Outlook, to send and receive email, allowing a wide range of content options. In most cases, Microsoft Exchange Server allows almost any type of content through its channels because Exchange Server never really deals with the message content, with the obvious exception of messaging gateway content conversions.

Let's take a look at the type of messages you can send and receive over your Microsoft Exchange messaging backbone. I will focus on discussing the types of messages that can be generated using Microsoft Outlook:

- **Rich text messages.** You can now add rich formatting to your mail

messages that includes formatted text, pictures, and embedded documents. In fact, there doesn't seem to be a limit to what your messages
can include. By having the ability to add robust content to your messages, you have the opportunity to express yourselves in a completely
enhanced way. Figure 3.1 is an example of an email that contains rich
message content.

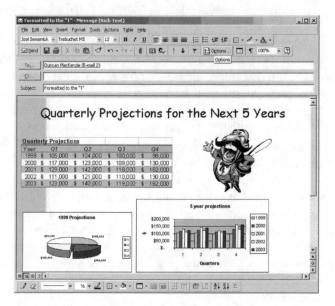

Figure 3.1   *You can see that this email contains some pretty
fancy content: clip art, tables, and Microsoft Excel charts
embedded directly into the message.*

- **HTML.** Who would have ever thought that we would someday be able
  to send HTML in an email message? Microsoft Outlook 98 and 2000
  provide the ability to compose and send emails in HTML format,
  allowing you to send richly formatted graphics and text along with hot
  links to other parts of the Internet in your mail messages. Additionally,
  the size of the message can be minimized by controlling where the
  graphical content is originating. For example, instead of sending all
  the pictures and background images as part of the email message,
  Internet links can be sent instead. When the user opens the email, his
  mail reader automatically connects to and downloads the additional
  graphics. A great example of this is Microsoft's weekly mass email
  "Microsoft: This Week!" This email is in HTML format providing
  summary information of the basic events and tips of the week. Because
  the message is in HTML format, users can click on hot links that take
  them to detailed Web pages on the Microsoft Web site.

- **Office documents.** The body of a message can also be composed of a Microsoft Office document. In fact, Microsoft Office is tightly integrated into Microsoft Exchange, providing the capability for users to save Office documents directly into public folders, email documents to others, and specify office document routing directly from the user interface of Microsoft Office applications. With Office 2000, you can build Team discussion groups and collaboration services, and you can even email PowerPoint presentations that will automatically run when the mail message is opened (however, I haven't quite figured out what that might be used for).

  One great aspect of Office documents is their capability to contain macros that do some work for you. All of the applications that comprise Microsoft Office, such as Excel, Word, and PowerPoint, have robust object models that can be manipulated with the macros embedded into the Office documents. In fact, the macros themselves are written with Visual Basic for Applications (VBA), thus they can call upon the language constructs and integration capabilities of full-blown Visual Basic. When you combine this with the fact that Office documents are easily manipulated and stored within your messaging infrastructure, you now have the facility to send usable Office data along with the applications that manipulate the data. This ability, as you will see in Chapter 9, "Microsoft Office Integration," is an extremely important concept.

- **Outlook message classes.** Enhanced message formatting is great when sending content from one user to another. However, what if the destination of the email is not a user but a process, and you want the process to perform some action based on the type of message sent? This is where Outlook message classes play a part. Outlook message classes are the heart of the default collaborative functionality that Outlook provides, such as appointment scheduling, tasking, journaling, and contact management. Microsoft Outlook uses different message classes to identify each type of message and uses this information to help interpret the data represented in the message.

  For example, if an email is created that has a message class of ipm.note, Outlook interprets the message as a simple email. However, if the email has a message class of ipm.contact, Outlook interprets the message as a Contact item. When the user double-clicks on the message, the contact details are read from the message body and displayedin a Microsoft Outlook contact form (see Figure 3.2). We will continue our discussion of Message Classes in Chapter 5, "Microsoft Outlook 2000 Collaborative Basics."

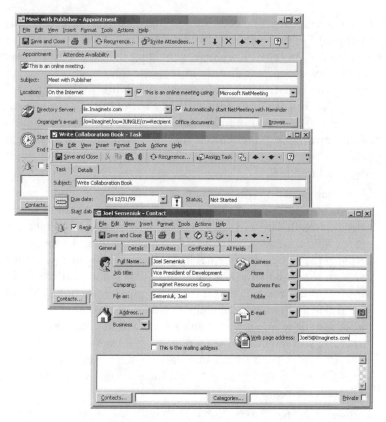

Figure 3.2   *Microsoft maintains a different message class for each type of Outlook item (Calendar items, Contact items, Task items, and so on). When developing collaborative solutions, new message classes can be created to support new functionality.*

Interface with Other Messaging Systems

Even though many messaging standards exist, like SMTP and X.400, not all messaging platforms are built to such conformance. To design and build a complete collaborative solution that can span one or more organizations with different messaging platforms, there must be some way of bridging the communication gap. Microsoft Exchange conforms to all major messaging standards and provides message gateways to many additional messaging systems (see Figure 3.3).

Note

The designation ipm stands for Interpersonal Message Format. This is an X.400 message format. ◆

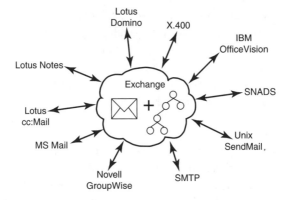

Figure 3.3 *Notice the extent of interconnectivity and integration*
Microsoft provides to and from other messaging systems.
Exchange can only provide messaging connectivity to some
foreign messaging platforms, while providing both messaging
and directory services to others, such as cc:Mail.

Microsoft Exchange Server can send and receive messages from the following messaging protocols and platforms:

- SMTP
- X.400
- Lotus Notes
- Lotus Domino v5
- Lotus cc:Mail
- Profs
- Novell GroupWise
- Unix SendMail
- SNADS
- IBM OfficeVision/VM
- MS Mail

Additionally, Microsoft Exchange supports access to the Information Store using the following protocols:

- HTTP
- POP3
- IMAP4
- NNTP

Please note that even though Microsoft Exchange can send and receive email and directory information from each of the preceding messaging platforms, this does not mean that you can easily build collaborative applications that span these environments. In fact, as you add the complexities of gateways and connectors, you typically sacrifice functionality that otherwise can be added to your collaborative solutions.

Collaborative Storage

Microsoft Exchange not only provides a strong messaging backbone, it also provides a powerful means to store and organize messages. Microsoft Exchange organizes messages in structures called folders. Every folder can contain messages and other folders. Additionally, very similar to a file system, such as NTFS, you can place usage permissions that govern who can manipulate content within the folders. However, unlike most file systems, Microsoft Exchange has a strong mechanism for sorting, filtering, and grouping the contents of folders. This functionality is called a *view*.

Without folder views, MAPI folders would seem to be one messy container of messages. Views allow users of the MAPI folders to organize the messages contained within a folder by placing filters on the messages, sorting the messages, and grouping the messages into message blocks. In fact, views are so powerful that I dedicate an entire section of this book to creating and managing views that will greatly enhance your collaborative applications. We will revisit Exchange Views in Chapter 5.

Speaking more specifically, there are two stores maintained by Exchange Server, the Private Information Store and the Public Information Store. Each user's mailbox is a small slice of the Private Information Store, which is used to store all mailboxes on the Exchange Server. When users use public folders, they are manipulating the contents maintained within the Public Information Store. We will spend most of our time and energy focusing on public folders because they allow users to share information easier than private folders, thus allowing additional types of collaboration to exist. Exchange public folders have a great deal to offer collaborative development. I mentioned earlier that public folders are accessible by anyone who has appropriate access permissions. In fact, by default, there are no restrictive permissions placed on public folders, which allows for instant collaboration. In basic form, public folders are a place for many people to store and review messages (see Figure 3.4).

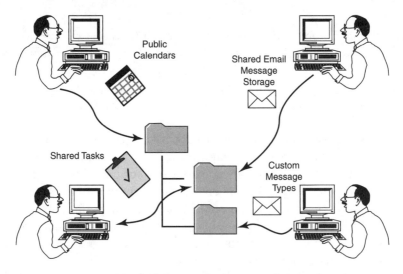

Figure 3.4   *Public folders provide the root collaborative storage mechanism for Exchange Server 5.5.*

Note

One new feature of Exchange 2000 is the provision of a collaborative Web Store that can store an extremely wide range of documents, including email messages, Web files, and Office documents. This feature is also available with Exchange Server 5.5 when Office 2000 and the Office Server Extensions are loaded on an Exchange Server containing IIS.

Exchange 2000's Web Store takes data storage to the next level by merging the best features of file system storage, the Web, and Microsoft Exchange together into one amalgamated method of saving and retrieving information. Expect the following functionality out of Platinum's Web Store:

- *Web browser accessible content for all content stored with Exchange*
- *URL access to all objects in the information store*
- *Consistent access via many different platforms including Outlook, any email client, Windows Explorer, and any browser*
- *Office application can save and open documents directly to and from Platinum's Information Store Web store*
- *Built-in content indexing for added searchability*

These new features will allow users to manage all forms of information (emails, tasks, contacts, office documents, and application data) in the same storage space using the same organizational advantages that Microsoft Outlook provides, such as views, filters, and groupings. ◆

Security

As you build more and more collaborative solutions that manage sensitive or confidential information, you will want the content of your messages to be as secure as possible. One of the primary ways that Microsoft Exchange can help implement your security requirements is by providing a high level of integration with the security models of Windows NT 4 and Windows 2000.

First, Microsoft Exchange mailboxes have one corresponding Windows NT account, and users must be authenticated by NT before they can access their mailboxes. Second, a unified logon environment exists, meaning that users do not face a secondary logon to gain access to their mailbox. If users have already logged in to Windows, they can automatically gain access to their mailboxes. Additionally, communication between Microsoft Exchange and its various clients can be encrypted using technologies, such as RPC encryption and Secure Socket Layers (SSL).

Included with Microsoft Exchange is a Key Management Server (KMS), allowing users of Exchange Server to digitally sign and/or seal their messages. Digital signatures provide a method by which the recipient of a message can guarantee that the sender is who the message states it is. Digitally sealing a message guarantees that only the listed recipients have the ability to open and read the contents of the message. In fact, Microsoft Exchange supports X.509 v3 certificates, which also allow other S/MIME-aware clients to send and receive mail to each other.

Utilizing the strong security mechanisms of Microsoft Exchange greatly enhances the features of your collaborative solution, especially in workflow scenarios. For example, using a combination of Windows (NT or 2000) security and additional Exchange Security, such as signed and sealed messages, you can now guarantee that a person's manager is the actual person who approved a purchase request. Signing documents with a pen might become a thing of the past.

Redundancy

When I discussed hot and fast backups, I stated that this functionality is extremely important because it allows the Exchange Server to perform backup maintenance without greatly affecting users of the server. What happens to your collaborative solution if an Exchange Server fails? If additional redundancy is added to message stores, it can prevent system wide failure if one server fails.

As mentioned before, it is extremely easy to add Exchange Servers to your messaging infrastructure. Typically, servers are added for one of two purposes—either load balancing or redundancy. Adding servers for data redundancy allows the storage of the same message content in more than one location. Redundancy is accomplished via multi-master public folder replication and is handled automatically by Exchange. All the content from all the servers participating in public folder replication has the same data. If one of the servers fails, the information can be accessible from other servers without having to reconfigure the Microsoft Outlook.

How does redundancy fit into a collaborative development project? It is extremely important that the developers of the collaborative application focus on designing and building the business components required for the resulting solution. By providing redundancy at the messaging infrastructure level, developers can assume that data is available all of the time, relieving developers from having to develop alternative data access components.

Robust Client Access
One of the most important collaborative functionalities of Microsoft Exchange is the wide variety of clients that Exchange Server can support. Microsoft Exchange allows for a wide range of clients to gain access to messages and services that are exposed by Exchange.

The following is a list of clients that can be used to access data and services in Microsoft Exchange:

- Microsoft Outlook 97, 98, and 2000
- Outlook for Microsoft Windows 3.X
- Outlook for Macintosh
- Outlook Web Access
- The Windows Messaging Client with the Internet Mail Service installed
- Any POP3, NNTP, IMAP4, and LDAP Client

More important than the number of clients that Microsoft Exchange can support is the level of interoperability the clients have with one another. Typically, it is very difficult to create a unified collaborative solution that supports such a wide variety of clients.

Here is an example of what this means. Suppose that you work for nine months creating a project management solution that is based on customized Outlook forms attached to public folders. Every employee in the organization is supposed to connect to certain Exchange public folders with Outlook to enter status reports, as well as to submit her working time. When the solution is rolled out, you realize that 10 percent of the company employees accesses their mailboxes using Netscape Mail (POP3 clients cannot access public folders or Outlook forms), and another 5 percent of the organization uses Outlook Web Access. Here, you have a total of 15 percent of the organization unable to use your solution.

When designing an effective collaborative solution, you must be conscious of the types of clients that exist in your environment and how those clients will interact with your solution.

Real-Time Collaborative Features

As discussed in Chapter 2, "Typical Collaborative Development Examples," real-time collaborative applications make up an entire category of collaborative solutions. Because we, the authors, have decided to write an entire book on how we can create collaborative solutions using Microsoft Exchange, it is quite safe to say that Exchange provides mechanisms to support and enhance real-time collaborative development.

Microsoft Exchange comes with a chat service that is capable of hosting 10,000 simultaneous users at a time. Users can use any IRC or IRCX client to participate in such chats. Exchange also provides an Internet Locator Server (ILS). The ILS tracks who is online and available to participate in some form of real-time collaboration. In fact, the ILS that Microsoft Exchange exposes is integrated directly into the Exchange directory eliminating the need to support more than one address list. Users who want to chat or meet online with other users can simply choose the user from the Exchange directory to initiate the communication.

Business Modeling

Business modeling is our final Microsoft Exchange topic. It is imperative that your collaborative environment provides methods of representing business entities in your organization. It is even more important that you have some means of manipulating the entities themselves or the communication between them. Again, Microsoft Exchange fulfills both requirements by providing two services: the Exchange Directory, which you can use to represent business entities, and the Exchange Event Service, which you can use to manipulate and enhance communication between items in the directory. Additionally, to exploit the functionality provided with the Exchange Event Service, you can use the Microsoft Scripting Agent, which is responsible for performing some action when events fire, and the Exchange Routing Objects, which provide the ability for you to create simple routing solutions.

Directory Services

The Microsoft Exchange Directory is a list of entities that consist primarily of exchange mailboxes, distribution lists, and custom recipients (which are mappings to external mail accounts). Associated with every directory item is a set of properties that is used to identify the object, such as address, phone number, and department. Upon initial examination, the Exchange Directory is simply a way of listing people or resources to which you can send mail.

Upon further observation, you can see that the Exchange Directory also provides the means of representing organizational hierarchy. It is this organization structure that is essential to many of your collaborative applications, especially those that deal with workflow and routing.

When developing collaborative applications, you should rely upon the organization infrastructure defined and maintained by the Microsoft Exchange Directory for two reasons. First, you should ensure that organizational information is represented and maintained in one place. This ensures that if there is any change to an organization's structure, it is automatically reflected in your applications after making the necessary modifications in the Exchange Directory. Second, because the Exchange Directory represents entities that are typical endpoints of communication, it makes sense that you use it as the primary organization reference in the solutions that you build.

Note

Exchange 2000 is tightly integrated with Windows 2000's Active Directory. In fact, Microsoft Exchange will no longer require its own directory store, it will use Active Directory. This is great for two reasons. First, this allows system administrators to create a single, unified enterprise directory. Second, this level of integration extends the scalability of Exchange to serve millions of users.

Exchange 2000 will expose the following features of Active Directory:

- *Unified administration. Both Windows 2000 and Exchange will be managed using the Microsoft Management Console (MMC). Adding a mailbox for a user will be as simple as enabling the Active Directory user for mail.*

- *Unified security. Because Exchange 2000 uses a Web Share for collaborative storage, the native Windows 2000 Access Control Lists (ACLs) will be used both on data stored in Exchange and Windows 2000 file shares. Additionally, Windows 2000 security groups can be used as distribution lists eliminating the need for redundant administration. There will no longer be any reason to separately administer information stored within Exchange and on the corporate e-file system, because they will be one and the same.*

- *Enhanced directory management. Exchange 2000 will scale easily to millions of users using Active Directory's distributed system topology. It will rely on Active Directory's replication model, as well as benefit from fast access protocols such as LDAP.*

In all, Exchange 2000 will be tied even closer to the operating system and networking and Web services provided by the Windows architecture than the current version of Exchange. Scalability and topology differences between your networking services and messaging infrastructure will be a thing of the past. ◆

Exchange Scripting Agent

One of newest features of Microsoft Exchange is the Exchange Scripting Agent, whose sole purpose is to extend the collaborative capabilities of Exchange. Microsoft Scripting Agent provides server-side scripting of events. Generally speaking, you can now write scripts to handle various events that occur on the Exchange Server without having to create complex custom Exchange Server extensions.

Microsoft Exchange Scripting Agent can be used for many purposes; however, I will focus on its role in implementing business logic when creating workflow applications. In this case, the business logic defines how different types of information are routed through your organization. You can use the functionality of the Exchange Scripting Agent to implement this flow.

Exchange Scripting Agents respond to events that occur within Microsoft Exchange Server. Such events include timer events and folder events, such as when messages are posted, edited, or deleted. In fact, Scripting Agents are associated with either public folders, as described earlier, or private folders, such as folders that exist within a user's mailbox. For added flexibility, Scripting Agents can be written in either VBScript or JavaScript in tools, such as Notepad (which is the default, unfortunately) or Visual Studio.

An additional feature that makes Scripting Agents so powerful is that scripts can be made to interact with COM objects written in any language that supports building COM components, such as Visual Basic or Visual C++. Calling custom COM objects provides an extremely high degree of functionality and extensibility to the Scripting Agents as well as to your workflow solutions (see Figure 3.5).

In addition, Microsoft Exchange provides a set of COM objects called routing objects that help simplify the design and implementation of routing and approval applications. These COM objects can be called and used from either inside your Scripting Agent or from other COM components or applications created in Visual Basic or Visual C++. I will discuss how to implement Microsoft Exchange Scripting Agents and Routing Objects in Chapter 14.

Microsoft Exchange Routing Objects

One of the newest features included in Microsoft Exchange Server 5.5 are Exchange Routing Objects. Microsoft Exchange 5.5 Routing Objects are a set of tools built to make the task of developing email-based routing and approval applications easier. Generally, Routing Objects provide developers a set of interfaces that allow business processes that involve some type of information routing and approvals to be modeled from within Exchange Server—which is exactly what workflow solutions require. The Exchange 5.5 Routing Objects are actually comprised of these three different components:

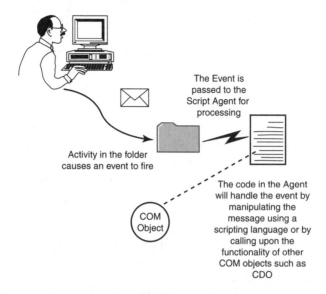

The Event is
passed to the
Script Agent for
processing

Activity in the folder
causes an event to fire

COM
Object

The code in the Agent
will handle the event by
manipulating the
message using a
scripting language or by
calling upon the
functionality of other
COM objects such as
CDO

Figure 3.5   *Scripting Agents are associated with events that fire within a public or private folder. You can take advantage of other objects that provide a COM interface (such as ADO or CDO) from inside your event scripts.*

- **The Routing Engine.** The Routing Engine is the core component of Exchange Routing Objects. The Routing Engine is a COM component (see "COM, DCOM, and COM+" later in this chapter for more information on COM) that works with the Exchange Event service responsible for implementing and tracking established routes, also called Maps. The Routing Engine was created to simplify email-based routing applications. The engine routes Work Items (see definition in the following bullet) to participants via email. Participants send email replies back to the engine to approve, reject, or comment on the item being routed. The engine tracks the responses and comments on the server and provides support for exception handling in the event a time-out occurs, duplicate mail is received, and so on. This implementation type is called a hub and spoke architecture, where the hub is a public folder or mailbox and the spokes are email messages sent to/from each recipient to the hub folder.

- **Routing Objects.** Routing Objects represent the items that can be manipulated by developers when creating workflow solutions. Routing Objects actually consist of a number of objects. The following is a list and brief description of each; Figure 3.6 illustrates these concepts:

  WorkItems. The original data to be routed or approved.

Maps. Represents the process map that will be used to execute and track particular WorkItems.

Rows. A single activity in a process map.

ProcInstances (Process Instances). Process Instances represent an executing process that consists of a WorkItem, state information, and map information.

Participants. Email addresses that are used in the routing and approval process.

Logs. Logs are used to track the execution of individual activities in a map.

RecipientEntry. An object that allows access and manipulation of status information regarding a process instance.

Vote Buttons. Provide a means for applications that are running on the server to programmatically create Outlook-compatible Voting Buttons on a message.

- **VBScript actions**. A default set of common VBScript functions for routing is supplied which includes functional activities, such as Sending and Receiving, Consolidating, and evaluation functions, such as TimeOut and NonDelivery detection.

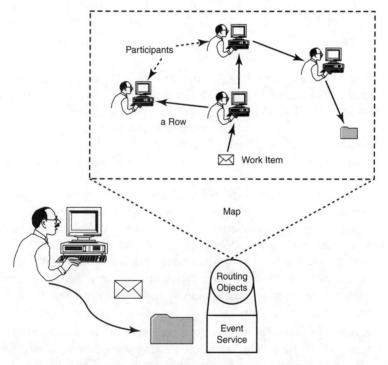

Figure 3.6 *Routing Objects work with the Exchange Event Service to aid developers when creating applications that require forms of workflow.*

Also included with the installation of Exchange 5.5 Routing Objects is the Exchange Routing Wizard. The Exchange Routing Wizard is an application, written in Visual Basic 5.0, that allows authorized folder owners to define and install simple sequential or parallel routes into a folder. After a route is installed into the folder, any document posted or dropped into that folder is automatically routed to the specified people, and the server automatically tracks the status of the item.

The Routing Wizard works by installing a process map into an Exchange Server folder. This is a definition of a parallel or sequential route. The map defines the steps in the route and how timeouts should be handled. The Routing Wizard guides users through a series of steps to help design and implement a routing solution without needing to write a line of code.

Additionally, the Routing Engine on the server automatically tracks the status of each item in the folder. It adds any comments made by recipients to the body of the original message, and it keeps track of who has approved or rejected the item so far. Users can view this status tracking information from within Microsoft Outlook by simply double-clicking any of the items in the folder in which the process map is defined.

> **Note**
>
> *We will learn how to use Exchange Routing objects and the Exchange Routing Wizard in Chapter 15, "Designing and Building Real-Time Solutions."* ◆

Microsoft SQL Server

You're probably wondering how SQL Server got worked into this book. I'm sure you are already aware that you cannot store all forms of data within Microsoft Exchange. What you cannot effectively store or retrieve from Exchange leads to the search for alternatives, and Microsoft SQL Server, in my opinion, is the only choice.

So where does SQL Server come into play when designing and building collaborative solutions? Well, if you haven't already noticed, Microsoft Exchange is a great platform for which to store messages. However, Exchange is a poor environment to store relational data, and in many cases, your collaborative solutions require access to many forms of relational data that must be stored in some type of relational DBMS. Additionally, SQL Server was built to store large amounts of relational data efficiently, which Microsoft Exchange was never meant to do.

> **Note**
>
> *The Exchange Stores are based on a Hierarchical model, whereas SQL Server data is maintained in a relational model.* ◆

Every time I start to discuss SQL Server 7.0, I have the overwhelming urge to go on forever, because this is how long it would take to fully exploit all of SQL Server's features. I'm going to suppress much of my urge and only write about the features that you will typically require during the development of a collaborative application. The following are some of the features of SQL Server that make it the best choice when selecting a data storage powerhouse:

- **Tight development integration.** One of the most important aspects of SQL Server is that it is tightly integrated into your development environment, which in this case is Microsoft Visual Studio. Visual Studio provides a rich set of tools to aid developers in the creation and testing of applications that interact with SQL Server. Some of the tools provide the ability to debug Transact-SQL from within a Visual Studio interface, ensuring that developers have the best set of tools to help reduce development costs while helping to add greater functionality and stability.

- **Development interfaces.** Storing and manipulating data on SQL Server is only one aspect of the power it provides developers. Another aspect is the rich set of interfaces developers can choose from when developing applications that interact with SQL Server. The following is a list of development interfaces that can be used to access data stored on SQL Server:

  ODBC. SQL Server 7.0 includes an updated SQL ODBC Server driver that is compliant with the Open Database Connectivity 3.51 specification and the ODBC Driver Manager. You should only use ODBC for low-level development of SQL database applications. Use ADO with the OLE DB Provider for SQL Server to develop business applications, and use OLE DB with the OLE DB Provider for SQL Server to develop your data access infrastructure.

Note

Visit `www.microsoft.com/data/odbc` *for more information on ODBC.* ◆

OLE DB. SQL Server 7.0 includes a native OLE DB Provider for SQL Server that complies with the OLE DB 2.0 specification. The provider fully supports SQL Server 7.0 and 6.5. It is recommended that you use OLE DB for low-level development of your data access infrastructure which is used by other COM components.

Note

You can get more information about OLE DB from the Web site `www.microsoft.com/data/oledb`. ◆

ADO, DAO, and RDO. All these are COM wrappers for some other underlying data access methods. For example, ADO is a COM wrapper for OLE DB, DAO is a COM wrapper for JET, and RDO is a COM wrapper for ODBC. ADO is a COM wrapper that not only supports OLE DB, but also JET and ODBC. ADO is an emerging technology and is designed to eventually replace DAO and RDO. We will use these interfaces for building line of business applications such as the collaborative solutions we are discussing in this book.

> **Note**
>
> *For more information, you can visit the Web site at* `www.microsoft.com/data/ado.` ◆

- **Multiple OS support.** New in version 7.0 is the ability to install the SQL Server database engine on virtually any computer running Windows NT, Windows 95, or Windows 98. You are no longer required to have Windows NT to run SQL Server. This is a particularly great feature for portable developers (a term I made up which refers to developers who do most of their coding and testing on laptop computers) where a complete development environment is required on each laptop. In the past, many laptops were not compatible with Windows NT (some of them were, but didn't perform well) thus requiring either Windows 95 or Windows 98. Because older versions of SQL did not run on these operating systems, two- and three-tier development was nearly impossible. We no longer face this problem because we can now write applications that interact with SQL Server running on a much wider variety of operating systems.

- **Security integration.** As with earlier discussions, providing a high degree of security to the applications that you build is a modern necessity. SQL Server 7.0 has greatly advanced how security is implemented and maintained over its previous version. Now, more than ever, SQL Server provides tight integration with the Windows NT security model (Integrated Security), while still providing the ability to maintain its own security mechanisms (SQL Security). It is extremely important to develop applications that leverage the security mechanisms provided by the operating system to take full advantage of features such as single logon environments and group security permission, which can all be administered from one convenient location.

- **Microsoft English Query.** Microsoft English Query provides users the ability to query data stored within SQL Server using English sentences. Users can ask SQL Server questions like, "How many Widgets were sold in Washington last year?" without having to understand the underlying database structure or Transact-SQL commands. Additionally, English Query has ActiveX support, which allows developers to embed this functionality into their applications. This, combined with other technologies, such as Direct Speak which converts speech to text and *visa versa*, can make a dramatic impact on the way people use computers. Like Captain Picard of the Star Trek Enterprise, we will all one day begin most of our advanced queries by saying, "Computer . . ."

- **OLAP Services.** OLAP stands for Online Analytical Processing. OLAP Services provide a way of retrieving and analyzing information from multiple sources. OLAP Services can be used to create corporate reporting and analysis solutions as well as data modeling and decision support solutions. In fact, you can use the services of OLAP in a workflow solution in which decisions must be made based on a set of complex statistics. An overly simplified example of this is a purchase request approval solution. In this simple situation, an employee requests approval for a particular purchase, such as purchasing this book for the corporate library. The receiver of the request is presented with a complex set of statistics that help him make his decision to approve or deny the request. For example, the receiver of the request is presented with a pivot table that represents information, such as summaries of the total amount requested by the employee, by category, by month, all while checking these totals against a corporate budget. Knowing this information up front allows the approver to make a more sound decision.

In short, as the complexity of your collaborative solutions increases, so does the need for SQL Server. Even collaborative solutions, which are not as complex, can benefit from the power and flexibility of a data storage powerhouse. As this is not a book dedicated to SQL Server, and I might add that there are many very good ones out there, I will not take my discussion of SQL Server any further; however, we will revisit SQL Server integration issues and examples much later in the book. If you want to get more detailed information on SQL Server for either administrative or developmental information, go to one of the following Web sites:

- General information about SQL Server: `http://www.microsoft.com/sql`
- General information about OLAP Services: `http://www.microsoft.com/sql/olap`
- General information about English Query: `http://www.microsoft.com/sql/eq`

Internet Information Server

There is a tremendous push for building more applications that run on the Web because there are so many inherent benefits of such application models. First, all the business data and logic can be centrally maintained. Second, presentation rules are stored centrally and can be modified with ease from one location. Finally, minimal to no client installation requirements exist, which means rollouts and updates are easily accomplished.

Microsoft provides a number of products that help us host, build, and deploy Web applications. At the heart of this technology is Microsoft Internet Information Server (IIS). Microsoft Internet Information Server is an Internet file and application server included with the Microsoft Windows NT Server operating system. IIS version 4.0 is shipped with the Windows NT 4.0 Option Pack, available via free download or shipped on CD-ROM. The Windows NT 4.0 Option Pack CD is also included with all new copies of Windows NT.

IIS contains a number of core Internet technologies that can be used in conjunction with Microsoft Exchange Server. These include the following:

- Web Server
- FTP Server
- NNTP Server
- Index Server
- SMTP Server
- Certificate Server
- Windows Script Host

IIS can be used alone as a Web server or in conjunction with compatible technologies to set up Internet commerce, access and manipulate data from a variety of data sources, and build Web applications that take advantage of server script and component code to deliver client-server functionality. The latest information is available on the IIS Web site at http://www.microsoft.com/iis/.

Because of its tight integration with Windows NT Server, IIS guarantees the network administrator and application developer the same security, networking, and administration functionality as Windows NT Server. Additionally, IIS also has built-in capabilities to help administer secure Web sites, and to develop and deploy server-intensive Web applications.

One of the best features of IIS 4.0 is its powerful application development platform. Active Server Pages (ASP) technology, server components, search and index features, and new transaction-processing capabilities are making development of server-intensive Web applications one of the fastest growing components of Web development. Web developers need access to features that enable commerce, database access, personalization, and dynamic content generation on the Web. Intranet developers also need these features—along with the ability to perform full-text search across all documents on their networks. This level of integration and extensibility is the basis for Web-enabled collaborative solutions.

The typical Web application is composed of many different components, scripts, and other applications. An ever increasing number of applications require the implementation of business rules that demand some type of transaction management, such as booking a flight, which requires a number of steps to be complete before the entire process is complete. Credit must be verified, tickets must be shipped, and customers must be billed. Updates for each booking typically occur in multiple databases on multiple servers. The failure of one of these components should not affect the success or failure of the entire application and should be handled correctly by the system to ensure successful transactions that persist even if there are system failures.

Transaction support in Windows NT Server and IIS, implemented through Microsoft Transaction Server (MTS) 2.0, tracks the success or failure of complete system processes (such as ordering or accessing and manipulating data) and correctly handles the process of aborting a transaction if necessary. When ASP pages are declared to be transactional, Transaction Server handles the details of creating the defined transactions that occur within the page. Transaction components are activated when needed and deactivated when not in use to save system resources.

The following are some additional development features to take note of:

- **Search/indexing.** The search and indexing features within IIS are particularly interesting to the collaborative solutions developer. Index Server indexes the full text and properties of documents that include Microsoft Office documents. Users search this index by sending queries through a Web browser, and Index Server returns the results to the user in an HTML page. Index Server searches can also be extended to support access to Exchange Server public folders.

- **Script debugging.** Microsoft Script Debugger 1.0 can be used to debug pages built with ASP technology.

- **Windows Script Host.** A scripting engine that allows the development and execution of scripts in a number of standard programming languages. Current supported languages include VBScript, JavaScript, REXX, and Perl.

Note

If you need more information on Microsoft Script Debugger, check out the follow-ing Internet Site: `http://msdn.microsoft.com/scripting`. ◆

After you have installed and configured IIS, you are not confined to using the functionality that is native to the product. In fact, you can use virtually any COM object to provide an entirely integrated set of functionality to your Web applications, just as you can with other development platforms, such as Microsoft Visual Basic. Here are a couple of technologies that you . can easily call upon to provide functionality to your collaborative Web applications built on IIS:

- Active Data Objects (ADO) version 1.5 can be installed from the Windows NT Option Pack to allow programmatic access to multiple types of data. As we observed in our discussion of SQL Server, ADO can be used to access, modify, and insert data into an RDMS, such as SQL Server. You can control the ADO objects you create using Visual Script or JavaScript.

- Microsoft Site Server, combined with Windows NT Server and IIS, provides a comprehensive solution for Internet commerce, site manage-ment, and Web publishing.

Note

You can get more information on Microsoft Site Server at the following Web address: `http://www.microsoft.com/SiteServer/Site`. ◆

- Microsoft Exchange Server provides messaging and collaboration infra-structure as we have already discussed. You typically gain access to messaging functionality through Collaborative Data Objects (CDO), which we will discuss in the section "Collaborative Programming Interfaces."

- SNA Server provides capabilities to access data on mainframe and AS400 systems within a Systems Network Architecture (SNA) network. This allows you to write applications that provide and store data on legacy mainframe systems, while a modern client interfaces through your browsers.

Note

Complete SNA Server information can be found at `http://www.Microsoft.com/SNA`. ◆

Internet Information Server provides an extremely robust and viable platform for which to construct a collaborative solution that is composed of many different underlying technologies. When designing your collaborative solution, you should always consider the extent of Web integration your solution will consist of, because as software products continue to evolve, you will see a continued escalation toward Web integrated components. One of the primary setbacks of developing Web-based collaborative solutions is that it is more difficult to develop enhanced user interfaces than you could in a tool like Visual Basic. However, I'm sure that, as time passes, this will no longer remain an issue, and the Web development environments will become even more robust.

Microsoft Outlook

I am not about to go through all of the functionality that Outlook provides to the power user because that would clearly be a topic for an entirely separate book. I will, however, focus on the specific functionality that Outlook provides to help you build advanced collaborative solutions.

Here are some of the features that make Microsoft Outlook one of the best collaborative clients you can use to enhance or build upon when developing advanced collaborative solutions:

- **Primary Exchange client.** Of course, Microsoft Outlook 2000 is the recommended client for Microsoft Exchange Server simply because it provides the richest feature set of all possible clients. Not only does it provide easy access to mailboxes and public folders stored on the Exchange Server, it also provides a rich set of tools to help manage daily messaging requirements.

- **Out-of-the-box collaboration.** Microsoft Outlook is an enriched messaging client that can be used to track calendar events, ongoing tasks, and contact information as soon as you install it, out-of-the-box. With no additional configuration, you can also use Outlook's features to instantly collaborate with others on your messaging infrastructure. For example, you can instantly invite others to meetings, check other user's free and busy time, assign tasks to one another, and share corporate contact lists.

- **Outlook views.** As discussed previously, views provide a way for users to better manage the hoard of messages that must be maintained on a daily basis by sorting, filtering, or grouping messages based on content or envelope information. Outlook greatly extends this capability by providing views to help manage special message folder types such as Calendar folders, Task folders, Contact folders, and Journal folders. Additionally, all of the default Outlook views can be extended to represent exactly what the users want to see.

- **Rules.** Rules are a powerful feature of Outlook. Messaging rules are not a new feature to any messaging client; however, the process of creating rules that Outlook provides is very impressive. Rules are definitions of actions that can be taken on messages as they arrive into certain folders maintained by Outlook. When defining rules, you must define the criteria that must be matched before the rule can execute ("all messages from Duncan"), as well as which action to perform ("mark as important and follow-up within two days"). Additionally, rules can be executed by the client, in this case Microsoft Outlook, or automatically by the Exchange Server, provided that the rules do not interact with a folder maintained by the client.

- **Web integration.** The level of integration between the Web and Outlook has dramatically increased over the last few product iterations. Today, you not only have a customizable Outlook Today page (the Outlook Today page is the Web page that Outlook displays when you display the Outlook Today folder), you also have the ability to assign folder home pages to private or public folders stored on the Exchange Server. This means that when you click on a folder that you have assigned a folder home page, rather than viewing the folder contents on the right hand pane, you view a Web page instead.

   You can typically display any Web page as the folder's Web page; however it makes more sense if the Web page you are pointing to provides some type of meaningful summary of the content in the folder. For example, you might have an Exchange public folder that holds corporate calendar events such as employee vacation schedules or shift schedules. You can create a Web page that automatically accesses all of this information and summarizes it on a useful HTML page. An example of this is a Web page that displays everyone's vacation schedules for the current month. We will talk much more about folder Web pages in Chapter 11, "Team Folders," and Chapter 12, "The Digital Dashboard."

- **Support for real-time collaboration.** One of my favorite features is Outlook 2000's better integration with applications, such as Microsoft NetMeeting or Microsoft NetShow. For example, instead of inviting people to a meeting, you can now invite them to an online meeting. At the time of the meeting, all attendees sign on using NetMeeting to discuss the meeting agenda.

- **Extensibility.** Perhaps Outlook's greatest accomplishment is the level of extensibility it provides developers. You can actually think of Microsoft Outlook as being a complete development platform, as well as a provider of a rich messaging object model that can be used by other development platforms, such as Microsoft Visual Basic. Here are some of the features that make Microsoft Outlook such a rich development environment:

Outlook forms extensibility. Outlook provides a number of default forms responsible for representing information on Contacts, Tasks, Appointments, and Journal Entries. More importantly, these forms can be extended to capture new data. Additionally, developers can create completely new forms to retrieve and display information not native to Microsoft Outlook. When extending existing forms or creating new forms, developers are provided with a rich development environment allowing them to use any installed ActiveX controls, communicate with any COM object, and use Visual Script to control the form's activity.

Enhanced events and object model. All the applications in Office 2000 provide enhanced programming models. In fact, Microsoft Outlook 2000 provides 10 new objects, 25 new methods, and nearly 50 new properties. Additionally, Outlook provides new methods for controlling and extending the Outlook Bar, including methods for creating or deleting Outlook Bar groups and shortcuts. Also, Outlook events have been extended from the form level, such as events firing within a message, to the application level, such as when new mail arrives or when mail is deleted.

Application level VBA. Outlook now has VBA at the application level. This means that, similar to all other Microsoft Office applications, you can write customized macros that can either be called independently or respond to events at the application level, such as when new messages arrive or when messages are deleted from certain folders. These macros can be used to extend the default functionality that Outlook provides to match any workspace.

Shared COM Add-In architecture. A COM Add-In is a special COM object that extends the functionality of an application. Until Outlook 2000, Outlook had a separate method for creating Add-Ins than its other Office counterparts. Outlook 2000 now allows for the integration of COM Add-Ins that follow the standard Microsoft Office COM Add-In specifications. This enables developers to easily add applications to Outlook's menus and toolbars, as well as have full access to the object model and events that Outlook provides.

Digital signatures for macros. As usage of document level macros increases, the need for enhanced security is required. Office 2000 provides developers with the means to digitally sign their macros to certify that they are virus free. Office 2000 recognizes digital signatures and does not display a macro warning screen unless the macro has been modified from its original version. This new functionality makes it easy for developers to distribute their macros without the worry of spreading infected code.

We will dedicate an entire chapter, Chapter 5, to discussing and learning how to use the rich set of collaborative development features that Microsoft Outlook provides.

Note

I recommend reading the Microsoft Press book Programming Microsoft Outlook and Microsoft Exchange *by Thomas Rizzo, Microsoft Press (ISBN: 0735605092). This book exploits the best new features of Microsoft Outlook 2000 and details the development and integration of Web applications and Outlook 2000.* ◆

Windows CE

Look out folks! Windows CE has entered the building. You might have already guessed that I have really taken a liking to the product. In fact, I can see an extremely important future ahead of Windows CE that will change the way we collaborate today.

Windows CE is a compact, highly efficient, scalable operating system that was designed for a wide variety of embedded systems and technologies. In fact, everything from gas pumps (Tokheim Systems, the world's largest provider of fuel dispensing systems signed a three-year contract with BP Amoco to provide future fuel dispensing systems based on Microsoft Windows CE) to hand held personal organizers are running the operating system.

So there you have it! Windows CE was not just created to provide calendaring or task management features. Windows CE is a fully functional development environment, which you should look toward to enhance any collaborative solution you build. Not only can you write applications that run on Windows CE, you can also use CE devices to browse your collaborative intranet. In addition, you use CE devices to be a fully functional Microsoft Terminal Server client, which allows you to capitalize on the power provided by mainstream workhorse NT Servers. Additionally, developers who want to write custom CE software can reuse their skills by employing tools such as Visual Basic and Visual C++ to do the job.

In fact, following are some of the more important aspects of Windows CE that make it an excellent component of a complete collaborative solution:

- **Support for Win32 APIs.** Windows CE supports more than 1,000 common Microsoft Win32 APIs including TAPI, which has been released in Windows CE version 3.0.

- **Support for COM objects.** Developers can create and use COM components on Windows CE. Version 3.0 of CE allows both in-process and out-of-process and supports all threading models (as opposed to single threading in previous releases). DCOM is not yet available in CE version 3.0 but might be released in a service pack by the time this book makes it to shelves.

- **Utilization of ActiveX controls.** Your wonderful investments in ActiveX controls are not lost to Windows CE. In fact, you can develop quite sophisticated applications by reusing the same ActiveX controls you use on other Windows operating systems.

- **Data synchronization.** One of CE's most important goals is to provide a high level of portability, while providing access to corporate information at any time. Windows CE provides data synchronization functionality when you need to take work with you. You can make changes while your portable device is offline; and when you return online, your changes are automatically synchronized with your desktop companion. This functionality holds true for both Office documents and Microsoft Outlook items such as email, calendar appointments, and tasks.

- **Multimedia.** DirectX 6.0 has made it to Windows CE version 3.0. This simply means that the operating system is capable of more advanced graphics, allowing the creation of a more aesthetically rich set of applications.

- **Network services.** Windows CE version 3.0 comes with a fully functional HTTP Server component that has support for ISAPI extensions. Additionally, version 3.0 implements a version of Microsoft Message Queue to help support the development of distributed applications.

- **Terminal Server client.** Use the Terminal Server client to turn your Handheld PC Pro device into a Windows-based Mobile Terminal. With a Mobile Terminal, you can now access full function Windows-based applications when connected to a Windows NT Terminal Server 4.0 and Windows 2000 Terminal Services over wired and wireless LAN or dial-up connections.

So how does the Windows CE operating system fit into a book that deals with collaborative development and Microsoft Exchange? My answer: How can we leave it out? Windows CE and the applications that you can write for it provide almost the exact features that you would expect from an operating system, such as Windows 98 or Windows 2000, except that you can fold it up and stick it in your pocket. Wouldn't it be great if you could build a collaborative solution that would allow its users to send vacation requests, approve purchase requests, review weekly status reports, and use the corporate intranet all on the commute home from work? Well, you can do all of this right now, with a little know how, with Windows CE.

Ties That Bind

I have discussed a great number of existing technologies (and will discuss many more) that seem to do certain jobs very well. Exchange sends and stores messages, SQL Server stores relational data, Outlook is an awesome

Exchange client, and so on. What you really need is some way of taking all the pieces and seamlessly combining them to create one unified solution. This seems to be the tricky part. You have a half dozen different applications each providing their own unique set of functionality. Your job is to understand what each provides while pulling them together to create an advanced collaborative solution (hence the purpose of this chapter). I will now take some time to describe what allows developers to take the best pieces of each of these applications and combine them to create one unified solution. The remainder of this chapter will be dedicated to looking at some of the underlying programmatic tools developers can call upon during the construction of all advanced collaborative solutions.

COM, DCOM, and COM+

If you're not familiar with COM, do not hesitate; go out and get a couple books on this topic right now! COM is too important to our cause to not fully understand its full potential and internal workings.

COM, the Component Object Model, is a specification on how to build components that can be dynamically interchanged by providing standards that components and clients must follow to ensure that the components operate together. COM components consist of executable code distributed as either dynamic link libraries (DLLs) or as executables (EXEs). Here are some other advantages of COM components:

- COM components are language independent. You can use virtually any development tool to create and use COM components.
- COM components exist at the binary level. Do not confuse a C++ class with a COM component.
- COM components can be upgraded without breaking old clients.
- COM components can be transparently relocated on a network.

Please understand that COM is not a computer language. In fact, as I stated a moment ago, you can use virtually any language to create COM components. Additionally, COM does not compete with or replace DLLs. In fact, COM uses DLLs to provide its components with the capability to dynamically link into the process space of a COM client application. COM is not a set of APIs (such as the Win32 APIs), nor is it a class library like MFC (Microsoft Foundation Classes). COM is a way that components can communicate with one another to share each other's services. In fact, I like to think that COM specifies a way for components to *collaborate* with one another.

One of the powerful features of COM is that the COM client does not know whether the COM component it is using is an in-process COM component (a COM DLL) or an out-of-process COM component (a COM EXE). More importantly, you can extend COM such that the calling application can be on a completely separate computer than the COM component, and the COM client doesn't even need to be aware of this. In fact, this is the benefit that DCOM (Distributed COM) provides to us. One of the primary benefits of DCOM is the capability to easily create multiple tiered applications, allowing developers to better separate and distribute the processing load of their applications. (See Figure 3.7.)

Note

There are three primary tiers of application architectures: Single Tier, 2-Tier, and N-Tier.

Single Tier applications are those that do not require the services of server or process. Single Tier applications are typically standalone and cannot distribute computing needs across a network.

2-Tier applications are those that are written to use the services of some back-end process. An example of a 2-Tier application is a custom contacts management application that stores its data on a Microsoft SQL Server. In this case, the application is broken into two components: the user interface and the back-end data store. However, in this scenario, when data is requested from the SQL Server, the processing required to retrieve the data from the database is actually performed on the computer running SQL Server.

An N-Tier system, which is sometime called a three-tier system, allows the user interface, business rules, and database to reside separately. When developing a multi-tier system, you can build intelligent clients with business rules that have been compiled into standalone DLLs. These DLLs can be written in Microsoft Visual Basic and reside on a server. Take note that there are two flavors of 2-tier applications. The first, intelligent client, assumes that all the application's business logic resides within the GUI. The second, intelligent server, assumes that all of the business logic resides at the same place as the data (such an example is usually implemented with stored procedures). ◆

COM+ fits into this picture by providing a single vision for creating component-based, distributed applications. It provides you with the tools to create transactional, n-tier applications. COM+ combines enhancements to COM, Microsoft Transaction Server 2.0, and many new services. Without going into too many details, generally COM+ is the newest release of COM supported by Windows 2000. The same general concepts apply to COM+ as COM and DCOM, with some added benefits.

I strongly urge all developers to research these technologies in greater depth as they will enhance your ability to create well designed, component-based applications. See the following note for some suggested reading.

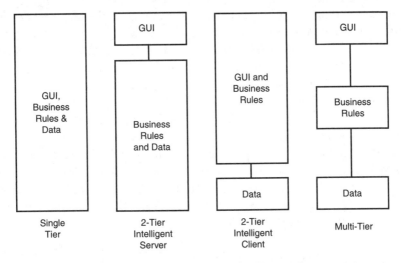

Figure 3.7   *Here is a diagram that explains what application tiers are.*

Note

A great place to start learning about COM is Inside COM, Microsoft's Component Object Model *by Dale Rogerson, Microsoft Press (ISBN: 1572313498).*

When you are ready to build distributed applications using the COM model, take a look at Microsoft Press's Inside Distributed COM *by Guy Eddon and Henry Eddon (ISBN: 0735607281).* ◆

Collaborative Programming Interfaces

In this section, we will focus on defining and explaining some of the more common programming interfaces you will use when developing collaborative solutions. These interfaces are as follows:

- CDO and MAPI
- ADSI

CDO and MAPI

CDO (Collaborative Data Objects) and MAPI (Messaging Application Programming Interface) provide developers with a way to provide messaging functionality to custom applications.

MAPI is an application-programming interface created by Microsoft that allows developers to create messaging aware or messaging based applications easily. In fact, applications that are written to the MAPI specification are not messaging system independent. They are either messaging system independent or they're not messaging system dependent, meaning that the application does not need to have any knowledge of the low-level details of the underlying messaging system to have the capability to send and receive messages, manipulate and save messages, and query addresses from a common address book. This programming interface frees the developer from having to write multiple versions of their application (see Figure 3.8). I like to think of MAPI applications much like Windows applications printing to a printer (in fact, I like to use this analogy for almost all APIs). It would be absurd to write multiple copies of an application for different models of printers. Application developers can write to one print interface, and the only thing that is required to change to allow printing to different printers is the print driver. MAPI is very similar to this. You can install many messaging services that allow your MAPI applications to talk to a wide variety of messaging systems at the same time.

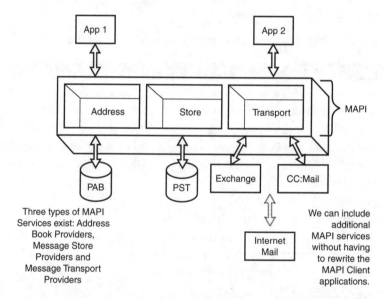

Figure 3.8   *MAPI provides a layer of abstraction between the programming interface it provides the client and the services it implements. This provides the flexibility of interchanging and adding services without needing to modify the client.*

In fact, MAPI can expose three types of MAPI services for applications to use. The first is, of course, the Messaging Transport. This allows your applications to send email to any installed and configured transport. For example, you can install transports for Internet Mail, Exchange Mail, and cc:Mail all at the same time, and your MAPI applications can send email to all of these messaging systems without requiring modifications. The second type of MAPI service exposed to applications is called the MAPI Address Book Provider. This allows applications to query address book information regardless of where the addresses are coming from. An example of a MAPI Address Book Provider is the Personal Address Book in Microsoft Outlook. The third type of MAPI Service is called the MAPI Store Provider that abstracts how messages are stored and manipulated on different messaging infrastructures. An example of a MAPI Store Provider is Outlook's Personal Folders (otherwise known as a PST file).

One of the main drawbacks of using MAPI is that you typically need to access the hundreds of MAPI functions through a lower level programming interface, such as Visual C++, making it more difficult for Visual Basic programmers to fully exploit MAPI to create messaging based applications. This is where CDO comes into play.

At its simplest, CDO is a COM wrapper for MAPI (see Figure 3.9). In fact, CDO is an object library that exposes many interfaces of MAPI allowing access from virtually any development tool that can create and control COM objects, such as Visual Basic, ASP, and Microsoft Visual C++.

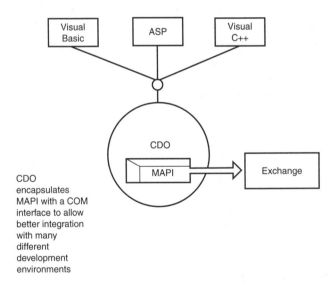

Figure 3.9 *Given its simplest definition, CDO is a COM wrapper for MAPI allowing developers to build much more robust messaging applications from a diverse set of development tools.*

The CDO object model is very comparable to the object model that Outlook 2000 provides, and many people have stopped me on the street asking, "When do I use CDO instead of the Outlook object model, because both provide nearly the same functionality?" I usually tell them that I usually use

CDO for creating Web applications because it provides some very nice functions to render various Exchange objects and messages into HTML format. It also provides users access to various content stored on the Exchange Server. The Outlook object model is a better choice if you need to retrieve Outlook-specific information, such as Task and Journal entries, custom Outlook forms, various Outlook properties, or if you need to access information in other mailboxes for delegate access.

Exchange 2000 and CDO 3.0

Exchange 2000 includes significant enhancements to the Collaboration Data Objects data model. CDO 3.0 is built on OLE/DB and not only provides a higher level of access to the Exchange Server data, but also provides access to Internet standard protocol services, such as LDAP queries and MIME message body parts.

CDO 3.0 will include system management objects, enabling administrators and developers to add admin capabilities to suit their technology and business needs —for example, automatically mailing reports to a list of recipients, enforcing corporate policies on folder creation, custom group calendaring application, or forwarding notifications to pagers and managing distribution list traffic. CDO 3.0 will also provide enhanced calendaring and contact management support and be dual interfaced for programming in C++, VB, VBScript, JavaScript, and Java.

Finally, Exchange 2000 will include CDO Workflow Objects, an enhanced library of workflow services based on transacted, synchronous events that will provide a high performance, reliable, and secure engine for workflow and tracking applications. ◆

ADSI

ADSI is a programming interface supported by the Microsoft Exchange Directory Service that enables developers to gain access to different directories through a common interface. ADSI supports access to Active Directory in Windows 2000, Windows NT 4.0 domain-based, Netware's Bindery, X.500-like directories, such as Netware's NDS Directory and Microsoft Exchange Server.

Note

Some people get confused about the meaning of the word directory. As we all know, the word is used to represent everything from a telephone list to a structure used to store files electronically. For the purpose of this book, we will assume that the directory refers to either the Microsoft Exchange Directory or Active Directory in Windows 2000. However, please note that this term generally refers to some structure that stores objects or data in some hierarchical fashion. This also includes any LDAP-compliant directory, Netware's NDS and Bindery directories, and even Window NT 4.0's domain-based directories. ◆

Like any programming interface, the goal of ADSI is to abstract the details of some underlying technology—in this case, directories. In fact, ADSI provides a standard COM interface so that every directory object can be treated in the same manner regardless of the type of underlying directory services. A directory not only holds simple email address information or phone numbers, it can also hold business process and organizational information such as employee/manager relationships and reporting paths. Directories can also be used to store personal information, such as home phone numbers and employee pictures, as well as resource information, such as location and ownership. Proper understanding of ADSI is essential for writing line of business applications, especially those that implement some form of workflow. We will learn how to use ADSI in the design and implementation of various collaborative solutions in Chapter 14, "Designing and Building Workflow Solutions."

Development Tools and Platforms

Let's discuss some of the tools that you can use to begin assembling all the pieces—all the wood, nails, and shingles. You need to take a look at your toolbox to find out what you can use to build your house—your collaborative house.

Thankfully, developers of collaborative solutions have a lot to choose from in terms of development tools. In this section, I will briefly (and I do mean briefly, because each of these topics is large enough for its own book) describe each of the development tools you can use to create collaborative solutions and highlight when each tool is generally used during the construction of complex solutions.

Visual Basic

Visual Basic 6.0 is perhaps the strongest business software development tool you can use to create collaborative solutions that tie together all of the products we have discussed thus far. Visual Basic 6.0 provides the capability to create standalone business applications using Rapid Application Development techniques. One of Visual Basic's strongest features is how simply developers can use and create COM components that can be utilized by any other development environment that uses COM components such as ASP.

Here are some additional key features of Visual Basic 6.0:

- **High-performance native-code compiler.** Developers can create applications including both client- and server-side components that are optimized for throughput with the Visual C++ 6.0 optimized native-code compiler.

- **Access to all of your enterprise data sources through ODBC, OLE DB, and Microsoft ActiveX Data Objects (ADO).** Visual Basic 6.0 introduces ADO as the powerful new standard for data access. Included OLE DB drivers are SQL Server 6.5+, Oracle 7.3.3+, Microsoft Access, ODBC, and SNA Server.

- **Integrated visual database tools.** Visual Basic 6.0 provides a complete set of tools for integrating databases with any application. Database features include design tools for creating and modifying SQL Server 6.5, Oracle 7.3.3 or later, and AS/400 databases.

- **Automatic data binding.** Virtually no code is needed to bind controls to data sources. Setting just two properties in the Properties window connects the control to any data source.

- **Data Environment designer.** Visually create reusable recordset command objects with drag-and-drop functionality. Bind to multiple data sources for data aggregation and manipulation.

- **Drag-and-drop creation of data-bound forms and reports.** Using the new Data Environment designer, developers can quickly drag-and-drop custom data-bound controls to create forms or reports with the new Data Report designer. Creation of custom data hierarchies is as easy as filling out a dialog box and dragging the command to the form.

- **Middle-tier testing and deployment tools.** Interactively debug Microsoft Transaction Server–packaged components and package and deploy components to remote servers.

- **Visual Basic WebClass designer.** Create server-side applications and components that are easily accessible from any Web browser on any platform.

- **Dynamic HTML (DHTML) Page designer.** Develop multimedia-rich applications using the document object model and Dynamic HTML design surface.

Note

For more information on Microsoft Visual Basic, check out the following Web page: `http://msdn.microsoft.com/vbasic.` ♦

So where can you use Visual Basic during the process of building collaborative solutions? The following list gives an idea of how and when Visual Basic can be used:

- **Create custom standalone applications.** Usually, Visual Basic is used to create standalone applications to model any number of business requirements. To further enhance application functionality without enormous amounts of work, Visual Basic can call upon the functionality of ActiveX controls and COM objects, such as CDO or ADSI, allowing developers to easily create applications that harness the power of other applications. For example, we stated that the Routing Wizard is a component of Exchange Routing Objects, which were discussed early in this chapter. The Routing Wizard is actually a Visual Basic 5.0 application that utilizes the COM interfaces of the Routing Engine and other Routing Objects to help establish a fast and easy routing scenario. In this case, Visual Basic provides the tools to allow developers to create a graphical interface for the Routing Objects provided by Exchange Server. Additionally, it enables developers to instantiate and control the Routing Objects remotely.

- **Create specialized COM objects.** Visual Basic provides developers with the necessary tools to create and expose their own COM objects including ActiveX controls. By easing this development burden, Visual Basic promotes the creating of applications that are broken down into distinct functional components.

VBA

Microsoft Visual Basic for Applications (VBA) is a powerful development technology for rapidly customizing packaged applications and integrating them with existing data and systems. VBA offers a sophisticated set of programming tools based on the Microsoft Visual Basic development system, the world's most popular rapid application development system, which developers can use to harness the power of packaged applications. VBA enables customers to buy off-the-shelf software and customize it to meet their specific business processes rather than build from scratch. This helps them save time and money, reduce risks, leverage their programming skills, and deliver precisely what users need.

VBA provides a complete integrated development environment (IDE) that includes the same elements familiar to developers using Microsoft Visual Basic, including a Project Window, a Properties Window, and debugging tools. Visual Basic for Applications also includes support for Microsoft Forms for creating custom dialog boxes and ActiveX Controls for rapidly building user interfaces. Integrated directly into a host application, VBA offers the advantages of fast, in-process performance (up to 200 times faster than other standalone development tools), tight integration with the host application (code behind documents, cells, and so on), and the ability to build solutions without the use of additional tools. Software programs that include VBA are called *customizable applications*, applications that can be tailored to fit specific business needs. This class of applications enables developers to quickly build solutions that require less end-user training. For MIS and business managers, customization means that solutions can be developed quickly and deployed easily, with minimal maintenance. In an industry familiar with two-year backlogs for new applications and high end-user training costs, these solutions provide a tremendous business bene-fit in terms of return on investment (ROI) and timeliness.

VBScript

Visual Basic Script is something else that you need to familiarize yourself with before embarking on your collaborative development challenge. Most people believe that VBScript is used only in Web development. Contrary to this belief, VBScript is used in many places including during Outlook Forms development and in the creation of Exchange Scripting Agents.

Microsoft Visual Basic Scripting Edition, a subset of the Microsoft Visual Basic programming language, is a fast, portable, lightweight interpreter for use in World Wide Web browsers and other applications that use Microsoft ActiveX Controls, Automation servers, and Java applets. In fact, you will be using VBScript quite extensively during the development phase of your col-laborative applications.

The following is a list of the areas where you are required to use VBScript when developing collaborative applications:

- **Developing Microsoft Outlook Forms.** Even though Outlook now sup-ports VBA, custom form development must be performed using VBScript.

- **Developing Scripting Agents.** All of the code in a folder Scripting Agent that responds to events handled by the Microsoft Exchange Event Service must be written in a scripting language. Developers who more often work with Visual Basic or VBA typically write code to handle folder events in VBScript.

- **ASP Development.** Although ASP can support both VBScript and JavaScript, developers normally use VBScript to write the code con-tained in an ASP page because many Web developers are also familiar with VBScript.

- **Windows Scripting Host.** Windows Scripting Host allows scripts to run right off of the Windows desktop, so to speak. Administrators can write VBScript code to manage common administrative processes, such as software upgrades and distribution.

Note

Although I have placed the focus on VBScript, JavaScript can be used interchangeably with VBScript in most cases. ◆

Significant Others

I have spent quite a bit of time looking at the most important tools and products that can be used to build advanced collaborative solutions. In this section, I will discuss a few more products that can be utilized to greatly enhance the collaborative experience. It is well worth the effort to seriously consider the integration of these products into your collaborative solutions.

Microsoft Chat

Microsoft Chat is Microsoft implementation of an IRC-compliant chat client that falls into the real-time collaboration category defined in the previous chapter. Microsoft Chat provides an interface to any compliant chat server such as the Chat server that comes bundled with Exchange Server 5.5. Another great feature of Microsoft Chat is its capability to represent chat participants as Chat Characters providing a graphical flair to the chat experience. During a chat, users have the ability to not only send textual information, but to send gestures to one another such as smiling or looking angry. More enthusiastic users can also customize or create new Chat Characters.

MSN Messenger

The MSN Messenger Service is a free application that can be used to collaborate between others on the Internet, specifically those with Hotmail accounts (see Figure 3.10). MSN Messenger tells you when your friends are online so that you can send an instant message to a friend or talk with several friends at once. You can also invite someone in your list to meet over the Internet using NetMeeting or to play an Internet game. In addition, it notifies you when email has arrived at Hotmail for you.

MSN Messenger Service and Hotmail are both Microsoft Internet products that work closely together through the same set of servers. (Hotmail is a free, Web-based email service.) You must have a Hotmail account to use MSN Messenger Service. Having a Hotmail account is not only essential for using MSN Messenger Service, but it can be very handy for reading and sending email when you're on the road; because with Hotmail, all you need is access to the Web.

Figure 3.10   *An example of a Microsoft Messenger screen.
Notice how, in addition to seeing who is part of the session,
you can also see what their status is (in this case,
Duncan Mackenzie is away from his computer).*

Both instant messages and email are ways to send messages over the
Internet, but they differ in the following respects:

- MSN Messenger Service sends instant messages in real time. Email
  collects messages for you and lets you look at them later.

- Instant messages in MSN Messenger Service have a temporary quality.
  Unless you deliberately save them, they are gone when you close the
  message window. Email messages remain until they are deleted.

- You can use MSN Messenger Service for more than sending or receiving instant messages. You can use it to set up an online meeting or an
  Internet game, or to receive other notifications, such as the arrival of
  mail. You can even use it to send email.

Exchanging messages with several MSN Messenger Service users at once
in an instant message window feels a lot like typing messages in a chat
window. But there are important differences:

- **Personalization.** In MSN Messenger Service, you communicate with
  the people you want to. No strangers allowed.

- **Privacy.** The only people who know about the conversation are the
  people who have been invited to participate. It is not publicized or
  open to the world.

- **Technology.** MSN Messenger Service uses a different instant messaging server technology than chatting does.

Microsoft NetMeeting

Microsoft NetMeeting is another real-time collaborative application that you can build upon in your applications. NetMeeting provides the following capabilities:

- **Video and audio conferencing.** Instead of textual communication over the Internet or intranet, users can send and receive full duplex audio and video.
- **Whiteboard conferencing.** Allows people to share a common whiteboard to collaborate graphically.
- **Chat.** Allows real-time collaboration using text.
- **Internet directory.** Allows users to locate other users on the Internet or intranet.
- **File transfer.** Provides the ability for users to transfer one or more files to one another.
- **Program sharing.** Users who are collaborating with NetMeeting can share the interface to applications such as Microsoft Word or Excel.
- **Remote desktop sharing.** Provides the ability to operate a computer remotely.
- **Advanced calling.** This feature gives you the flexibility to send a mail message to a NetMeeting user or initiate a NetMeeting call directly from your mail address book.

Of course, the drawback of using such applications is the bandwidth that is required to send and receive such information. Many large organizations use the features of NetMeeting on the corporate LAN/WAN for various forms of communication.

One of NetMeeting's best features is that it allows developers to leverage its capabilities by integrating real-time multipoint data conferencing into customized solutions (see Figure 3.11). In fact, with NetMeeting, developers can do the following:

- Create custom conferencing solutions (for example, a medical application that allows many doctors to review medical information, such as x-rays, to provide enhanced medical diagnosis) using the Microsoft

NetMeeting Software Developers Kit (SDK) and development tools such as Visual Basic or Visual C++.

Note

You can download the NetMeeting SDK from http://www.microsoft.com/ windows/NetMeeting/Authors/SDK/. ◆

- Integrate conference functionality into Web pages by utilizing ActiveX controls and scripting interfaces provided by the latest version of NetMeeting.

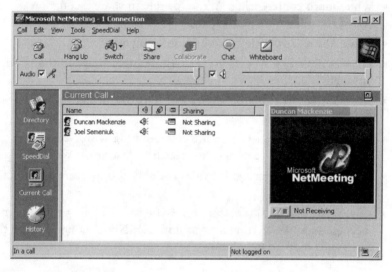

Figure 3.11   *A sample Microsoft NetMeeting session with only two participants.*

Chapter Summary

In this chapter, I took a bold step and described all of the technologies that can be called upon during the design and implementation of advanced collaborative solutions. This was done to ensure that all readers have a common understanding of how each of these products and technologies can be brought together to form one unified collaborative solution. Please take note that even though this book deals primarily with Microsoft Exchange Server, you must understand that building collaborative solutions requires you to go beyond the functional boundaries of Microsoft Exchange and call upon the technologies that fulfill your functional requirements.

In this chapter, we discussed the following:

- What makes Microsoft Exchange Server a superior messaging infrastructure for your collaborative solutions.

- The functionality that SQL Server provides to advanced collaborative solutions.

- The role Microsoft Outlook plays in your collaborative playground.

- The benefits and potential that Windows CE provides collaborative applications.

- The technologies (COM, DCOM, COM+) that allow developers to combine the services from many different applications to form one unified set of services used to collaborate.

- A set of general programming interfaces, such as CDO, MAPI, ADSI, at a very high level, to help clarify the part they play during the construction of collaborative solutions.

- The set of development environments you can use to construct collaborative solutions that include Visual Basic (all of Visual Studio), VBA, and VBScript.

- An additional set of applications that can be easily integrated into virtually any collaborative solution you can define.

4

The Heart of Collaboration: Microsoft Exchange Server

In this chapter, we will focus on the following topics:

- The Microsoft Exchange Server architecture
- Configuring Exchange for collaborative development and operations
- Understanding the functional roles of the Exchange client
- How to effectively implement Exchange public folders
- Understanding and configuring the Microsoft Event Service

The Importance of Architecture

We have spent enough time summarizing the products we are going to work with. Let's change our direction and dig into some of the finer details of the process of collaborative solution development.

Before we go any further, however, it should be stated that the primary goal of this book is to provide a comprehensive reference to collaborative development. One of my pet peeves with other development-related books is that they rarely describe the underlying architecture of the applications that the book describes. Many development books do not address setting up a proper development environment to house collaborative solutions. They often fail to cover issues related to the physical implementation of the products on which you are building your applications that could lead to developmental nightmares. When you develop collaborative applications, you must be cognizant of the underlying architecture of your messaging infrastructure and supporting network because their organization and topology will greatly affect the design and implementation of your solutions. That is where this chapter fits into the puzzle. I'm going to spend some time outlining the architecture of our main product, Microsoft Exchange, as well as introduce procedures that can be followed to help create the development and production environments of your collaborative solutions. I am hoping that this will provide you with an understanding of the complexities of the underlying architecture of Microsoft Exchange.

Setting Up a Collaborative Development Environment

One of your first steps, as collaborative solutions developers, is to create a development environment that provides all the services you require for your solutions and mimics the actual implementation of your messaging and collaborative infrastructure.

Many times, I have walked into an organization and found that the developers were not in sync with the implementation of the network. Although this shouldn't pose too much of an issue theoretically, and many developers argue that this is not the job of the application developer, I am a strong believer of the opposite approach. Collaborative development should always begin with your messaging infrastructure. By possessing insight into the physical implementations and constraints of your underlying messaging topology, you can choose and implement the appropriate design that will produce a successful collaborative solution.

Here are some of the most common Do's and Don'ts that you might want to strive for and avoid when developing collaborative applications:

- **Do** make every effort to familiarize yourself with the implementation of the messaging infrastructure. After you understand all of the components of your organization's infrastructure, meet with the network designer and administrators to discuss topics, such as technical constraints, weaknesses, and future plans of your network and messaging solution.

- **Do** make every effort to share the design and assumptions made regarding your collaborative solution with network engineers and administrators. These people can give you the required insight into networking and architectural features that could lead to functional constraints in your solutions. I encountered an example of this recently. It involved an application that was designed and implemented assuming that all parts of the network, even servers and services across WAN links, were available, which was not the case.

- **Do** make every effort to gather input from system architects and administrators regarding the design and implementation of your solution. Remember, half the job of creating a successful collaborative application is meeting the needs of its users. The other half of a successful solution is ensuring that it can be easily managed and understood by those who need to support it.

- **Don't** assume that your application will perform the same under intense load. Take some time to load and test all of your collaborative applications before you roll them into a production environment. A great method of load testing your applications is by using a utility that is shipped with Exchange Server called LoadSim. The LoadSim utility simulates messaging load on the Microsoft Exchange messaging infrastructure, allowing you to gather metrics regarding the performance of your collaborative processes and how they are affected by load.

- **Don't** assume that your application will perform in the same manner at all times of the day, month, or year. As a collaborative developer, you cannot simply live inside the functionality of your application. You must always be aware of the surrounding processes that can make your application respond or act differently. For example, suppose that you have written an emergency response system that requires immediate action within a given time threshold—for our purpose, assume that this time threshold is two minutes. If a response is not obtained within two minutes, an alternative action must be taken. This type of system could be greatly affected by normal networking activity, such as in the morning when all users log on to the network at roughly the same time, or during times of online backup when the servers might not respond as fast as they do normally, causing the threshold to be reached more often than during normal work times. Try to avoid letting normal networking operations add a level of variability to the functionality of your solutions.

- **Do** design your application to work with temporarily disconnected users. Now, more than ever, we are working with technology that allows users to take their computers home or on the road with them. Ensure that you always handle disconnected usage in your application by either providing some level of functionality to your application in a disconnected state or, at a minimum, by gracefully acknowledging the fact that the user is not connected to any back-end servers. Microsoft Outlook is a great example of an application that provides a great deal of offline functionality. When online, you can send and receive messages and work with public folders. Microsoft Outlook provides a comparable set of features when it is not connected to Microsoft Exchange by allowing users to send (the messages sit in the Outbox until Outlook is connected with Microsoft Exchange) messages as well as work with content contained in public folders. Also, Outlook can automatically detect when it cannot connect to Microsoft Exchange and can switch to an offline state. We will talk more about Microsoft Outlook's service capabilities in Chapter 5, "Microsoft Outlook 2000 Collaborative Basics."

To develop and test your collaborative solution, you must first construct a development and testing environment that adequately simulates the main architectural features of your underlying messaging system. The following are some tips you can follow to help establish your collaborative development and test environment:

- First, make the strongest effort to establish a development and test environment that mimics the real architecture of your networking and messaging infrastructure. If your production system is comprised of routers and subnets, you should set up routers and subnets in your development/test environment. The same concept holds true for parameters, such as Exchange Sites, third party connectors and gateways, and public folder replication scenarios. The closer you can make your development environment like the environment your application will eventually be deployed on, the less headache you will encounter during the integration testing and rollout phases of your project.

- When setting up your development environment, try to work closely with the networking and messaging architects that have designed and implemented the production environment. This saves a great deal of time, effort, and guesswork during the planning stages of the project.

- Perform incremental tests on computers other than your development computers. This may seem fairly obvious, but some developers wait until well into the development process to install and test their applications on other computers. In my experience, you should build and test as often as possible.

- Ensure that you create an installation image of all the different client installation configurations that will exist in the production system. An installation image quickly allows you to erase and reconfigure test clients easily.

- If you have taken the time to create client installation images, use them often. When you are testing the installation or functionality of new builds, it should always be on a newly restored image of a valid client configuration. This eliminates any functional inconsistencies that can crop up due to residue from previous installations of your solution.

Generally speaking, developing and testing your collaborative applications in an environment that directly correlates to the environment provided by the production infrastructure guarantees to minimize any integration issues that I discussed at the beginning of this chapter. As a rule of thumb, build often and test even more often.

I'm not going to spend much more time preaching good methodology and development practices. What I do recommend, however, is that you read some good books on software development. They will certainly provide insight into successfully building and deploying applications. In addition, I like to follow the Microsoft Solutions Framework (MSF) for enterprise development. You can find more information on MSF at `http://www.microsoft.com/msf`.

> ### Note
>
> *I recommend that all developers read the following titles:*
>
> Rapid Development: Taming Wild Software Schedules *by Steve McConnel, published in July 1996, by Microsoft Press; ISBN: 1556159005.*
>
> Code Complete: A Practical Handbook of Software Construction *by Steve McConnel, published in May 1993 by Microsoft Press; ISBN: 1556154844.* ◆

The Microsoft Exchange Architecture

Before you can start the processes of developing your collaborative solutions, it is always a good idea to familiarize yourself with the architecture and functionality of your underlying messaging platform, which is, in our case, Microsoft Exchange. Because we spent a great deal of time summarizing the functionality that Exchange provides to the collaborative process in Chapter 3, "Overview of Collaborative Tools and Techniques," the only thing that is required is to define the architecture of Exchange. This section will accomplish exactly that.

As stated earlier, the complete functionality that you reap from Microsoft Exchange is simply a number of well-defined Windows NT services that interact with one another in well-defined ways. Some of the services are considered core, meaning that their absence would cause Microsoft Exchange to stop sending and receiving messages. Other services are considered to be non-core, meaning that their absence would not cause Microsoft Exchange to stop performing its messaging services. Figure 4.1 displays these services.

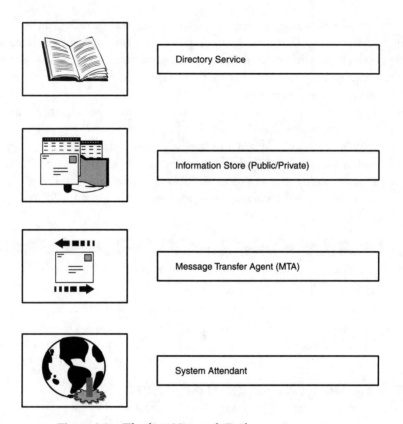

Figure 4.1   *The four Microsoft Exchange core services.*

The System Attendant Service

I like to think of the System Attendant Service as being the head honcho of Microsoft Exchange because every other Microsoft Exchange service depends on the System Attendant in one form or another. In fact, a sure way to stop all of the services that comprise Microsoft Exchange is to shut down the System Attendant Service.

The System Attendant Service is responsible for many functions within Microsoft Exchange. The following is a summary of the functions it performs:

- Every time a new recipient is created within a Microsoft Exchange environment, the System Attendant automatically generates the new recipient's related email addresses. For example, if the Exchange messaging environment contains mail connectors to foreign messaging implementations such as cc:Mail or SMTP mail, the System Attendant must generate additional cc:Mail and SMTP mail addresses for each new recipient, in addition to the address assigned by default by Microsoft Exchange. Refer to Figure 4.2 to see how multiple email addresses can be defined for one Microsoft Exchange recipient.

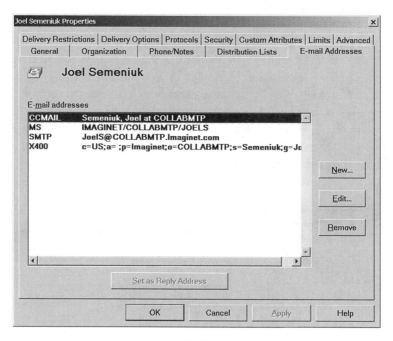

Figure 4.2   *Example of multiple email address types created by Exchange Server.*

- When objects are deleted from the Exchange Directory, this wasted space is automatically reclaimed by the System Attendant Service.

- The System Attendant is also responsible for building the routing tables that are used to transfer messages from one server to the next within or between sites.

- Microsoft Exchange provides a special piece of functionality called a Link Monitor to automatically check connection links between other Exchange Servers. This method uses ping messages between servers to verify connection state. The System Attendant is responsible for managing these Link Monitors to help alert administrators when a possible messaging failure exists.

- If message tracking is enabled by Exchange administrators, Exchange keeps track of the location and route of each message inserted into the system by recording entries in a log file. The System Attendant is responsible for overall maintenance of the tracking logs that support this functionality.

The Information Store Service

The Information Store is the service that manages the databases that Microsoft Exchange uses to store messages. In fact, Exchange manages messages in two separate databases: the Private Information Store and the Public Information Store.

The Private Information Store is a database (Priv.mdb) that maintains all of the messages sent to a particular mailbox managed by the Exchange Server. The messages (and folders) that exist within the Private Message Store can only be accessed by those users who have been granted specific access—the owner of the mailbox or assigned delegates.

The Public Information Store (Pub.mdb) is the most essential collaborative component that is provided by Microsoft Exchange 5.5. It is in the Public Information Store where Microsoft Exchange stores and manages public folders, as shown in Figure 4.3.

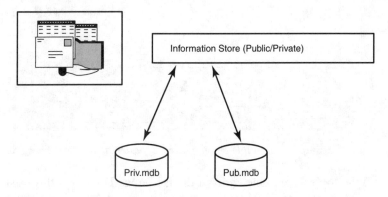

Figure 4.3   *The Information Store Manages two databases: the Private Information Store (`Priv.mdb`), which stores personal mailboxes, and the Public Information Store (`Pub.mdb`), which stores public folders.*

In short, the Information Store Service manages all access to and from clients and the data stored within either of the separate message stores. In fact, the Information Store Service provides data access interfaces for the following client types:

- MAPI clients, such as Microsoft Outlook or Microsoft Exchange Client.

- Any Post Office Protocol version 3 (POP3), such as Eudora, Netscape Mail, or Outlook Express.

Note

Users of POP3 clients cannot gain access to messages contained in any other folder than their inbox, including messages stored within public folders. This is a major implementation constraint for many organizations. ◆

- Any Network News Transfer Protocol (NNTP) clients, such as Netscape Mail or Outlook Express.

Tip

By exposing an NNTP interface to your information stores, setting up NNTP newsgroups becomes as simple as creating a public folder and clicking an option indicating that it is an Internet News Group. This couldn't be much simpler. ◆

- Any Internet Message Access Protocol version 4 (IMAP4) clients, such as Microsoft Outlook Express and Eudora.

Note

IMAP4 is a newer protocol that was created to provide a much richer feature set than POP3. With IMAP4, users now have the option to view folder contents other than the contents of their inbox. In addition, users no longer need to download messages from the server. Users can now store and manage messages on the IMAP4 server, in this case, Microsoft Exchange Server. ◆

As you can see, the Information Store Service presents a rich set of interfaces that provides access to a wide variety of clients with varying degrees of functionality.

The Directory Service

As we discussed in the previous chapter, the Microsoft Exchange Directory is a place that stores information about everything within the Exchange messaging infrastructure. Not only does it store information, such as mailbox and recipient names, it also stores an extremely large amount of organizational information and custom attributes. The service that manages access to all of this data is the Microsoft Exchange Directory Service.

The Microsoft Directory Service provides the following functionality to clients and other components of Exchange:

- The Directory Service stores and manages information regarding mailboxes, custom recipients, public folders, distribution lists, and configuration information about sites and other Exchange services.

- The Directory Service acts like a simple telephone book for all other Microsoft Exchange services that require directory lookup information. Because many other services within Microsoft Exchange require access to directory information for actions such as routing and delivery of messages, it is imperative that these services use a single point of reference for all directory-related queries, thus alleviating any problems associated with providing direct directory access.

- The Directory Service also participates in directory replication where the Directory Services throughout your Exchange organization share their Directory databases through multi-master directory replication.

Note

Remember that Exchange 2000 is tightly integrated into Windows 2000 by leveraging the Active Directory features that are now native to Windows 2000. Generally, this means that Microsoft Exchange no longer maintains its own Directory Service. All recipients and distribution lists are created and stored within Active Directory. ◆

The Message Transfer Agent Service

The Message Transfer Agent Service does exactly what its name suggests—it transfers messages between Microsoft Exchange Servers within the same messaging site. That's not all it does. It also submits, routes, and delivers messages to foreign X.400 MTAs, the Information Store Service, and Microsoft Mail Connectors. In addition, if the MTA needs to submit messages to a foreign X.400 MTA, it converts the content as required from MDBEF (Microsoft Database Exchange Format) to native X.400.

The Message Transfer Agent Service is also responsible for a process called Distribution List expansion. In many cases, users send email to a group of users, such as the "Sales Department," instead of each person in the sales department individually. Microsoft Exchange always must determine which mailboxes (and other distribution lists) are comprised in a given distribution list. It is the job of the MTA to unravel the contents of a given distribution list to help specify who is the ultimate recipient of a piece of email.

The Microsoft Exchange Event Service

This is the first Exchange service we have discussed that is not considered mandatory for messaging—that is, it is not an Exchange core service. However, when it comes to the core services that collaborative applications depend on, no other service provides more value. As we discussed in the previous chapter, the Microsoft Exchange Event Service is responsible for providing a programmatic way of processing data that is stored in Exchange folders (public or private). Collaborative developers can write scripts that are activated whenever some event takes place in the script's associated folder (such as a new posting). We will spend a great deal of time learning how to implement such scripts later in the book, so for now let's put this topic aside.

The Microsoft Exchange Chat Service

The Microsoft Exchange Chat Service is not one of the core services of Microsoft Exchange; it isn't really a part of Microsoft Exchange at all. It is an extremely important service for those who want to implement some level of real-time collaboration very easily.

The Microsoft Exchange Chat functions as an Internet Information Server add-on more than anything. The reason that this product is shipped with Microsoft Exchange is because both of them fit nicely into the collaboration category. The Exchange Chat Service was discussed in the last chapter.

The Microsoft Exchange Key Management Service

How do we know that the sender of a piece of mail is really who she claims she is? What if the message was sent by an imposter? Worse yet, what if the message received was somehow altered from its original form during transit? You can prevent these questions from being asked when you use the functionality provided by the Microsoft Exchange Key Management Server. Microsoft Key Management Server allows users to digitally sign and seal their email messages. Generally speaking, Microsoft Key Management Server provides an extremely high level of security for those organizations that are concerned about implementing such levels of protection. You can additionally utilize the functionality of such services from within your collaborative solution. For example, suppose you create a routing and approval solution that requires a high level of validation. Let's further suppose that you want to ensure that the recipient of an approval message is who it was intended for. Your routing and approval solution can encrypt all of the messages destined to your recipients, and if the mail can be opened, you know that the correct person has read the message. Also, you can incorporate message signing in your routing applications to verify whom your requests are coming from.

There are actually two types of components that make up the functionality of the Key Management server: the server components and the client components. The server-based components can reside on any Exchange

Server computer in the organization (however, there can be only one Key Management server in the organization). The following components define the server-based portion of the Key Management Service:

- **Security Administration DLL.** This provides the administrators of Microsoft Exchange the ability to administer and control the Key Management Service.

- **Key Management Service.** This is a Windows NT service that accepts and processes requests from the Administrator program.

- **Key Management Database.** The Key Management Database is a file database that manages advanced security information for the entire Exchange organization.

- **Key Management Security DLL.** The Key Management Security DLL reacts to Key Management security requests initiated by the user. This DLL is responsible for extracting message-based requests and sending them to the Key Management Service.

Additionally, the Exchange System Attendant is used by the Key Management Server components to receive user requests to activate advanced security and store signing and sealing keys in the Key Management database. The client requires the capability to request participation with the advanced security options as well as have the capability to sign and seal messages. This means that there must be some component of advanced security that resides on the client; this component is called the Security DLL. Client applications use this DLL for any type of advanced security activity.

> ### Note
>
> *There is a substantial difference between signing and sealing messages. When you sign the bottom of a letter or a personal bank check, your signature verifies to someone else that you are authorizing a payment. A digitally signed message is exactly the same thing; you are putting a calculated stamp on your messages that can be used by others to verify authenticity.*
>
> *A sealed message is one in which the content is completely encrypted. In fact, only the destined recipients can open and read the contents of your messages when they are digitally sealed. This is different from a signed message where the actual message content is not hidden from others.* ◆

Other Microsoft Exchange Services

We have been focusing a great deal on the services that we, as developers of collaborative solutions, rely upon to provide the heart of our messaging applications. Here are a few other services that are also very important to

Microsoft Exchange; however, they are probably more important to the messaging architects who require Exchange to integrate into other messaging platforms:

- **Internet Mail Service.** Provides SMTP mail exchange with other SMTP servers. POP3 is provided by the Information Store, as was previously mentioned.

- **Internet News Service.** Replicates content to and from Usenet news-groups using NNTP. It also provides a connection to the Exchange server for NNTP clients.

- **Microsoft Mail Connector.** Allows Microsoft Exchange to send and receive messages from Microsoft Mail.

- **Directory Synchronization.** Allows Microsoft Exchange to synchronize directory information with post office information stored in a Microsoft Mail Post Office.

- **Schedule + Free/Busy Connector.** Exchanges Calendar free and busy time between Microsoft Exchange and Microsoft Mail.

- **Connector for Lotus Notes, GroupWise, and cc:Mail.** Provides Microsoft Exchange with the functionality of exchanging directory information and messages with Lotus Notes, GroupWise, and cc:Mail messaging systems.

Although we have not completely defined the services I have just listed, these services are extremely important to the overall functionality of Microsoft Exchange and are of great interest and importance to the Exchange Messaging architect.

I want to stress that, as developers of collaborative solutions, you must be very decisive when it comes to the scope of your overall solution. Please take note of the functional nature of the preceding listed services. Most of the non-collaborative-related services are meant for messaging integration with other platforms. This means only one thing; your collaborative application might have to integrate with a completely foreign messaging system that may or may not have the same capabilities as Microsoft Exchange. This would definitely be listed as a functional design constraint on your whiteboard.

Installing and Configuring Additional Collaborative Components

If you can type **Setup**, you can install Microsoft Exchange Server. However, what do you need to install or configure to make Microsoft Exchange ready to be your collaborative development platform? Now, we are going to take a look at some of the extra steps you must take to effectively bring your Microsoft Exchange Server from a simple messaging server to a collaborative workhorse. In fact, from this point on, I will assume that all of the appropriate messaging infrastructure elements are in place (sites, site connectors, third party connectors, directory replication) so that we can focus solely on the collaborative components.

Outlook Web Access

When deciding which Exchange component to discuss first in this section, I had to revert to the first component I generally configure after I install Microsoft Exchange Server: Outlook Web Access.

Outlook Web Access is an additional component that can be installed during the installation process of Microsoft Exchange, specifically during a custom installation.

> ### Tip
>
> *Outlook Web Access can be installed on the same computer as Microsoft Exchange or on a different computer altogether. Please note that Outlook Web Access requires Internet Information Server version 3.0 or later. Typically, when creating a collaborative development environment, you will install Exchange, IIS, and Outlook Web Access all on the same computer. Of course, when testing your application, you should work closely with your messaging and networking architects to help define the exact nature of the production system. I will not spend time discussing all of the different aspects of installing and configuring Outlook Web Access on production systems because that exceeds the goal of this book.* ◆

Before you install Outlook Web Access, please ensure that your development server has the following properties:

- Windows NT 4.0 with Service Pack 3 or later
- IIS 4.0 and the NT Option Pack
- Windows NT TCP/IP Patch
- Any required language packs
- All users must have *Log On Locally* rights

Now, you need to configure your Microsoft Exchange server to support Outlook Web Access. You do this by controlling the HTTP object in the Microsoft Exchange Administrator program. To be honest, you don't have to change any of the default settings of the HTTP object for Outlook Web Access to work; however, you might want to tweak some of the settings to conform to your environment. Figure 4.4 displays the HTTP object in the Exchange Administrator program.

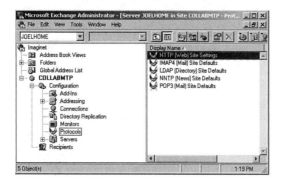

Figure 4.4   *The HTTP object in the Exchange*
Administrator program.

The following are some of the HTTP protocol options that you can configure using the Exchange Administrator program:

- **Enable Protocol.** Enables or disables the protocol at the site level, server level, or user level.

- **Allow anonymous users to access the anonymous public folders.** Allows anonymous users access to any public folders published with Anonymous access privileges. (We will discuss folder permissions later in the section, "Exchange Public Folders.")

- **Allow anonymous users to browse the global address list.** Allows anonymous users to browse the GAL.

- **Maximum number of address book entries returned.** Limits the number of address book entries returned to the user.

As you can see, with the possible exception of the Enable Protocol setting, the preceding settings do not dictate how you will design your collaborative applications.

Tip

You can actually set the HTTP Protocol settings to one of three levels. The first level is at the site level, which allows you to configure HTTP settings for the entire site. The second level is at the server level. HTTP settings set at the server level override those at the site level. And finally, the third level is the user level. Here, you can simply enable or disable certain users' ability to participate in Outlook Web Access. ◆

After you have installed and configured Outlook Web Access, the first thing to do is try it. By default, Outlook Web Access is initiated when you launch your browser (which must support frames and JavaScript) and visit the following URL: http://<IISServer>/Exchange, where <IISServer> is the name of your Web server supporting Outlook Web Access.

Key Management Server

After the Key Management Server is installed, it must be configured to provide advanced security functionality for selected users in your Exchange organization. In fact, there are two stages that must be completed before an administrator enables advanced security. Stage 1 consists of the Key Management administrator granting advanced security functionality to a given user. Stage 2 consists of the client initialization of advanced security options based on information presented to the client as a result of the first stage (see Figure 4.5).

Note

You should be cognizant of some installation requirements that exist when deciding on which server to install the Key Management Server.

Use the following guidelines when deciding which server to use as the KM server:

- *Advanced security must be administered using the Microsoft Exchange Server Administrator program.*

- *The Administrator program must be running on a Microsoft Exchange Server computer that has remote procedure call (RPC) connectivity to the KM server.*

- *The server should be physically secure.*

- *The key management archive database should be backed up regularly.*

- *The server must be using the Microsoft Windows NT file system (NTFS) format for maximum security.* ◆

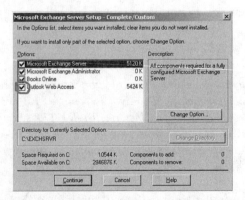

Figure 4.5   *The process of enabling advanced security.*

Stage 1: Enabling Advanced Security for a Mailbox

When you enable advanced security for a mailbox, you give users temporary keys that are used to digitally sign and encrypt mail. A temporary key is used only once for a user to enroll in advanced security, and it secures the connection between the KM server and the client.

When you start the process of enrolling users in advanced security, an RPC is made to the KM server. The KM server generates a one-time temporary key and returns it to you. You must then transmit the temporary key to the user so the user can complete the advanced security process on the client.

A local private key file is created and can be copied to any computer that the user wants to use to digitally sign and encrypt mail.

Perform the following steps to make all of this happen:

1. Navigate to the property pages of the specified user's mailbox.

2. Select the Security tab (see Figure 4.6).

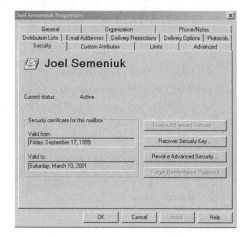

Figure 4.6   *Here is the Security tab of a recipient after advanced security has been enabled.*

3. In the Key Management Server Passwords box, type the required number of advanced security administrator passwords and choose OK after each password.

4. Choose Enable Advanced Security. A dialog box appears prompting you to select the method you want to use to transmit the temporary key to the user.

5. Transmit the temporary key to the user in a secure manner.

Tip

When writing applications that take advantage of advanced security, it is a good idea to understand how you can revoke advanced security permissions for users. Revoking advanced security permanently disables the certificate for a mailbox. When security is revoked for a mailbox, anyone attempting to open an encrypted message previously sent from that mailbox is prompted with a warning stating that the message was secured with a revoked security certificate. The same things happen with a digital signature.

To revoke advanced security for a user, perform the following procedure:

1. *Navigate to the property pages of the specified user's mailbox.*

2. *Select the Security tab.*

3. *In the Key Management Server Passwords box, type the required number of advanced security administrator passwords, and choose OK after each password.*

4. *Choose Revoke Advanced Security.*

5. *In the Key Management Server Passwords box, type the advanced security administrator password, and choose OK.* ◆

Tip

Of course, there is much more to Key Management administration than setting up and revoking advanced security permissions. I will not touch any of those topics in this book. I regretfully pass these topics on to other authors who are specifically writing books on such topics.

Here are some additional administrative tasks you should learn how to perform on the Key Management Server:

- *Enabling additional sites to use the KM server*
- *Enabling security for users in remote sites*
- *Backing up and restoring advanced security data*
- *Viewing the security log*
- *Moving users from one KM server to another*
- *Moving the KM server from one site to another* ◆

Stage 2: The Role of the Client

As mentioned earlier, you must first enable advanced security from the Microsoft Exchange Administrator program. The second part of this process involves configuring the client to use this new feature.

A portion of the enabling process involves the generation of a token that will be given to the client in some secure fashion. For the purpose of testing and software development, it really doesn't matter how the token is provided to the client. Microsoft Exchange Server also has the capability to email the token to the destined user, and the token is displayed in clear text in a mail message. Included with the token are instructions on how to enable advanced security from the client component.

The following note is a sample of a message that was sent to enable advanced security on the client. Notice the message includes instructions for enabling this feature.

Note

Your advanced security temporary key is TABTNDHTKDGG. To enroll in advanced security and start generating security credentials, please do the following:

From the Tools menu in Outlook 98 or Outlook 2000, choose Options, Security. Select Get a Digital ID and then select Set Up Security for Me on the Exchange Server. Click OK and enter your temporary key.

If you are using earlier versions of Outlook, from the Tools menu choose Options, Security. Select Set Up Advanced Security. ◆

Chat Server

To be blunt, setting up Microsoft Exchange Chat Server is a joke when it comes to installation. Configuring the Chat Service is slightly more complicated. Typically, the next job in setting up a Chat Service is to create a chat room. You can create one or more chat rooms by following these steps:

1. Launch the Microsoft Exchange Chat Service Manager from the Start menu.

2. Select a chat server under Microsoft Exchange Chat Service in the left pane.

3. Select Channels (Rooms) under that server in the left pane.

4. From the Action menu, choose New, Create channel.

5. Type the name of the channel in the Name box and choose OK. Be sure to precede the channel name with a valid channel prefix (#, &, %#, or %&).

   #: Denotes an IRC global channel

   &: Denotes an IRC local channel

   %#: Denotes an extended IRC global channel

   %&: Denotes an extended IRC local channel

The channel name is the only parameter required for a persistent channel (see Figure 4.7). To customize a persistent channel, modify the channel properties as needed using the following property sheets:

- **General.** Set the channel topic or subject, or create the messages that clients see when joining or leaving the channel.
- **Access.** Choose a member account, set joining restrictions, or assign passwords.
- **Settings.** Set the member limit, specify the language, rate the channel's content, or provide client-specific data.
- **Modes.** Set the channel visibility (private, hidden, or secret), impose speaking restrictions, or set message parameters.

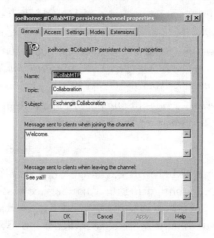

Figure 4.7   *The property page for a persistent channel
from the Microsoft Exchange Chat Administrator program.
After you have created your channel (room),
test it out by launching your chat program, such
as Microsoft Comic Chat (see Figure 4.8).*

Of course, there are many other settings you can use to fine-tune how your chat room will function. Here are some of the extra settings you might want to modify to fit your environment:

- **Intranet Mode.** Designates that the Chat server is operating on a private network and cannot accept connections to clients whose IP address cannot be validated.
- **DNS Lookup Mode.** Requires a valid IP address from the client.

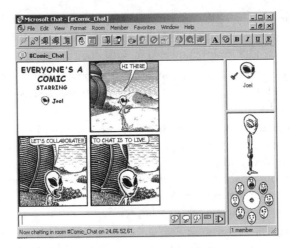

Figure 4.8   *Here we have a Microsoft Exchange Chat room in action.*

- **Server Protocol.** Designates the protocol that the server can accept connections from.

- **Maximum Server Connections.** Indicates the maximum number of client connections to the server.

- **Maximum Anonymous Connections.** Indicates the maximum number of unauthenticated users allowed on the server.

- **Dynamic Channels.** Allows clients to create dynamic channels on the server.

- **Communication Ports.** Specifies the TCP and UDP ports that will be used for the Chat server.

- **Authentication.** Specifies authentication methods available.

- **Messages Sent Upon Connection.** Specifies what message will be sent to the client when the client connects and disconnects.

Exchange Public Folders

Undoubtedly, one of the first things you will do after you install Exchange is start working with Microsoft Exchange public folders, because, as we have already discussed, public folders are used as a basis for most of your collaborative solutions. In this section, we will look at what you need to do to create and manage Microsoft Exchange public folders and begin collaborating.

At the most basic level, the administrator establishes the base-level folders, and sets permissions and other usage parameters. However, a great deal of complexity can be built into public folders, depending on the complexity of the uses. In most cases, when building collaborative solutions, you must extend public folder maintenance to include the following:

- Adding custom forms for contributing or reviewing information. We will spend quite a bit of time in future chapters discussing how to build Outlook forms.

- Defining views to organize and find information. In short, views allow you to customize the way you look at information stored within a public folder. You can use powerful mechanisms such as grouping, sorting, filtering, and content rules to define much more useful ways of organizing and retrieving your data. We will be discussing how to create and manage views in Chapter 5.

- Creating rules to process new information. Rules are defined to execute whenever new content is added to a public folder. Rules allow you to react to messages as they are inserted into the public folder, providing a mechanism to enhance the way you handle information.

- Creating Scripting Agents to provide custom event handling for a folder. Scripting Agents allow you to manipulate messages or perform other actions when the content of a folder is changed in any way by writing code that gets executed by the Exchange Server.

- Assigning individual access permissions for public folders that allow the definition of custom security for users using both individual accounts and distribution lists. Implementing security on public folders is absolutely essential to collaborative applications.

Creating and Structuring Exchange Public Folders

As we discussed at the beginning of this chapter, Microsoft Exchange public folders are governed by the Information Store Service of Microsoft Exchange. In fact, all public folders are actually stored in a file called Pub.mdb on the Microsoft Exchange Server. One of the great aspects of public folders is that the Exchange user never needs to know any of this. The underlying architecture, including server locations, is completely isolated from the Exchange client.

Public folders are typically created with a MAPI-based client such as Microsoft Outlook running in Workgroup mode. They can also be created using the Exchange Server Administrator program using the Import mode or programmatically through the Microsoft Collaboration Data Objects library.

Note

There are a number of different public folders that exist that do not appear in the list of public folders in Microsoft Outlook. These types of public folders are used specifically for system services. For example, Microsoft Exchange stores all of our Calendar Free and Busy information inside a special public folder. To get a better understanding of the type and number of public folders used by Microsoft Exchange, take a look at the list of public folders in the Microsoft Exchange Administrator program under System Folders (see Figure 4.9). You should observe the folders responsible for managing Exchange Forms, Offline Address Books, and Schedule Free and Busy Time. ◆

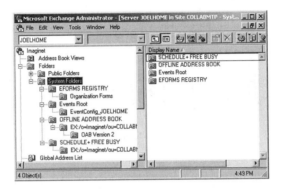

Figure 4.9   *Where to find System Folders in the Microsoft Exchange Administrator program.*

If you have created any folder in your own mailbox, you can easily comprehend what is required to create a public folder. Before we get into greater detail, let's take a look at what we have to work with.

Figure 4.10 depicts an empty set of public folders, meaning that no public folders have been created by any user. Take note of the initial hierarchy of folders presented. The root of all public folders is called, ironically enough, public folders. It is under this formation that all public folders in the Exchange organization are listed, regardless of their physical location. Under the Public Folder root exists two additional folders called Favorites and All Public Folders. If you take a close look at All Public Folders, you can see one folder called Internet Newsgroups, which happens to be the only user-level public folder created during the installation of Microsoft Exchange. For the time being, we will only focus on the contents of the All Public Folders folder, which happens to be the location where you normally gain access to public folders when you are connected to the Exchange Server (as opposed to Favorites, which you typically access when offline).

Let's take a little time to discuss who can create public folders. By default, everyone in the organization has the ability to create public folders. Moreover, when users create public folders, they are automatically the owners of the folder and have the ability to set the folders permissions to allow or block access to other users. There are actually two levels of public folders: top level folders, which are the folders that appear directly under the root of All Public Folders, and non-top-level folders, which are sub-folders of top level folders. I recommend that you modify the default setting that allows all users to create top level folders to allow only a given subset of users, perhaps a group called Exchange Folder Administrators, to create and manage top level folders.

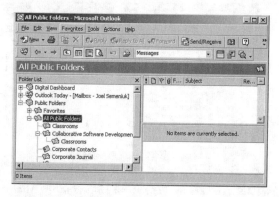

Figure 4.10   *Where to find the root of all public folders.*

Note

In a multiserver/multisite environment, Microsoft Exchange clients have the ability to view the public folder hierarchy even if they cannot see the content of the public folder, as long as they have permission (the folder is visible). This is because Microsoft Exchange replicates the hierarchy of public folders separate from the actual content of the public folders. ◆

To modify who can and cannot create top level folders, follow these steps:

1. View the properties of the Information Store Site Configuration object (see Figure 4.11).
2. Select the Top Level Folder Creation tab (see Figure 4.12).
3. Add and revoke permissions as necessary.

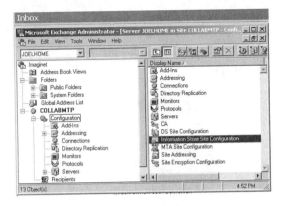

Figure 4.11   *The location of the Information Store Site Configuration object.*

Figure 4.12   *The Top Level Folder Creation tab.*

After you have designated who can add new top level public folders, you can now progress to the process of creating public folders. As mentioned earlier, the only place that you can create a new public folder is through the client interface—in our case, through Microsoft Outlook.

Perform the following procedure to create a new public folder:

1. Choose the folder you want your new folder to appear under. If the new folder is to become a top level folder select All Public Folders.

2. Create the new public folder by right-clicking on the folder you selected in the previous step and select New Folder.

Or, select the folder you chose in the previous step and select File, New, Folder from the menu bar of Microsoft Outlook.

3. After completing the previous step, the dialog box in Figure 4.13 appears.

Figure 4.13   *The Create New Folder dialog box.*

This dialog box allows you to provide a name to the new folder and specify the location and content type of the folder. Specify these parameters and click the OK button. You have successfully created a public folder.

In the Create New Folder dialog box, when selecting from the Folder Contains list box, you are presented with the following list:

- **Appointment Items.** Creates an Outlook Calendar folder
- **Contact Items.** Creates an Outlook Contacts folder
- **Journal Items.** Creates an Outlook Journal folder
- **Mail Items.** Creates a normal folder that contains mail item views
- **Note Items.** Creates an Outlook Notes folder
- **Task Items.** Creates an Outlook Tasks folder

By selecting one of the preceding folder content types, you are actually telling Microsoft Outlook how to display the folder and its contents from within Outlook. This is meaningless when these folders are accessed from clients other than Microsoft Outlook. In fact, these folders look like ordinary folders with ordinary mail messages from clients, such as the Microsoft Exchange Client, which was the first client for Microsoft Exchange (hence the name).

Tip

Many people stop me on the street and ask, "Hey, mister, when I create a new Exchange public folder, where would that folder be created physically?" I simply answer, "That's easy, on your Public Folder server determined by the settings on your Private Information Store object for which your mailbox is defined!"

Every mailbox has an assigned home server that specifies on which server's Private Information Store the mailbox resides. Each server's Private Information Store object can specify a server for which it uses to create and reference public folders for every mailbox residing in the Private Information Store. By default, a Private Information Store's Public Folder Server is the same one the Private Information Store resides on (see Figure 4.14). ◆

Figure 4.14   *Where to specify the default public folder creation location.*

Many organizations dedicate Exchange Servers for storing and managing nothing but public folders and their contents. This means that all other Exchange Servers' Private Information Stores will point to one server to house all public folders. This relieves a great deal of stress on Exchange Servers that simply manage mailboxes when your collaborative applications become resource intensive (see Figure 4.15). ◆

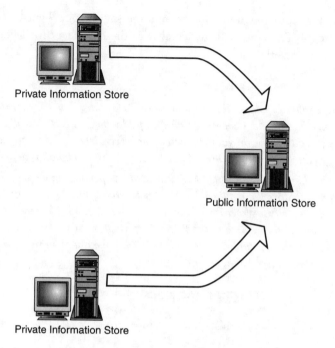

Figure 4.15   *Microsoft Exchange Servers can share a Public
Information Store or maintain their own.*

Adding the Public Folder to the Global Address List

By default, the public folders are not added to the Global Address List,
which makes it difficult for users to send messages to a public folder.
You can configure a public folder to appear in the Global Address List
by following these steps:

1. Log on as an Administrator and launch the Exchange Administrator
   application. Find the public folder you want to view in the Global
   Address List under the list of public folders in the Administrator program. Press Alt+Enter to view the properties of this public folder.

2. Select the Advanced tab from the public folder's Properties page
   (see Figure 4.16).

3. Uncheck the Hide from Address Book check box.

The public folder will now appear in the Global Address Book. Users can
address their email messages to the folder by selecting it from the Global
Address List.

Figure 4.16   *Adding a public folder to the Global Address List.*

Implementing Security on Exchange Public Folders

Now that we have learned how to create different types of public folders (at least as they apply to Microsoft Outlook), let's take a look at how to apply security to those folders.

Establishing folder level security is a key aspect to many organizations. Some companies want to have all information completely public for all to enter and modify. Some organizations take the extreme opposite approach and lock down all public folders ensuring that only those with explicit permissions can gain access to folder content. Other organizations take a mixed approach to managing security by locking down some areas and exposing others.

I will add that you can control the security of public folders from either the Administrator program or the client application, such as Microsoft Outlook. To access public folder permission settings from the Microsoft Exchange Administrator program, perform the following:

1. Under the Folder object, select the folder you want to configure.

2. View the properties of the folder you selected in the previous step by pressing Alt+Enter or by selecting Properties from the File menu of the Administrator program (see Figure 4.17).

3. Click the Client Permissions button that is displayed on the resulting screen.

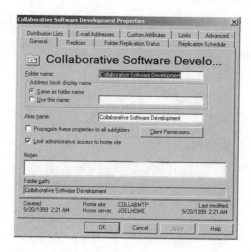

Figure 4.17   *The properties of a public folder in the Exchange Administrator program.*

To access folder security settings from Microsoft Outlook, perform the following procedure:

1. Select the folder that you want to modify from under All Public Folders. Note that you must be the folder's owner to be able to modify security attributes of the folder.

2. Right-click the folder and select Properties from the pop-up menu.

3. Select the Permissions tab at the top of the folder's Properties dialog box.

Using either method, you should see a dialog box that looks similar to Figure 4.18.

Figure 4.18   *The Client Permissions page for a public folder.*

As you can see from Figure 4.18, the Client Permissions dialog box (or Permissions tab, if you are viewing permissions from Microsoft Outlook) displays the current permissions settings, as well as a set of permissions controls. You can use these permissions controls to create select predefined permissions roles or create new permissions configurations.

Let's take a look at the meaning of individual permissions and what they mean. Table 4.1 summarizes the permissions you can grant to users of a folder.

Table 4.1   Folder Permissions

Permission Name	Permission Description
Create Items	Grants permission to create new items in the folder.
Read Items	Grants permission to read the contents of items in a folder.
Create Subfolders	Grants users permission to create subfolders within the folder.
Folder Owner	Grants users folder owner status which essentially grants all permissions to the folder.
Folder Contact	Grants users folder contact status. Folder contacts receive notifications from the folder, such as replication conflict error messages.
Folder Visible	Grants users permission to view the folder in the Public Folder hierarchy.
Edit Items	Permissions can be set such that: • Specified users cannot edit any items in the folder. • Specified users can only edit items that they have created in the folder. • Specified users can edit all items in a folder.
Delete Items	Permission can be set such that: • Specified users cannot delete any items in the folder. • Specified users can only delete items that they created in the folder. • Specified users can delete any item in the folder.

In addition to specific permissions, you have the benefit of choosing from a preset group of permissions roles. Roles are pre-canned sets of permissions that you can apply to users of a folder. Table 4.2 summarizes the permissions given to each of the roles you can select from the Roles drop-down box.

Table 4.2   Roles Permissions

Role Name	Create Items	Read Items	Create Subfolders	Folder Owner	Folder Contact	Folder Visible	Edit Items	Delete Items
Owner	Yes	Yes	Yes	Yes	Yes	Yes	All	All
Publishing Editor	Yes	Yes	Yes	No	No	Yes	All	All
Editor	Yes	Yes	No	No	No	Yes	All	All
Publishing Author	Yes	Yes	Yes	No	No	Yes	Own	Own
Author	Yes	Yes	No	No	No	Yes	Own	Own
Non-Editing Author	Yes	Yes	No	No	No	Yes	None	Own
Reviewer	No	Yes	No	No	No	Yes	None	None
Contributor	Yes	No	No	No	No	Yes	None	None
None	No	No	No	No	No	Yes	None	None

To add users and configure their permissions, perform the following actions:

1. Click the Add button, select a recipient or a distributions list from the global address list, and click the Add button again. You can add as many different mailboxes and distribution lists as necessary. Click the OK button when you are finished.

2. Configure the permissions for each of the recipients or distribution lists you chose in step 1 by either selecting a role or configuring the permissions independently according to your needs.

Tip

Make sure that you always address the security of the default users and the anonymous users listed by default in your folder's Permissions dialog box.

The Default user refers to a valid Exchange user who is not explicitly listed in the Permissions dialog box for a given folder. By default, the security for the Default user is none, so if that person hasn't been explicitly granted permissions, she cannot access folder content.

The Anonymous user refers to users who are not actually logged on to the Exchange Server. Again, by default, these users have no permissions to any of the folder content but can still see the public folder in the folder hierarchy. ◆

Offline Public Folders

The greatest features (in my opinion) Microsoft Outlook provides to users with laptops are offline folders. In this section, you will learn how to implement offline folders in Microsoft Exchange.

One of the problems with having a laptop, besides being expected to work 24 hours a day, is that you are not always connected to Microsoft Exchange. Offline folders allow users to gain access to data that resides in public folders that are stored on the Exchange Server, even when they are not connected to the corporate network in any way.

Note

With the advent of Windows 95, it was much easier to be an efficient laptop user. One of the features that Windows 95 provided was the Briefcase. The Briefcase was a special folder that you could create on the hard drive of the laptop running Windows 95. A user could then copy files into the Briefcase from the corporation's network location and a synchronous relationship would instantly be formed between the files stored in the Briefcase and the original files stored on the network. Users could then take the laptop offline, modify the files, and then resynchronize the files when they returned online. This was all too amazing to the typical laptop user.

As the Briefcase worked really well for files, what about mail stored in Microsoft Outlook? Wouldn't it be great if there was a way to keep my mail in my mailbox at the Exchange Server while accessing the mail when offline? The answer: offline folders.

Laptop users very quickly began seeing an insurgence of technology that allowed them to access remote data even while they were not physically connected to any network. In fact, Microsoft Internet Explorer allowed users to choose whether they wanted to view Web pages offline.

Windows 2000 provides even better tools for laptop and roaming users, such as the Active Sync set of technologies. I like to think that Active Sync is the Briefcase on steroids. ◆

The secret to offline folders is, of course, the seamless mechanism that Outlook uses to ensure that messages are replicated between the user's inbox with that of the local data store, without the requirement of any user interaction. What users "see" when they are offline is what they will see when they are online, and they don't need to do anything special to accomplish this.

The same holds true for public folders that you want to reference when you are offline. By default, there are no public folders available to the user when she is offline. It is the job of the individual user, or administrator, to configure a public folder to be available offline. Unfortunately, configuring a public folder to be available offline is not as straightforward as you might expect. Earlier, I mentioned where to find public folders from inside

Outlook and a set of public folders called Favorites. A user must copy a reference to a public folder to the Favorites folder before he has the option of making the folder available for offline use.

The following set of steps details the process of configuring a folder for offline usage. Take note that, for any content to be available offline, you must have the Exchange Service settings in Outlook configured to use an offline folder:

1. From the hierarchy of folders under the All Public Folders folder, select the folder that you want to make available offline. Drag this folder to the Favorites folder. This makes a reference to the original folder from the Favorites folder.

2. Right-click the folder you just copied into the Favorites folder, and select Properties from the pop-up menu. When the folder's Properties dialog box appears, select the Synchronization tab.

3. Select When Offline or Online, and you are done.

You might want to place a filter on what you want to view offline because the contents of a public folder can be quite large. When you implement filtered synchronization, only the items in the folder that match the filter criteria are synchronized to local storage. To apply a filtered synchronization, simply click the Filter button from the Synchronization tab of the Public Folders properties and define what criteria the filter should use to select which folder item will participate in offline synchronization.

Here are just a few of the filters you can place on synchronization:

- Messages containing specific words in fields, such as frequently used fields for that folder type
- Items that match specific item categories
- Items that are unread, have attachments, or are of a given size
- Items that contain ranges of information, such as contacts that have birthdays this month

The complexities of the filter definitions can be quite extreme; however, they should provide a sufficient level of power to those who require it.

Public Folder Content Moderation

Content moderation is nothing new, because many different Internet new services have been doing this for some time. Public folder content moderation allows administrators to set up an environment in which all items posted to the folder are forwarded to a designated recipient or public folder for review. Reviewers must then move the moderated content back into the folder after it has been reviewed and approved for viewing by others. Until the items receive approval, they are usually held in an interim public folder. Using a moderated folder, rules can be defined to specify who is allowed to post information into a folder, as well as who is allowed to approve the posts that users submit. Because this capability is built into public folders, no code needs to be written to provide it. Figure 4.19 shows the interface for creating a moderated folder.

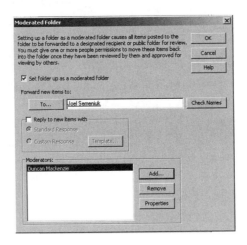

Figure 4.19   *An example of a public folder that has been set up for moderation.*

Let's take a look at how you can enable moderation for a given public folder.

To set up a public folder for moderation, right-click on the public folder you want to moderate and choose the Properties option from the pop-up menu. Next, select the Administration tab. From there, you can select the Moderated Folders button. Table 4.3 allows you to configure who can moderate the folder.

Table 4.3   Configuration Options for Public Folder Parameters

Option	Description
To	Specifies the name of the moderator(s) who will screen the incoming messages or the name of an alternate public folder where the messages are stored for the moderators to review.

continues ▶

Option	Description
Reply to New Items with Standard Response	Sends the standard response message. The standard response reads:
	"Thank you for your submission. Please note that submissions to some folders or discussion groups are reviewed to determine whether they should be made publicly available. In these cases, there will be a delay before approved submissions can be viewed by others."
Reply to New Items with Custom Response	Sends the custom response message specified by the moderator.
Moderators: Add, Remove, Properties	Enables you to specify the names of the people who are moderators for this public folder.

Preparing for Outlook Forms Development

Our next step is to prepare your Microsoft Exchange environment for Outlook form development and deployment. There isn't much that you need to configure in Microsoft Exchange to handle Outlook forms development; however, you do need to configure organizational storage containers for these forms. In this section, we will take a look at form libraries and what you need to do with them before you can build, test, and deploy Outlook forms.

Form Libraries

Form libraries are repositories for forms that are commonly used in the collaborative environment. There are three general locations for form libraries:

- **Organization Forms Library.** A repository for forms that are commonly accessed by all users in a company.

- **Public Folder Forms Library.** Designed to store forms that are used with a specific public folder.

- **Personal Forms Library.** Exists on a specific user's computer. Users can save forms to this library, but other users cannot view or modify them. This is a great location to use as a staging area during the development process. It is a good idea to publish your forms to your Personal Forms Library before you publish them to the Organization or Public Folder Forms Libraries.

Configuring an Organization Forms Library

Let's take a look at how to create an Organization Forms Library (because this is the only forms library that isn't created for you by default). The following instructions detail the steps required to create custom system folders using the Exchange Administrator. The custom folders will become the Organizational Forms Library:

1. Log on to your Exchange as Administrator. Open the Microsoft Exchange Administrator by clicking Start and selecting Programs, Microsoft Exchange, Microsoft Exchange Administrator. Expand Folders, System Folders, EFORMS REGISTRY in the Explorer tree view (see Figure 4.20).

2. From the Tools menu, select Forms Administrator.

3. In the Organization Forms Library Administrator dialog box, click New.

4. In the Create New Forms Library dialog box, Organization Forms already appears in the Library Folder Name field. Click OK.

5. In the Organization Forms Library Administrator dialog box, click Close.

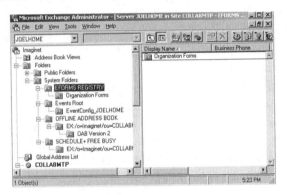

Figure 4.20   *The EFORMS REGISTRY is a*
system public folder.

Now you have a organization-wide, central storage location for forms that you create. We will revisit this when we learn how to create and public customized Outlook forms.

The Exchange Event Service

The Microsoft Exchange Event Service allows for the creation of folder agents, a new feature in Exchange 5.5, which allow a developer to write scripts that execute upon certain events. A folder agent can be implemented for four different events:

• **When a new message arrives into a folder.** This type of agent is useful for building applications that need to check new items as they arrive.

- **When a message is changed.** This event is useful if the contents of a public folder need to be synchronized with another data source, such as a SQL database or another Exchange folder.

- **When a message is deleted.** This event can be used to provide synchronization capabilities between different data sources and the Exchange public folder.

- **A timer-based event.** Agents can fire based on timer events. For example, in the expense report scenario, a manager needs to approve expense reports to allow them to be processed and paid. A public folder agent can be created that checks to see if expense reports have not been approved by the manager every 24 hours. If a manager has not approved the expense report, the agent could then reroute the expense report to another manager for approval.

To make sure that you can begin developing folder agents, there are only a few things you need to do:

1. Make sure that the Microsoft Exchange Event Service is running on the computer that maintains the public folder on which you want to implement the agent.

2. To install and administer event scripts, the user must be granted at least Author permissions on the `EventConfig_<servername>` object in the Exchange Server directory. To configure the appropriate permissions:

   In the Microsoft Exchange 5.5 Administrator, select the `EventConfig <servername>` object from the Folders,System Folders,Events Root container.

   From the File menu, select Properties. On the General tab, select Client Permissions.

   In the Client Permissions dialog box, click the Add button.

   Select one or more users who will be managing scripts on the server and grant them a role of at least Author. Click OK twice.

3. Make sure that the Server Scripting add-in is active from within Microsoft Outlook.

We will spend a considerable amount of time building folder agents later in the book.

Note

Please note that routing objects are automatically installed with Exchange Server Service Packs 1 and 2. To get more information on routing objects, please refer to the agents.hlp *file on the Exchange Server Service Pack CD-ROM.* ♦

Chapter Summary

You should be ready to begin the design and implementation of your collaborative solutions. This chapter focused on some key issues regarding the architecture of Microsoft as well as configuration of some of its core elements. This chapter discussed the following topics:

- The core services of Microsoft Exchange
- Installing and configuring Microsoft Exchange components such as the Exchange Chat Service and the Key Management Service and the Event Service
- Creating and managing public folders
- Configuring organizational forms libraries

5

Microsoft Outlook 2000 Collaborative Basics

In this chapter, we are going to focus on the features of Microsoft Outlook that can be exploited to create collaborative solutions without writing a single line of code. I have included these topics in this book because, for the most part, many businesses have a lack of knowledge and understanding regarding the collaborative possibilities that Microsoft Outlook provides in its base form. Outlook is a powerful product that can be configured in an endless number of functional possibilities. Understanding how to manipulate Outlook without employing some programmatic method is an extremely important first step toward developing collaborative solutions with Outlook.

As I have mentioned before, the extent of your collaborative solutions typically relies on the functionality of your underlying collaborative client. So it makes sense to take you through the built-in collaborative functionality of Microsoft Outlook 2000, which is the collaborative client we are focusing on throughout this book.

To effectively cover all of the collaborative features of Microsoft Outlook 2000, we are going to break apart Outlook's functionality into categories and cover each category in separate chapters. The following is a list of how we are going to segment the collaborative features of Microsoft Outlook:

- Out-of-the-box collaboration
- How to organize your information using Outlook

In this chapter, we will focus on the collaborative functionality that is available to everyone using Microsoft Outlook on a Microsoft Exchange messaging platform. In fact, the features described in this chapter require absolutely no custom programming. I'm sure that the programmers reading this book are ready to flip to the next chapter; however, I urge everyone to continue reading to ensure that there is a common understanding of all such features.

Outlook 2000's Out-of-the-Box Collaboration

Out of the box, Microsoft Outlook fills the role of a generic messaging client as well as a generic contact, tasks, and appointment management application. In the first section of this chapter, we are going to review the features of Outlook as they apply to the following:

- Appointment management
- Contact management
- Task management
- Journal management

I am going to make the assumption that Microsoft Outlook is configured to run in Workgroup mode on a Microsoft Exchange messaging backbone so that focus can be made on using these built-in features with others within your collaborative infrastructure.

Appointment Management

As you already know, the Microsoft Outlook Calendar provides users with the ability to schedule and maintain appointments. Outlook appointments can store information, such as the following:

- The appointment subject
- The appointment location
- Start and end times (or none if the appointment is an all day event)
- Reminder settings
- Appointment details
- Contact information
- Category information
- Real-time collaboration information, such as what applications to launch or documents to share during the start of a NetMeeting session

Let's take this base functionality and extend it to the collaborative realm. If you look closely at the top of the Appointment definition window in Figure 5.1, you will see that there is a button called Invite Attendees. For the purposes of collaboration, this is a very useful button because it allows you to set up meetings with other people and resources in your collaborative environment. More importantly, it allows you to book appointments that meet every attendee's schedule in a much easier fashion.

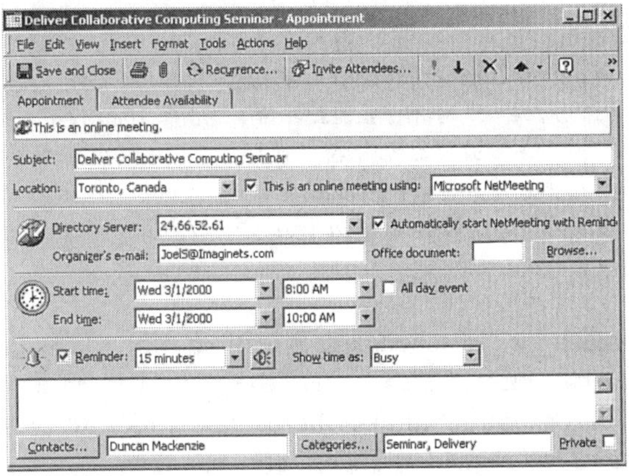

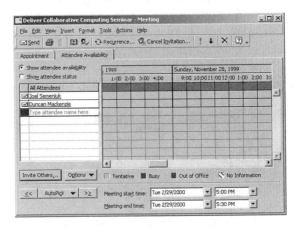

Figure 5.1   *A representation of an appointment in Microsoft Outlook.*

To invite someone to a meeting, you can either click the Invite Attendees button or select the Attendee Availability tab (which you must to do if you want to view the schedules of those you want to invite). Let's take a closer look at the Attendee Availability tab (see Figure 5.2).

Figure 5.2   *The Attendee Availability tab in an Outlook meeting request displaying the free and busy times of chosen attendees.*

As you can see in Figure 5.2, the Attendee Availability tab displays the exact information you might expect—the free and busy times for all selected attendees.

> **Tip**
>
> *You can invite a distribution list to a meeting. Outlook displays the name of the distribution list in the list of attendees. Additionally, the organizer of the meeting might want to expand the distribution list to view the individual recipients in the list. This can be accomplished by clicking the + symbol next to the name of the distribution list. Please take note that you cannot collapse the list after it has been expanded. ◆*

When larger meetings are scheduled, it is often more difficult to find a time when everyone can meet. This is where the AutoPick feature comes into play. The AutoPick feature allows Microsoft Outlook to pick the next available time that all the invited attendees are available.

> **Tip**
>
> *If you have been granted at least Read Delegate access to the Calendar of another user, you might see the subject of appointments that appear as busy areas in the Attendee Availability form when you hover the mouse over the busy area. ◆*

When you have found a time when all users can meet for a given meeting, click the Send button at the top of the appointment form to send out a meeting request. A specially formatted email is sent to all attendees.

Each attendee receives an email requesting confirmation of the scheduled appointment. Figure 5.3 is an example of a meeting request that appears in the inbox of an employee who has been added to the meeting attendee list.

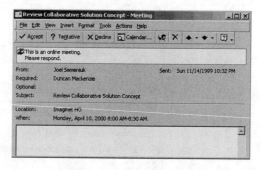

Figure 5.3   *When a user receives a meeting request, he has the ability to accept, decline, or tentatively accept.*

The invited user can choose to accept, decline, or mark the meeting request as Tentative. Users also have a convenient way of viewing their schedules for that particular time period by clicking the Calendar button. Any response causes an email to be sent to the organizer of the meeting. Upon receiving the appointment request response, Microsoft Outlook automatically updates the details of the meeting event. Figure 5.4 displays the status of a meeting after one of the attendees has accepted the meeting request.

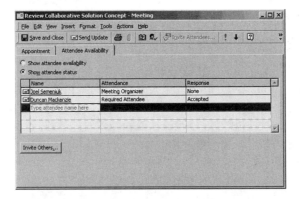

Figure 5.4   *Example of a meeting status report.*

Resource Scheduling

Sometimes, there is a battle finding available meeting resources, such as projectors or even the meeting rooms themselves. Organizations might want to set up schedules for individual resources so that they can be included in the list of attendees to help in picking availability times. Typically, resources correspond to a mailbox on an Exchange server. However, you cannot expect a projector to check its email every day to accept or decline meeting requests.

Microsoft Outlook recognizes this problem and provides the ability to automatically handle meeting requests without any user intervention. To configure these settings, log on to Outlook as the Resource Mailbox; select Tools, Options, Calendar Options, and Resource Scheduling to produce the Resource Scheduling dialog box. You can configure the mailbox account to automatically accept meeting requests and process cancellations, automatically decline conflicting meeting requests, and automatically decline recurring meeting requests.

Appointment Collaboration over the Internet

In the previous examples, we have assumed that all the people on the appointment attendee list have mailboxes on a Microsoft Exchange Server. In many cases, you will be inviting others to a meeting who are not part of your Exchange organization. This is where you can apply some Internet standards.

In comes Internet Calendaring (iCal or iCalendar). You can use the iCalendar standard to send meeting requests to people who are not in your Exchange organization, such as people across the Internet. Basically, iCalendar allows you to define an appointment and send the request using the iCalendar standards. Anyone using an iCalendar-compliant mail reader can view the appointment and accept or decline the event.

Here is how you can create an appointment and forward it as an iCalendar appointment to a user on the Internet:

1. Create an appointment as you would for someone in your Exchange organization. Invite all of the required and optional attendees.

2. Select the attendee from the attendee list who is not in the Exchange organization but is an Outlook Express user on the Internet. Click the envelope icon to the left of the attendee and select Don't Send Meeting to This Attendee from the pull-down list.

3. In the Actions menu of the appointment form, choose Forward as iCalendar option.

4. A dialog box is displayed that allows you to forward the appointment information to users that you specify in the To box. Type in the email address of the remote user or users and click Send.

Note

Not all scheduling software can read iCal files. If you need to forward an iCal attachment to a user or a group of users on the Internet, you might want to be sure that they can import the attachment into their scheduling software. If the destined recipients are using Outlook 2000, they will have no problem opening the iCal attachment as a Calendar item. ◆

The result is the transmission of the appointment in iCalendar format in the form of an attachment to a mail message. The recipient of the message can simply open the attachment, provided he has a valid iCalendar messaging client, and respond to the appointment request as necessary.

Tip

The specifications for iCalendar are defined by the following RFCs:

RFC 2445—Internet Calendaring and Scheduling Core Object Specification (iCalendar) http://www.imc.org/rfc2445

RFC 2446—iCalendar Transport-Independent Interoperability Protocol (iTIP): Scheduling Events, BusyTime, To-dos and Journal Entries http://www.imc.org/rfc2446

RFC 2447—iCalendar Message-based Interoperability Protocol (iMIP) http://www.imc.org/rfc2447

continues ▶

Please note that the iCalendar specification was based on an earlier specification called vCalendar. Outlook also allows you to save an appointment as a vCalendar file type. This vCalendar file can be attached and sent to a recipient who can process vCalendar attachments. Outlook 2000 can read both iCalendar and vCalendar files. ◆

Contact Management

One of the most important assets of an individual or an organization is its contact list. In this section, I will examine the basic functionality that Outlook provides to users who use its built-in contact management features. I will also take a look at some ways that you can enhance collaboration using Outlook contacts.

In its basic form, Microsoft Outlook provides a mechanism for creating and managing contacts electronically. By default, you can record a great deal of information regarding a contact, including the following:

- Typical contact information, such as full name, address(s), phone numbers, and so on
- Additional contact information, such as spouse's name, birthdays, anniversaries, and nicknames
- Internet specific information, such as Web page, NetMeeting settings, and Internet Free and Busy Address

Additionally, Outlook provides many folder views to help organize contacts in the Contacts folder. You can use default views to organize your contacts by the following:

- Category
- Company
- Location
- Follow-Up Flag

Outlook allows users to work with their contacts more seamlessly by providing access to a number of common functions with a simple right click of the mouse. Figure 5.5 displays the default options available to users when they right click on an Outlook Contact item. Right clicking an Outlook contact provides easy access to functionality that includes the following:

- Send a mail message to the selected contact
- Set up a new appointment and associating the selected contact with the appointment
- Set up a meeting with the selected contact
- Create a new task assignment for the selected contact

Figure 5.5   *The default right-click options of an*
Appointment item in Outlook 2000.

- Enter journal information regarding the selected contact
- Cause Outlook to dial the phone number of the selected contact
- Instantiate a NetMeeting session with the selected contact

Microsoft Outlook can also use a contact folder as an address book. In fact, the MAPI service called Outlook Address Book allows Outlook to use any contacts folder as a MAPI Address Book Provider. This functionality provides two very important features.

First, when composing an email, the Outlook Address Book allows you to select Outlook contacts recipients(as long as they have email addresses) as well as recipients from the Global Address List on Microsoft Exchange.

Second, Outlook uses the Outlook Address Book during name resolution. Name resolution takes place when composing a new mail message. Instead of selecting a recipient from a list of contacts, the recipient's name is typed into the To field. Outlook must then verify that the name typed in the To field matches a valid email recipient defined in either the Global Address List or from a Contacts folder being used by the Outlook Address Book.

Using Contacts in Collaboration

Up to this point, we have focused on the general ways you can use Microsoft Outlook to manage contacts. However, what if you need to share contact information throughout the entire organization or even to certain groups of users? Using Outlook and Exchange, this couldn't be much simpler to accomplish.

The secret here is, of course, a contacts public folder, which instantly gives Outlook users the ability to share contacts with one another. As discussed in the previous chapter, you can place a great deal of security at the Public Folder level by restricting and granting access to users and groups of users in your Exchange environment.

Here are some examples of contact public folders:

- **Corporate contact folder.** This list is available to every user in the organization and contains contacts that are important to the organization on a whole.

- **Internal employee contact folder.** This contact folder contains details of all of the employees in an organization and should be accessible only by executives and Human Resource employees.

- **Accounting contact folder.** Accountants typically deal with the accounts payable and accounts receivable ends of a business. A contacts folder containing just this type of information is useful.

- **Project contact folder.** A project contact folder typically contains the names and addresses of individuals involved with certain projects.

As a reminder, here are the steps you can take to create a contacts public folder:

1. Select the appropriate folder you want to create your new folder under. If you want the new contacts folder to be a Top Level Folder, select the All Public Folders from the Public Folder root.

2. Right click the parent folder and choose New Folder from the pop-up menu or Select File, New, Folder from Outlook's menu bar. This displays the dialog box depicted in Figure 5.6.

Figure 5.6   *The Create New Folder dialog box allows you to specify the type of folder you are creating.*

3. Give the folder a name

4. From the Folder Contains drop-down list, select Contact Items.

You can then configure your new folder's security as you see fit.

Sending Contacts to Others

As you might have guessed, it is extremely easy to email contacts to others, especially if the recipient is another Outlook 2000 user. You simply create a new mail message, then select Insert, Item from the message windows menu bar. This gives you the opportunity to select a contact from any contact folder that you have access to.

However, what if the destined user is not using Microsoft Exchange? Even worse, what if the destined user is not using Outlook at all? How can contact information be sent to these types of users? The answer is vCard. vCard is an industry standard developed to unify how contact information is passed and interpreted over the Internet.

Tip

The vCard specification is defined in the following RFCs:

RFC 2425—MIME Content-Type for Directory Information
http://www.imc.org/rfc2425

RFC 2426—vCard MIME Directory Profile http://www.imc.org/rfc2426 ◆

To send a contact as a vCard, perform the following steps:

1. Open the contact you wish to send in vCard format.
2. From the File menu, select Save As.
3. From the Save As Type pull-down list, select vCard Files (*.vcf).

You can now send this file as an attachment.

When a vCard contact is received as an attachment, you can easily add the contact to your list of contacts in any contact folder that you have permissions to write to. Simply drag the vCard attachment to a contacts folder, add any new information to the resulting window, and click Save. It couldn't be easier.

Contact Activities

Being able to view all the activities that you have performed with a given contact is essential in this day and age. To make this more complex, there are so many ways that you interact with your contacts: emails, meeting requests, appointments, tasks, phone calls, assignments, and status reports. Outlook 2000 makes contact activity tracking an extremely simple process.

The default form for an Outlook Contact item contains an Activities tab. When selected, the activities form displays all of the activities you have performed with the selected contact. This information is assimilated from all of your mail in your inbox, Journal items, Calendar items, Task items, and

Note items. Outlook simply scans these folders looking for items that are addressed to or linked to the currently selected contact. It's simple.

You can modify and enhance where Outlook searches for activities for a given set of contacts. Simply display the Properties dialog box of a folder and select the Activities tab, as shown in Figure 5.7.

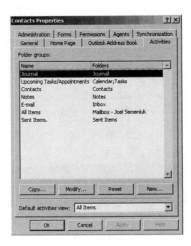

Figure 5.7   *You can specify where to look for activities regarding a contact in the properties of a folder.*

You have the ability to delete locations, modify existing locations, or create new locations for Outlook. Let's take a look at how you can create a new location for Outlook to search for contact activities:

1. Display the properties of an Outlook contacts folder. Select the Activities tab and click New.

2. The resulting dialog box allows you to name the new location as well as choose the location from a tree view of your mailbox and public folders. Give the location a name and click the check box beside the corresponding folder.

Task Management

Microsoft Outlook also lets users create and manage tasks. By default, Outlook provides a task form, shown in Figures 5.8 and 5.9, for recording various task details, such as the due date and start date for the task, the priority of the task, the percentage of the task complete, reminder information, and other details, such as billing information and actual work effort.

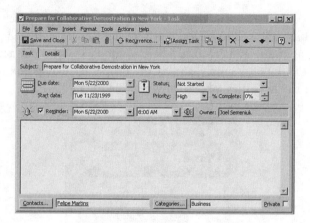

Figure 5.8   *General task details.*

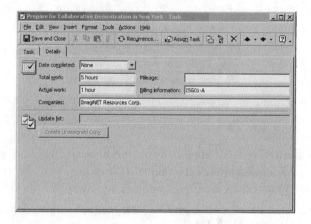

Figure 5.9   *Extended task details.*

Typically, tasks are only created and maintained in a user's mailbox, and are viewable by the user and those who have at least Read Delegate access to the folder.

If you look very closely at the default Outlook task form, you will see a button named Assign Task. Using task assignments can really enhance collaboration.

Clicking the Assign Task button allows you to send a task definition to other Outlook users in the organization. Figure 5.10 depicts the process of assigning an Outlook task to someone.

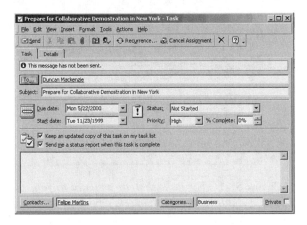

Figure 5.10   *An example of a task assigned to Duncan Mackenzie. Duncan will receive a task request email in his inbox where he can accept or decline the task.*

Similar to sending Outlook Calendar meeting requests, when you assign a task to someone, a specially formatted email (the message class is identified as ipm.TaskRequest) is actually sent to the user. The person that you assign the task to has the opportunity to accept or decline the task request. If the task is accepted, it is added to the user's Task folder in his mailbox, and an acceptance email message is sent back to the creator of the task. If the task is declined, an email is sent back to the person who issued the task assignment and the task is moved into the deleted items folder.

After a task has been assigned, the assigned user can update the details of the task by modifying the task from his Task folder or by sending regular status reports. Whenever an assigned task is modified by either the creator of the task or the person that the task is assigned to, a Task Update message is generated. This message is automatically addressed to the creator of the task and appears in his Inbox as a new message. Outlook automatically integrates any changes indicated by the Update message into the original task (only if the option to maintain assigned tasks is turned on) or when the user reads the message.

Additionally, users who have been assigned tasks can generate regular status reports that are sent back to the tasks' creator by default. To send a status report for an assigned task, simply open the assigned task and select Send Status Report from the Actions menu. This displays a pre-addressed message window that allows status information to be entered and sent. Figure 5.11 displays the Task Status Report windows that are displayed when sending a status report.

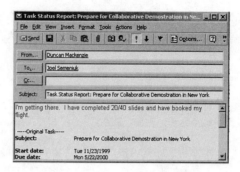

Figure 5.11   *For tasks that are assigned to you,*
you can send status reports to the users who assigned the tasks.

There are some additional options that you can configure with regard to task assignments, as displayed in Figure 5.12. The option Keep Updated Copies of Assigned Tasks on My Task List allows the creator of the task to view updated task information. The second option controls what happens when you mark a task that you have been assigned as complete. The option Send Status Reports when Assigned Tasks Are Completed indicates whether a Task Completion message is sent to the creator of the task.

To reach these properties, follow these steps:

1. Select Tools, Options from Outlook's menu bar.
2. Click the Other tab.
3. Click the Advanced Options button.
4. From the resulting screen, click the Advanced Tasks button (see Figure 5.12).

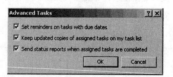

Figure 5.12   *Setting advanced task options.*

Journal Management

Journaling is a great way to keep track of various day-to-day activities. Here is a list of some of the more common uses for journaling in Microsoft Outlook:

- Track email correspondence to users or a set of users.
- Track contact activity such as phone calls, notes, faxes, letters, and conversations.
- Track Microsoft Office documents.

Journaling can be automatic or manual. Automatic journaling is performed by Outlook whenever you perform certain actions. For example, Outlook can be configured to create a journal entry every time you send an email to your clients. Or, Outlook can create a journal entry every time you send and receive meeting invitations to certain users. In fact, the following list summarizes the automatic journaling capabilities of Outlook.

These following items can be automatically recorded in the Outlook Journal:

- Email message
- Meeting request
- Meeting response
- Meeting cancellation
- Task request
- Task response

Documents created in the following programs can be recorded:

- Microsoft Access
- Microsoft Excel
- Microsoft Office Binder
- Microsoft PowerPoint
- Microsoft Word

Automatic journaling can be a powerful tool for those who track contact activity closely.

The other method of using Outlook journaling is, of course, to create journal entries manually. You can manually journal just about anything from files to other Outlook items, such as Contact or Appointment items. The best and easiest way to create a Journal item that relates to either a file or an Outlook item is to simply drag the file or item onto the Journal folder. Next, a Journal definition screen appears where you can enter more information regarding the Journal item.

The pending question is, "How can I use the journal to collaborate?" Again, the plain and simple answer is to create a Journal public folder.

By creating a Journal public folder, you are creating a public repository where people can manually record new Journal items. These journal entries can then be viewed by all who have the appropriate permissions. One of the great features that you lose when you use a public folder as a journal location is automatic journaling. Unfortunately, Microsoft Outlook can only automatically create journal entries into the user's default Journal folder in his Exchange mailbox. Fortunately, you can rectify this problem with a little bit of programming. As I always say, "We programmers make our own rules!" I will show you how to do this in Chapter 7, "Microsoft Office 2000 VBA."

A Journal public folder can also be included in the source of an Outlook contact activities section. This means that Journal items that are linked to certain Outlook contacts are stored in any contact folder. This makes viewing activities of a contact much more organizational than personal.

Organizing Information

The key to getting the most value out of Microsoft Outlook is learning how to organize and access your information in the easiest possible manner. If you are like so many other computer professionals, you probably receive 50 to 100 emails per day, have over 200 people in your contacts list (perhaps in the corporate contact list), keep a running set of 30 or more tasks, and keep every email, task assignment, and meeting request you have ever sent. This environment leads to a whole lot of glut. If you cannot manage this information effectively, it all becomes wasted chunks of information.

Microsoft Outlook, thankfully, provides a number of features that turns glut into extremely valuable information. In this section, we are going to discuss those features that make managing your Outlook data more plausible. These easy-to-use features are rules, folders and fields, and views.

Rules

With Microsoft Outlook, you can automatically manage incoming, outgoing, and previously delivered mail with a feature called rules. Rules simply manipulate mail in some fashion based on a set of user definable conditions. Rules are typically created in your inbox using the Rules Wizard or a public folder using the Folder Assistant. In fact, you can define many rules, all performing different actions on the same message in the same location.

Rules, no matter where they are defined, are typically comprised of three elements:

- A set of conditions that identifies which messages to apply the rule to
- A set of actions that specifies what to do with the message if it meets the rule conditions
- A set of exceptions that specifies when *not* to apply the rule even when the set of primary conditions have been met

The Rules Wizard

To create rules that apply to messages in your inbox, use the Rules Wizard. The Rules Wizard, which has been greatly enhanced in Outlook 2000, is comprised of a series of steps that take even the novice user through the steps of rule creation.

The Rules Wizard first asks the user what actions to take after mail has arrived or mail has been sent. Next, the wizard gathers any conditions that the message must meet. Some conditions include messages sent by particular people, specific words in the subject or the message body, messages assigned with specific categories or flagged for certain actions. In the third step, the Wizard requests the user to specify which actions to perform on the messages that meet the rule's criteria. Rules can move messages, copy messages, print messages, delete messages, flag messages, automatically reply to messages, or even run applications. The last action the Rules Wizard takes is to request that the user specify any exceptions to the rule being defined. Exceptions are similar to the conditions except they specify when *not* to run the rule. Figure 5.13 displays the final stage of the Rules Wizard.

Figure 5.13 *Here I have configured a rule that copies all messages sent from Duncan to a specific public folder while marking the message as important (because all mail from Duncan is important).*

Here are some examples of rules that can be defined in your inbox using the Rules Wizard:

- Sort messages as they arrive by project. All messages from contacts of a given company are moved into the corresponding Project or Company folder.
- Display a message box when messages of high priority are received.
- Move personal email into a separate folder as they arrive.
- Automatically file messages that you sent into folders relating to their associated company or project.
- Automatically archive messages that have been read and were received three months ago into a mail archive folder.

The Folder Assistant

Setting up rules in public folders is generally performed by the more advanced Outlook user. Public folders do not use the Rules Wizard to create and maintain rules. Public folders use the Folder Assistant to define new rules and are not as powerful as the rules that can be defined with the Rules Wizard.

When defining rules using the Folder Assistant, in the properties of a public folder, you can specify the following criteria to determine when the rule will be executed:

- The sender of the message
- The recipient of the message
- Whether the message was sent directly to the recipient or if the recipient was carbon copied the message
- Specific words in the subject and message body
- The message size in kilobytes
- The dates that the messages have been received
- The importance and sensitivity of the messages

The number and complexities of actions are greatly simplified when compared to the actions you can take in rules defined by the Rules Wizard. An example of a Folder rule is depicted in Figure 5.14. The following is a list of the actions that can be taken if a message meets the defined rule criteria:

- Return to sender
- Delete
- Reply with (a message that you could specify)
- Forward to (a list of recipients and/or distribution lists) with the message intact or as an attachment

Figure 5.14   *An example of a Folder Assistant rule.*

Additionally, you can create a rule stating that no other rules should be processed. This is quite important when many rules are defined for a given folder. This would indicate that there is some order to the execution of rules, and in fact there is. Figure 5.15 reflects how rules are represented and ordered in Outlook 2000.

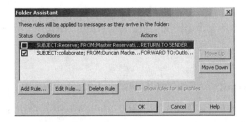

Figure 5.15   *You can control which rules are activated and what order the rules execute using the Folder Assistant.*

When many rules are defined for a public folder, you can control their order by using the Move Up and Move Down buttons. You can also control them by making them inactive. Be careful when using rules that prevent subsequent rules from firing, because they can cause unexpected results.

Folders and Fields

You are most likely aware that Microsoft Outlook stores messages in folders. Additionally, you are probably conscious that Outlook separates messages into components called fields (which depend on message type) and displays these fields as columns in Outlook folders. What you might not already know is that you can customize the number and type of fields for any folder managed by Outlook.

Let's take a look at the process of creating new fields for a folder. First, choose the folder for which you want to add a new field to. Next, right click the column headings of the folder and select Field Chooser. The Field Chooser is a dialog box that helps you customize views, which we will talk about in the next section. Field Chooser is also a venue for creating customized fields for a folder. To create a new field for a folder, click the New button from the Field Chooser dialog box. Specify the new field's name, type, and format in the resulting New Field dialog box.

When defining a new field, you must specify the name of the field, the type of the field, and the specific format of the data type you selected (for example, the Number type can have formats that include All Digits, 1 Decimal, 2 Decimal, Scientific, Truncated, and so on).

A field can be one of the following types:

- **Text.** Stores text strings of up to 255 characters (for example, "This is some text")
- **Number.** Stores standard number forms (for example, 1234.56)
- **Percent.** Stores numeric data expressed as a percentage (for example, 11.8%)
- **Currency.** Stores numeric data stored as currency (for example, $12.95)
- **Yes/No.** Stores a True or False value (for example, "Yes" or "No" or "On" or "Off")
- **Date/Time.** Stores time and date values (for example, 10:30 p.m.)
- **Duration.** Stores a numeric value representing elapsed time (for example, 12 hours)
- **Keywords.** Holds multiple text values separated by commas (for example, "High, Medium, Low")
- **Combination.** Stores the combined values of other fields with literal strings (for example, FirstName = "Joel", LastName = "Semeniuk", FullName = "Joel Semeniuk", where FullName is the Combination field)
- **Formula.** Stores the results of a formula typically expressed as a Visual Basic expression (for example, Hour(Now()), which displays the current hour)
- **Integer.** Stores nondecimal numbers. (for example, 1234)

I will discuss how to use Combination and Formula fields when I begin the discussion on building customized or modified Outlook forms in the next chapter, Chapter 6, "Microsoft Outlook 2000 Forms Development."

Views

In Outlook, a view is a way of looking at messages that exist within a folder. Views are a powerful tool because they not only provide the means for users to easily manage and find information but they can be used as a very basic reporting tool that is extremely easy for users to use, modify, and extend.

Outlook provides many built-in views. In fact, every time you look at the default Contact, Calendar, Journal, Notes, and Task folders, you are witnessing examples of built-in Outlook views. And, as you might have guessed, you not only have the ability to customize existing Outlook views, but you can create new views that display information exactly as you want. Basically, Outlook supports the following views:

- **Table.** This view looks much like a table represented in an application such as Microsoft Access. This view consists of rows (messages) and columns (fields). The Table view is one of the more common views in Outlook. The default Task view is an example of a Table view.

- **Timeline.** The Timeline view displays entries in a chronological order represented by a timeline. The default Journal folder view is an example of a Timeline view.

- **Card.** The Card view displays information much like a Rolodex card. The default Contacts folder view is an example of a Card view.

- **Day/Week/Month.** This view is essentially a calendar view. In this view, users can view items for a particular day, week, or month. Fields that express date and time values are best displayed in this view. The default Calendar folder view is an example of a Day/Week/Month view.

- **Icon.** The Icon view is by far the simplest view, displaying only an icon and subject for each message in a folder. This view hides all item details from the interface. The default Notes folder view is an example of an Icon view.

Creating Views

Generally, when creating new views, Outlook provides one of two options. The first is to create a view from scratch. The second is to copy and modify an existing view, which is by far the most common method of creating new views.

Let's take a look at how you can create a new view for an Outlook folder:

1. Select the folder you want to create the new view for.

2. Select View, Current View, Define Views. The resulting dialog box displays a list of views that have been created for the folder you have chosen. Please note the built-in views that exist for every Outlook folder.

3. To create a new view from scratch, click the New button. A dialog box is displayed requesting properties of the new view, as depicted in Figure 5.16.

4. Click the desired options to specify the name of the new view, the type of view you are creating, and the scope of this view.

Figure 5.16   *Specify the name, type, and scope of the new view.*

The Scope of a View

When creating a new view, users can identify the scope of the view. A view's scope determines what other folder the new view will be accessible from. There are three options:

- *This Folder, Visible to Everyone. With this scope selected, any user who has access to the folder for which the view has been created can use the view itself. This option is great for public folders that have customized content.*

- *This Folder, Visible Only to Me. With this scope selected, the new view will only be available to the user who has created the view.*

- *All <Folder Type> Folders. This scope specifies that every folder of a given type will inherit the new view. In a way, this is a great way to "distribute" your view of a given folder type to everyone in the organization.* ◆

5. After you have entered the folder's name, type, and scope, click OK to display the View Setting dialog box and make all the appropriate changes to the new view's settings. To save the view, click OK on the View Settings dialog box.

Applying Views

After a view has been created, it can be applied at any time. You can select the view using one of the following methods:

- Choose View, Current View from Outlook's menu bar and select one of the listed views.

- Ensure that the Advanced toolbar is displayed. This toolbar contains a Views pull-down box. Clicking on the Views pull-down box displays a list of views defined for the currently selected folder.

Setting View Options

When I discussed how to create a new view, I didn't spend a lot of time discussing how to customize the view. There are many different options available to a view. You can control the way information is presented by specifying the field sort order, field groupings, data filters, formatting options, and other view functionality such as in-cell editing. In this section, I will present a more comprehensive look at these features.

Selecting Fields

When defining a new view or even redefining an existing view, one of the first options you modify is the list of fields that are displayed in the view. When you first looked at the View Settings dialog box, you should have noticed that the first button was Fields. Oddly enough, this is the place where you can modify the list of fields the view will display.

The Show Fields dialog box, shown in Figure 5.17, has two forms. The first form is the normal Show Fields dialog box that displays a list of available fields on the left side of the dialog box and a list of selected fields on the right side. You can select any available Outlook field to be included in your view. Because there are a great number of fields to choose from, Outlook has grouped the fields into general field types. These field groups can be selected from the Select Available Fields from pull-down box at the bottom of the Show Fields dialog box.

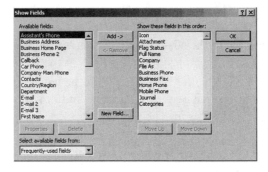

Figure 5.17   *Specify the fields and where you want them to be displayed in the view.*

In this dialog box, not only can you select the fields that you want to be present in a view, you can also change the order of the fields by using the Move Up and Move Down buttons.

The second version of the Show Fields dialog box only appears when modifying the field list for a Calendar view. The information that is displayed in a

Calendar view is pretty specific to data and time formats. In fact, in this instance, the Show Fields dialog box is now called the Date/Time Fields dialog box, as shown in Figure 5.18. The Date/Time Fields dialog box allows you to specify which item component that stores date and time information will be used to represent the start and end times of a Calendar item.

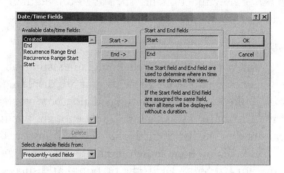

Figure 5.18   *Certain views can only display certain fields, such as a Day/Week/Month view.*

You don't need to use the Show Fields (or Date/Time Fields) dialog box to choose or modify the fields that appear in a view. You can actually perform all of this activity using the Field Chooser dialog box that we discussed before (when we were creating new fields).

For example, here's how to perform some actions using the Field Chooser:

- **To Add a Field to the View.** Select the field in the Field Chooser, and drag the field to the appropriate position in the view.

- **To Delete a Field from a View.** Click on the column heading of the field you want to remove from the view and drag down until the mouse cursor changes into an X.

- **To Change the Position of a Field in a View.** Click on the column heading of the field you want to move and drag it to its new position. You will notice a red marker that indicates its new position as you drag the field.

Grouping
Outlook's grouping feature allows you to group items together that contain similar field contents.

If you look closely at the View Settings dialog box, you will see that you can control view grouping using the button called Group By. When you click on the Group By button, you are given the opportunity to define up to four groups. Each group is defined by selecting a field that will be used to assimilate items by.

Here is an explanation of some of the other settings you will find on this dialog box, as shown in Figure 5.19:

- **Show Field in View.** Specifies that the selected field will also appear as a column in the view.

- **Ascending/Descending.** Defines the sort order of the group.

- **Expand/Collapse Defaults.** Specifies the default settings for the groups. Groups can be expanded, showing all group contents, or collapsed, showing the group header only. It is sometimes convenient to specify this property at the View level.

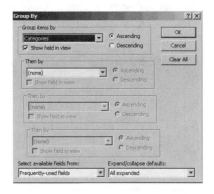

Figure 5.19   *You can specify up to four levels of groupings in a view.*

Of course, you do not have to use the Group By dialog box to establish field grouping. You can use the Group By box. You can access the Group By box, which appears directly above the view pane and depicted in Figure 5.20, by selecting the Group By button on the Advanced toolbar.

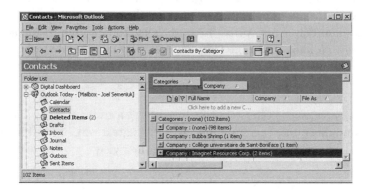

Figure 5.20   *You can use the Group By section of an Outlook view to specify grouping parameters.*

To add or remove groups, all you need to do is drag and drop the column headings in or out of the Group By box.

Sorting

Sorting is probably the easiest view feature to manipulate. When viewing the View Settings page, you can configure how a view is sorted by clicking the Sort button. With the Sort dialog box, which is very much like the Group By dialog box, you can select the fields that you want to sort the contents of the view by as well as indicate whether the sort is in ascending or descending order. You can specify up to four fields to sort on. Figure 5.21 depicts the options that you can select on the Sort dialog box.

Figure 5.21   *A view's Sort dialog box allows you to specify the sort order and direction of up to four fields that appear in the view.*

Actually, the easiest way to sort the contents of a view is using the View pane from within Outlook. Simply click the column heading of the field you want to sort the view by, and it's done. Clicking the column twice reverses the sort order (from ascending to descending order, or *vice versa*).

Additionally, if you want to sort more than one field at a time, you can hold down the Shift key while you click on the columns. By default, clicking on a column that is not sorted forces the view to be sorted by the new column only. Holding down the Shift key allows you to sort on up to four fields at once.

Filters

Learning how to use filters effectively is key to learning how to manage large amounts of data within Outlook. Filters are a way of blocking the display of items that do not fit certain criteria in a view.

Here are some of the common criteria you can use to filter items in a view. You can apply these filters one by one or in any combination:

- Specific words in the item's subject, message body, or other frequently used text fields
- Items sent to or received from certain recipients
- Items received during a given time period
- Items assigned to certain categories
- Items only read or unread
- Items with or without attachments
- Items with Normal, High, or Low importance
- Items that fit certain size criteria

Additionally, you can choose just about any field and add any number of criteria to a filter. Figure 5.22 shows the Filter dialog box and some additional criteria placed on the filter being defined. Note how you can define many different sets of criteria for one filter.

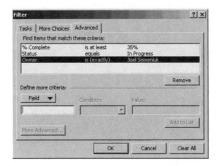

Figure 5.22   *In a view's Filter dialog box, you specify the exact parameters that each field in the view must fall into for the item to be displayed in the view.*

Tip

Unfortunately, there is no easier "GUI" way of creating filters. Filters must be created using the Filters dialog box. ◆

Other Settings
You can specify additional formatting in Outlook views. These additional view properties are accessed from the Other Settings button in the View

Properties dialog box, as shown in Figure 5.23. The Other Settings dialog box allows you to control the following:

- Column heading fonts and sizing
- Row fonts
- Row editing features such as in-cell editing and the new item row
- Auto preview font settings
- Gridline format
- Preview pane format

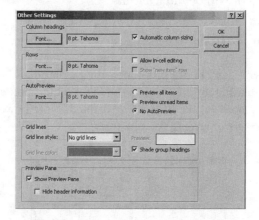

Figure 5.23   *Specify how the view is graphically displayed in the view pane with the view's Other Settings dialog box.*

Tip

In-cell editing allows you to modify the contents of a field without having to open the item. For example, if your view is a simple contact list, you can modify the names of contacts by clicking in the cell and editing the contents, saving the trouble of opening the item and using the default Outlook form for all editing. ◆

Automatic Formatting

Automatic formatting allows Microsoft Outlook to format each row separately depending on the content or state of the item represented by the row.

I must admit that I use the Automatic Formatting feature of views like it was going out of style. The gist of automatic formatting is to define certain criteria that must be met before the formatting is applied. In fact, you have probably seen the effects of automatic formatting every time you have ever received any email messages in Outlook—they appear bold!

Here are some examples of built-in automatic formatting:

- **Unread messages.** Change the item font to bold
- **Expired email.** Change font of the item to strikethrough
- **Overdue email.** Change font color of the item to red
- **Overdue tasks.** Change font color of the item to red

Let's take a look at how you can define new conditions for your views:

1. Open the Automatic Formatting window by clicking the Automatic Formatting button in the View Properties dialog box.
2. Click the Add button to add a new formatting condition.
3. Enter the name of the condition in the Name field.
4. Click the Condition button to enter the conditions of the format. Please note that this is the same dialog box used when defining filters.
5. Click the Font button to define the font that will be applied to items that fit the condition specified in step 4.

Additionally, you can choose which automatic formatting options are enabled at any given time by checking or unchecking the boxes next to each format definition.

Some Examples of Useful Views

This section provides some examples of how I typically use views. I will revisit the design and implementation of views when I discuss Outlook forms development in the next chapter.

Color-Coded Emails

I receive anywhere from 40 to 60 emails per day, and I need a way to filter out the signal from the noise.

First, I create a view that increases the size of the font and changes the font color to red whenever mail messages are sent directly to me.

Second, I change the font color of all emails that are more than a month old to a light gray.

Finally, I ensure that all of the emails I have received from my primary clients are purple with a bold font.

These modified views make all the important email stand out to ensure that it has my utmost attention.

Folders That Act as Tables

A great aspect of Outlook views is you can create a folder that acts very much like a Microsoft Access table. For example, I am currently working with a client that wants to maintain a list of classrooms as well as a set of information associated with each classroom. Our decision was to represent these classrooms as items in a specially formatted folder.

Representing information in this way is a great means of creating a table-like environment without the need of a database engine such as Microsoft Access or SQL Server. Additionally, this information is accessible through Outlook at any time, alleviating any dependencies that might be experienced if the same information was stored in another fashion. You can use the standard Find features, and of course View features, such as sorting, grouping, and filtering, to manipulate and find the data stored within such a table. Figure 5.24 is an example of such a solution.

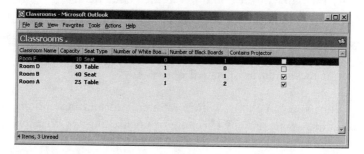

Figure 5.24   *A view that displays a list of classrooms. Each classroom is represented by an Outlook Mail item. Each column of the view is a custom field.*

Chapter Summary

In this chapter, we discussed the built-in collaborative features of Microsoft Outlook and the importance and ease of using such features when designing and implementing more complicated collaborative solutions. We discussed the following:

- How to collaborate with Outlook contacts
- How to collaborate using the Outlook Calendar
- Using Outlook tasks to collaborate with others
- Outlook journaling and how it can be used to collaborate with others
- How you can extend the functionality of Outlook folders by adding fields, rules, and views

6

Microsoft Outlook 2000 Forms Development

As I promised, this chapter is where we get a little more into the development details of slightly more advanced collaborative solutions. And, as you know, coding is more fun than anything else in the world.

In this chapter, we will discuss Outlook forms development. Truthfully, when I considered the topics I wanted to cover in this chapter, I listed enough topics to form a book dedicated solely to the process of developing Outlook forms. Because we cannot cover every aspect of Outlook forms creation, I will focus on the hard stuff, such as building forms that contain VBScript, and breeze through the more obvious aspects of this process. If you require more introductory information on forms creation, you should begin with the Outlook 2000 Help and work from there.

Overview of the Forms Development Process

Let's take a moment to put everything into perspective. Why would you want to develop Outlook forms? Well, as we discussed in Chapter 5, "Microsoft Outlook 2000 Collaborative Basics," Microsoft Outlook is a simple email client. In fact, Outlook provides a rich environment for storing and manipulating information. You can use Outlook's existing functionality to store information regarding your contacts and appointments, and you can also define new types of objects and associated properties to store within the same environment, leveraging Outlook's phenomenal data management capabilities. Looking at it from this point of view, the reason for developing new Outlook forms is quite apparent—to store and manipulate new types of information within Microsoft Outlook.

There are a couple reasons why organizations embark upon the process of Outlook forms development. My experience suggests that the most common reasons organizations choose to design and implement forms is to extend existing contact, task, or appointment forms to capture more information, or to capture the same information in a different way. This is a great start, and there is absolutely nothing wrong with it. In most situations, however, organizations do not develop solutions that are more complicated, because they do not see the benefit of doing so or because they believe that alternative solutions, such as stand-alone applications that use Microsoft Access or SQL Server, are better (and, of course, in many cases this is true).

I am not going to spend any time discussing how you can simply extend existing Contacts, Tasks, and Appointment forms to capture a few additional parameters. I am going to focus on some of the more complex solutions that can be built using Outlook forms.

This leads me to my next train of thought: overly complex Outlook form solutions. You can accomplish a lot using Outlook forms; however, in my opinion, there is a limit to how much functionality you should really provide in an Outlook form. If your Outlook forms get overly complicated, you might want to try implementing your solutions using Visual Basic. I spend a great deal of time working with organizations, attempting to create solutions to meet their needs while at the same time ensuring that I provide a stable and supportable environment. I have found that stability and supportability both get compromised when overly complex Outlook forms are constructed. So as a rule of thumb, don't get too crazy creating technically complicated forms, unless you're just doing it for fun.

The process of designing and implementing forms is really no different than designing and implementing forms using Microsoft Access, with a few differences, of course. I recommend using the following approach:

- **Folder Design and Implementation.** Carefully design how data will be organized in the folders that your new form will be associated with. Remember, you are not working with a relational model of your data. Although you can implement some degree of data normalization, the more normalized your data becomes, the more difficult it is to work with in your Outlook forms because there is no structured query language to retrieve relational data from a public folder. I like to define the contents of the folders as objects with properties. Each property of an object corresponds to a field that needs to be created to house data storage, and I strongly recommend that you create these fields before you begin developing your forms.

Exchange 2000 and OLE DB

Exchange 2000's Web Store provides support for OLE DB and ADO. This allows developers to access data from Exchange 2000 as they would access data on a SQL Server or Access database.

Exchange 2000 provides two OLE DB providers. The first is a remote provider giving access to Web Store contents from remote computers. The second is a local OLE DB provider that is optimized for local access. The local provider provides access to content to applications, such as Virus Scanning software.

The overall benefit of using OLE DB providers to provide access to Exchange 2000's Web Stores is to allow applications developers the ability to use ADO to navigate, query, filter, and sort data stored on Exchange Server. Developers who are already skilled SQL developers will have no problem reusing their skills to access data stored in the Web Store. ◆

- **Form Design and Development.** Interestingly, you cannot really create a form from scratch like you can in other development environments, such as Visual Basic or Visual C++. In other words, when a form is created, it must begin with a base form. These base forms can be any form that is installed by default in Outlook, including Post forms, Mail forms, Contact forms, Appointment forms, Task forms, and Journal forms.

  After you have selected your base form, you can then start developing your new form by launching the base form in design mode. Placing a form in design mode invokes Outlook's form's development environment. This is the mode where you can add and modify your graphical elements, such as text boxes, combo boxes, list boxes, check boxes, and pictures, as well as write the necessary VBScript code to support the required functionality of the form.

- **Publishing and Saving Forms.** Your final step is typically distribution of your new form. This process is called publishing. Typically, new forms are published in forms libraries, such as the Organizational Forms library, or in the folder where the form will be used. This obviously depends on what the form will be used for. You should always save the form into a file that can be maintained in a code storage facility such as Visual Source Safe.

Outlook Items and Forms

What is the relationship between Outlook items and forms? I think the best way to describe this relationship is to look at a list of all of the default forms that come with Microsoft Exchange, because when you create new Outlook forms, you will always begin with one of these. Table 6.1 displays these forms.

Table 6.1   The Standard Outlook Forms

Form Name	Description
Contact	Used to gather or display information about a person or an organization.
Distribution List	Used to create a list of contacts and/or email addresses that can be used as a single email address.
Task	Used to gather or display information about a task.
Mail Message	Used to send information to another user.
Post	Used to gather information that is inserted into a public folder (or any other folder).
Appointment	Used to gather information used to schedule an appointment or an event.
Journal Entry	Used to log information regarding another Outlook item or event.
Office Form	Used when the primary item content is a Microsoft Office application such as Microsoft Excel or Word. Additional customization can be implemented within these applications using Visual Basic for Applications (VBA).

How does Outlook know what form to display when you click on an item? This is actually quite simple. Every item has an associated *message class* that is stored with the item as a property. The message class of an item is a property that uniquely identifies the Outlook form that the item is associated with. Table 6.2 displays a list of the more common Outlook message classes and their associated Outlook forms.

Table 6.2   Message Classes and Built-In Outlook Forms

Message Class	Associated Form
IPM.Appointment	The Appointment form used to create and modify calendar events in a Calendar folder.
IPM.Contact	The Contact form used to create and modify contacts in a Contact folder.
IPM.Activity	The Journal form used to create and modify Journal entries.
IPM.Schedule.Meeting.Request	The Meeting Request form used to invite others to a calendar event.
IPM.Note	The default form for a Mail Message.
IPM.StickyNote	The Note form used to create an item in a Notes folder.
IPM.Post	The Post form used to gather and submit information to a folder.

Message Class	Associated Form
IPM.Task	The Task Folder form used to create or modify an Outlook task.
IPM.TaskRequest	The Task Request form used when assigning an Outlook task to another user.

Displaying the Message Class for an Item

You can display the message class that is associated to each item in a folder by creating or modifying a view that contains the Message Class field. ✦

When you create or open an Outlook item, Outlook looks at the Message Class property of the item and begins searching for the corresponding Outlook form. The following is a summary of the steps that Outlook takes to launch an item's corresponding form:

1. Outlook determines if the form is a standard form or a customized form. If the message class indicates a standard form, such as IPM.Note, Outlook opens the item using the appropriate built-in form.

2. If the message class does not correspond to any standard Outlook forms, Outlook checks its form cache on the local computer for the appropriate form.

The Outlook Forms Cache

Outlook uses a chunk of local storage to cache Outlook forms to improve performance. The form cache is found in a directory located in your Windows Profile (usually C:\Windows\ . . . \Application Data\Forms on Windows 95 or C:\Documents and Settings\User\Local Settings\Application Data\Microsoft\Forms in Windows 2000). Centralization is maintained by ensuring that every user is working with the most current version of the form. Hence, if the original form, which is typically stored in a public folder or an Organizational Forms library, is modified, the modified copy replaces the copy that is on the local cache. When a form is activated for the first time, the form definition file is copied from its forms library to the Forms folder.

Additionally, users have the ability to modify the maximum amount of storage that Outlook will use for the forms cache. Users can change this maximum value by selecting Options from the Tools menu, clicking the Other tab, clicking the Advanced Options button, and then clicking the Custom Forms button. Setting this option to 0 effectively disables the forms cache; however, users cannot open any custom forms.

continues ▶

Avoid publishing forms that have the same name. This can cause some confusion in the form cache because Outlook uses the name of the form to determine which form to use. If you publish different forms with the same name into different locations you might be in for some unexpected surprises. ◆

3. If the form is not in the forms cache, Outlook searches the forms library of the folder that is currently in use.

Publishing Forms

Remember that forms can be published to organization forms libraries, personal forms libraries, Web forms libraries, and folders. Additionally, form definitions can be stored with the item itself. ◆

4. If the form is not found in the folder's form library, the user's personal forms library and organizational forms library are then checked. If the user has Web Services enabled, Outlook also searches the Web forms library.

5. Finally, if Outlook cannot find the customized form, it opens the item using the built-in form from which the customized form was based.

On another note, forms can be stored along with the item that uses it. This gives other Outlook users the ability to use the form even when the form definition is not located in any other forms library.

Outlook always knows the base form of any customized form because the message class of the standard form is always a part of the message class of the resulting form. For example, if you create a form that is based on the Contacts form to collect additional employee related information, you might call this new form Employee. Because your new Employee form is based on the Contacts form, the resulting message class looks something like IPM.Contact.Employee. Notice how Outlook preserves the base message class in every new message class created when you define new forms.

On a different note, you can change the message class for any item using a little programming, because it cannot be changed directly through the Outlook user interface. There are many reasons why you might want to change an item's message class. For example, suppose a company is a big user of Microsoft Outlook and has created a Corporate Contacts public folder. Let's further suppose that the company has entered over 10,000 contacts into the public folder over the last two years using the default Contacts form. Management has decided that some additional information should be stored about the contact, such as the name of the employee who acquired the contact and some sales and marketing related data. The company's development team has created a new Contact form and is ready to use it; however, all the existing contacts in the folder are not configured to use this new form. All the existing contact items in the folder have a message class of IPM.Contact. The new form is called IPM.Contact.CorpContact. All the existing items must have their message class changed to IPM.Contact.CorpContact to ensure that users will use the new form when opening the items.

Example 6.1 shows some code, written in Visual Basic, that cycles through every item in Outlook's default Contacts folder and changes each item's message class from the default IPM.Contact to the new message class IPM.Contact.CorpContact associated with the new form.

Example 6.1   *Using Visual Basic code to change message class from IPM. Contact to IPM.Contact.CorpContact.*

```
Private Sub UpdateMessageClass()

    Dim olApplication As Outlook.Application

    Dim olNameSpace As Outlook.NameSpace

    Dim ContactsFolder As Outlook.MAPIFolder

    Dim Itm As Outlook.ContactItem

    Set olApplication = New Outlook.Application

    Set olNameSpace = olApplication.GetNamespace("MAPI")

    Set ContactsFolder = _

        olNameSpace.GetDefaultFolder(olFolderContacts)

    Set ContactItems = ContactsFolder.Items

    For Each Itm In ContactItems

        If Itm.MessageClass <> "IPM.Contact.CorpContact" Then

            Itm.MessageClass = "IPM.Contact.CorpContact"

            Itm.Save

        End If

    Next

End Sub
```

Of course, the preceding code is a little oversimplified, because it deals exclusively with the default Contacts form and not a public folder—and of course the name of the form is hard coded (I can see my university professors looking at this code and saying, "Oh boy!"). However, you can use this code as a basis for a function to use in your environment.

Customizing Outlook Forms

When developing new Outlook forms, you must first choose an existing form to work from, to act as a form template for your new form. You can choose from an existing, built-in, or another customized form. After you have selected your base form, you are ready to begin customizations. In this section, I will discuss the process of selecting base forms and form customization, which encompasses how to manipulate the Read and Compose pages, form properties, and form actions.

Choosing the Correct Standard Form

As I stated earlier, every new Outlook form that you create is based on some existing Outlook form, such as the Post or Message forms. Your biggest challenge is to choose which form you will use as the basis for your new form. Here are some guidelines I use when building Outlook forms:

- What is the primary functionality of the form? If you are building a form that will be used to send someone else information, the Mail form is the best. If you are posting information to a folder, you could use the Post, Contacts, Appointment, or Task forms.

- If you are building a Post form, what kind of information are you gathering? Obviously, you have a range of forms to use that capture tasks, contacts, and appointments. However, if you are capturing a completely new set of information, such as classroom information, you might want to start with a blank Post form.

- When customizing forms, be cognizant of which pages on the form are customizable. For example, all of the fields on the primary pages of the Contact, Mail, and Post forms are customizable. However, some pages, such as the primary pages of Task, Journal, and Appointment forms, are static. If you want to customize these forms, you must do so by adding additional pages to the form.

Understanding some of these limitations up front also helps you predict what is required to perform the task at hand and then explain those requirements to others. For example, if someone asks you how much time it takes to add one more field to a Contacts folder, you could probably tell them that it takes five minutes. However, if someone asks how long it takes to add one more field on the main page of the Task form, you could probably say that it takes a good part of a day, because you effectively have to re-create the functionality of the main task page on a new page and then add the new text box. It might only take five minutes if the user can accept having the text box located on a separate page from the rest of the Task properties (which is typically what happens).

Customizing a Form

After you have chosen the form you want to customize, you should also have a clear understanding of what you are building. (Design before you build—what a concept!) You should consider the following things, for example:

- How many pages does your form display?
- How many of the pages you display are from the original form?
- How many new fields does the form require and what are their types?
- Do you require a separate read form that functions differently from the compose form of an item?
- Which fields are visible on the form?
- What are the default values of the required fields?
- What are the ranges of acceptable data for each field displayed on the form?
- What built-in fields are used on the form?
- Does the form contain a Microsoft Office document?
- What are the types of controls that are used to capture data for each of the fields? (List boxes, text boxes, check boxes, option buttons, labels, and combo boxes are just some of the controls that you can use to capture data.)

The remainder of this chapter is dedicated to the processes of creating, testing, and deploying forms using Outlook. You will be using a feature called the Outlook Forms Designer to create new Outlook forms. When working in this environment, especially when you are extending your forms using Visual Script, it is a good idea to install Microsoft Script Debugger or Visual Interdev and make sure that all of your help files are installed.

Creating a New Form

There are a couple ways you can begin designing a new form. Choosing one of these methods depends on whether or not the form will contain a Microsoft Office document. For now, let's just focus on customizing forms that do not contain Office documents. Perform these steps to begin customizing an Outlook form:

1. From the Outlook menu bar, select Tools, Forms, and Design a Form to display a list of forms that you can use as a basis for your new form.

2. Search for the base form you want to design using the Look In pull-down box. The Look In pull-down box displays the contents of various form libraries that you have access to. If you want to customize one of the default Outlook forms, select Standard Forms Library in the Look In pull-down box. It is a good idea to display the Details of the forms you have selected. Click the Details button from the Design Form dialog box to show additional information about a selected form.

3. After you have found the base form, click the Open button to open the form in design mode, which looks similar to Figure 6.1.

As you can see in Figure 6.1, when viewing a form in design mode, there are a number of extras that appear on the screen. First and foremost, some additional pages are displayed on the screen, such as (P.2), (P.3), (Properties), and (Actions). These additional pages allow you to better organize your form, set the form's properties, and control how the form can be used.

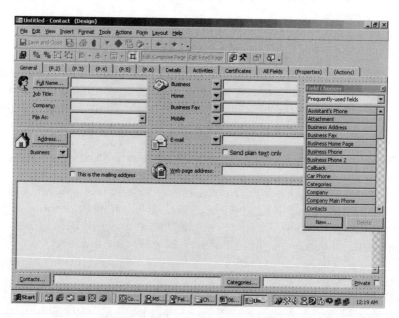

Figure 6.1   *The Outlook Contact form in design mode.*

When in design mode, you will also see that the Form and Layout items are added to the design window's menu bar. These menu items allow developers to control the development environment and control how the form and its contents are displayed. Many of the new menu items correspond to the development toolbar, which is also automatically displayed. The Outlook Field Chooser is started as well.

Read/Compose

As I mentioned earlier, one of the decisions you need to make before you implement your form is whether there will be separate read and compose pages. Separating the read page from the compose page allows you to specify how users interact with a form when composing and reading an item. Typically, you ensure that your form has a different read form when there are a number of fields that must not change after the item has been created. A customer reference number is a good example of this. If you create a Customer form and record a customer number, you probably do not want this reference number to change. To prevent this, you can create a specific read form that displays the customer number but does not allow edits.

By default, Outlook does not enable separate read and compose pages. To enable separate read and compose pages, select Separate Read Layout from the Form menu. You can enable this option at any time during the development process. Additionally, you can switch between editing the compose page and read page using the Edit Compose Page and Edit Read Page buttons on the toolbar.

Disabling Separate Read Layout

When you disable Separate Read Layout, you discard all modifications made to the read page. This is a great option after you have made extensive changes to the compose page and you want the read and compose pages to mesh. When you re-enable this option, the read page copies the entire layout of the compose page.

In most cases, the read page is very similar to the compose page. If this is the case for your form, I suggest leaving the Separate Read Layout option turned off until you have finalized your compose page, at which point you can enable this option and tweak the read page. ◆

Pages

An Outlook form contains pages that are used to separate the user interface into segments. Take a look at the Appointment form in design mode as shown in Figure 6.2.

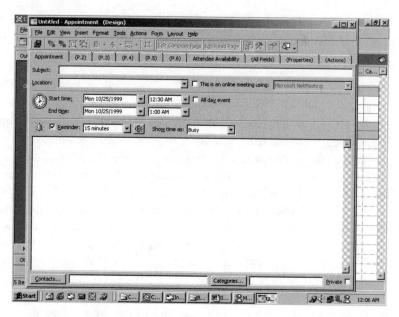

Figure 6.2   *The Appointment form in design mode. Notice all of the additional pages you can use to extend this form.*

Notice how the Appointment form in design mode displays 10 separate pages, even though only two pages are displayed at run time. Pages whose names are not surrounded by parentheses are displayed during run time. All other pages are hidden.

Some Outlook forms allow developers to customize a form's default page; others do not. It is a good idea to know which ones can be customized and which ones cannot before you begin design and development. To help you out, Table 6.3 summarizes this information.

Table 6.3   *Built-In Forms and Customizable Default Pages*

Form Name	Level of Page Customization
Appointment	No default pages are customizable.
Contacts	Only the General page; no other pages are customizable.
Distribution List	No default pages are customizable.
Journal	No default pages are customizable.
Mail	All default pages are customizable.
Post	All default pages are customizable.
Task	No default pages are customizable.

You can enable or disable any page in an Outlook form, even on forms that contain non-customizable default pages. To enable or disable a page, select the page by clicking its associated tab, then check or uncheck Display This Page from the Form menu. There must be a minimum of one page on any Outlook form. Unfortunately, there is a static number of pages that can exist in a form, and this number is limited to using only the pages that are displayed in design mode.

Need More Than Six Pages?

If you need to display more than six pages to capture or display data, you should look at using the multi-page control, which I will talk about in the section "Fields and Controls" later in this chapter. ♦

You should rename your new form pages to match their content—Anything is better than (P.1). Unfortunately, pages that are not customizable do not allow the name of the page to change. To change the name of a new page or a customizable default page, select its tab, select Rename this Page from the Form menu, and type in the new name of the page in the resulting dialog box.

Form Design Tidbit

Some Outlook forms developers employ the design-as-you-go approach. I, however, am a huge advocate of planning no matter what size the project. I like to begin with a paper sketch of what I want my form to look like, detailing the number and order of pages and the content each of my pages contains. Most of these ideas are obtained from the clients the form will be used by. I then implement a prototype of a screen and take it to the client for discussion. Nine times out of ten, extensive modifications are required before the client is happy with the form. This method minimizes rework, and any time you can minimize work, the better life becomes. ♦

Form Properties

When in design mode, you can set many properties that are associated with your new form. Table 6.4 summarizes the form properties that can be configured for your new form.

Table 6.4   Form Configuration Options

Property	Description
Category	To help organize forms in the New Form dialog box, you can assign a category to the form. Some organizations choose to use department names as form categories, such as Marketing, to better classify who might use a particular group of forms.

continues ▶

Table 6.4   continued

Property	Description
Sub-Category	Using sub-categories allows you to further categorize your form. Many organizations describe how the form will be used in a department in the sub-category property of the form. For example, if the category is Marketing, a sub-category might be Client Tracking for a form that tracks information about client marketing activities.
Always use Microsoft Word as the email editor	This property allows you to specify Microsoft Word as the editor in the message portion of your form. All formatting options inherent to Microsoft Word are available in the message body. Be careful with this option because some users get aggravated at the excess time forms require to load when this option is enabled.
Template	This parameter specifies the Microsoft Word template that is used if Microsoft Word is enabled as the email editor. Remember that you can add VBA code to Microsoft Word templates to provide additional functionality to your messages.
Contact	This field contains a list of individuals who are responsible for maintaining and distributing the form. This information is displayed in the Forms Manager window and the Properties window of the form.
Description	This field contains a brief description of the purpose of the form. It is also a good idea to briefly describe how to use the form in this field. This information is displayed in the Properties dialog box and in the Help, About portion of the form.
Version	You can enter version information into the form. Typically, a form that is in development mode has an 0.X format. Upon initial release, this value should be changed to 1.0. Any version of the form that is a result of bug fixes should increment the version number by 0.1.
Form Number	You can specify a form number to help identify your form.

Property	Description
Change Large Icon	You can change the icon for your form. The large icon is displayed when an item with which the form was created with is displayed in Icon mode.
Change Small Icon	You can change the icon that is used in a normal list view.
Protect Form Design	When you select this option, a password is required to access the form definition. Protecting a form definition is a very common practice in many organizations.
Set Password	This is where you can set the password that must be entered to design the form.
Send Form Definition with Item	Selecting this option causes the form definition to be stored along with the item that the form is creating. This is useful when users who access the item do not have access to the form libraries that typically hold form definitions. This is great for forms that have been created for one-time uses.
	When users open an item that contains the form definition of a form that is not part of the recipient's trusted organization forms library, a warning dialog box is displayed indicating that the form may contain scripts. Users have the option of disabling the scripts in the form at that time.
Use form only for responses	When you want the form to be used for replying to an open item only, use this option. You can specify the reply form in the form that is used for reading and creating the item.

Form Actions

It is extremely important that you understand how to control the actions a user can take with a form. First of all, let me describe what an action is. An action is a way of controlling which options are available to users who are interacting with a form. You use a form action every time you click the Reply, Reply All, Forward, or Forward All buttons when reading your email. Reply, Reply All, Forward, and Forward All are actions you can be take when reading your email.

When you create custom forms, you use actions to do the following:

- Provide the users with a clear set of activities that can be performed from inside a form
- Implement some type of process, such as a wizard, guiding the users through a sequence of steps

Let me give you a few examples of this. Suppose you have a public folder called Classrooms that is used to track all of the training classrooms your organization maintains. You represent each classroom using a folder item, capturing all the details of the classroom in a set of custom fields such as ClassroomName, ClassroomLocation, NumberOfSeats, and ContrainsProjector. To ease the process of entering data into each item, you have created a nice little Classroom form that looks a little like Figure 6.3.

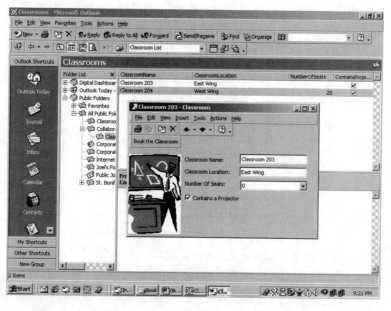

Figure 6.3   *The Classroom form, which uses a custom action.*

Let's further suppose that you would like to provide the ability to book a class in a classroom at a certain date and time. In this case, you could create a custom action called Book the Classroom that launches a form allowing the classroom to be booked by a user. An example of such a form is depicted in Figure 6.4. After the user has booked the room, the Book Classroom form closes, and focus is returned to the Classroom form.

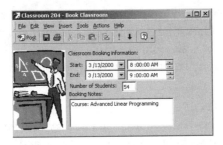

Figure 6.4   *The Book Classroom form. This form launches when a user clicks on the Book the Classroom button on the Classroom form shown in Figure 6.3.*

Setting up new actions and modifying existing actions for your forms is actually a fairly simple process. Figure 6.5 is a form that is displayed when the user selects the Book the Classroom action from the Classroom form. To create a new action for a form, follow these steps:

1. When in design mode of your form, select the Actions tab.

2. Click the New button to produce the Form Action Properties dialog box.

3. Give the action a name.

4. From the Form Name pull-down box, select the form you want the action to launch.

5. Specify the characteristics of the new form, such as what to do with the original message when responding and how to address the form.

6. Specify whether to show the action and where to show it—in the Menu and Toolbar or in the Menu Only.

7. Specify what the action does with the form: Open the Form, Send the Form Immediately, or Prompt the User to Open or Send.

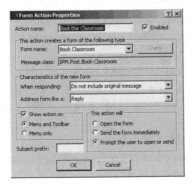

Figure 6.5   *The Form Action Properties dialog box.*

In addition to creating your own actions, you can control how Outlook's built-in actions work just as you control your custom actions. If you want to prevent Outlook's actions from occurring, you can disable Outlook's custom actions, or you can replace these actions with your own custom actions.

Fields and Controls

To really capture the data you need and display it in a way that makes sense, we need to discuss how you can use fields and controls in your forms. You probably are familiar with these, but let's briefly review them.

A field is simply a place where you can store information in a folder. The subject line of a message is classified as a field; so are the message body and list of recipients. You can easily add fields to any folder to allow you to capture the data you need. Controls, on the other hand, are constructs that you can use on your forms to help gather and present data. Examples of controls range from a simple button to check boxes, list boxes, and combo boxes. By reading this book, I assume that you already have an understanding of what controls are.

In this section, I will discuss some of the more important fields you typically need, especially when extending some of the built-in forms, such as the Appointment form or the Contact form. I also want to acquaint you with the process of creating custom fields. Then, we will delve into the world of controls by describing how to use the basic ones. We will even discuss how to use custom controls, controls that are not standard with Microsoft Outlook, to further enhance your forms. So, without further delay, let's begin.

Built-In Fields

It is important to know that Outlook provides a whole bunch of built-in fields that you can use in your applications. Don't think for one second that the fields you see on Outlook's Appointment form are the only appointment-related fields in Outlook.

If you have ever used the Field Chooser to help create a view, you have probably observed the vast extent of built-in fields you can choose from. To refresh your memory, take the time to launch the Outlook Field Chooser and browse through some of the listed fields. For example, choose All Contact Fields from the Field Chooser dialog box and look at the number of fields you can choose from. There are many more fields in this list than most organizations require.

I am trying to say that you should always try to use the built-in Outlook fields before creating your own. If you can't find a field that fits your requirements, which is generally the case if you want to store information that is specific to your organization, feel free to create as many custom fields as your heart desires.

Take time to review some of the more common fields that you can use from the list of available fields. Because there simply isn't enough room in this book to discuss every field (and because that would be an incredibly boring endeavor), I leave that exercise up to you.

Custom Fields

When you begin building customized solutions for specific users or companies, you will quickly realize that you cannot store all of the required data in built-in Outlook fields. You need to resort to defining your own custom fields.

For example, suppose that you are creating a public folder that will be used by a training organization to track instructors. This solution will not only track the names and contact information of each instructor, but a list of all of the courses that he can teach, as well as any additional certification he has. As you could probably guess, using built-in fields will not fit the bill. At this point, you need to create your own fields.

Luckily, Outlook provides such a feature. You can create as many different types of fields as you need, as described in Chapter 5. Please remember that deciding on the details of the fields you are creating should not be taken lightly. Obviously, you wouldn't create a Microsoft SQL Server database without performing some level of design. In fact, developing Outlook applications should follow the same development methodologies you use when developing other solutions using Visual Basic or Visual C++. Take the time to carefully plan each of the fields that you create to ensure that you create fields of the correct name and type. Unfortunately, after you have created a field, there is no easy way to change any aspect of it, including the field's name or type, without first deleting the field and recreating it from scratch.

Of course, not every field you create in a public folder is used in every form. Take the Classroom and the Classroom Booking forms, for example. Both of these forms are published to the same public folder, and both forms use custom fields. However, each of the forms uses different custom fields to gather information from the user. So, just to add clarity to our discussion, fields that are defined at the folder level are called *folder level fields* and can be referenced in the Field Chooser by selecting the User-Defined Fields in Folder option. Fields that are used in a particular form define *item level fields*. Item level fields are a subset of folder level fields. You can view all item level fields for forms you are creating by selecting the (All Fields) page and selecting User-Defined Fields in This Item from the drop-down list when your form is in design mode. This option is depicted in Figure 6.6.

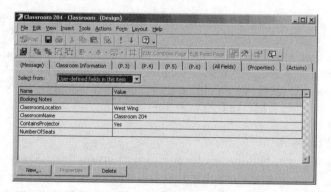

Figure 6.6   *You can view the custom fields that have been used on a form using the (All Fields) tab that is available when a form is in design mode.*

Using Controls

Like so many other development environments, you can greatly enhance the forms that you create using form controls. In this section, I will describe how you can take advantage of and use built-in controls and custom controls for any form you create.

Overview of Built-In Controls

As I stated earlier, Outlook provides a number of built-in controls that you can use when you create your own custom forms. Examples of these controls are depicted in Figure 6.7. The following lists the controls that come built into every installation of Microsoft Outlook 2000:

- **Label.** Presents read only text to the user.
- **Text Box.** Presents or gathers text to/from a user.
- **Combo Box.** Allows a user to enter text or select from a preset list of text entries.
- **List Box.** Allows a user to select an entry or entries from a preset list of entries.
- **Check Box.** Allows a user to toggle an option on or off.
- **Option Button.** Allows a user to select an option from a preset set of options all displayed as option buttons.
- **Toggle Button.** Allows a user to toggle an option on or off.
- **Frame.** A container for additional controls. Used to group controls into logical sections.
- **Command Button.** Allows a user to perform some action by clicking a button.
- **Tab Strip.** Provides a strip of dialog box tabs that can be manipulated to control options displayed to the user.

- **Multi Page.** Provides a strip of dialog box tabs and separate frames that can be manipulated to control options displayed to the user.
- **Scroll Bar.** Provides the ability for users to move the viewing area of a display up or down, left or right.
- **Spin Button.** Provides an up/down set of arrows that allows users to increment values represented in other controls on the form.
- **Image.** Displays an image on the form.

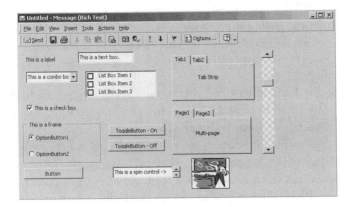

Figure 6.7 *A dialog box that displays all of the built-in controls provided by Outlook.*

Because this is not an introductory book, I will not describe how to use each of these controls. I will explain how to access the basic properties of Outlook controls, how to bind these controls to built-in or custom fields, and how to validate data captured by each of these controls.

Properties of Controls

When working with controls, you must have the ability to specify how the control interacts and is displayed to the user of the form and how the controls handle data that is entered or displayed in the control. Outlook provides a means of controlling all these aspects by accessing the properties of a control. Accessing the properties of a control, built-in or custom, displays an Outlook window that allows the collaborative solutions developer to control some of the basic aspects of a control, such as the following:

- Name and caption (if applicable)
- Position on the form
- Font specifications
- Whether the control is visible, enabled, read only, sunken in the form, multi-line (if it is a text box), and whether it resizes when the form is resized

Additionally, the Properties dialog box of a control allows you to specify the following:

- Outlook field the control is bound to
- Display format of the data in the field
- Possible values of the field the control is bound to
- Initial value of the field the control is bound to
- Validation formulas and messages

I believe that the basic properties of a control (name, position, visibility, and so on) are fairly self evident, so let's move on to field binding.

Field Binding

When you bind a field to a control, you are specifying which field the control saves information to and displays information from. Basically, the bound field acts as a form level variable.

So what does field binding mean to forms development? Remember that the forms themselves do not store any data. Data is actually stored in an item, whereas the form is stored as a form definition in a forms library or in the message itself. Microsoft Outlook dynamically constructs a form and binds each of the forms controls to fields at run time.

Binding of a field to a control is performed using the Value tab in the properties of a control. Click the Choose Field button to select an existing field from the list of available fields, or create a new field by clicking the New button.

You can use the Field Chooser to automatically bind controls to fields. From the Field Chooser window, which appears automatically when a form is in design mode, simply drag one of the displayed fields from the list of available fields onto the form. Microsoft Outlook automatically creates a control and binds it to the field that was selected. The type of control that Outlook chooses to create depends on the type of field that was selected. For example, Yes/No fields appear as check boxes when dragged onto a form; most other types appear as simple text boxes.

You should be aware that there are some of built-in fields that, when dragged onto an Outlook form, provide features that cannot be duplicated by simply binding a field to a control. For example, if you choose to drag the To field onto your form, the result is a button and a text field. However, without any additional programming, the resulting To allows the user to select a list of recipients from the standard Select Names dialog box.

You can also bind a field to a control in code. Example 6.2 binds two fields on a form to a couple of built-in fields when the form is opened using VBScript.

Example 6.2   *Binding two form fields to built-in fields.*

```
Function Item_Open()
'Manually Bind Controls to Fields at Run Time
'Comments:
'   Use the ItemProperty property to set this make this relationship.

    Item.GetInspector.ModifiedFormPages("Classroom Information").txtSubject.ItemProperty =
➡"Subject"
    Item.GetInspector.ModifiedFormPages("Classroom
➡Information").txtBillingInformation.ItemProperty = "Billing Information"
End Function
```

Obviously, there are pros and cons to this method of field binding. The con is that you need to write code. The pro is that you can control data binding very specifically and make modifications to the bind behavior quickly in one place. As you can see, the code is not overly complicated, and if significant code needs to be written anyway, this might not be a bad option. Personally, I prefer to control everything in code. I like to have all settings laid out in one place, leaving nothing to guesswork, which you might have if you configure all field bindings through the GUI.

Field Validation

For every piece of data collected, you probably want to verify that the entered data is correct. There are basically two ways of validating field data. The first is to use the validation features provided in the properties of bound form controls. The second is to use code to validate your values. In fact, you could probably use a combination of both, if necessary.

In most cases, validation can be broken into two levels: property validation, where each property value is analyzed independently of all other properties, and object validation, where the entire object is analyzed as a whole. Take, for example, a form that allows a user to enter address information. Your job is to validate that the information is correct. Property validation checks to see that the ZIP code is correctly formatted or the city is spelled correctly. Object validation verifies that the ZIP code is correct for the specified city and state by referencing a master database of ZIP codes, states, and cities. Unfortunately, Microsoft Outlook only provides the capability to perform property validation, leaving object level validation to you and code.

To perform basic field level validation on a control, you must first bind the control to a field. To bind a control to a field, access the properties of the form and select the Validation tab. The resulting screen allows you to specify the validation rule that the contents of the field must adhere to and the message that appears when the contents of the field break the validation rule.

Table 6.5 shows some examples of validation formulas that you can use in your forms.

Table 6.5   Examples of Field Validation Rules

Validation Formula	Explanation
< 50	Value entered must be less than 50.
=ucase("WEST WING") or ucase("EAST WING")	Ensures that the value entered into the field is either "WEST WING" or "EAST WING."
>=Now()	Ensures that a date and time that was entered is not in the past.
<>[ContainsProjector]	Specifies that the given field must not have the same value as the field [ContainsProjector]. This is useful to ensure that two options are not enabled at the same time.
=(IIf([ClassroomLocation] = "WEST WING" , 10 , 20))	If you have a [NumberofSeats] field, you could specify that, if the location of the classroom was in the WEST WING, the number of seats must be 10; otherwise, the number of seats must be 20.

Descriptive Validation Error Messages

You should always take the time to make sure that you are displaying meaningful error messages to the user of the form. Users don't like to make mistakes, so treat them nicely when they do. Always explain what might have caused the validation error. For example, you can display messages such as, "You have entered an invalid number of seats for the location of the classroom you have entered. You entered 20 seats for a WEST WING classroom instead of 10." This can be achieved by placing the following in the validation error message field:

```
"You entered " & Cstr([NumberOfSeats]) & " for a " & [ClassroomLocation]  & "
classroom instead of " & cstr(IIf( [NumberOfSeats] = 10 , 20 , 10 )) ♦
```

Because we haven't discussed how to use VBScript to enhance your forms, I will not go into great detail at this time about how to perform field validation using VBScript. I will say that you can use VBScript to validate each property, control the display properties of other controls, and utilize more advanced development techniques, such as calling Component Object Model (COM) objects that reside on the client or on a middle tier such as in Microsoft Transaction Server (MTS). Typically, you resort to VBScript when there is no easy way to perform the same action in the GUI.

We will revisit VBScript later in this chapter in the section "Using VBScript in Outlook Forms."

Using Custom Controls

Sometimes, built-in controls do not provide the level of functionality you require on your forms. For example, you might need the user to enter a date. Microsoft Outlook does not provide its own date control to ease this process. For these cases, Outlook allows you to use a custom control, such as the Microsoft Calendar control, on your form that gathers the data using a calendar.

Custom controls are COM components that you can place on your forms. There are many different custom controls, many of which are installed when you install Visual Basic. You can also create your own custom control using tools like Visual Basic or Visual C++; however, that is a topic for another book.

Before you can add a custom control to your forms, you must first add the control to Outlook's control toolbox by right-clicking the control toolbox and choosing Custom Controls. This displays a list of all available custom controls that you can add to your form.

Every control, custom or built in, shares the same basic Outlook-specific set of properties, as displayed in Figure 6.8, as well as an advanced set of properties that allows you to customize the functionality and look of the control in one place, as shown in Figure 6.9. Standard Outlook properties are displayed by right-clicking the control and choosing the topmost Properties option on the pop-up menu. Advanced properties are accessed by right-clicking the control and choosing Advanced Properties from the pop-up menu.

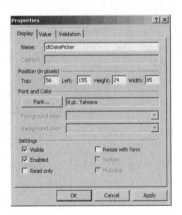

Figure 6.8 *Outlook-specific properties of the Date Picker control.*

Figure 6.9   *The Advanced Properties*
of the Date Picker control.

Many controls have an additional properties sheet that can also be accessed
through Microsoft Outlook. If a control has its own custom properties
sheet, you can access it by right-clicking the control and choosing the
bottommost Properties selection from the pop-up menu. The custom properties page for the Date Picker control is displayed in Figure 6.10.

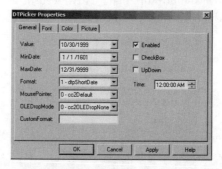

Figure 6.10   *The Date Picker's own properties page.*

Not every control has its own properties sheet. For example, you can use
Visual Basic or Visual C++ to create your own custom control to use in
your Outlook forms. The custom controls that you create do not necessarily
need to have a their own properties pages. For controls that you buy, or for
the controls that come packaged with Visual Studio, refer to product help to
learn how to use each control.

Custom Controls and Published Forms

When you publish a form, the required custom controls the form uses are not published along with the form. This means that if a user wants to use your published form, he must have the same controls installed and registered on the computer from which he is launching the form. For this reason, many organizations try to minimize the use of custom controls on their Outlook forms.

One way around this is to email all users an installation package that simply contains all the required custom controls. Users receive the email and double-click the attached setup program. The program then copies the controls to the local computer and registers them appropriately. Thus, when users launch the new form, all required controls are ready for action. Of course, there are endless ways to ensure that the controls you require reside on each local computer. Always ask your network administrator to advise you of the recommended method for your network. ◆

Using VBScript in Outlook Forms

Sometimes, it is not enough to simply capture the information in fields and controls on your form. Sometimes, you need to control the form and manipulate data programmatically. In walks VBScript to the rescue.

As I have already discussed, VBScript is a scaled-down version of Visual Basic that you can use in your forms to control objects, folders, items, and controls within a form, as well as write procedures that respond to events that occur within a control or a form.

VBScript Tutorial?

Obviously, this is not a reference book for VBScript or Visual Basic. I assume that you know or have the ability to learn how to program using VBScript. If you are not as proficient using VBScript as I am assuming, you might want to visit this Web site: `http://msdn.Microsoft.com/scripting.` ◆

There are two primary reasons to use VBScript in the Outlook forms you develop. The first is to enhance the overall functionality of the form you are developing. With VBScript, you can programmatically control all of the form elements, provide custom event handling for form and control level events, or access the services of other COM applications. For example, you can use VBScript to populate list box and combo box controls during the form load event, perform additional validation on data entered into form level fields, or automatically perform an action, such as sending out bulk email messages to users on a distribution list, based on some action and data captured by the form.

The second reason you might want to use VBScript in your forms is to perform some level of business processing. VBScript is a perfect candidate for accessing and controlling business objects that exist either on the local client machine or in a middle tier, such as MTS. For example, suppose you have created an expense tracking form that allows users to simply enter and categorize their business-related expenses. You can use VBScript to use the data provided to the form in a call to a middle-tier business object that was responsible for recording this information into a SQL Server located somewhere on the network. As you can clearly see, the more sophisticated you want your Outlook forms to be, the more you need to use VBScript. You should, however, take note of the following conditions of using VBScript:

- VBScript has only one data type: Variant.
- VBScript uses late binds all COM objects.
- You cannot use built-in constants in VBScript. You must refer to the literal the constant refers to in code.
- VBScript has minimal error handling capabilities.
- You can only declare 127 procedure level variables and 127 global or script level variables.

The VBScript Development Environment

Unfortunately, the development environment you would use to write Visual Script functions and procedures is only a little more functional than Microsoft's Notepad. The nice development environment you are accustomed to, which is provided by products such as Visual Basic, is not available to you when you develop Outlook forms. However, even though this development environment is fairly straightforward, I will still take time to discuss how to use it to add Visual Script to your forms.

Visual Script Editor

Microsoft Outlook provides a tool called the Script Editor that gives you the ability to add VBScript code to your forms.

The Integrated Development Environment (IDE) for VBScript

The Script Editor is little more than an enhanced text editor. When you launch the Script Editor for the first time when creating a new form, you are presented with a completely blank screen. You are responsible for defining all of the functions, procedures, and event handlers in the provided window. To help you with this process, the Script Editor provides an Event Handler and an Object Browser. The Event Handler allows you to select from the many form level events that you can handle in your code. For example, if you want to perform some action when the form closes—property validation, for instance—you simply open the Event Handler window and choose Close from the list box. Outlook automatically adds a function in the Script Editor that you can use to perform a series of actions and/or checks.

Microsoft Outlook exposes an extremely rich object model that can be used by applications that are external to Outlook, such as from a Visual Basic application, or internal, such as from an Outlook form. You can use the Object Browser in the Script Editor to view all of Outlook's objects, properties, and methods. The Object Browser allows you to insert these functions directly into your code, as well as find help on the usage of these objects.

I will discuss each of these features in more detail later in the "Object Browser" section of this chapter. ◆

Let's take a look at when and how you can launch the Script Editor. The Script Editor is available only in the design mode of a form and is depicted in Figure 6.11.

Launch the Script Editor by selecting View Code from the Form menu when in the design mode of a form.

Figure 6.11 *The Script Editor contains no contents when launched for the first time during the creation of a form.*

Event Handler

One of the handiest features of the Script Editor is the Event Handler. As I described before, the Event Handler displays a list of form level events that you can write code behind. As you can see in Figure 6.11, which has a number of event handling functions defined (such as Item_Close and Item_Open), you can use the Event Handler to insert skeleton code for the many events that you can handle in code.

Before we go further into how to use the Event Handler, I should spend some time discussing events. Microsoft Outlook automatically fires many form level events as described in Table 6.6.

Table 6.6   Automatically Fired Outlook Form Events

Event	Description	Is Cancelable
AttachmentAdd	Occurs after an attachment has been added to an item.	No
AttachmentRead	Occurs when a user has requested to read an attachment.	No
BeforeAttachmentSave	Occurs before an attachment is saved to the item. Data has not been written to the item yet.	Yes
BeforeCheckNameS	Occurs before Outlook attempts to resolve names listed in any of the destination fields, such as To, CC, or BCC.	Yes
Close	Occurs before Outlook closes the item that is currently displayed.	Yes
CustomAction	Occurs before Outlook performs some custom action defined in the form.	Yes
CustomPropertyChange	Occurs after a user defined property (field) of an item has changed.	No
Forward	Occurs immediately before the item is forwarded to a new destination address.	Yes
Open	Occurs after opening an item and directly before the item is displayed on the screen.	Yes
PropertyChange	Occurs when a built-in item property (field) has changed such as the Subject field.	No
Read	Occurs when an existing item is opened by a user.	No

continues ▶

Event	Description	Is Cancelable
Reply	Occurs immediately before Outlook executes the Reply method of the item.	Yes
ReplyAll	Occurs immediately before Outlook executes the ReplyAll method of the item.	Yes
Send	Occurs immediately before Outlook sends the item to the Outbox.	Yes
Write	Occurs before information gathered by the form is actually saved.	Yes

The Is Cancelable column in the preceding table is quite significant. As you can see, many of the listed events have been marked as cancelable. This means that you can override the event in your code if certain conditions are not met. To prevent the event from firing, simply set the return value of the event to False. Take a look at the following code snippet:

```
Function Item_Write()
    ' Ensure that the ClassroomLocation Field is valid
    If not IsValidLocation(item.UserProperties.Find("ClassroomLocation").value) Then
        Item_Write = False
        msgbox "You must enter a valid Classroom Location before saving this item."
    End If
End Function
```

As you can see, I have written an event handler for the form Write event that will execute just prior to Outlook saving the contents of form elements to an actual item. I want to ensure that the value entered into the ClassroomLocation field is a valid classroom location. In this case, I call a function called IsValidLocation, passing the value that was entered into this field by the user. If this function returns False, I set the return value of this function to False, effectively canceling the Write operation.

Form Events Versus Application Events

Form events have a much narrower scope than Outlook application events, which are discussed in Chapter 7, "Microsoft Outlook 2000 VBA." Application events correspond to events that occur independent of any specific Outlook form. For example, when new mail arrives in your inbox, an application level event fires. ◆

In many cases, multiple events fire one after another automatically. It is important to understand when this happens and in what order these events fire. Table 6.7 summarizes these events.

Table 6.7   Cascading Events

Event	Sequence of Events
Sending an item	Send, Write, Close
Posting an item	Write, Close
Opening an existing item	Read, Open

Similarly, form controls also fire events—well, they fire only one event: the Click event. Just to make this more interesting, only controls that are not bound to fields will fire the Click event. This means that if you want to write code that must react to the modification of a certain field on an item, you must use the PropertyChange event for built-in item fields or CustomPropertychange for all user defined fields. To create an event handler for an unbound control, define a function that has a name like *<ControlName>_Click*. For example, if you want to react to a click event on an unbound text field called txtFullName, you would write a procedure that would look something like this:

```
Sub txtFullName_click()
     'Insert event handler code here.
End sub
```

Let's get back to using the Event Handler to insert event handler skeleton routines into the Script Editor. To quote an old friend of mine, "This isn't rocket surgery." If you want to stick an event handling routine into your code, launch the Event Handler by selecting Event Handler from the Script menu in the Script Editor. Select the event you want to handle and click the Add box.

Empty Event Handler

I double-dog dare you to insert the same event handler into your code more than once. What happens? Outlook doesn't stop you. I must divulge a little secret. I once spent a whole hour looking through my code wondering why one of my event handlers wasn't working. I realized, with a silent curse of course, that I had accidentally inserted an empty event handler earlier in my code. Outlook was calling the empty event handler instead of the procedure I wanted it to call. Needless to say, I quickly removed the extra routine.

Outlook always runs the first event handler it sees when it searches for an event handling procedure, because Outlook interprets VBScript. ◆

Object Browser

As I mentioned earlier, Outlook exposes an extremely large and useful object model that you can access from the VBScript code that you write in your forms. Obviously, the more complicated an application's object model, the more difficult it becomes to write code that exploits it. Outlook's Script Editor provides a feature called the Object browser to help.

You can launch the Script Editor's Object Browser by pressing F2 or selecting Object Browser from the Script menu. The Object Browser window, as depicted in Figure 6.12, has two frames. The left-hand frame shows all of the available Outlook classes; the right-hand pane displays the properties and methods of the selected class. When you find the class method or property that you want to use, click the Insert button and Outlook inserts the name of the selected method or property in the current position of the Script Editor. To get help on any of the objects, properties, or methods, click the Object Help button.

Figure 6.12   *You can browse through Outlook's object model using the Object Browser.*

Accessing Help

You can also access help regarding the Outlook object model in all of its glory by accessing Microsoft Outlook Object Library Help from the Help menu in the Script Editor. I recommend that you leave the Help Window open and minimized when you are using the Outlook objects—It saves time. ◆

Uses of Visual Script

To give you an idea of how you can use Visual Script to extend your forms, here are some examples of when I have used it:

- **Control of GUI elements.** In many cases, form elements change based on the content or state of certain controls. If this is the case, VBScript can be used to change the state of controls on forms when values in built-in or custom fields change.

- **Population of list and combo boxes.** In many cases, the population of list and combo boxes is performed at run time. Additionally, many forms require the contents of these controls to be dynamic, based on data contained within a folder or some other storage, such as a SQL Server. VBScript can be used to populate list and combo boxes when the form opens. Because VBScript supports ADO, you can use it to access data from just about any data source. For forms that need to be used offline, I typically retrieve data from a public folder that is set as offline. This is the easiest way to locally cache data you need to reference in your forms.

- **Enhanced property level validation.** As you have seen, you can perform substantial field validation using the Validate fields of a control. Sometimes, you will require more complex levels of validation. In these cases, I almost invariably use VBScript.

- **Object Level Validation.** As I mentioned before, Outlook does not provide facilities to perform object level validation. Whenever object level validation is required, you must use VBScript to either pass data to business objects that perform the validation or perform the validation directly in script. This depends on the architecture of your resulting solution.

- **Data synchronization.** On many occasions, I have had to create forms that capture data such as contacts or tasks. On almost as many occasions, I have had to write code that would store the same information into other data sources such as SQL Server. You can write VBScript that takes the information that you have entered into the form and inserts or updates information stored on a SQL Server, depending on the state of the form (compose = insert, read = update).

For example, Example 6.3 shows code that populates a list box from items that exist in a public folder. I essentially treat this public folder like a lookup table you would commonly use in a relational database system. Because the public folder can be set to be offline, this function works regardless of connection state. Additionally, any changes to the public folder are automatically updated whenever the users work online.

Example 6.3   *Populating a list box from items in a public folder.*

```
Function Item_Open()

' Purpose:  To Populate automatically populate controls
'           from the contents of a selected folder

        dim olFolder        'This is a MAPIFolder
        dim olNS            'This is a NameSpace
```

continues ▶

```
dim iCount
dim oCTRL              'Will Point to the List Box Control

' First get the namespace - this will always be MAPI
Set olNS = Application.GetNameSpace("MAPI")

' For simplicity's sake, get the user to select a folder
' that will be used to populate our list box control
set olFolder = olNS.PickFolder

if not (olFolder is nothing) then
        if olFolder.Items.Count > 0 then

                ' Get a reference to the List Box Control
                set oCTRL =
➥Item.GetInspector.ModifiedFormPages("Populate").lbSubjects

                ' For every item in the folder, grab the subject and add it to
➥the listbox
                For iCount = 1 to olFolder.Items.count
                        oCTRL.AddItem (olFolder.Items(iCount))
                Next
        End If
End If

End Function
```

Testing Outlook Forms

After you have completed designing and building your form, you need to
test and deploy it. Of course, in the case of Outlook forms development,
you call it testing and publishing.

Form testing can be done at any time during the development process.
Remember, forms and the VBScript code that they may contain are not
compiled but are interpreted by Outlook. To test a form, select Run This
Form from the Form menu on your form's design window. This option
loads and runs the form just as the form would if Outlook launched it.

Testing Is Good

*I test my forms continuously throughout the development process, especially when
my forms contain VBScript code. Because the Script Editor development environment does not provide automatic syntax checking, I find it useful to test often to
catch as many bugs, syntactic or logic, as early as possible. ✦*

One of the things you have to remember when testing your form is that
Outlook is really running the form. For example, if I were to build a Post form
and run it in design mode, enter data, and close the form, Outlook creates a
new item in a designated folder. So, as a rule of thumb, I generally run the

form, use the form, and then cancel the form to prevent the excess cleanup work I normally have to perform afterwards. Of course, this is not an option if you want to test code that occurs during an item send or an item post event. In this case, it might be wise to place some debug code in your VBScript that cancels the Write and Close events at the last minute. Always ensure that you remove this code before you publish your forms or users cannot create any new items.

Of course, whenever you test, you invariably need to debug. Unfortunately, the Outlook Script Editor does not provide any debugging features to help you in this area. If an error occurs in your VBScript, Outlook reports the line number of the error. Fortunately, the Script Editor allows you to go to any line number by choosing Go To from its Edit menu.

One way to help you during the testing process is to use a product called the Microsoft Script Debugger. Personally, I typically use Visual Interdev to help debug the script that I write behind my forms, as shown in Figure 6.13. Either of these products can be used to help with the following debugging techniques:

- **Set breakpoints.** To insert a breakpoint that launches the Script Debugger or Visual Interdev, insert a Stop statement in your VBScript code.

- **View and change values at run time.** When debugging using the Script Debugger or Visual Interdev, you can use the Command windows to change values of variables immediately. The values are discarded the next time the script runs.

- **Trace the call stack.** You can list the currently running procedures in your script. This helps determine how a procedure or function was called.

- **Control script execution.** You can change the execution of the script using the Set Next Statement or Run to Cursor features.

Occasionally, you might want to launch a form that you have been working on without executing any VBScript event handlers. You can accomplish this by launching the form while holding down the Shift key. This is a great option if you do not want to have code in the Open event that is responsible for establishing a database connection or presetting form level variables to be executed when the form runs.

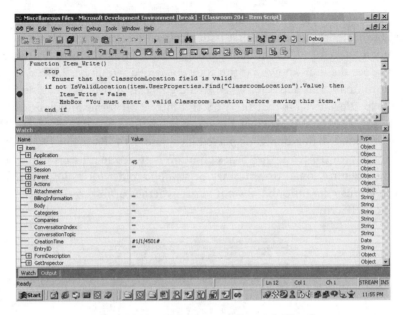

Figure 6.13 *You can use Microsoft Visual Interdev to help debug VBScript code.*

Deploying Outlook Forms

The last step in the process of Outlook forms development is to make the new form or forms available to others. This process is called form publishing.

There are three ways you can make a form available for others to use:

- **Save the form with each item it creates.** This option is best suited for one-off forms where the form is only used once and never used again. You can save the form definition with each item the form creates by selecting the Send Form Definition with Item option in the Properties page of your form in design mode.

- **Save the form definition to a forms library.** You use this method for forms that are commonly used, such as expense report forms, vacation request forms, and so on. Remember that a forms library can be the organizational forms library, a folder forms library, a personal forms library, or a Web forms library. Remember that a folder forms library can exist in a public folder or in a .PST file. In most cases, you publish your form to an organizational and folder forms library.

- **Save the form as a file (.oft).** Saving a form in an .oft file format gives you the ability to distribute your form to others, giving them the option to install the form in their own forms library of choice.

There are a couple minor issues you should be aware of when saving form definitions with items. The first issue deals with security. When a user receives an item, such as a mail message, that contains a form definition, how does the user know that the code contained within the form does not perform malicious activities when executed? The answer is they don't know. To help alleviate fears that the VBScript in one-off forms are malicious, Outlook always asks whether the script execution should be enabled. This confirmation dialog box is displayed in Figure 6.14. Basically, Outlook considers a form trusted if the form definition is stored in a forms library such as the organizational forms library or a public folder forms library. If a form is trusted, Outlook does not verify whether or not to enable the execution of VBScript.

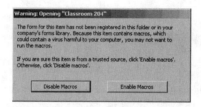

Figure 6.14   *Outlook verifies the execution of VBScript code in one-off forms because they cannot be inherently trusted.*

Sample Forms

All of the forms associated with this course are provided in .PST file format from the following Web site: http://www.newriders.com/exch_prog ♦

Here are the steps required to publish your form:

1. When designing your form, from the form designer's menu, select Tools, Forms, Publish Form As.

2. Using the pull-down list or the Browse button from the Publish Form As window, select the form library that you want to publish your form in.

3. Enter the Display name for the form. Outlook automatically assumes that you want to have the same form name as you have entered as the display name. Depending on your organization's form naming conventions, this might not be the case. You simply override the form name field if it does not follow your conventions.

4. Click the Publish button. Take note of the message class of the form that is automatically constructed by Outlook based on the root form type and the text in the Form Name text field.

After you have published your form, it is instantly available to other Outlook users. Outlook handles everything else.

Chapter Summary

In this chapter, I discussed the process of Outlook forms development. Outlook forms development is typically the bulk of the development most organizations experience with Microsoft Outlook. As you can see, you can develop a wide range of customized solutions using Outlook forms.

Not only can you create your own forms, which are based on built-in Outlook forms, but you can extend your forms using VBScript. VBScript can be used to enhance your forms' functionality by supporting the form directly by adding additional control over data and controls. It can also be used to provide links into other COM applications that reside locally or remotely within MTS.

Outlook forms are typically created to gather or manipulate information that is stored within Microsoft Exchange. As you can see, when a front end connects to other systems, such as SQL Server, you should consider other implementations, such as Visual Basic, or Outlook VBA, which is the primary topic of the next chapter.

In this chapter, we discussed the following:

- The general process of developing customized forms in Microsoft Outlook, from effective form design to development to deployment.
- The relationships that exists between items and forms.
- How to extend built-in Outlook forms by adding controls, pages, and actions, and setting form properties.
- How to use fields and controls to gather and display information the way you want.
- How to use Visual Script to extend the functionality of your forms.
- How to test the custom forms you create before deployment.
- How to deploy Outlook forms for others to use.

7

Microsoft Outlook 2000 VBA

One of the newest and, in my opinion, most useful features of Microsoft Outlook 2000 is the addition of Visual Basic for Applications (VBA). In Chapter 6, "Microsoft Outlook 2000 Forms Development," I discussed how you can add functionality to your forms by writing VBScript that executes when certain form level and control level events occur. Outlook 2000 has taken this further by including an environment to create macros, developed in VBA, that can be executed at the application level instead of at the form/item level. These macros can be executed manually by the user of Outlook or automatically based on various events that can occur from within Outlook, such as when new mail is received or when items have been modified or added to a folder.

You typically create an Outlook macro when there is no other means of implementing your solution using Outlook forms, rules, or views. For example, you generally use Outlook rules to manipulate messages as they arrive in your inbox. If your manipulation exceeds the functionality provided by rules, however, such as a requirement to process information contained in messages, you have two choices: create a macro to perform the task or use some other development technique to develop your solution, such as using Visual Basic to create a standalone application or an Outlook COM add-in.

In this chapter, I will introduce how to manipulate Microsoft Outlook at the application level by showing you how to create Outlook macros, written in VBA, that manipulate Outlook items and folders; modify the Outlook interface by adding buttons and menu items; and exploit many of the objects, events, and properties that are exposed by Outlook. Chapter 9, "Microsoft Office Integration," will show you how to use Visual Basic, rather than VBA, to manipulate and extend Outlook by either creating Outlook standalone applications or Outlook COM add-ins.

What Is VBA?

VBA allows users and developers to customize an application from within the application itself. The birth of this concept was not with VBA. In fact, products like Microsoft Excel have been customizable using macros for a number of years. Microsoft Excel had its own macro language that was much different from the macro language of other applications, such as Microsoft Word. In an effort to unify the process of macro development, Microsoft introduced VBA as the common development environment and macro language for all its Office products. To expand on this idea, Microsoft now licenses VBA to other software vendors, allowing more than just off-the-shelf Microsoft applications the capability of VBA-enabled expansion.

So, why is VBA the macro language of choice? VBA is a derivative of Visual Basic. Programmers of VBA can use the same syntax and a similar development IDE and debugging environment as they use in Visual Basic to extend VBA's host application. This means that any VB programmer can easily write VBA code in any host application that supports VBA. This is extremely important if you want to save time and money and reduce learning overhead by reusing skills. This is good any way you look at it.

Any application that hosts VBA is called a customizable application. Each customizable application exposes an extensive object model that can be used to control various aspects of its behavior and interface. The customizable application, in our case, is Outlook 2000. This means that any developer who is familiar with VB or VBA can easily extend the functionality of Microsoft Outlook to help fit his/her own needs or the needs of an organization. You get a lot of bang for your buck with Outlook. It provides a rich set of functions to help users manage contacts, tasks, notes, journal entries, appointments, and email. If you need something specific added to your Outlook environment, you can simply build it. How can you go wrong?

When to Use VBA

Many developers ask if they can use VBA in customized Outlook forms. You can use VBA to extend the functionality of Outlook, but unfortunately you cannot use it to extend the functionality of your forms.

VBA in Forms

Saying that you cannot use VBA in your Outlook forms is a little misleading. You can, as long as your form is an Office document form. Because you can include VBA in just about any Microsoft Office document, you can expect the same when you embed the Office document into a form. The VBA is actually executed by the

Office application that supports the document type. For example, if I embed an Excel spreadsheet in a form, the VBA code within the spreadsheet is actually executed by the Excel application.

To create a new form based on an Office document, select Office Document from the File, New menu in Outlook. From there, place the form in design mode, and away you go. ◆

The Outlook VBA environment is slightly different than the VBA environments of other applications, such as Microsoft Excel or Word. In Excel or Word, VBA can be stored in a template file, which is extremely easy to distribute and use by many users. In Outlook 2000, however, all VBA is contained within a project file called VBAProject.otm, which is different for each Windows user. This touches on another very interesting point: Outlook 2000 can have only one set of VBA macros per user. This is extremely limiting when you consider that other applications, such as Microsoft Excel, can run a completely new set of macros with every document that it opens. So, if Outlook VBA places so many constraints on developers, why would we use it? Surely there are other methods of doing the same thing? In fact, we can use other methods. When it comes to modular components that work well to extend Outlook's functionality, COM add-ins are the perfect fit. Not only are they modular, packaging functionality into bite-sized pieces, but they are much easier to distribute than VBA macros.

Why not create Outlook add-ins all the time? Well, sometimes it's just not worth the effort. I spend a great deal of my life tinkering with things. I am continually creating snippets of code that perform specific and well defined tasks for myself. I call this activity One-Off development. Generally, I write these small pieces of code to either test a theory or implement something that I desperately need. I don't want to waste time creating, debugging, and managing COM add-ins. Hence, I use VBA. In a nutshell, I write Outlook VBA code for the following reasons:

- **To experiment with new technologies or new product functionality.** For example, as soon as I installed Outlook 2000 on Windows 2000, I wrote some Outlook VBA code that used Direct Speech to announce when I had new mail. It also checked if the sender matched an item in my contact list. If there was a match, I programmed Outlook to call out the name of the sender: "You have new mail from Duncan Mackenzie and Jeremy Leduc." I like that one.
- **As a learning tool.** One of the easiest places to play with Outlook's object model is from inside Outlook using VBA.

- **To create proof of concept code that could eventually be used as a COM add-in.** For example, I created the code that caused Outlook to announce my new messages in VBA first. Other people liked the idea and asked if I could make something more generic and distributable. So, I created a COM add-in; however, in this case, I was essentially able to cut my code from VBA and paste it directly into Visual Basic to create my COM add-in.

Author's Note

I use Outlook VBA 60 to 70 percent of the time when testing out new ideas or creating proof of concept extensions to Outlook. My project file becomes really messed-up after a while, which is why I always keep a clean VBAProject.otm file handy. As it turns out, when my current VBAProject.otm file gets really messy, I just erase it and replace it with a nice and fresh VBAProject.otm. Of course, it's not completely empty, because I like to have a few basic code snippets hanging around.

This method can also be used to deploy Outlook VBA to other users. For example, instead of writing a COM add-in for Microsoft Outlook, you can send someone your VBAProject.otm. They can simply replace theirs with yours and magically have your VBA code. I don't recommend this, though. ◆

The Outlook VBA Development Environment

If you have worked in other VBA environments, such as the one provided in Microsoft Excel, the Outlook VBA development environment is similar and you might skim through this part until something catches your interest. However, for those who have never used VBA in any application, pay attention!

If you have already used Microsoft Outlook but have never had the time to look at Outlook macros, which are snippets of VBA code, you can launch the VBA development environment by selecting Visual Basic Editor from the Tools, Macro menu option, or you can press Alt+F11.

The Outlook Visual Basic Editor

The Outlook Visual Basic Editor provides you with the development environment that is required to write VBA code in Outlook 2000. If you are an experienced VB or VBA developer, you will immediately notice the similarities this development environment has with VB or other VBA editors. The Outlook Visual Basic editor consists of many windows, such as the Project window, the Properties window, and the Code window. Many of these windows can be docked on the screen to provide a more robust development environment.

Take a close look at the Project window. Notice that you can only work with one project at a time. Outlook stores its VBA project code in a file called VBAProject.otm. You can change some of the properties of this project by choosing Tools, Project Properties. Outlook's Project properties dialog box allows you to specify the name of the project, the project's description, the associated help file and help context ID, conditional arguments, and project protection to prevent unauthorized users from modifying the code of the project.

Like other VB projects, you can add different modules, classes, and forms to the default VBAProject.otm file. To insert additional modules, classes, and forms into your project, use the Insert menu in the Visual Basic Editor.

In many cases, you will want your VBA code to use other COM objects that are installed on your computer or on a middle tier server, such as Microsoft Transaction Server. Before you can make use of these objects, you must first add the object to the list of references for the project. To add additional object references to your project, select Tools, References and select the appropriate set of object references from the resulting dialog box. Figure 7.1 displays the object references that are used for many of the examples provided in this chapter.

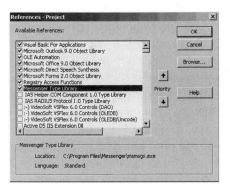

Figure 7.1   *The Outlook VBA project's references used to create many of the examples presented in this chapter.*

Referencing COM Objects

Adding many references to your project negatively affects the load time required to launch Microsoft Outlook. Generally, the more references you have in your Outlook VBA project, the more time it takes to load Outlook and initialize the VBA environment. ◆

Outlook VBA Projects

Microsoft Outlook does not store its VBA macros in documents like other Microsoft Office applications, such as Microsoft Word or Excel. This is due to one simple reason: Outlook does not create documents. Outlook stores all the code that you create in a file called VBAProject.otm. Interestingly, there is a different VBAProject.otm for every user on a computer. This means that if you intend to provide more than one user with the same set of VBA macros on the same computer, they must either be logged on as the same user or you must ensure that your VBA code is written and stored in two places.

Writing VBA code from inside Outlook has its advantages. Your code runs inside Outlook, meaning that you never have to create or instantiate the Outlook.Application object. It's just there for your development pleasure. The biggest advantage also happens to be its biggest disadvantage: Your code runs inside Outlook. This simply means that Outlook must always be running for your code to work, even if it does not refer to or use the Outlook object model.

Outlook VBA Hello World

I am going to start with something really simple, such as the reoccurring "Hello World." However, I have decided to add a little twist to this really boring app and get Outlook to greet me by name—verbally, when I start the application. It's always so nice when your computer greets you at the door, isn't it?

Before I show you some code, I want to point out that you must have Direct Speech installed before attempting to run this code. I use Windows 2000, which has Direct Speech installed by default. If you don't have Direct Speech installed, you can substitute the speech with message boxes.

Before you begin, you must ensure that your project knows how to reference the Direct Speech COM components. I'll talk more about this later; for now, simply select Tools, References in the Visual Basic Editor, and check off Microsoft Direct Speech Synthesis from the Available References list box.

Don't Have Direct Speech?

If you don't see Direct Speech Synthesis in the list of references, you don't have Direct Speech installed. You can simply exclude all of the lines of code that use Direct Speech Synthesis from the examples provided in this chapter. ◆

After you have the appropriate reference in place, you are ready to type the code listed in Example 7.1.

Global Variables

Global variables are declared in the (General) section of the code window for your project. ♦

Example 7.1 *Modified version of "Hello World." Outlook greets the user by name and announces the number of unread messages in the user's inbox.*

```
' Global Variables
Dim objSpeak As DirectSS              ' The Direct Speech Object
Dim olNameSpace As Outlook.NameSpace  ' The Outlook NameSpace Object

Private Sub Application_Startup()
' This macro will run every time Outlook is started.
' This will greet the currently logged on user
' at the same time providing the number of unread messages
' that exist in the user's inbox.

' Local Vars
    Dim strCurrentUser As String      ' Temp string to hold the user name
    Dim strMessage As String          ' Used to construct the message

On Error GoTo errApplication_Startup

' Instantiate objects
    Set objSpeak = New DirectSS
    Set olNameSpace = Application.GetNamespace("MAPI")

    strCurrentUser = olNameSpace.CurrentUser

    strMessage = "Hello " & strCurrentUser
    strMessage = strMessage & ". " & "You have "
    strMessage = strMessage & olNameSpace.GetDefaultFolder(olFolderInbox).UnReadItemCount
    strMessage = strMessage & " unread messages "
    strMessage = strMessage & " " & " in your Inbox.  Have a great session!"

    objSpeak.Speak strMessage

    Exit Sub

errApplication_Startup:
    ' Place error handling routines here
    Resume Next
End Sub
```

First, I want to explain why I placed the olNameSpace object and the objSpeak object into the (General) section of the project. First, the olNameSpace object is used many, many, many times. I like to keep it global and assume that it is there, much like how Outlook provides the

Application object ready for you to use. With regard to the objSpeak object, when you initiate the object's Speak method, the code falls right through, in this case, to the end of the procedure. When it reaches the end, VBA discards the object. In most cases, the objSpeak object doesn't get a chance to speak its mind before being obliterated, and you don't get to hear much of the constructed message. So, keep this object global so that it doesn't go out of scope when the procedure ends.

Take notice that you don't have to create a reference to Microsoft Outlook in the references section of the Visual Basic editor. The reason for this is apparent. Also note that you can just begin using the Application object without having to declare or instantiate it in any way. Outlook provides you with that object automatically. This is sufficient because you can gain access to all other objects from the Application object. You can prove this to yourself by taking a look at the Outlook object hierarchy in Outlook Help.

Outlook Namespace

You might have noticed that I used the function GetNameSpace, a member of the Outlook.Application object, to obtain a reference to the current Outlook NameSpace object. If you are wondering why, the answer is that I use this function purely out of habit. To gain access to Outlook's NameSpace object, you can alternatively reference the Application.Session property. ◆

One of the properties of the Outlook NameSpace object is the name of the currently logged on user, appropriately called CurrentUser. I use the CurrentUser property and the GetDefaultFolder method to string together a simple message. With the GetDefaultFolder method, I can specify a default folder, represented by an Outlook constant called olFolderInbox. I can then reference the UnReadItemCount property of the user's inbox. I tag that onto the message string as well. When I'm done building the message string, I simply invoke the Speak method of the DirectSS object. Just like in movies—Outlook can talk. As you will see in later examples, it will also become apparent how to make Outlook say, "You've got mail."

The Macro Security Warning

If you have written a similar "Hello World" example, you might have noticed that the next time that you start Outlook a new dialog box is displayed asking if you want to enable or disable any of the embedded VBA macros. The Macro Security Warning dialog box is there to help protect users against inadvertently running VBA macros that could potentially harm their data, computer, or network.

The macros you can create in Microsoft Outlook are a little more difficult to distribute than those created in Microsoft Excel or Microsoft Word. You can't just stick VBA code in a file and have it run automatically when Outlook starts (even though, technically, all of Outlook's VBA code is stored in VBAProject.otm). In Outlook, the macro warning message is there simply to remind users that VBA macros exist in case the VBAProject.otm file is replaced without the user's knowledge.

The fastest way to get rid of that nasty warning dialog box is to set your security options to Low (by selecting Zone Settings from the Outlook Security option tab). I don't recommend this method because it leaves you completely vulnerable to someone who wants to replace your VBAProject.otm file. The method I recommend is to digitally sign your code.

What does a digital signature mean to VBA code within Outlook? A digital signature reassures the user that the creator of the code is who he claims to be and that the code has not been modified since it was signed. For publicly available code, such as the ActiveX control you download in your browser, the digital certificate is authenticated by an independent authority. For code that you write for yourself or your organization, you might not need to have your certificate authenticated this way. You can use a utility called SelfCert.exe (provided by Microsoft Office 2000) to create a personal digital certificate.

The first step in using SelfCert is to install it. Make sure that the Digital Signature for VBA Projects option is installed when you install Microsoft Office. The second step is to generate a digital signature for yourself by running SelfCert.exe from the C:\Program files\Microsoft Office\Office directory (assuming that you have installed Office 2000 in that location). SelfCert simply asks for your name and confirms the creation of the certificate.

You must perform one additional step to digitally sign the VBA code you write in your Outlook project. From the Outlook VBA editor, choose Tools, Digital Signature and choose the personal certificate that you just created. The dialog box that displays a list of digital certificates actually comes from the operating system. Windows OS stores all digital signatures, for which you have the private key, in the My Certificate store implemented in the Registry in \HKEY_CURRENT_USER\Software\Microsoft\SystemCertificates\My\Certificates store.

This is not the only method of code signing at your disposal. You can also use products such as Microsoft Certificate Server to generate code signing certificates. If you need to publicly distribute your Outlook VBA code (although I'm not sure when you would want to do this), you can obtain your certificates from certificate authorities such as Thawte Consulting or VeriSign for a nominal fee. Of course, if you are developing solutions for your own corporation, it is acceptable to use SelfCert or Microsoft Certificate Server for code signing. ◆

Outlook Objects and Events

One of the biggest challenges that most programmers face when dealing with VBA application development is learning how to utilize the many diverse methods, properties, events, and types that each application exposes. There are lots of books dedicated to the explanation of application object models. This is not one of them. As you might have already learned, Outlook has an extensive application object model that you can easily call upon when developing your collaborative applications. The secret to learning this object model is not to go and buy some expensive book that speaks to every property, method, or event, but to actually dig in and use it.

For this reason, I will not explain the Outlook object model in detail. I will, however, provide sufficient information to get you started, show you how to get help, and provide you with examples to get you going; the rest will remain in your hands. Besides, books that simply list and describe methods and properties are really boring, and that's not what I want this book to be.

Where to Find Objects and Events

The first place to look for information regarding any object that you are using in your application is the Object Browser, as shown in Figure 7.2. The Object Browser is my personal best friend (that doesn't say a lot for my personal life, does it?). Generally speaking, the Object Browser displays all of the methods, properties, and events that are exposed by a COM object that you are referencing in your Outlook VBA project. The Object Browser not only lists these items, but it also describes parameters and return values for methods and events.

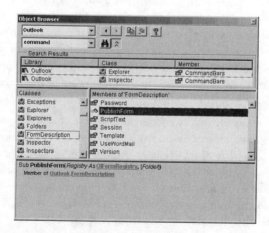

Figure 7.2 *The Outlook Visual Basic Editor's Object Browser.*

In many cases, the Object Browser does not provide information, such as extended help and examples of object usage. If this is the case, most objects do provide an associated help file that supplies all of this information. The entire object model that Microsoft Outlook exposes is fully documented and can be accessed from the Object Browser or directly from the Visual Basic Editor by pressing F1.

Overview of Outlook Objects

As I mentioned earlier, we (the authors) have decided not to detail Outlook's extensive object model for one very good reason: Why would you want to read about it here when you can get extremely good help, fully equipped with explanations and examples, at the click of a button?

We do provide a quick rundown of some of the more important objects that Outlook provides. Table 7.1 describes some of the more common objects that are presented to you in the examples provided in this and upcoming chapters. ◆

Table 7.1   Some of the More Important Objects That Are Referenced in This Book

Object Name	Description
Application	Represents the entire Outlook application. All other Outlook objects can be derived from the Application object. The Application object is intrinsic to Outlook VBA, meaning you don't need to declare it to use it.
NameSpace	Represents the root for Outlook's data storage. You can retrieve the NameSpace object using the Application.GetNameSpace function or using the Application.Session property. There is only one datasource that is supported by Outlook's NameSpace object: MAPI.
PropertyPages	PropertyPages are custom pages that have been added to Outlook's Options dialog box or to a folder's Properties dialog box.
SyncObjects	SyncObjects specify what data is stored locally when the Outlook client is not connected to Exchange. You can use SyncObjects to specify which folders are available offline as well as what synchronization filters are placed on each folder to control the items that are synchronized between offline storage and online storage.
AddressLists	Provides access to the transport provider's address book for the current Outlook session.

continues ▶

Table 7.1   Continued

Object Name	Description
Folders	Also called MAPIFolders; this is the set of all available Outlook folders. To gain access to items stored in Outlook, you must first understand how to manipulate Outlook folders.
Items	The Items collection refers to all of the items that are stored in a given folder.
UserProperties	When you create a new field in a folder or an item, that field is accessed from the UserProperties collection. Every Outlook item has a UserProperties collection that identifies which custom fields have values in the item.
Explorers	Represents sets of windows in which the contents of folders are displayed. You typically use the ActiveExplorer or GetExplorer methods to return an Explorer object.
CommandBars	If you need to make or modify Outlook toolbars, you will use the CommandBars collection.
Panes	You can manipulate panes, such as the Preview pane, using the Panes collection.
Inspectors	An inspector represents the windows in which an Outlook item is displayed. You typically use ActiveInspector or GetInspector to return an Inspector object. The Inspectors collection represents a collection of all Inspectors.

Again, you can use Outlook's Help to learn how to use each object.

Declaring and Using Outlook Objects and Events

Before you can use any of the objects that your project references, you must declare them. There is one exception to this rule when you write code in Outlook VBA: the Outlook.Application object. This only makes sense because your code is running *in* Microsoft Outlook, therefore you can always be sure of its existence.

All other Outlook objects can be derived from the Outlook.Application object. For example, suppose you want to see how many items exist in your inbox. If you take a look at the Outlook object model, you can see that if you need to make a reference to the Items collection of any folder, you need to traverse the object hierarchy displayed in Figure 7.3.

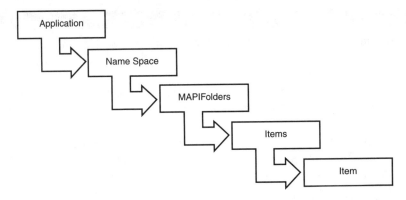

Figure 7.3   *The objects that you must traverse to reference an item in a folder.*

Example 7.2 shows some code that will help you get there.

Example 7.2   *Traversing the Outlook object model in VBA.*

```
Dim olNameSpace As Outlook.NameSpace
Dim olInbox As Outlook.MAPIFolder
Dim olInboxItems As Outlook.Items
Dim olInboxItem As Outlook.MailItem

Set olNameSpace = Application.GetNamespace("MAPI")
Set olInbox = olNameSpace.GetDefaultFolder(olFolderInbox)
Set olInboxItems = olInbox.Items
Set olInboxItem = olInboxItems.GetFirst
```

First, I declare all the objects that I use to gain reference to the first item in my inbox, with the exception of the Application object. Sometimes, the definition is not as you would expect. For example, you might assume that an Outlook folder would be represented by the Outlook.Folder object, not the Outlook.MAPIFolder object. Thankfully, the VBA development environment provides context-sensitive pop-up menus to help you when specifying objects, methods, and properties.

The next step is to traverse the object tree until I get to the desired level. Notice that I begin with the NameSpace object. In this case, the GetNameSpace method, passing the string "MAPI" to specify the type of NameSpace to return, provides me with the required NameSpace object. I then use a method called GetDefaultFolder from the NameSpace object to retrieve a reference to my default inbox folder, which is specified using the Outlook constant olFolderInbox. (This value conveniently pops up when you start typing the method in your code module.) After I receive a reference to the Inbox folder, I can refer to the Items collection that contains all of the inbox messages I can reference as MailItems.

Outlook Namespace

You might have noticed that I used the function GetNameSpace, a member of the Outlook.Application object, to obtain a reference to the current Outlook Namespace object. If you are wondering why, the answer is that I use this function purely out of habit. To gain access to Outlook's NameSpace object, you can alternatively reference the Application.Session property. ◆

Of course, I didn't need to declare all those variables just to reference the first message in my inbox. I could have written something like this:

```
Dim olInboxItem As Outlook.MailItem
Set olInboxItem =
Application.GetNamespace("MAPI").GetDefaultFolder(olFolderInbox).Items.GetFirst
```

Both methods work just fine; however, the first method eats up a bit more memory than necessary.

Event Handling

You might have noticed, when browsing through the Outlook object model, that a great many events fire automatically when certain events occur, such as when new mail arrives. Wouldn't it be great to trap those events and write custom event handing routines that serve your purposes? Wait a second, you can do that! You can write VBA that can respond to any event you choose just by declaring the object a little differently and writing specific event handling procedures.

For example, suppose you want your computer to announce the timeless expression "You have mail" when new mail arrives in your inbox. First, notice that the Outlook.Application object has a NewMail event. Because the Application object is the top-most object, and is already defined and instantiated, all you need to do is write a simple event handling procedure that looks like this:

```
Private Sub Application_NewMail()
    objSpeak.Speak "You have mail"
End Sub
```

Figure 7.4 displays how events are handled in Outlook.

For any object other than the Outlook.Application object, you must declare the object in such a way that you can also trap its events. The secret is to use the WithEvents keyword when declaring objects that fire events you want to handle. For example, suppose you want to write a routine that performs some action whenever a new post is made to a folder. You can write the code shown in Example 7.3.

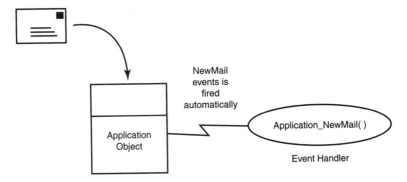

Figure 7.4 *You can write event handlers for Outlook objects that automatically fire events.*

Example 7.3   *Handling an ItemAdd event for an Items collection.*

```
Private WithEvents olItems As Outlook.Items

Public Sub TrapFolderPost()

' Execute this sub to specify the folder that you wish
' to trap an item add event.  This code assumes the global
' variable olItems - declared WithEvents

    Dim olNameSpace As Outlook.NameSpace
    Dim olMapiFolder As Outlook.MAPIFolder

    Set olNameSpace = Application.GetNamespace("MAPI")

    ' Choose the folder that you would like to trap the
    ' event for.

    Set olMapiFolder = olNameSpace.PickFolder
    Set olItems = olMapiFolder.Items

End Sub

Private Sub olItems_ItemAdd(ByVal Item As Object)
' This code is fired when an item is added to the
' olItems collection

    MsgBox "You added an item"

End Sub
```

As you can see, the preceding code starts with the declaration of a global object called olItems with the WithEvents keyword. This allows you to create specific event handlers for the events this object will fire. The first procedure, TrapFolderPost, basically initializes the global variable by requesting that the user select the folder in which he wants to trap item addition events. The final procedure, olItems_ItemAdd, is simply the event handler. Notice that the event handler always has the following format:

```
<Declared Object Name>_<Event Name>
```

In this case, the object was called olItems, and I wanted to trap the ItemAdd event for the Outlook.Items collection. This event handler simply lets the user know that the event was handled.

You can use the previous sample code to get your feet wet. However, I thought that I would also provide you with some sample code that is extremely useful. Take a look at the code in Example 7.4.

Example 7.4   *A real-world example of handling events in VBA.*

```
Public WithEvents olPersonalJournal As Outlook.Items
Public olCorporateJournal As Outlook.MAPIFolder


Public Sub Initialize_Handler()
' Initialize all Global Objects

    Set olCorporateJournal = GetPublicFolder("All Public Folders\Corporate Journal")
    Set olPersonalJournal = Application.GetNamespace("MAPI").
GetDefaultFolder(olFolderJournal).Items

End Sub

Public Function GetPublicFolder(sFolderPath As String) As Outlook.MAPIFolder
' This function will return a Public Folder in the Public Folder
' tree from a path such as:
'    Public Folders\All Public Folders\Corporate Contacts

    Dim sFolderPaths() As String
    Dim olFolder As Outlook.MAPIFolder
    Dim olNS As Outlook.NameSpace
    Dim i As Integer

On Error GoTo errGetPublicFolder

    sFolderPaths = Split(sFolderPath, "\", -1, vbTextCompare)

    If UBound(sFolderPaths) > 0 Then
        Set olNS = Application.GetNamespace("MAPI")
        Set olFolder = olNS.Folders("Public Folders")
        For i = 0 To UBound(sFolderPaths)
            Set olFolder = olFolder.Folders(sFolderPaths(i))
        Next i
    End If
```

```
    Set GetPublicFolder = olFolder

    Exit Function

errGetPublicFolder:
    Resume Next
End Function

Private Sub olPersonalJournal_ItemAdd(ByVal Item As Object)
' Move the new item to the central journal folder
    Item.Move olCorporateJournal
End Sub
```

The code in Example 7.4 was written to ensure that every journal entry that is created in a user's personal Journal folder is moved to a central Journal public folder. Microsoft does a great job of automatically journaling events for you, such as meeting requests, task assignments, office documents, and so on. The only problem with this is that these journal items are created in a user's personal Journal folder, which is not much use to everyone else. Using the preceding code, you can guarantee that every journal item that is automatically created for you in your own personal Journal folder is moved to a central location. Take note that you do not copy personal journal entries to the Corporate Journal public folder.

Working with the Outlook Interface

There will be many cases where you will want to modify aspects of Outlook's default user interface. For example, you might want to add things like custom button bars, custom menus, and custom pop-up menus to help users enjoy the functionality provided by your COM add-ins or macros.

Because I cannot effectively cover how to add or modify GUI elements, I will not cover this topic at length in this book. I will say that the object model that Outlook exposes, which allows you to add menus and buttons and property pages, is very similar to the way all other Office applications expose their GUI objects. If you are well versed in manipulating Microsoft Excel GUI elements from VBA, you will have absolutely no problems doing the same with Outlook GUI objects.

For reference purposes, here is a list of objects and collections that you can manipulate to change the general look and feel of Outlook:

- PropertyPages collection / PropertyPage object
- CommandBars collection / CommandBar object
- Panes collection / Pane object
- OutlookBarPane object
- OutlookBarStorage object

- OutlookBarGroups collection / OutlookBarGroup object
- OutlookBarShortCuts collection / OutlookBarShortCut object
- Pages collection / Page object

For further information, please refer to Outlook's Visual Basic Help.

Outlook 2000 VBA Programmers Reference

If you are serious about getting nasty with Outlook and the GUI objects you can work with, you might want to pick up one of the following books: Outlook 2000 VBA Programmers Reference *by Dwayne Gifford, Wrox Press, Inc. (ISBN: 186100253X) by Dwayne Gifford, John Green, and Duncan Mackenzie, Wrox Press, Inc. (ISBN: 1861003005).* ◆

So I don't leave you hanging on this topic, Example 7.5 shows some sample code that utilizes the CommandBar object. The following code snippet creates a new toolbar in Microsoft Outlook that lists all of your MSN Instant Messenger contacts. Users can select a contact to begin a conversation with. I kept this fairly simple because I didn't want to have to describe how to use the Messenger object model. With a little effort, you could easily modify this code to display only those contacts who are online, but again, this would require further explanation of the Messenger object.

Example 7.5   *Modifying the Outlook User Interface sample.*

```
Private WithEvents olCommandBarControl As CommandBarComboBox

Public Sub InstantMessageAddOn()

' This sub will create a new CommandBar and ComboBox
' that will list all of the contacts stored in Microsoft
' Instant Messenger.  This will allow the user to select
' a contact and launch the Instant Messenger window.
'
' Note: This procedure uses the publicly declared object:
'    olCommandBarControl

    Dim objMo As Messenger.MsgrObject
    Dim olCommandBars As CommandBars
    Dim olCommandBar As CommandBar
    Dim i As Integer
    Dim intContactCount As Integer
    Dim oimState As Messenger.MSTATE

On Error GoTo errInstantMessageAddOn

    Set objMo = New Messenger.MsgrObject
```

```
' Get the current Explorer's Collection of CommandBars
Set olCommandBars = Application.Explorers.Item(1).CommandBars


' Add a new Command Bar
Set olCommandBar = olCommandBars.Add("Instant Messenger", msoBarTop)


' Add a new control to the Command Bar
Set olCommandBarControl = olCommandBar.Controls.Add(msoControlDropdown)


' Set the Properties of the new ComboBox
With olCommandBarControl
    .Caption = "List of Online Users"
    .TooltipText = "List of Online Instant Messenger Contacts"
    .DescriptionText = "List of Online Users"
    .Enabled = True
    .Width = 145
    .DropDownWidth = 145
End With


' Fill the Combo Box with all users in the list
intContactCount = objMo.List(MLIST_CONTACT).Count
If intContactCount > 0 Then
    For i = 0 To intContactCount - 1
        olCommandBarControl.AddItem objMo.List(MLIST_CONTACT).Item(i).FriendlyName
    Next i
End If


olCommandBar.Visible = True


Exit Sub


errInstantMessageAddOn:
'Place error handling here
    MsgBox Err.Description


End Sub



Private Sub olCommandBarControl_Change(ByVal Ctrl As CommandBarComboBox)


' We declared the olCommandBarControl WithEvents meaning we can now
' trap when the value of this control changes.  When it does, we are
' going to grab it's value and launch an Instant Messaging Window


    Dim objMa As Messenger.MessengerApp
    Dim objMo As Messenger.MsgrObject
    Dim strLogonName As String
    Dim i As Integer
    Dim intListCount As Integer
    Dim bNotFound As Boolean


    Set objMa = New Messenger.MessengerApp
    Set objMo = New Messenger.MsgrObject
```

continues ▶

Example 7.5   *continued*

```
intListCount = objMo.List(MLIST_ALLOW).Count

i = -1
bNotFound = True

' Since the ComboBox lists the Friendly names, we must
' first resolve to logon names

While bNotFound And i < intListCount - 1
    i = i + 1
    If objMo.List(MLIST_ALLOW).Item(i).FriendlyName = Ctrl.Text Then
        bNotFound = False
    End If
Wend

If Not bNotFound Then
    objMa.LaunchIMUI (objMo.List(MLIST_ALLOW).Item(i).LogonName)
End If

End Sub
```

Distributing Your Project

As I mentioned earlier, distributing your Outlook macros isn't the easiest or most common thing to do. Distributing macros created for other applications, such as Microsoft Word or Excel, is a piece of cake comparatively. Simply email the Office document containing the macro to someone or place a template containing the macro in a central location for anyone to use. Unfortunately, you don't have this luxury in Outlook.

Here are some suggestions that you might choose to follow if you need to distribute your code to other machines, as shown in Figure 7.5:

- **Don't distribute macros, distribute COM add-ins.** I typically use Outlook macros for one-off solutions for myself or my colleagues. If I need to disperse my solution to many users, I typically write an Outlook COM add-in. This makes distribution and installation more manageable.

- **Export your code to a class or a module so that it can be imported into the destination Outlook client.** When in your Outlook Visual Basic editor, use the Import File and Export File options under the File menu to exercise this option.

- **Replace the destination client's VBAProject.otm file with your own.** Just one comment on using this method: Don't use it! It's just not nice.

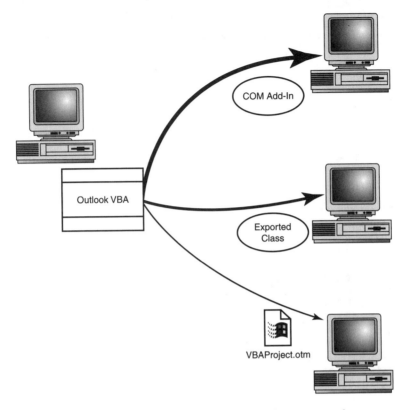

Figure 7.5 *Three possible ways to distribute your code.*

Additional Examples

Just for fun, I have included a couple of other interesting examples of Outlook VBA. In fact, I simply took this code from my current VBProject file. Enjoy!

Makeshift List Server

This first example isn't really useful in the real world, however the provided code should demonstrate what you can do with messages as they arrive in your inbox. The code shown in Example 7.6 makes Outlook perform somewhat like a list server. Basically, Outlook will react to every message that this recipient receives. Mail that is received by this recipient is processed in one of three ways. If the incoming mail message's Subject field reads "subscribe," the email address of the message's sender is added to a special distribution list that is located in the recipient's default Contacts folder. If the incoming mail message's subject field reads "unsubscribe," the sender is removed from the distribution list. All other messages sent to this recipient are forwarded to the specified distribution list.

Example 7.6   *Makeshift List Server sample code.*

```
' List Server

Private WithEvents olInboxItems As Outlook.Items

Private Const DLNAME = "CollabDL"
Private Sub Application_Startup()
    Initialize_handler
End Sub
Public Sub Initialize_handler()
    Set olInboxItems = Application.Session.GetDefaultFolder(olFolderInbox).Items
End Sub
Private Sub olInboxItems_ItemAdd(ByVal item As Object)
' Make a call to ProcessMessage.
' Notice that ProcessMessage accepts a MailItem and we are passing an
'        object
    ProcessMessage item
End Sub
Private Sub ProcessMessage(olNewMessage As Outlook.MailItem)
' This procedure will determine if the message is in fact a mailitem
' if it is, it will add or remove the senders email address to the
' distribution list that this mailbox corresponds to.

    Dim olOutgoingMessage As Outlook.MailItem
    Dim olDL As Outlook.DistListItem

    ' Set the Distribution Folder
    Set olDL = Application.Session.GetDefaultFolder(olFolderContacts).Items(DLNAME)

    If LCase(olNewMessage.Subject) = "subscribe" Then

        'Add User to DL
        Set olOutgoingMessage = olNewMessage.Reply
        olDL.AddMembers olOutgoingMessage.Recipients
        olDL.Save

        ' Send a Confirmation Notice
        olOutgoingMessage.Body = "Subscription Succeeded"
        olOutgoingMessage.Send

    ElseIf LCase(olNewMessage.Subject) = "unsubscribe" Then

        'Remove User from DL
        Set olOutgoingMessage = olNewMessage.Reply
        olDL.RemoveMembers olOutgoingMessage.Recipients
        olDL.Save
```

```
        olOutgoingMessage.Body = "You are now unsubscribed"
        olOutgoingMessage.Send
    Else

        'Send Message to DL

        Set objOutgoingMessage = olNewMessage.Forward
        olOutgoingMessage.Recipients.Add DLNAME
        olOutgoingMessage.Recipients.ResolveAll
        olOutgoingMessage.Send

        Set olOutgoingMessage = Nothing

    End If

End Sub
```

Centralized Category Management

One of my pet peeves is that there is no easy way to centrally manage Outlook categories. Categories provide an excellent way to organize the massive number of emails, tasks, contacts, and journal items that you use day to day. Categories are even more powerful if they are common across an organization. The code snippet in Example 7.7 shows how you can use a central folder to control the contacts on a local machine. This code parses each item in a folder and extracts all of the categories. The extracted categories are appended to the list of categories maintained in the system Registry or used to replace the entire list.

Again, this code should give you an idea of how this might work. You can easily add logic that sorts the categories or reduces the amount of user interaction.

Example 7.7   *Centralized category management sample code.*

```
Public Sub SetLocalCategories()

' Define the location that Outlook stores it's categories
    Const REG_MCL = "Software\Microsoft\Office\9.0\Outlook\Categories"
    Const REG_MCL_VALUENAME = "MasterList"

    Dim olFolder As Outlook.MAPIFolder
    Dim strCategories As String
    Dim strOldCategories As String
    Dim olItem As Outlook.PostItem
    Dim olNS As Outlook.NameSpace
    Dim intEraseLocal As Integer
    Dim objRegAccess As REGTool5.Registry
```

continues ▶

```
On Error GoTo err_SetLocalCategories

' Instantiate objects
    Set olNS = Application.GetNamespace("MAPI")
    Set objSpeak = New DirectSS
    Set objRegAccess = New REGTool5.Registry

    objSpeak.Speak "Erase Local Categories?"
    intEraseLocal = MsgBox("Would you like to replace local categories?", vbYesNoCancel, _
➡"Erase Local Categories")

' Get the location of the folder that will be used to extract categories from
    objSpeak.Speak "Please select the Master Category folder"
    Set olFolder = olNS.PickFolder
    objSpeak.Speak "Thank you"

    If intEraseLocal <> vbCancel Then

    ' For each item in the selected folder, extract the categories
        If Not (olFolder Is Nothing) Then
            For Each olItem In olFolder.Items
                If strCategories = "" Then
                    strCategories = olItem.Categories
                Else
                    strCategories = strCategories & "," & olItem.Categories
                End If
            Next
        End If

        If intEraseLocal = vbNo Then
            ' This will get the previous categories if the user
            ' selected not to erase them.
            If objRegAccess.GetKeyValue(HKEY_CURRENT_USER, _
                                    REG_MCL, REG_MCL_VALUENAME, _
                                    strOldCategories) Then

                strCategories = strCategories & strOldCategories
            End If

        End If

        ' Remove non unique categories, sort if necessary
        strCategories = FilterNonUnique(strCategories, True)

        ' Update the registry key
        If Not objRegAccess.UpdateKey(HKEY_CURRENT_USER, _
                                    REG_MCL, _
                                    REG_MCL_VALUENAME, _
                                    strCategories) Then
            objSpeak.Speak "There was a problem updating the categories"
        End If
```

```
        End If
    Exit Sub

err_SetLocalCategories:
    MsgBox Err.Description
End Sub
```

Chapter Summary

There are always times when you require more functionality than you receive by default with Microsoft Outlook. For just those cases, Microsoft has added the capability for users and developers to write VBA to help expand the default functionality that Outlook 2000 provides. Although Outlook's VBA development environment is similar to every other VBA environment in Microsoft Office, the key difference between writing Outlook VBA and VBA in other applications is that Outlook VBA is difficult to distribute and centrally maintain. For this reason alone, many companies have decided not to use VBA macros for line-of-business applications.

Although Outlook VBA is harder to distribute to network users, we (the authors of this book) believe that it still serves an extremely important role in the creation of one-off collaborative solutions. Additionally, Outlook VBA is a great way to develop proof-of-concept applications that can easily be turned into Outlook COM add-ins, which are easier to distribute and manage as a whole.

At its base, however, we believe that the Outlook VBA development environment is an extremely useful tool for both expert developers and those who are just beginning to harness the power of the Outlook object model. Using Outlook VBA should be the first stop for any developer on the road to developing advanced collaborative solutions that utilize the many objects and events Outlook provides.

8

Visual Basic, CDO, and MAPI

Microsoft Outlook is the primary client for any Exchange-based solution, but sometimes it cannot meet your collaborative development needs. In such a situation, you either need to build an alternative application to work within your solution or create additional components to add to Outlook's functionality.

Now, before I go any further into discussing alternatives to developing in Outlook, let me make one thing clear: You can do almost anything in Outlook! Often, we turn to an alternative tool (like Visual Basic, which will be the focus of this chapter) not because we cannot do it in Outlook, but because it is easier or more convenient to build within the other tool.

Outside of Outlook, the key tool for Exchange development is Visual Basic, which can access Exchange through Outlook itself, the Collaborative Data Objects library (CDO), or the Messaging API (MAPI). All three of these methods of integrating VB will be discussed in this chapter, giving you a full picture of how you can use VB to build part of your collaboration system.

In this chapter, we will cover the following:

- The role of VB in collaborative solutions
- CDO and MAPI—What are they and which one should you use?
- Differentiating and deciding between server and client-side components of your solution

Visual Basic's Role in Building Collaborative Applications

Visual Basic can be integrated with Exchange in a wide variety of ways, working as a part of another application or as a completely standalone program. You can put a VB application or component into every stage and system that is part of a collaborative solution. This is due in most part to the power of COM (Component Object Model), the component communication standard that is supported by every part of a collaborative system, including Outlook, VB, and VBScript. This common foundation allows you to leverage code created with VB in a wide variety of ways. Following are the more common ways in which VB can be used as part of a collaborative solution. Although quite a few examples are listed here, this is by no means a complete list.

VB, used in combination with Microsoft Outlook, can do the following:

- Create COM add-ins.
- Call VB component(s) from within a VBA macro (which could be attached to a menu item or toolbar button, or associated with an event in the Outlook application).
- Call VB component(s) from the VBScript code that you can write behind an Outlook form.
- Place and script an ActiveX control (built with VB) onto your Outlook form.
- Use Automation to control Outlook from VB code—for example, to send messages.
- Call VB component(s) from the Dynamic HTML code that you use in Outlook Today.

Other client uses for VB include the following:

- Create COM add-ins in VB that integrate with Microsoft Office and communicate with Outlook or (through CDO) directly with the Exchange Server.
- Build standalone VB applications that use Exchange to send/receive information by using CDO from the client machine.

VB can be used with Exchange Server to do the following:

- Use CDO to manipulate and act on the contents of public folders from VB code. Can provide Auto-Response capabilities.
- Call VB component(s) from the VBScript code used for event scripting in public folders. Can be part of a routing (workflow) system in this manner.
- Connect (with CDO) to multiple inboxes to provide group task or schedule functions beyond what Exchange/Outlook already provides.

VB can be used with Outlook Web Access to call VB components from the VBScript in the Active Server Pages (ASP) that make up Outlook Web Access.

VB can be used with Windows CE Devices (Handheld PCs, Palm PCs) to do the following:

- Build applications that run on the CE device and provide a portable solution for handling contact, email, task, or scheduling information.
- Work with Pocket Outlook to send messages or manipulate the content of the user's inbox.

VB can be used with Real-time collaboration tools to do the following:

- Control NetMeeting or MSN Messenger (both covered later in Chapter 15, "Designing and Building Knowledge Management Solutions") to start up communication sessions.
- Use the exposed COM functionality of either of these products to add real-time communication features to your own programs through Visual Basic.

Every one of the preceding examples is a method of using VB as part of your collaboration solution, but there are really only four things you will build with VB (for use in this type of system):

- **Message processors.** These are standard VB applications (.exe) that connect to your Exchange system (through MAPI, CDO, or the Outlook object model) and manipulate the contents of public or private information stores.
- **ActiveX controls.** These components (which usually have a visible interface) can be placed onto many different containers, including Web pages, forms in Visual Basic, and (most importantly to us) Outlook forms. A special text entry box that validates credit card numbers is an example of an ActiveX control, one that can be useful when creating an Outlook form. These controls might not be specifically designed for this purpose.
- **COM DLLs.** Similar to ActiveX controls, these components are designed for use with any compliant environment, not just in collaboration systems. Acting as libraries, holding objects that expose properties and methods, the usefulness of these DLLs is dependent on what code they contain. In a collaborative solution, these libraries can be used in many locations, including the code in Outlook forms, the script behind Active Server Pages (in Outlook Web Access), and within other VB code.
- **COM add-ins.** A new type of component that is possible with Office 2000, the COM add-in is a special code library that is designed to plug in to any or all of the Office applications. COM add-ins can be created directly in the VBA environment of Office 2000 (if you have the Developer version of Office), or you can take advantage of the full VB language and build them through its environment.

Taking each of those items individually, the following sections provide a brief description to illustrate how each fits into your collaborative development toolkit.

Message Processors

Message processors are a very broad class of VB applications that include anything that is designed to act on the messages (items) in an inbox or public folder. You can think of these programs as the external equivalent of Outlook's rules (Inbox Assistant) on the client and of the Exchange scripting on the server.

These utilities are designed to allow automated processing of received messages, usually sent to a system mail account, such as ReportRequest@Imaginets.com or info@scribe.mb.ca. Functioning as (semi) intelligent software agents, a message processor can parse each message to determine its intent and then execute code to create an appropriate reply or simply route the message to another folder.

You might be thinking, "Can't I do all that with the Rules Wizard?" That is a very good point; you can accomplish at least some of what message processors do using the built-in rules features of Outlook and Exchange, but you'll reach the limits of those tools quickly. Actually, in addition to the limits you will reach in complexity, there is a physical limitation to the total size of all your rules that can prevent you from creating a large number of them. In the example that follows, we'll go through a scenario where a message processor written in VB is the best solution.

The system administrator for a television production company is responsible for compiling reports on the show's weekly ratings (detailing how many people watched the show that week) and number of plays (how often the show was played across the world).

To create these reports, which she builds using Microsoft Word 2000, information is collected from many different sources. These sources include Microsoft Excel spreadsheets emailed from a company that compiles all the appearances of the show worldwide, and comma-delimited text files posted to a secure FTP site (for which she has a user ID and password) containing the latest Nielsen ratings. When new information is available (a new spreadsheet has arrived in the administrator's mailbox, and a new text file appears on the FTP site), all that data is used to create several key reports for the marketing staff of the production company. Some of these reports are needed every time, others are needed only once a month, and certain reports are generated only upon request.

The building of these reports involves a lot of manual effort from the system administrator and is dependent on her available time. Even if new information arrives at 6 p.m. on Friday, it might take until the end of business on Monday before all the necessary reports are compiled. To make matters worse, sometimes the data that arrives is corrupt or for the incorrect time period, requiring an email to the appropriate company to request the information again. All in all, there is sometimes up to a week's backlog in producing the correct reports for the marketing group.

In the preceding example (based on a real-life situation), there are many different issues. One solution that handles all of them is to create a Visual Basic program that handles the time-consuming details of this problem. An application can be written that runs all the time and periodically checks the contents of a specific mailbox, or a public folder. To make it simple to get information into the correct location, a public email address can be created for it.

When a new message is found in the mailbox or public folder, the program could save the attached spreadsheet to disk and then delete the message. When it is saved, the spreadsheet could be parsed using the Excel object model, and all the appropriate information could be preserved in some way so that it is available for future use. (In most cases, this information could be inserted into a database.) At the same intervals that the application is checking for new email, it could also connect to the ratings company's FTP site and download the latest file, if it exists. The information from this file could also be parsed and persisted into a database. After both files have been found and processed, the system could query the database for all the information it needs to produce the weekly report and then use Word's object model to programmatically build the actual report document.

For more information about using Word and the other Office 2000 applications to programmatically produce documents, see Chapter 9, "Microsoft Office Integration."

Expanding this solution to automatically produce reports in response to user requests is easy. Simply have the application look for and parse a second type of email message, a request message. This allows the employees of our fictional company to request unusual reports or reports of a past time period. Those reports are generated and emailed back to the requesting user within a matter of minutes. This type of system has one huge advantage: It removes the dependency on the system administrator for what could be essential marketing information. This type of automated system works 24 hours a day, 7 days a week. If someone needs a copy of the show's ratings from November, 1998, he can order that information at 3 a.m. on Saturday and still receive a full report within a few minutes. To allow our application to easily parse the report requests, a very specific format would have to be used. However, if all of our users are on our Outlook system, we could provide a simple form (see Figure 8.1) that takes care of any formatting issues.

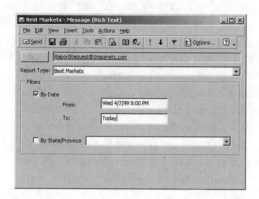

Figure 8.1   *An Outlook form can provide an easy way to send structured information through email.*

A rough flowchart of how such a system works is shown in Figure 8.2, with key sections shaded. These sections interact directly between our Visual Basic application and Exchange, through either CDO, Outlook, or MAPI. The code for these sections will be used later in the chapter to demonstrate the different technologies that you can use to accomplish the same task.

Possible Solution with Exchange Server Scripting

It is important to point out that the solution illustrated in Figure 8.2 for our television production company system administrator could have been written using at least some Exchange Server scripting. Scripts can be set up to automatically run on every new message arriving into a public folder and could have accomplished much of this work. In the real-world, though, sometimes you have to consider the development complexity in addition to the rest of the system's requirements. Although you could code this solution completely in VBScript on the Exchange Server, that is not a very developer-friendly environment and you would likely end up wanting to use at least COM DLLs written in VB. In the end, it is likely that a server scripting solution would take a great deal more effort and produce a substantially more complex system than simply building an application directly in VB. ◆

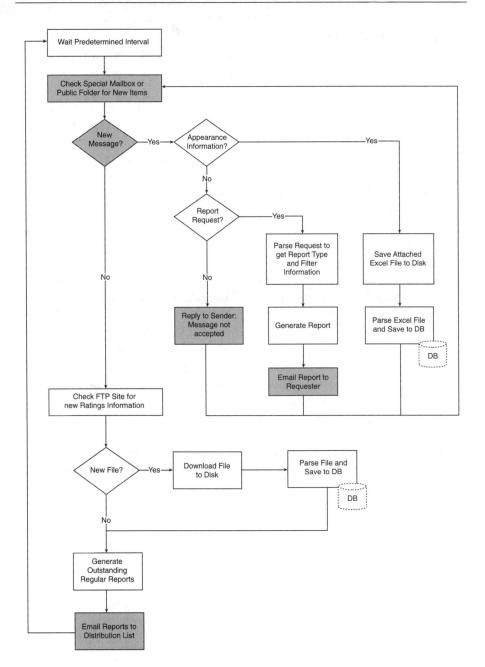

Figure 8.2 *System flow chart highlighting the messaging-related areas.*

ActiveX Controls for Outlook Forms

ActiveX controls, or OCX's as they are sometimes called, are a form of COM-compliant component that you can build in VB or Visual C++. These components are very similar to any other type of COM object in that they expose properties, methods, and events, and function as easily distributed code libraries. But they are different in one key aspect: Unlike a COM DLL, an ActiveX control can have a visual interface. Due to this difference, ActiveX controls are designed to be placed onto forms, and their properties and methods are manipulated by the code on that form. These controls can be placed on forms in many different development environments, including Visual Basic, Visual C++, Access, PowerBuilder, Delphi, and (most importantly for this book) Outlook forms.

In the running example shown in this section, credit card information is being stored as a property of the contact items in a folder. In such a situation, security must never be ignored as that information is extremely sensitive and needs protection. Proper use of folder level security settings combined with good NT security practices can ensure the safety of your data. Chapter 4, "The Heart of Collaboration: Microsoft Exchange Server," provides more detail on how to set up your server correctly for this type of system.

Although custom controls are used for a wide variety of purposes, their most common use on an Outlook form is to provide some type of data entry and validation that is beyond the capabilities of a simple text box. An example of this type of control is a credit card entry control, an entry field that validates the credit card number typed into it, telling you whether the card number is correct and determining what type of card it is (American Express, Visa, MasterCard). You can build this control in VB, as shown in Figure 8.3, and then compile it into an .ocx file. That .ocx file would have to be installed onto the machine you are using to create your Outlook form(s) before the .ocx file could be placed onto the forms, and the .ocx file would have to be installed onto every client machine that was going to use your form. The need for client distribution makes the use of these controls less appealing because one of the advantages of Outlook forms is that they are automatically installed when used.

To place an ActiveX control onto one of your Outlook forms, you first must register it on the machine where it is to be used. The registration process is beyond the scope of this book, but is discussed in the Visual Basic documentation. After the registration is complete, you have to make the control available to the form designer by placing it onto your toolbox. To accomplish this, you need to bring up the Additional Controls dialog box by right-clicking on the toolbox and selecting Custom Controls, as in Figure 8.4.

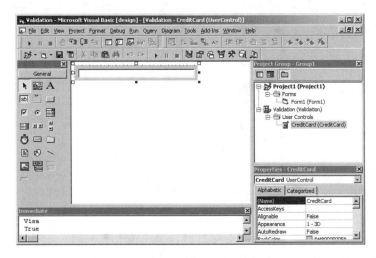

Figure 8.3   *Visual Basic can be used to create ActiveX controls to provide advanced User Interface functions to your Outlook forms.*

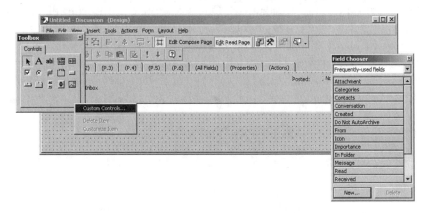

Figure 8.4   *To use an ActiveX control on an Outlook form, you must first bring up the Toolbox window, right-click on it, and select Custom Controls.*

The Additional Controls dialog box, shown in Figure 8.5, shows all the custom controls (.ocx files) that are available on the machine. Every one that is checked off will appear in the toolbox as an icon that you can select. After the controls appear in the toolbox, they work exactly like the standard ones—simply click to select, and then click and drag onto the form to place.

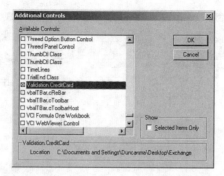

Figure 8.5   *The Additional Controls dialog box allows you to choose which ActiveX controls you want to have available on the toolbox.*

After you have placed one or more of these controls onto your form, you need to perform a few setup tasks before starting to use the control(s). You can use the control's properties dialog box (right-click and choose the bottommost properties menu item) to set up various control-specific features. You can use the standard Outlook supplied properties dialog box shown in Figure 8.6 (right-click and choose the uppermost properties menu item) to change the control's name and associate the control with a particular field of your form. After the information has been set up in the two property dialog boxes, you can write code that uses your control's properties or responds to various events that are raised by the control.

Figure 8.6   *After a control has been placed on your Outlook form, you can set up its corresponding form property and other settings using the properties dialog box.*

The built-in methods that the form uses for controls provide for a single value coming out of each control, which is true for most data entry fields, and that value can be associated with a particular form property through the Outlook-supplied property dialog box. When associated, values stored into that property display in the control, and values entered into the control are stored into the associated property. In most cases, this behavior is perfect, and because it is provided for you, you don't have to do anything for it to work. With certain controls, though, it is not quite as simple because there is more than one property association that you want to make. An example of this can be found with our Credit Card ActiveX control, which provides properties not only for the value entered into its text entry area (.CardNumber) but also for the type of credit card entered (.CardTypeName). If you want a property beyond the first to be linked to a form property, you have to write code that saves the specific control attribute into the corresponding property of the form. That code is best written into the item's Read and Write events, copying the appropriate values from the form to the control in the Read and back again in the Write. In Example 8.1, CardTypeName is a Read-Only property, so there is no need for code in the Read event.

Example 8.1   *Using script to synchronize a custom control's properties with custom properties of your form/folder.*

```
Function Item_Write()
Dim sCardType

sCardType = Item.GetInspector.ModifiedFormPages("Message").ccEntry.CardTypeName
Item.UserProperties.Find("Card Type").Value = sCardType

End Function
```

With the preceding code in place, the additional properties of a control persist when the form itself is not open. This means that you can even create views that show you the custom properties populated by the ActiveX control. Overall, these controls remove many of the limitations of Outlook forms, because you can now create an interface, such as the one shown in Figure 8.7, capable of doing anything that you can build in Visual Basic. The biggest limitation of ActiveX controls is the need to install the controls onto the client's machine; but if you can get around that problem, they become very useful.

Figure 8.7   *The use of ActiveX controls can greatly enhance the appearance and functionality of your forms.*

Checking Credit Card Numbers

Figure 8.7 shows the creation and use of an ActiveX control that performs validation of credit card numbers, ensuring that they are at least the correct format and determining what type of card they are from. Complete code for that control is supplied on the Web site for this book along with a text file containing the demonstration VBScript code that you could use in conjunction with the control on an Outlook form. If you plan to use this control in your own project, note that it checks only the validity of the number itself and cannot determine whether the card number refers to a real account or that the account has any credit available (because this control never communicates with the financial institution). ◆

COM DLLs for VBScript and Active Server Pages

One of the greatest strengths of the scripting model of ASP, Outlook, and Exchange is that they all have the capability to create instances of COM objects. This means that your script can use the code encapsulated in an ActiveX EXE or DLL, components that you can create in any one of several development environments, including Visual Basic. The code required to instantiate these objects is different in each case, as it is not a feature of VBScript but instead is provided as a method (CreateObject) of the Application object in Outlook and the Server object in ASP. When created, you can use these objects just like any other object in your script, calling their methods and manipulating their properties. Example 8.2 shows the Visual Basic code for a sample component, Sample.clsNameBuilder, which you would compile into a DLL and install onto any machine that is going to need to create instances of it.

Example 8.2   *A class module in Visual Basic can be compiled into an ActiveX DLL, giving your script access to its methods and properties.*

```
Option Explicit
Public Function FullName(ByVal FirstName As String, ByVal LastName As String) As String
    FullName = FirstName & " " & LastName
End Function
```

To use CLSNAMEBUILDER.CLS from script, you would create an instance of the object with the appropriate object's CreateObject method. The following VBScript code (Example 8.3) demonstrates how you would create and use an ActiveX DLL from the code behind an Outlook form.

Example 8.3   *The Outlook.Application object exposes a CreateObject method, giving you the ability to create instances of COM objects from your script.*

```
Sub BuildName
      Dim sFirstName
      Dim sLastName
      Dim objNameBuilder

      sFirstName = "Duncan"
      sLastName = "Mackenzie"

      Set objNameBuilder = Application.CreateObject("Sample.clsNameBuilder")
      MsgBox objNameBuilder.FullName(sFirstName,sLastName)
End Sub
```

By creating useful classes and building them into COM DLLs (or ActiveX DLLs, as they are labeled in VB), you are creating libraries of code that can be accessed from almost anywhere. This is a very common and useful way to integrate or migrate existing Visual Basic business logic into a collaborative development solution.

Author's Note

When building business logic into your code, always encapsulate that logic into a component, such as a COM DLL. This allows you to have a single source of that functionality that can be used from each and every application that needs it.

If, for instance, you are building a mark tracking system for a university and you have code that calculates a student's grade point average, you might have need for that code in many places: an Excel spreadsheet used by the student advisors, a Web page provided for the student to view his progress, the main reporting system that produces transcripts, and so on. Due to the wide support for COM, you could simply build the code into a DLL and then call that same DLL from each and every one of those locations. By creating your application in this manner, you are guaranteed that every part of the system behaves in the same manner, and every calculation of a student's grade point average is done exactly the same way. ◆

COM Add-Ins

A new feature of Office 2000, COM add-ins are a special case of the COM DLLs discussed previously. These components are built in much the same way, classes in VB that are compiled into DLLs, but they are specifically designed to plug in to one or more of the Office 2000 applications. By integrating themselves closely with Office, these components have the capability to manipulate the user interface of the application they plug in to and to respond to events within that program. That close integration is what makes these components so useful. They enable you to provide very advanced customization to that application's user interface. In Outlook, for instance, you add your own tab into the Options dialog box for the application, as shown in Figure 8.8, and into the Properties dialog box for individual folders, creating a very professional look to your custom solution.

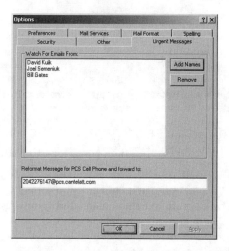

Figure 8.8   *Having your own custom tab in Outlook's Options dialog box makes your add-in look like a part of Outlook instead of something thrown on top of it.*

COM add-ins are normally built in VB. But with the Developer Edition of Microsoft Office 2000, you can create them directly in VBA, which is especially useful if you do not have VB. Otherwise, there is no functional difference between an add-in created in VB and one created directly in Office 2000.

Understanding CDO and MAPI

We have discussed a wide variety of ways in which you can use VB as part of a collaborative Exchange/Outlook solution. The one common point between all these items is that your VB code needs to talk to the underlying messaging system to carry out its tasks. There are three main ways in which this can be accomplished:

- The Messaging API (MAPI) provided by Windows
- Through a set of COM objects known as Collaborative Data Objects (CDO)
- OLE Automation, controlling Microsoft Outlook

MAPI is the base method for communicating with Exchange and is provided as a part of the operating system for that purpose. CDO is a new interface into the messaging system and is actually just a wrapper around MAPI (see the diagram in Figure 8.9), providing you with a COM-compliant way to communicate with Exchange. Although it isn't covered in this chapter, there is also a special form of CDO called CDO for NT Server, or CDONTS, which is worth a bit of discussion. Finally, you have the choice of using Outlook itself, programmatically controlling it through OLE Automation (basically using Outlook as a COM component). Each of these methods has its advantages and disadvantages, but you can generally accomplish a messaging task through any one of them. In any case, all three methods take into account the user's settings on the machine (although they can be overridden) and can even transparently use the user's offline store (.ost file) instead of connecting.

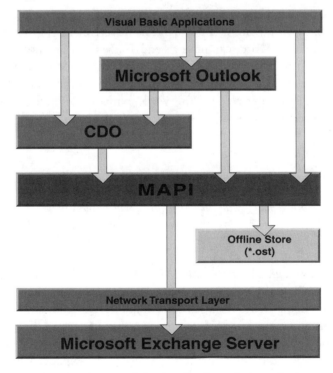

Figure 8.9   *CDO and Outlook both work through MAPI to talk to Exchange Server and/or an offline store.*

Relationship between Outlook, CDO, CDONTS, and MAPI

As all of these interfaces are attempting to accomplish the same goal of providing a communications interface between your applications and the messaging system, there is a great deal of functionality that overlaps between the interfaces. Due to this overlap, you have the ability to choose between these interfaces. As with many situations, sometimes a choice is worse than no choice at all. In this case, each of the different technologies has some serious advantages and disadvantages, and the choice should be relatively easy.

MAPI

Starting with the lowest level interface, MAPI is the actual underlying OS-provided method for a client program to communicate with a messaging system. Because the OS provided API, this interface is actually not just limited to Exchange-based systems. Many other email systems are MAPI compliant, which means that programs can use MAPI commands to communicate with them. It is through this feature of MAPI that programs, such as Microsoft Word, can have a Send To, Mail Recipient menu option that works with Outlook, Netscape's email client, the Microsoft Exchange client, and others. Code was written once for that purpose and (because it makes all its calls through MAPI) it works with any of these systems. MAPI calls have been available in Windows for quite some time (since Windows 3.1) and can be declared and called from your program(s) just like any other API call.

> ### Author's Note
>
> *Microsoft Office actually works with more email systems than MAPI. This is because Office uses both MAPI and VIM (Vendor Independent Messaging) to communicate with messaging systems.* ♦

MAPI is often divided into Simple MAPI, Common Messaging Calls (CMC), MAPI, and CDO. All of these are really just interfaces into MAPI, but programming MAPI itself is rather complicated (relatively speaking), so these alternatives are provided. Simple MAPI is a set of 12 functions that enable you to log on to the messaging system, use the address book, send and read mail, and other common functions. CMC exposes a similar set of functionality but is a cross-platform interface developed by a standards body called XAPIA (the X.400 Application Programming Interface [API] Association), which makes it a good choice for code that is intended to run on multiple operating systems. We will not look at CMC, because it is rather difficult to code on multiple operating systems using VB, and because CMC on Windows is simply a layer over MAPI.

CDO

The latest interface to MAPI is the Collaborative Data Objects library. This library, known as CDO, was created to provide an object-based interface that uses COM and is easy for VB and VBA programmers to use. There is also a special version of CDO that is designed to provide a similar interface to non-MAPI-compliant messaging systems that Microsoft has provided with IIS and MCIS on NT Server. This version, which (although simpler) is somewhat compliant with the regular CDO, is known as CDONTS. It is important to note that you can choose to use either CDO or CDONTS when working with Exchange 5.5, but that when working with IIS or MCIS you can only use CDONTS. An important point about CDO versus directly programming against MAPI is that CDO can be called from a scripting language, such as VBScript or JavaScript, allowing it to be used as part of an Active Server Page (ASP)-based application. While on the topic of Web applications, there is another set of components that is really an extension of CDO: CDOHTML. These components are used by Outlook Web Access to render items (messages, appointments, or tasks) into HTML. With these components available, it is a relatively easy task for your code to take advantage of them and quickly generate HTML to display any particular item. CDO is installed onto client computers running Outlook 98 or 2000 and onto your server if you have installed Exchange Server (or Outlook Web Access), but not onto client computers running Outlook 97.

Outlook (97, 98, and 2000)

Outlook is not another interface of MAPI, it is actually an application that is a MAPI client, designed to provide access to the functionality of the underlying mail system. This application, like the rest of Microsoft Office, exposes a complete object model through COM and, therefore, can easily be controlled from VB. Using this object library, you can easily send mail, browse the contents of the inbox or other folders, and work with the address book. Anything you can do with Outlook manually can be done through its object library. In relation to the other components here, when you use Outlook from VB, you are making requests through Outlook that it turns into calls against MAPI. How Outlook communicates with MAPI internally is not relevant, but it is likely that Outlook features use MAPI directly for most things and might use CDO to implement some of the trimmings.

Deciding Which Messaging Tools to Use

As stated earlier, each of these methods has advantages and disadvantages, so you might pick a different one for different situations. Working through Outlook is relatively simple but involves more overhead, CDO is not available on some client machines, and MAPI involves using API calls. To simplify your decision, here are the key factors to consider when picking between the various interfaces: where your code will execute, what development language you plan to use, you or your team's skill in using APIs, and, of course, what you need to accomplish.

Where Your Code Will Execute

This is an important factor mainly because it determines which of the interfaces is likely to be available, but also because applications designed for servers generally have different characteristics than those made to run on client computers.

Server Applications

If you are writing code to execute on the server, you probably don't need any form of visual interface and don't need to work with those parts of the Outlook object model that are dealing with non-messaging issues (like user settings). This eliminates Outlook, which is good because it wouldn't likely be installed anyway. This leaves CDO, CDONTS, and MAPI. Normally, you would take MAPI out right away, because CDO is simpler to use in general and much easier to use from VB. Choosing between CDO and CDONTS is simply a matter of knowing whether you are going against Exchange or another Microsoft messaging system (such as the SMTP service in IIS or Microsoft Commercial Internet System [MCIS]) and whether you plan to move this solution from one of these systems to another. If you are using Exchange, you should generally use CDO unless you are planning to switch to MCIS at some point in the future.

Client Applications

The question to ask when building a client application is "Is Outlook available?" If so, "Is it Outlook 98 or better?" The first question determines whether or not you have the option of using Outlook; the second tells you if you can use CDO without installing it yourself (which is not a Microsoft supported configuration, so I generally don't recommend it). MAPI is always available, of course, but for the reason of complexity (see the next two factors: development language and API development skill), you might want to stick with CDO or Outlook.

To choose between Outlook and CDO, consider whether you are using Outlook's user interface, taking advantage of its capability to print or display items, or if you are simply working with folders, items, and the address list. In general, don't use Outlook if you don't need it (or if CDO is installed), CDO provides you with almost all the functionality of Outlook without the user interface and the additional overhead.

Author's Note

One important piece of functionality that Outlook has and CDO does not is the capability to initiate synchronization between the server information store and your offline store (.ost file). This capability can be critical to your application, requiring you to use Outlook instead of CDO.

This feature, although it was part of the original Exchange client and is present in every version of Outlook, was not available programmatically until Outlook 2000. On a project that used Microsoft's Exchange client, we sorely needed that functionality and had to resort to a complicated method of sending key presses (made a little more elegant through the use of the SendMessage API) to the Exchange client. As with most things, it would be so much easier to go back and implement that solution with today's technology. ◆

Impact of Your Skill Set on the MAPI/CDO Decision

The development language you plan to use and your skill in using API calls really determine whether MAPI is a viable option. Outlook, CDO, and CDONTS are all designed to be used from VB or VBScript, so they expose a COM interface to make that interaction as easy as possible. Because MAPI itself does not provide this simple means of interaction, you must use the C-style API calls to communicate with it. If your team is not familiar with this type of programming, you have good reason to avoid it—especially if your team is programming in VB because API calls are even more difficult and can often cause problems when used from VB. If VBScript is the language you plan to use (in an ASP system, for instance), you have little choice; MAPI cannot be called directly from VBScript.

What You Need to Accomplish

Finally, you need to always fall back to your system's requirements. How difficult an interface it is to use doesn't really matter if that is the only interface that does what you need. It is difficult to break down every single possible use of a messaging system and map that to these interfaces, but Table 8.1 provides a simple listing of the interfaces and some key capabilities or limitations of each:

Table 8.1   Pros and Cons of Outlook, CDO, and CDONTS

Pros	Cons
Microsoft Outlook Object Model	
Provides fully-featured interface for displaying messages, appointments, and the like.	Generally not installed on server machines.
Provides functionality not found in other interfaces, such as initiating or configuring synchronization.	More or greater overhead than other interfaces.

continues ▶

Table 8.1   Continued

Pros	Cons
CDO	
Provides COM-based object model that covers most mail functions.	Limited to MAPI-compliant Systems.
Simple to use from VB and compatible with VBScript.	Not installed on Outlook 97 client machines.
Provides HTML rendering of items (used extensively in Outlook Web Access).	HTML mail functionality not provided.
CDONTS (CDO for NT Server)	
Compatible with Exchange, IIS, and MCIS.	Not as full featured as CDO. Doesn't provide HTML rendering.
Simple to use from VB and compatible with VBScript.	Server only.
Can send HTML mail and has `NewMail` object that allows the sending of email with only four lines of code.	Doesn't provide user authentication, designed for outbound mail purposes.
MAPI	
Full functionality of client interface to Exchange.	API calls only. Difficult to use.
Available on any Windows client or server machine.	Cannot be used from scripting languages (like VBScript).

When Only CDONTS Will Do

It seems like there is an exception to everything, and the CDO versus CDONTS comparison also has one. Although these two libraries are very similar, CDONTS can send HTML email and CDO cannot. This is a big problem for many different programs and can cause you a great deal of trouble, which is why it is being fixed. CDO for Windows 2000 has added the capability to send email along with several other helpful features (such as the posting of NNTP or newsgroup messages). So, if you are planning to implement your system on a Windows 2000 machine, you are in luck. ◆

Choosing Your Development Tools

The preceding information should be very helpful in choosing which tools to use for communication with your messaging system, but that section does not provide you with a definitive answer to the question "What should I use?" As a wrap-up of that material, here are some simple rules to help you choose when to use what:

- If you don't need to integrate directly with Outlook or use its actual forms for display, do not program using the Outlook object model.
- If CDO is available to the application, regardless of whether it is a client or a server component, use CDO.
- The exception to the second rule (isn't there always an exception?): If you need to connect to and use the services of IIS's SMTP mail services or Microsoft Commercial Internet System instead of (or in addition to) Exchange, you should look at CDONTS.

With CDO seeming to be the most likely choice for most of your applications, the next section will provide a brief overview of these objects and some sample code demonstrating their use.

Programming with CDO

After going through all the pros and cons in the preceding sections, you probably have come to the conclusion that your VB application should use CDO. This is rapidly becoming the standard method of accessing your messaging system and is being chosen over MAPI or Automation of Outlook. This section will provide an overview of the object model of CDO and cover a series of examples. These examples will show how to accomplish a large number of the most commonly needed tasks and can serve as a starting point for your own application. Code to perform many of these examples is compiled into a single sample application for you to look through, and it is also provided in snippet form on the Web site associated with this book (www.newriders.com/exch_prog).

The CDO Object Model

The CDO object model (CDO 1.2, corresponding to Outlook 98 and 2000), along with the available properties and methods, will be documented in more detail in Appendix A, "The CDO Object Model," but this section provides a brief description of the major objects available through this library (see Figure 8.10).

Session

The Session object is the main or top-level object in CDO. It represents a single connection to the Exchange Server and has methods and properties that expose all the other objects you will need. In addition to exposing the collection of available information stores (InfoStores), this object also has several properties and methods that make it easy to obtain the more commonly needed objects, such as Inbox and Outbox, two properties that return the user's default folders for incoming and outgoing mail, respectively.

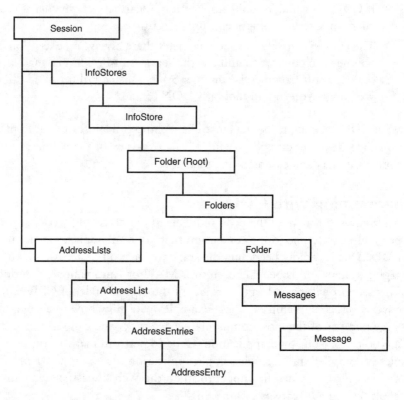

Figure 8.10   *A simplified view of the CDO object model.*

InfoStore and InfoStores

This object, and its corresponding collection, represents a single set of folders and associated settings, Information Stores. For instance, in my Outlook folders (shown in Figure 8.11), there are two InfoStores: Mailbox Duncan Mackenzie and Public Folders. Notice that both of these InfoStores are provided by the same service—Exchange. It is possible, and even likely, for several different services (such as Personal Folders) to be involved, each capable of supplying any number of InfoStores.

Figure 8.11   *For most users, there are several different information stores available, such as their own mailbox and the public folders.*

Folder and Folders

Within each information store, there is a collection of folders, each one represented by a Folder object. These Folder objects are the means by which you get to individual messages, as each folder exposes a Messages collection containing all of the items contained within that folder. A Folders collection is exposed by every Folder object and can be used to access or create folders that exist underneath that folder in the information store.

Message, Messages, and MessageFilter

All of the items in a folder are exposed as a Messages collection, a potentially large object that can be filtered using the MessageFilter object and the Messages collection's Filter property. Each individual item is represented as a Message object, which will quickly become a very common object in your code. Although there is another object available when dealing with Appointment items, all types of items are Messages regardless of whether they are Tasks, Appointments, Notes, Emails, or Contacts. To accommodate the wide range of possible properties, the Message object exposes a Fields collection in addition to several standard properties like Subject. Through this Fields collection, it is possible for you to retrieve any property value desired, such as fields that would exist on one type of item but not on any other (the Pager telephone number field, CdoPR_PAGER_TELEPHONE_NUMBER, which exists on Contact items, but not on regular email messages). The values needed for retrieval from the Fields collection are available through the CDO library as members of the enumerated type: CDOPropTags.

AddressList and AddressLists

Another object and collection pair, an address list represents an individual container within the address book, such as the Global Address List (GAL), your Outlook Contacts folder, and any number of sublists within these containers, such as individual departments set up within the GAL (see

Figure 8.12). The AddressLists object, which is available as a property of your Session, represents all the lists available to that particular session. The available address lists correspond to those lists you see in the GAL when you are picking addresses for an email message, as shown in Figure 8.12.

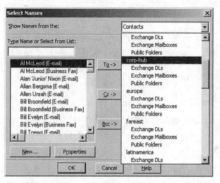

Figure 8.12   *Within a single address list (such as the Global Address List), there can be many sublists defined to simplify searching for an address entry.*

AddressEntry, AddressEntries, and AddressEntryFilter

Closely related to the previous collection pair, these objects deal with the actual addresses within the lists exposed by the AddressLists collection. Due to the potential size of an AddressEntries collection (at least as many entries as you have Exchange users), your code shouldn't loop through these entries unless absolutely necessary. To find a particular entry without looping, you can use the Filter property of the AddressEntries collection (which is an object of type AddressEntryFilter), narrowing the list down to a manageable number of entries. When you have the list filtered as desired, you can access the individual AddressEntry objects to work with their properties directly.

Common CDO Tasks

Whether you are using CDO for use on a Win32 platform or from a scripting language like VBScript for use in the server-side execution of a Web system, there are certain common tasks that you need to perform. Several of these commonly needed bits of functionality are provided in the sections that follow.

Getting Ready to Work with CDO

If you are planning to work with CDO from VB, the first step is to set a reference to the Microsoft CDO 1.21 Library in the Project References dialog box (see Figure 8.13). With this reference in place, you will have access to the Intellisense features of VB (such as drop-down lists of properties and methods and the tool tip display of method parameters) for the CDO objects you create in code.

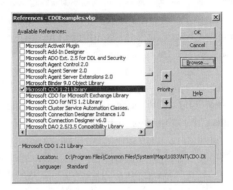

Figure 8.13   *As a first step in programming with CDO in VB, set a reference using this dialog box available through the Project\References menu option.*

Creating a reference is not required in VB, and is not even possible in a Web environment like an Active Server Page application. The alternative is to simply declare a variable as Object or (in script languages, which do not support any other data type) Variant and then use the CreateObject function to create instances of the appropriate objects. Either way, the result is the same, but there are performance benefits to having set a reference to CDO directly in your project. Examples of both methods for using the CDO objects are shown in Examples 8.4 and 8.5, but the remaining examples in the chapter will assume that you are using VB and have set a reference to CDO 1.21.

Example 8.4   *Creating instances of CDO objects with and without setting a reference to it.*

```
Public Sub Using_a_Reference_to_CDO()
Dim objSession As MAPI.Session

    Set objSession = New MAPI.Session
    ' Work with the object
    '....
    Set objSession = Nothing

End Sub

Public Sub No_Reference()
'This is how the code would look in VB
'with no reference, or in ASP.
Dim objSession

    'Note that this would be Server.CreateObject in ASP
    Set objSession = CreateObject("MAPI.Session")
    'Work with the object
    '....
    Set objSession = Nothing

End Sub
```

These two code listings demonstrate the two different ways in which you can use COM objects: Early or Late Binding. The difference is in when your application determines the internal name of the object to be loaded (the Class ID of the COM object). In the case where a reference has been set, this is Early Binding, because your application knows about the object before it is compiled. The other possibility, using no reference, is known as Late Binding because the object is only determined at run time.

Creating a New Session and Logging In
After you have your reference, you must create an instance of a Session object and use it to log in to MAPI. Until you have logged in, you are not connected to the MAPI services and cannot work with any of the CDO objects. To log in, you use the Session object's Logon method, which takes several parameters that control its behavior. The key elements you need to use describe the MAPI profile to use, whether any UI elements should be used, and if an existing MAPI session should be used, if one exists.

Creating Temporary Profiles
The three parameters that deal with profiles are ProfileName, ProfilePassword, and ProfileInfo. The first two allow you to specify the name of an existing profile on the current machine and to use that profile, in combination with the password, to log in to your information sources. This is rather simple and is the method to use if you have a certain profile on the machine that you want to use, as shown in Example 8.5.

Example 8.5   *This code logs you into MAPI using the supplied profile "Microsoft Outlook."*

```
Private Sub Logon()
Dim objSession As MAPI.Session

    Set objSession = New MAPI.Session
    objSession.Logon ProfileName:="Microsoft Outlook", ShowDialog:=False

    'Work with the object
    '....
    Set objSession = Nothing

End Sub
```

If you do not specify a value for ProfileName, you need to have the user select one by setting ShowDialog to True.

This brings up the standard dialog box used by MAPI for this purpose. After the profile is selected (see Figure 8.14), it might also bring up the dialog box that allows the user to choose between connected and offline modes (see Figure 8.15).

Figure 8.14   *Not providing a profile name and setting* ShowDialog *to True tells MAPI to raise any dialog boxes it needs, like this one to choose a profile.*

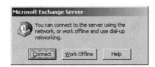

Figure 8.15   *If the profile chosen, or created, supports both offline and online modes and is set to Choose Connection Type in the Exchange service's property pages, a dialog box displays to allow the user to choose.*

This works well for client-side applications, because it is likely that the user will be present for this logon and will also have defined at least one profile. It isn't suited for use on a server, where there shouldn't be any user profiles, and this code has to run without any user interface. To accommodate this scenario, you can skip the ProfileName and ProfilePassword parameters and provide values in ProfileInfo to allow the system to create a temporary profile. Temporary profiles allow you to connect to a specific mailbox on an Exchange Server. They are created at logon and destroyed after logoff. This method of logging in involves supplying two pieces of information as parameters to the call: the server name and the mailbox name separated by a linefeed character (vbLf), as shown in Example 8.6, which logs in to the mailbox Duncanma on the server EXCHANGE-01.

Example 8.6   *Supplying the ProfileInfo parameter frees your code from dependence on profiles which have been created and still exist on the machine.*

```
Private Sub Logon_TemporaryProfile()
Dim objSession As MAPI.Session

    Set objSession = New MAPI.Session
    objSession.Logon ProfileInfo:="EXCHANGE-01" & vbLf & "Duncanma"

    'Work with the object
    '....
    Set objSession = Nothing

End Sub
```

Using an Existing Session

Sometimes, most notably behind an Outlook form, you want to use an existing MAPI session, if one is currently active. The NewSession parameter allows you to specify whether or not you wish to reuse an existing session. Setting this parameter to True indicates that a new MAPI session should be created, while a value of False indicates that any existing session should simply be reused. Using an existing session has the advantage of avoiding the object instantiation overhead, although it must be set to True (to force a new session) when your code wants to use a different profile than the current session (to log on as someone else, for instance). Two code examples are provided next (see Examples 8.7 and 8.8), one that logs on using the existing Session object, if any are currently available, and one that has to create a temporary profile.

Example 8.7   *Setting NewSession to True forces MAPI to create a new Session object.*

```
Private Sub Logon_ForceNewSession()
Dim objSession As MAPI.Session

    Set objSession = New MAPI.Session
    objSession.Logon NewSession:=True, _
        ProfileInfo:="EXCHANGE-01" & vbLf & "Duncanma"

    'Work with the object
    '....
    Set objSession = Nothing

End Sub
```

Be Careful When Reusing an Existing MAPI Session

If you reuse an existing MAPI session, NewSession set to False, you do not need to supply any profile information (Name, Password). If the call has to create a new session because one is not currently available, the absence of those profile parameters cause the appearance of the Choose Profile dialog box, or an error if ShowDialog is set to False. Never call this method without a profile name unless you do not mind the MAPI user interface coming up if there is no existing session. ◆

Example 8.8   *Setting NewSession to False allows MAPI to reuse an existing Session object if one exists, and to create a new session if one doesn't already exist.*

```
Private Sub Logon_ReuseExistingSession()
Dim objSession As MAPI.Session

    Set objSession = New MAPI.Session
```

continues ▶

```
objSession.Logon NewSession:=False, ShowDialog:=False

'Work with the object
'....
Set objSession = Nothing

End Sub
```

As mentioned at the beginning of this section, the perfect place for this code is in the VBScript behind an Outlook form, because at that point, with your form loaded and running, you know that a session must already exist. In that case, the code would look a little different because VBScript does not support any data type other than variants. Example 8.9 shows the adjusted code using no strongly typed variables:

Example 8.9   *When using CDO from VB Script, you cannot use object variables (Dim x as MAPI.Session) because it only supports variants, and you cannot use named arguments in your method calls.*

```
Function Item_Open()
Dim objSession

    Set objSession = Application.CreateObject("MAPI.Session")
    objSession.Logon ,,False,False

    MsgBox objSession.Inbox.Messages.Count

End Function
```

Working with InfoStores

InfoStores, or information stores, are the individual sets of folders that are available to the current profile and generally include a mailbox information store and the public folders. Although the Session object does give direct references to several key folders, including the Inbox, Outbox, and any other default folder (through the GetDefaultFolder method), to walk the complete set of available folders requires direct access to these InfoStore objects. The objects themselves are rather simple, exposing useful properties like Name and RootFolder (which returns the uppermost folder in that particular store).

Those simple properties are sufficient for most of your needs, as you can use the RootFolder and its child folders to access the entire contents of that information store. The code shown in Example 8.10 demonstrates using the InfoStores collection as the start of a procedure that walks the entire folder tree of every loaded information store.

Example 8.10 *The InfoStore object is your method for getting at all of the content available inside that particular set of folders.*

```
Public Sub WalkInfoStores()
Dim objSession As MAPI.Session
Dim objInfoStore As MAPI.InfoStore
Dim sIndent As String
    sIndent = ""

    Set objSession = New MAPI.Session
    objSession.Logon NewSession:=False

    For Each objInfoStore In objSession.InfoStores
        Debug.Print objInfoStore.Name
        WalkFolders objInfoStore.RootFolder, sIndent
    Next

    Set objSession = Nothing

End Sub
```

The WalkFolders procedure, which demonstrates how to navigate through a folder hierarchy, is covered in the following section, "Working with Folders."

In most cases, when working with an Exchange system, the only two of these stores that you can be sure of is the user's mailbox and the server's public folders. A common need is to obtain the root of the Public Folder collection itself, but you do not want to work with InfoStores collection in every piece of code that needs to access this root folder. Using a function to simplify this is usually the best method, as demonstrated in Example 8.11, which returns a reference to that specific InfoStore directly. Also provided is a simple procedure demonstrating how you would use this function in your code, calling it with an already logged in Session object.

Example 8.11 *Breaking common functionality into separate procedures makes it easy to reuse that code in multiple projects.*

```
Public Function GetPublicFolders(objSession As MAPI.Session) As MAPI.InfoStore
Dim objPublicFolders As MAPI.InfoStore
Dim objInfoStores As MAPI.InfoStores

    Set objInfoStores = objSession.InfoStores
    Set objPublicFolders = objInfoStores.Item("Public Folders")

End Function

Public Sub TestGetPublicFolders()
Dim objSession As MAPI.Session
Dim objPublicFolders As InfoStore
```

```
Set objSession = CreateObject("MAPI.Session")
objSession.Logon NewSession:=False

Set objPublicFolders = GetPublicFolders(objSession)

'Work with the objects
'....
Set objSession = Nothing

End Sub
```

Working with Folders

The individual folders in any information store, regardless of the type of items the folder is designed to hold, are all represented by the Folder object in the CDO Library. Each folder is part of a hierarchy and therefore has both a Parent property, representing the Folder or InfoStore object that is directly above it, and a Folders collection that represents the child folders that are below it. Through this Folders collection, it is easy to add a new folder below the object, or to simply iterate through those folders for processing. Anytime you have an object hierarchy of this form, where each child object can in turn contain a collection of child objects, you can build a relatively short and simple procedure that uses recursion to process every object. An example of this type of procedure, WalkFolders, is shown in Example 8.12, demonstrating the key functions you need to work with both individual folders and the Folders collections. For an example of using this function, look at Example 8.10 earlier in this chapter for the WalkInfoStores procedure.

Example 8.12   *Using the WalkFolders procedure.*

```
Public Sub WalkFolders(ByVal objRootFolder As MAPI.Folder, _
                           ByVal sIndent As String)
Dim objCurrentFolder As MAPI.Folder
Dim objChildFolders As MAPI.Folders

    Set objCurrentFolder = objRootFolder

    'Just dump out the name to see that this code is working.
    Debug.Print sIndent & objCurrentFolder.Name
    Set objChildFolders = objCurrentFolder.Folders

    'Use this value to produce a properly indented list _
        of folders in relation to each other.
    sIndent = sIndent & vbTab
```

continues ▶

Example 8.12   *Continued*

```
For Each objCurrentFolder In objChildFolders
    'Call this same routine (Recursion) to handle the _
        sub-tree beneath this child folder.
    WalkFolders objCurrentFolder, sIndent
Next

End Sub
```

Within each individual folder, there are several key properties that you should use, beyond the two used previously (Name and Folders). Every Folder, InfoStore, or Item has a specific value that is used to identify it to the MAPI system; given that value, you can easily obtain the object itself through the Session methods GetFolder, GetInfoStore, and GetMessage, all of which take these unique identifiers as parameters. In the case of a Folder object, the property ID provides this value, and the property FolderID actually provides the identifier for the parent folder. In addition, there is also a property StoreID which gives the identifier of the InfoStore that contains this folder.

It is difficult to allow the user to pick a certain folder from all the available InfoStores. Just having the user type in an actual folder name requires a search through all the folders to find that name, and it is possible that more than one folder will have the same name (but in a different place in the hierarchy). This is a common need in any MAPI client, and Outlook provides a dialog box, shown in Figure 8.16, for this purpose. Using the Outlook object model, it is possible to bring this dialog box up (using the NameSpace object's PickFolder method), but that function is not provided to the CDO programmer.

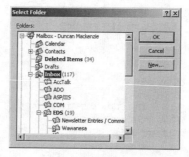

Figure 8.16   *The Outlook object model provides the ability to bring up this dialog box for selecting a folder.*

CDO is generally used in a non-interactive mode; there is no user and therefore no user interface, which means that you often do not need a dialog box like the one shown in Figure 8.16. Once in a while though, you do, which forces you to choose between two evils: using the Outlook object model for that purpose alone or building your own dialog box. Neither of these is a great idea, but I provide you with a COM DLL that allows you to put up a dialog box (see Figure 8.17) that is functionally similar to the preceding one, although it's not as attractive. This DLL is available from the Web site for this book. There, you can see all the code that was used to build it and examples showing how to use it.

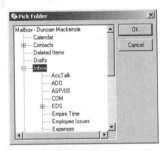

Figure 8.17   *The CDOUtilities DLL provided on this book's Web site allows you to pop up this dialog box to allow the user to select a folder.*

In addition to the GetFolder method and the InfoStores collection, the Session object offers several other ways to get at important folder objects. These include the Inbox and Outbox properties and the GetDefaultFolder method. The two properties are rather self-explanatory, but GetDefaultFolder is a little more complicated; it takes one of several parameters and returns the corresponding special folder. The available default folders are: Contacts, Calendar, Deleted Items, Notes, Journal, Tasks, Sent Items Inbox, and Outbox. The GetDefaultFolder method provides a quick and easy way to get directly to any one of these folders after you have logged on with your Session object. Several examples of this method, accessing the various default folders, are given in the following sections on items.

Working with Items

The next level in CDO below the InfoStore are folders, and below the folders are messages, the objects corresponding to the individual items (mail, tasks, contacts) that reside within each folder. The entire group of items under a particular folder is available through the Messages collection of that folder, and each individual item is represented as a Message object. The code shown in Example 8.13 demonstrates the simplest code you can use to work with these items, using a For Each . . . Next loop to process each item.

Example 8.13   *Every type of item in CDO is really a message, whether Outlook treats them as email, tasks, or contacts.*

```
Public Sub SimpleMessageLoop(objSession As MAPI.Session)
Dim objMessageFilter As MAPI.MessageFilter
Dim objMessages As MAPI.Messages
Dim objTasks As MAPI.Folder
Dim objCurrentMessage As MAPI.Message

    Set objTasks = objSession.GetDefaultFolder(CdoDefaultFolderTasks)
    Set objMessages = objTasks.Messages

    For Each objCurrentMessage In objMessages

        Debug.Print objCurrentMessage.Subject

    Next

End Sub
```

This particular example prints out a listing of all the tasks in the user's default task folder, regardless of whether those tasks are complete, expired, or still outstanding. To obtain a filtered list of messages, you use the MessageFilter object, which allows you to configure a filter through its various properties. These properties, such as Sender, Importance, Unread, and others, collectively describe the desired filter. Example 8.14 shows how you can loop through only the unread items in the user's default inbox. Note that to run the example, you need to call it with a logged in Session object.

Example 8.14   *Setting the properties of the MessageFilter object to reduce the number of messages to only those that you need to work with.*

```
Public Sub SimpleMessageFilter(objSession As MAPI.Session)
Dim objMessageFilter As MAPI.MessageFilter
Dim objMessages As MAPI.Messages
Dim objInbox As MAPI.Folder
Dim objCurrentMessage As MAPI.Message

    Set objInbox = objSession.Inbox
    Set objMessages = objInbox.Messages
    Set objMessageFilter = objMessages.Filter

    objMessageFilter.Unread = True

    For Each objCurrentMessage In objMessages
        Debug.Print objCurrentMessage.Subject
    Next

End Sub
```

To allow for the most flexibility in filtering messages, the MessageFilter object exposes a Fields collection, and the field/value pairs placed into that collection are used as filter criteria. An example of this is shown in Example 8.15, but more information on the Fields collection and Field object is provided in the following section.

Example 8.15   *Using the Fields collection to specify complex filter criteria.*

```
Public Sub ComplexMessageFilter(objSession As MAPI.Session)
Dim objMessageFilter As MAPI.MessageFilter
Dim objMessages As MAPI.Messages
Dim objContacts As MAPI.Folder
Dim objCurrentMessage As MAPI.Message
Dim objFields As MAPI.Fields

    Set objContacts = objSession.GetDefaultFolder(CdoDefaultFolderContacts)
    Set objMessages = objContacts.Messages
    Set objMessageFilter = objMessages.Filter
    Set objFields = objMessageFilter.Fields

    objMessageFilter.Or = True

    objFields.Add CdoPropTags.CdoPR_BUSINESS_ADDRESS_CITY, "Winnipeg"
    objFields.Add CdoPropTags.CdoPR_HOME_ADDRESS_CITY, "Winnipeg"

    For Each objCurrentMessage In objMessages

        Debug.Print objCurrentMessage.Fields(CdoPropTags.CdoPR_DISPLAY_NAME)

    Next

End Sub
```

Earlier, we discussed that the objects under every folder are messages, but there is an important exception to this: Appointment items. Although Appointments are part of the Messages collection in a folder, they are not Messages; they are AppointmentItems. This can cause a problem with your code, if you want to use the same looping routine to deal with more than one folder's contents, an error will occur if you attempt to assign an Appointment item to a Message object. To avoid this, you can use code like the modification, shown in Example 8.16, of the SimpleMessageLoop routine.

Example 8.16   *By using a variant for your loop counter, and checking the Class property of each item, you can write code that works with both Messages and Appointments.*

```
Public Sub SimpleMessageLoop(objSession As MAPI.Session)
Dim objMessageFilter As MAPI.MessageFilter
Dim objMessages As MAPI.Messages
```

continues ▶

Example 8.16   *Continued*

```
Dim objFolder As MAPI.Folder
Dim objCurrentItem
Dim objAppointment As MAPI.AppointmentItem
Dim objMessage As MAPI.Message

    Set objFolder = objSession.GetDefaultFolder(CdoDefaultFolderCalendar)
    Set objMessages = objFolder.Messages

    For Each objCurrentItem In objMessages
        If objCurrentItem.Class = CdoObjectClass.CdoAppointment Then
            Set objAppointment = objCurrentItem
            Debug.Print objAppointment.Subject & " (" & objAppointment.Location & ")"
        Else
            Set objMessage = objCurrentItem
            Debug.Print objMessage.Subject
        End If
    Next

End Sub
```

Message Fields

As discussed earlier, all items in CDO (with the notable exception of appointments/meetings) are message items, and therefore the properties of the Message object do not provide all the information that is available on items that are really Contacts, Tasks, or Journal entries. All that additional information is available either as one of the built-in fields or a custom field. Custom fields are set and retrieved by name, but the built-in fields are available by special constant values known as property tags. For instance, the value CdoPR_PAGER_TELEPHONE_NUMBER refers to a Contact item's pager number. A listing of all these values is provided as an enumerated type, CdoPropTags, of the CDO library.

Creating New Items

The simplest means of adding an item when using CDO is to use the Add method of the Messages collection. This method adds and returns a new item into the Messages collection, adding the item into that folder. You can set several simple properties directly in the Add, but you are better off holding onto the returned Message object and setting its properties through the standard Message or AppointmentItem interfaces. Example 8.17 creates and sends a new email message, followed by Example 8.18, which contains the code required to add a new contact to the user's default contact folder. Both examples need to be called with a logged in Session object as a parameter.

Example 8.17   *Creating and sending a new email message.*

```
'Sample code to call this procedure.
'NewEmailMessage objSession, "TestMessage", "Duncan Mackenzie", _
                 "duncanma@microsoft.com", "SMTP", "Testing"

Public Sub NewEmailMessage(objSession As MAPI.Session, sSubject As String, _
                           sToName As String, sToAddress As String, _
                           sToAddressType As String, sBody As String)
Dim objNewMessage As MAPI.Message
Dim objRecipients As MAPI.Recipients

    Set objNewMessage = objSession.Outbox.Messages.Add
    With objNewMessage

        Set objRecipients = .Recipients
        objRecipients.Add sToName, sToAddressType & ":" & sToAddress,
CdoRecipientType.CdoTo
        .Subject = sSubject
        .Text = sBody
        .Send ShowDialog:=False

    End With

End Sub
```

Although the preceding code uses the built-in properties of the Message object, adding a contact or other object type requires knowing the PropTag IDs for the appropriate fields. An example of this type of code is shown in Example 8.18.

Example 8.18   *Adding a contact requires knowing the PropTag IDs for the appropriate fields.*

```
Public Sub NewContact(objSession As MAPI.Session, sFirstName As String, sLastName
As String)
Dim objNewMessage As MAPI.Message
    Set objNewMessage = objSession.GetDefaultFolder(CdoDefaultFolderContacts).Messages.Add
    With objNewMessage
        .Type = "IPM.Contact" 'Default Type is Email Message
        .Fields.Add CdoPR_GIVEN_NAME, sFirstName
        .Fields.Add CdoPR_SURNAME, sLastName
        .Fields.Add CdoPR_DISPLAY_NAME, sFirstName & " " & sLastName
        .Update
    End With
End Sub
```

Cleaning Up

When you are finished working with your CDO objects, you should go through the following steps:

1. Set any object variables other than the Session to Nothing (Messages, Folders).
2. Log off the Session object.
3. Set the Session object to Nothing.

Following these steps will help ensure that you have released any reference you might have been holding to the CDO Library. This is a key element of your code because an unreleased reference could keep the MAPI session open longer than required. The following code snippet gives an example of some simple cleanup code; yours might be more complicated if you have created and kept any other MAPI objects open (such as an InfoStore object):

```
objSession.Logoff
Set objSession = Nothing
```

Server-/Client-Side Applications

In the earlier section that described the various programmatic interfaces to MAPI, there were a number of places where a distinction was made between server- and client-side applications. To determine what type of application you are building, it is important to understand the difference between the two, beyond the simple fact of where they run.

In many cases, the decision to create a client- versus a server-side application is simply a matter of two things:

- Who, if anyone, is going to use this program?
- How often is it going to be run?

If the answer to the first question is that individual users will interact with the program, through a dialog box for instance, you are likely talking about a client application. If the answer is that no one in particular is going to use it, because it is designed to run against a system inbox or public folder, this suggests a server application. The second question is also equally revealing and can be phrased as, "When will the application be run?" If you expect it to run whenever a message is received, regardless of the date or time, you need it to be on a machine that is always available, suggesting the server. If it is only to be run at the request of a user, a client machine is possible.

The answer of where to run your application is, as you read in the preceding paragraph, almost completely dependent on the purpose of the system. In general, if there is a specific user associated with the program (such as an inbox agent for each user), think client side; whereas if it is an overall system utility, it should be on the server where it can run continuously.

There is little restriction on how you can use CDO or Outlook from a client-side program, but if you choose to work as a server-side program, the implementation of your program is more complicated. Server-side applications designed to work with Exchange are generally running whenever an event occurs, such as a new message, or in some cases are designed to always be running. In either case, your code will often be executing when there is no user logged on to the machine, which raises the complexity of creating a VB program. To create an application for this type of use, you have to choose between a COM DLL that you call from Exchange's event scripting interface or a true VB executable.

The COM DLL option is the simplest. As long as you do not attempt to put up any form of user interface elements (and suppress any attempt by CDO to do so), you should be fine. However, if you create an executable, you need to run that program as an NT service, which raises other issues in addition to the requirement for no user interface elements. The complexities of using a VB application in this role are beyond the scope of this discussion, but details on some of these issues can be found on the Microsoft support site at the following URL: `http://support.microsoft.com/support/kb/articles/Q177/8/51.asp`. (This points to the knowledge base article #Q177851, "HOWTO: Build a VB/Messaging Application to run from a Service.")

Chapter Summary

Between Outlook forms, VBA, and the scripting you can do on the Exchange Server, there is little that cannot be accomplished. Functionality is not everything though, and, in some cases, the convenience and portability of components created in VB is very appealing to the collaboration developer. Fortunately, we do have the choice; several interfaces are provided to make it easy for us to take advantage of the power of Exchange and Outlook as well as the features of the full VB language.

These interfaces (MAPI, CDO, and Outlook) are all methods of working with the same underlying system(s), but each of them has advantages and disadvantages. By looking at the requirements of your particular program, you can determine which of the interfaces is best suited for your purposes, and this chapter has provided you with an overview of each interface for just that purpose.

In addition to a general overview of the interfaces available, a number of examples of using CDO were provided, as it is the messaging interface you will likely use most often. For more information on CDO, and programming against it, see the following chapters (which contain a number of topics that touch on CDO) and a detailed coverage of the CDO object model (including a section detailing the different error codes received for common problems) in Appendix A.

9

Microsoft Office Integration

The concept of using the Microsoft Office suite as part of a business application (collaborative or otherwise) is not unusual. In fact, it is extremely common, and a large number of applications are taking advantage of the features of Office from within their code. In this chapter, we will discuss this trend and how your programs can benefit from some form of integration with Microsoft Office. The following topics will be covered:

- **An argument for integration.** Why people are building systems around Microsoft Office, and why you should do the same.
- **Office documents for transmitting information.** How you can use an Office document as a method for entering and submitting data into a collaboration system.
- **Office as a report generator.** How to use Office to create richly formatted reports out of your application.

To help demonstrate the power of this approach and the advantages it gives to your development project, I will walk you through a sample collaborative development application that takes advantage of both Exchange and Microsoft Office 2000. All the code you will need for this sample (a COM add-in application) is provided on the book's Web site at http://www.newriders.com/exch_prog.

An Argument for Integration

There are two main reasons to leverage the features of Office: one is primarily an advantage for you, the developer or designer of the system, and the other is an advantage for the users of that same system. We'll cover both of these reasons, starting with the one that appeals to you as the developer or designer of the system.

In the olden days of computing, there were many situations where programs had to be written without any operating system available. This meant a great deal of additional work for the programmer because disk access, serial port communication, and other features of the platform had to be managed completely by each individual program. This was bad. Each program ended up doing a lot of the same work, memory management, communicating with the display hardware, and so on, as the others. The creation of various operating systems, such as Windows, UNIX, and others, helped to eliminate this problem. Programmers no longer had to worry about those mundane details, which had been left to the operating system. Today, the productivity of the development team is much greater, and the time-to-market of a new application is much shorter.

Programmers Still Have to Worry

Let me point out that most programmers still have to think about memory management and other functions that are supposedly handled by the OS. This is not the way it is supposed to be; this happens because there are either flaws with how the OS deals with a particular issue or the application doesn't like the restrictions the OS places on it. Either way, the ultimate purpose, which we can all agree has been at least partially realized, was to free programmers of those issues. ◆

Programmers had to start worrying about bigger issues—how to communicate with email systems, telephony applications, and so on—but one by one, the OS has taken over these common tasks (with the likes of MAPI and TAPI) and again has attempted to simplify the life of programmers by allowing them to concentrate on the function of their applications. I am not alone when I say, "Thank you!" to the OS developers for this: I can now develop a business application and focus on the business, not on all the details about loading my program into memory or figuring out how to configure my I/O stream to the Comm port. The OS provides a set of base services that we can easily take advantage of, and this is a good thing all around.

Try to think of Microsoft Office as another layer on top of the OS. If your application's environment (your company's standard desktop) includes Office, it is always available to you, like the OS itself. If you think of it as just another set of base services and you don't take advantage of those services you are making life hard for yourself. There is an advantage to the programmer by using Office: You gain a huge number of features that you didn't have to build yourself, features that are being upgraded and tested by a huge team of developers independent from your project.

The next big advantage is from the user point of view: The use of Office can make it simpler for users to interact with your system. There is no shortage of complexity in the computer world, and this complexity is a main reason why many people find computers and computer applications difficult to use.

It is a generally accepted fact that making your program integrate well with the operating system (such as Windows) results in consistency between applications, and that makes the entire computer easier to use. This is true because the operating system is an ever-present part of the system, something that the user sees every day and is likely to be familiar with. Likewise, if Microsoft Office is the main suite of applications for those users, it also is something that the user sees every day and is likely to be familiar with. If you can leverage that existing user knowledge by using Office dialog boxes and documents from within your program, you'll avoid a lot of training issues and reduce the overall complexity of the user's computing environment.

Take, as an example, the act of picking the name or email address of another person in the company. Your application can provide any number of dialog boxes that ask for this information and supply the list of users using a wide variety of user interface elements (tree view, icons, and so on). By building your own dialog box, however, you are now responsible for training and supporting users on the use of that dialog box. If you instead use the Address book function provided to you by the OS (see Figure 9.1), you still might have some training issues, but you are dealing with a common dialog box that is used across many different applications and is more likely to be understood by the user. In addition to the usage benefits, you also get a dialog box that will be updated in the future to deal with new technologies (such as a switch from Exchange 5.5 to Exchange Platinum or beyond) without having to recompile your code.

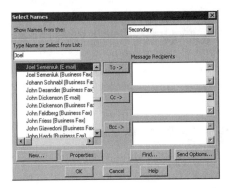

Figure 9.1   *Common OS-supplied dialog boxes, such as this address picker, provide a high degree of consistency across multiple applications.*

Office became a good choice for me when I realized that I could solve an entire group of client requirements at once by utilizing the power of Microsoft Word in my application. The client wanted to be able to produce reports that were saved onto disk for archive purposes, and the copy on disk should be capable of being reprinted without the report being re-run. They also wanted to be able to change a large number of the generic parts of the report (such as header, footer, and font styles) without having to pay me to do it. The final requirement: The reports had to able to be sent to several other offices where they could be printed out, and those offices were not running the main application I had written.

I puzzled over this for some time, working with HTML files (which are hard to bundle up and email, and are not well suited for printing), PDF files (which solved several parts of the problem, but producing them and supporting all those font and text changes was very complicated), and my own custom report document formats (heavily dependent on my code and hard to send out to other offices). Finally, I settled on Word documents, provided the users with a template (that they could modify to their hearts content), and I started and finished the reporting part of my system in almost no time at all. This choice even prepared me for future change.

A pair of new requirements cropped up a few months after the system was implemented: Two new offices joined the group of people that had to receive and print these reports (which were being sent out as .doc files by email). One office didn't have Microsoft Office and the other had Macintosh computers. Simply downloading the Word 97 Viewer for the first office and purchasing Office 98 (the Mac version of Office) for the second easily solved the problem without any new development. There are other ways to solve this problem as well, and many other word processors would have easily been able to convert the files, but almost any solution could have been implemented without changing my code.

In summary, we use Office in our applications to provide a consistent user experience and to take advantage of its functionality without having to rewrite the code for that functionality ourselves. These two reasons are very powerful and cover a host of smaller reasons, making a very good argument for this integration.

Why Office 2000?

Office 2000 has had many features added that make collaboration easier, including great features like the Office Web Components and (my personal favorite) COM add-ins. In general, though, the features in Outlook 2000 will have the greatest affect on your collaborative development. Those features are the focus of Chapter 5, "Microsoft Outlook 2000 Collaborative Basics." In this chapter, we will focus on more generic use of Office within your system, and all our examples will be designed to work with both Office 97 and Office 2000. Any 2000-specific information will be flagged as such to avoid any confusion. ◆

Office Documents for Transmitting Information

When creating a collaborative system, you often need to receive input into the system. This input can take many forms, and in the context of Outlook and Exchange, it is often in the form of an email message. Even with custom Outlook forms, though, email isn't always the best method for submitting information, and other methods must be found. The submission of files is a commonly chosen root, using TEXT, RTF, or binary files to upload a set of data as one item. Of course, these files could be uploaded through email, which allows for the submission of information through external (not part of your Exchange system) email networks, such as Hotmail. The resulting flexibility might be just what you need, depending on the type of system you are building.

In this chapter, the system that we'll be discussing needs just that type of functionality. It is an information updating system for a company (ImagiNET Resources Corp.) that has a large staff of trainers and consultants. These employees are often located at a client's site and therefore do not always have access to their Exchange email. Sometimes they do not even have access to the Internet version of their email, Outlook Web Access, and are limited to using an internal email system or accessing/sending mail from home after hours. This company's problem is a common one—how to communicate information to and from these employees in an electronic fashion to allow automatic processing of that data.

The working conditions of a consultant point toward a file-based system for this type of information because files are offline ready, allowing the consultant to create the file whenever and wherever he is and to update that file as needed without being connected. When completed, the submission or return of information is easily accomplished through any available means, whether that is an email system or the Web. As described previously, the file format chosen can be any one of a variety of choices, such as TEXT, XML, RTF, and others, but all of these choices require a certain amount of user skill in creating them so that the system can understand their contents. Office documents allow you to provide all of this functionality and still have a very rich data-entry environment and structured data that makes the file processing as simple as possible. This choice leverages the existing investment the company has made in Microsoft Office, instead of going forward with some form of custom entry program and creating additional expense. To build a solution like this, there are several distinct phases, as follows:

- Creating the template document for the data entry.
- Developing a transfer mechanism to get the files out to the user and back into the system.

- Writing code to process the files when received.
- Saving that processed information into a structured storage format like a database.

We'll go through each of these phases, using a simple example based around the needs of a company like ImagiNET and utilizing Outlook and Word for most of its functionality.

Our Simple Example

As an example of using these Office documents (in this case, Word and Excel files) to gather data from users, you will build a system to verify people's addresses. This system will consist of several functions, as follows:

- Scanning through a list of contacts in Outlook and generating a document containing each contact's current address information.
- Sending each document to the associated contact along with a request to please update the file as needed and return it.
- Processing received email as it comes in, grabbing the attached file and scanning it for address changes.
- Making any necessary changes to the original Contact item in Outlook.

All these steps will be accomplished through the creation of a COM add-in using Visual Basic. This add-in will run inside Outlook 2000 and allow the user to send off an address verification request for any Contact item desired and will automatically handle any responses received.

Looking for the Finished Add-in?

Many parts of this add-in are not directly related to the topic of this chapter and will be only briefly covered, but the complete code is available on the ImagiNET Web site at http://www.imaginets.com. ◆

Creating the Templates

To allow the user to enter information, you need to provide him with a document in which to do so. Regardless of whether this is an Excel workbook or a Word document, the same requirements exist for them both. You need to format the document so that the user can enter information into the areas you want him to and cannot make any changes to any other area. In Excel, you accomplish this with a combination of named ranges (they allow you to refer to a particular cell by name, not by its row/column location) and the worksheet protection features. In Word, the procedure is similar, but the addition of forms makes it even easier to accomplish.

Documents Can Be Templates Too

The term template can be misleading when used in this context, because you could simply be creating an actual document file (.doc or .xls, for instance), not an actual template (.dot or .xlt). ◆

For our simple example, we will create templates that will be filled in twice: once by the COM add-in when it puts the contact's current information into a new document to be emailed out, and once by the contact when it updates its information. For the purposes of this example, we will demonstrate this process using both an Excel workbook and a Word document, but in practice you would likely choose only one.

Setting Up Named Ranges in Microsoft Excel
The procedure for creating an entry form in Microsoft Excel consists of four steps. First, create a new worksheet and completely format it, creating all the labels and using sample data to populate the cells that will be used for data entry. Next, name all the data entry cells (name the range corresponding to that cell, if you are interested in the underlying details of this procedure) so that you can refer to them by that name in later code. Next, before you can complete the final step of protecting the worksheet, make sure that the data entry fields will be editable by unchecking the Locked option in the cell's property dialog box. At the same time, any cells that are performing calculations can have their formulas hidden by checking the Hidden option in that same dialog box. Finally, protect the worksheet and assign a password using the Protect Sheet menu option.

To demonstrate this process, let's walk through a simple example consisting of a worksheet with one data entry field. You need Microsoft Excel if you want to follow along and complete this example:

1. Open Microsoft Excel and create a new blank worksheet by clicking the New icon on the toolbar, or by choosing New from the File menu and then selecting Workbook from the dialog box that is displayed.

2. In the upper-left corner of the worksheet, cell A1, put the label for your data entry field, Your Full Name:. You can resize the column to fit the text and format it the way you want.

3. In the second column of that same row, cell B1, enter some sample data as a placeholder for your data entry field—Bill Gates, for example. Resize the column as needed so that it accommodates most names.

4. Select cell B1 and give it a name by typing one into the Name box (the drop-down combo box located on the left end of the Excel toolbar, just above cell A1), as shown in Figure 9.2, and then pressing the Enter key when you are done typing the name. For this particular example, give it the name YourName.

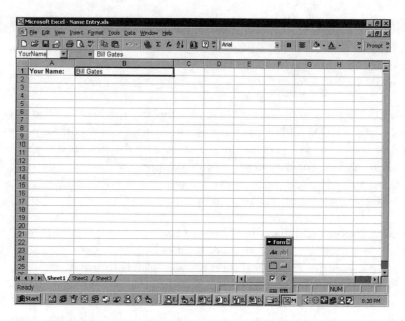

Figure 9.2   *The Name box is used to select cells by name,
display the current cell's name, and define new names.*

5. With cell B1 selected, view the Format Cells dialog box by selecting
    Format, Cells. Switch to the Protection tab and uncheck the Locked
    setting. This ensures that, after you protect the worksheet, you can edit
    values in this cell. Click OK.

6. Protect the worksheet by selecting Tools, Protection, Protect Sheet. In
    the dialog box that appears, as shown in Figure 9.3, ensure that all the
    options are selected (Contents, Objects, and Scenarios), and then click OK.

7. Save the worksheet as Sample.xls. Close Microsoft Excel and then
    reopen it by finding and double-clicking the Sample.xls file on your
    computer (wherever you saved it).

8. Note that you can edit the data entry cell for your name, but you can-
    not change anything else, and you can save the workbook as desired.
    This is the way the file will be given out for data entry.

The end result of this little exercise is a Microsoft Excel file that only allows
the entry of information into a single cell, information that can easily be
retrieved from code because it has been given a meaningful name. From VB
(or VBA), you can simply write code like that shown in Example 9.1 to
open the document and pull out the entered value.

Example 9.1 *Sample code showing how to pull the value from a named range in an Excel worksheet.*

```
Private Function GetNameFromXLSFile(sFilename As String) As String
Dim objExcel As Excel.Application
Dim objWorkbook As Excel.Workbook
Dim objWorksheet As Excel.Worksheet

    Set objExcel = CreateObject("Excel.Application")
    Set objWorkbook = objExcel.Workbooks.Open(sFilename)
    Set objWorksheet = objWorkbook.Worksheets("Sheet1")

    GetNameFromXLSFile = objWorksheet.Range("YourName").Text

End Function

Public Sub TestGetName()

    MsgBox GetNameFromXLSFile("D:\Documents and Settings" & _
    "\Duncanma\My Documents\Name Entry.xls")

End Sub
```

The actual file that will be used for your address verification system will have several more data entry fields (address, city, phone) and will be more richly formatted, but the concept is the same. To create a professional appearance, always remember to get rid of anything unnecessary for your application, such as any extra worksheets in the file, and to rename everything that is needed, including the worksheets you are using (don't leave them named as Sheet1 and so on) and every data entry cell.

Author's Note

When I am creating a template in either Word or Excel, I assign names to everything I think I might ever want to access programmatically. Therefore, although you only need names on your data entry fields, I always give names to the captions as well. This gives me the ability to change the contents of those areas of the document from code without having to ever change my original template. Doing things in this manner means more work in the short term, but has the potential to make things much easier in the future. ◆

We will detail the code required to create and send out the individual copies of this workbook in the section "Office as a Report Generator."

Microsoft Word Documents
When working with Microsoft Word documents to create a data entry form, the process is very similar to building them in Microsoft Excel. Your end goal is the same—to create a document where the user can enter information

in to certain places and not anywhere else, and where you (the programmer) can easily retrieve information out of the document. To achieve these goals, here are the three steps to create a data entry form in Word. First (as with the Excel document), create your document with all the formatting you want, using sample data as placeholders for all your data entry fields. Next, ensure that the Forms toolbar is visible (if it is not, right-click anywhere on another toolbar and click the Forms menu option) and replace each of your data entry placeholders by using the items on this toolbar (like the Text Form Field and the Check Box Form Field). As you insert each form field, right-click on it to view its properties, set its Bookmark property to a name for this field, and set its default text to whatever value you want to appear in the field before the user has entered anything. Finally, protect the form by selecting Tools | Protect Document or by clicking the padlock icon on the Forms toolbar.

With these steps completed, you have created a data entry form in Word, with data fields that can be easily filled in by the recipient and then programmatically retrieved by you. To demonstrate these steps, another exercise is provided for you to walk through and create a simple data entry form that you can try out. Just follow these steps, and you'll have a Word document that contains a single data entry field and only allows you to work with that field. You need Microsoft Word to complete this exercise:

1. Open Microsoft Word and create a new blank document by using the New icon on the toolbar or selecting File | New.

2. Type in the prompt for your single data entry field, Your Name:, and format it the way you want.

3. Ensure that the Forms toolbar is visible (see Figure 9.3). If it is not, right-click on another toolbar and select the Forms option from the menu that appears.

4. Move the cursor in Word to the end of the prompt you just typed in. Click the first toolbar icon, the Text Form Field icon, to insert a form field at the current cursor location.

5. Right-click the form field you just added and select Properties. A dialog box is displayed, as shown in Figure 9.4.

6. Put the text <Enter your name here> into the Default Text property, and put the name for this field (YourName) into the Bookmark property. Click OK to close this dialog box.

7. Click the Padlock icon on the Forms toolbar to protect the forms on this document. This protects them without using a password; to do this with a password (which is preferable in a real application), select Tools | Protect Document.

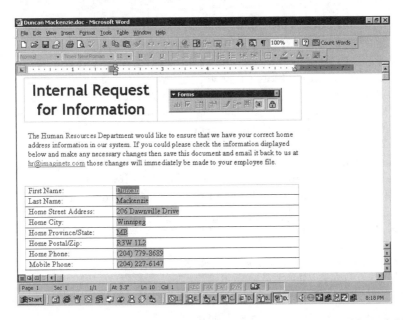

Figure 9.3   *The Forms toolbar allows you to insert various types of form fields into a Word document and to turn the protection features on and off.*

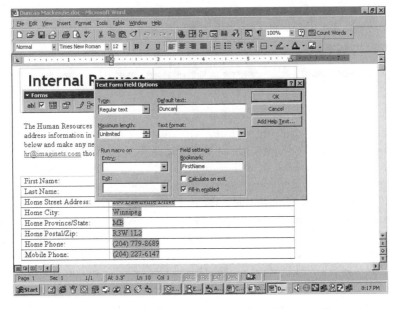

Figure 9.4   *The Text Form Field Properties dialog box allows you to set up a variety of useful values, including the maximum length of entered text, the default value, and some formatting information.*

8. Save the document with a name and location that you can easily find, and then close Word.

9. Find that document using the Windows Explorer, and double-click it to open it in Word. Notice that you cannot even select text outside of the data entry field and that the field is automatically selected when the document is opened. Replace the default text with someone's name and then save and close the document.

Because you provided a bookmark name for your data field, it is very easy to retrieve its contents using VB or VBA code. Example 9.2 shows how this could be accomplished—pulling out the text the user has entered.

Example 9.2   *This VB code retrieves the text entered into a Word data entry form.*

```
Private Function GetNameFromDOC(sFileName As String) As String
Dim objWord As Word.Application
Dim objDoc As Word.Document

    Set objWord = CreateObject("Word.Application")
    Set objDoc = objWord.Documents.Open(sFileName)

    GetNameFromDOC = objDoc.FormFields("YourName").Result

End Function

Public Sub TestGetName()

    MsgBox GetNameFromDOC("D:\Documents and Settings\Duncanma\Desktop\Data Entry Form.doc")

End Sub
```

As with the previous example using Microsoft Excel, the actual document that will be used by your Address Verification system will contain many more data entry fields and will be richly formatted. Despite its simplicity, the preceding example demonstrates all the techniques used in the creation of the final document. The full document (with several more fields) is available from the book's Web site at http://www.newriders.com/exch_prog. When actually creating the document (using VB code, of course), you will also add a piece of functionality by storing the contact's ID into a special document property, which makes it rather simple to associate this document with the appropriate Contact item. Accomplishing this requires code like the following:

```
Set objNewDoc = objWord.Documents.Add("HRAddressVerification.dot")

objNewDoc.CustomDocumentProperties("EntryID") = objContact.EntryID
```

Transferring the Files

Whenever you are dealing with Office documents as part of a collaborative solution, you need to transport them to and from the users in some manner. There are two main choices for moving documents around: emailing attachments or using Web sites and Web pages. The choice of emailing attachments is the most common and simple to implement. This method doesn't even require the user to have a certain email system, only that he has the ability to send and receive attached files along with his messages. It is not uncommon to want an alternative to this approach, though, and the idea of using the Web for this submission is also appealing. The sections that follow provide some brief coverage of these two topics.

Using Email Attachments to Transport Your Files

If you decide to use email to move the files to and from your clients, there are two main things you need to know how to program: putting attachments into email messages and taking them out. You can expect the user to manually detach the files to edit them and then re-attach the files for the return trip, but you still need to programmatically handle both of these tasks because the files need to be attached for sending out in the first place, and the edited responses need to be removed from the message after they have been sent back. Both of these tasks will be documented by using CDO to access the message from Visual Basic.

Attaching File(s) to an Email Message

The key CDO elements of attaching a file are the message itself, the Attachments collection, and the Attachment object. Generally, all you need to do is use the Attachments collection's Add method because it allows you to specify the four most important pieces of information and avoids the use of an individual attachment object all together.

Following are the parameters for this method:

- **Name.** This value allows you to specify a display name for the attachment that will appear in the Outlook interface. If not supplied, CDO picks an appropriate value for it, such as the filename if you are attaching a file.

- **Position.** When your goal is to just get a file into your email, this parameter is not all that important, but it affects the appearance of your message by determining at which character position the attachment should appear. Specifying 0 for this value places the file(s) at the very beginning of your message.

- **Source.** Depending on the attachment type, this can specify the file path to the file to load, a path to be used as a shortcut, or even the ID of a message you want to embed.

- **Type.** This parameter determines if the attachment is a file (CdoFileData), a link (CdoFileLink), an OLE document (CdoOLE), or another MAPI message (CdoEmbeddedMessage).

You can also specify these parameters using the individual properties of the Attachment object, but if you use the Add method, it saves you a couple of steps. Example 9.3 shows some code that does just what you might need. To test it out, create a VB project with a single form and a reference to the CDO library, place a command button on that form called cmdNewMessageWithFiles, and put this code into the module behind the form.

Don't Be a Spammer

Be sure to change the file path and address information before trying it out. You are not likely to have a file by that name in that location, and you should use the email address of someone who won't mind the spam. Sending email to yourself is often the best choice when testing. ◆

Example 9.3   *Use this code to send a file with an email message using CDO and VB.*

```
Private Sub cmdNewMessageWithFiles_Click()

    SendFileByEmail "Joel Semeniuk", _
                    "SMTP:JoelS@Imaginets.com", _
                    "D:\Documents and Settings\Duncanma\Desktop\Data Entry Form.doc", _
                    "Please Look At This File (Just a Test)"

End Sub

Private Sub SendFileByEmail(sToName As String, sToAddress As String, sFileName As String, sSubject As String)
Dim objSession As MAPI.Session
Dim objNewMessage As MAPI.Message
Dim objAttachments As MAPI.Attachments
Dim objRecipients As MAPI.Recipients
Dim objRecipient As MAPI.Recipient

    Set objSession = CreateObject("MAPI.Session")
    objSession.Logon ShowDialog:=True, NewSession:=False

    Set objNewMessage = objSession.Outbox.Messages.Add

    With objNewMessage
```

```
    .Subject = sSubject

    Set objRecipients = .Recipients
    Set objRecipient = objRecipients.Add(sToName, sToAddress, CdoRecipientType.CdoTo)
    objRecipient.Resolve

    Set objAttachments = .Attachments
    objAttachments.Add Position:=0, Type:=CdoFileData, Source:=sFileName
    .Send

End With

Set objRecipients = Nothing
Set objAttachments = Nothing
Set objNewMessage = Nothing
Set objSession = Nothing

End Sub
```

When attaching a file to an email message that is to be sent to an internal user (someone on the same network as you), it might be beneficial to send him a link to a file and not the file itself. To accomplish this, simply use CdoFileLink in place of CdoFileData in Example 9.3, and make sure you are using a path that will be available to the user from his machine. This usually means that you should refer to items using a UNC (Universal Naming Convention) path, such as `\\CorpServer\Documents\Data Entry Form.doc`; but in some environments, it could also mean using a common drive letter or even an URL to a file located on a Web server.

Saving Files(s) from an Email Message
When you receive email messages that contain attachments, you need to save them to disk before you begin processing them, which is a rather simple process thanks to the handy WriteToFile method of the Attachment object. Example 9.4 demonstrates how to use this method and save attachments to disk, along with several other useful techniques as it loops through the unread messages in a folder and saves the attachments of every one of them. To run this code as is, you need to create a VB project containing a form and, with a reference to the CDO library, create a button on that form named cmdRemoveFiles and place this code into the form's code module.

Complete Code Is On the Web

This code, and the code from the previous section, is available on the book's Web site (`http://www.newriders.com/exch_prog`) along with the rest of the samples from this book. ◆

Example 9.4   *This code demonstrates how to save attachments from messages and save them to disk.*

```
Private Sub cmdRemoveFiles_Click()
Dim objSession As MAPI.Session
Dim objFolder As MAPI.Folder

    Set objSession = CreateObject("MAPI.Session")
    objSession.Logon ShowDialog:=True, NewSession:=False

    Set objFolder = objSession.Inbox

    RemoveFilesFromAllUnreadMessages objFolder, "C:\Attachments\"

    Set objFolder = Nothing
    Set objSession = Nothing

End Sub

Private Sub RemoveFilesFromAllUnreadMessages(objFolder As MAPI.Folder, sSaveToPath As
String)
Dim objMessages As MAPI.Messages
Dim objMessage As MAPI.Message
Dim objAttachments As MAPI.Attachments
Dim objFilter As MAPI.MessageFilter
Dim objAttachment As MAPI.Attachment
    On Error Resume Next

    MkDir sSaveToPath

    On Error GoTo 0

    Set objMessages = objFolder.Messages
    Set objFilter = objMessages.Filter
    objFilter.Unread = True

    For Each objMessage In objMessages

        If objMessage.Attachments.Count > 0 Then

            Set objAttachments = objMessage.Attachments

            For Each objAttachment In objAttachments

                If objAttachment.Type = CdoFileData Then
                    objAttachment.WriteToFile sSaveToPath & objAttachment.Name
                End If

            Next

            Set objAttachment = Nothing
            Set objAttachments = Nothing
```

```
    End If

    objMessage.Unread = False
    objMessage.Update

  Next

End Sub
```

In this particular example, you are saving all the files from all the unread messages. In an actual system, you will likely want to filter the messages to find those with specific subjects or senders.

Using the Web to Submit Files

The alternative to submitting files through email is to submit them using a Web page. This method uses a relatively new HTML syntax that makes it browser dependent (basically, you need a 4.0 browser or later, if you don't want to require any additional browser configuration). On the Web page itself, the following snippet of HTML code is used:

```
<INPUT id=file1 name=file1 type=file>
```

This creates an entry field and a File browse button that allows you to enter or select the path to a file on your local machine (see Figure 9.5).

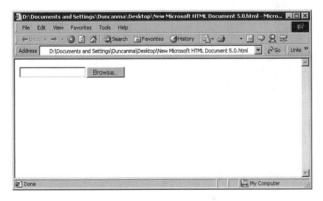

Figure 9.5   *This type of Web page allows you to upload files directly to the Web server.*

When the entire form is submitted, the file is encoded into a MIME format and sent along with any other form information to the server. At this point, you need to use some form of server-side code (such as ASP) to handle the uploaded file. The process involved in obtaining the file out of its encoded form and saving it to disk is rather complicated and is often handled by some form of third-party control. The site `www.15seconds.com` has several good articles dealing with this subject at `http://www.15seconds.com/focus/Upload.htm`. It is worth checking out.

Processing the Files

Regardless of the exact method you choose for uploading the files, you need to process them at some point. This is usually done through some form of COM code at the back end, but you have the choice of processing the file immediately upon its arrival or processing all the files at some point using a batch type of processing. Either type has its advantages. If you process immediately, you can respond to the user within moments, instead of potentially long after the submission; batch processing can allow for more efficient use of server resources over time. In either case, there is likely to be a single procedure that is the start of processing each file. It is not important whether this is called directly by code when the page is submitted or the email received or whether some form of batch process calls it. The actual code involved is basically the same in each case. Following along with the earlier example (the document requesting that people update their personal information), the next sections show the code that is needed to pull data from that document and update the appropriate contact record. The entire process consists of the following four steps:

- Opening the document
- Finding the contact item
- Updating the contact
- Closing the document and contact

Step 1: Open the Document

You just saved the document to disk, so you have the filename readily available, making the task of opening the file into Microsoft Word rather simple. The following code opens the document using a filename stored in the variable sFileName:

```
Set objNewDoc = objWord.Documents.Open(sFileName)
```

Step 2: Find the Appropriate Contact Record

Using the Outlook object model, you want to obtain the particular contact record that corresponds to this particular received file. An important point here is that when you first created the document, you placed the EntryID of the contact into the document's EntryID property to make it easy to find the appropriate item when you get the document back. This was discussed earlier in this chapter in the section "Microsoft Word Documents" when we showed how to use the CustomDocumentProperties collection of the Document object to save a value for future reference.

Avoid Ambiguous Values as Identifiers

This EntryID property and the appropriate values are added so that there is no chance of selecting the wrong contact record. If names or addresses are used, there is a chance of confusion, and the nature of this code (modification of the contact records) means that any mistake in identifying the contact would likely result in a loss of information. ◆

Given that EntryID, it is a simple matter to get the correct item using the Namespace object's GetItemFromID method, as follows:

```
sEntryID = objNewDoc.CustomDocumentProperties("EntryID")
Set objContact = OLNamespace.GetItemFromID(sEntryID)
```

Step 3: Pull the Information Out of the Document and Update Contact

After you have the Document object and the Contact object, the next step is to get the actual data and update the original Contact item. There are two ways you can do this: check whether a value has changed before updating the contact or (and this is usually my choice) update everything and save regardless of whether or not the actual values have been modified. This type of decision only matters if the act of updating is something you want to avoid at all costs, in a situation where updates are extremely resource intensive or a large number of these items are being processed. Either way, the values are retrieved from the document using the Result property of each individual form field and assigned to the corresponding contact item property. Example 9.5 shows how to do this.

Example 9.5   *Using the Result property to update the contact object.*

```
With objContact

    .FirstName = objNewDoc.FormFields("FirstName").Result
    .LastName = objNewDoc.FormFields("LastName").Result
    .HomeAddressStreet = objNewDoc.FormFields("HomeStreet").Result
    .HomeAddressCity = objNewDoc.FormFields("HomeCity").Result
    .HomeAddressState = objNewDoc.FormFields("HomeProvince").Result
    .HomeAddressPostalCode = objNewDoc.FormFields("HomePostal").Result
    .HomeTelephoneNumber = objNewDoc.FormFields("HomePhone").Result
    .MobileTelephoneNumber = objNewDoc.FormFields("MobilePhone").Result

    .Close olSave

End With
```

Step 4: Close the File and the Contact

This is basic cleanup. Release every object that you have created as you moved through this process. Although VB does a fair amount of this type of cleanup for you, it is always best to code it in explicitly, then it is never missed. For example:

```
Set objContact = Nothing
objNewDoc.Close wdDoNotSaveChanges
Set objNewDoc = Nothing
Set objWord = Nothing
```

In the end, the key to working with these data entry forms is to build something that the recipient doesn't have much chance of misusing. The system being built in these examples (and given in its entirety on the ImagiNET Web site) can accept one or more documents back from any combination of contacts, with any subject from any email, and still process them correctly. The other key to this type of system is the creation of the actual document, which is described in more detail in the following section. But before moving on to that information, the completed code for processing your incoming files is included in Example 9.6.

Example 9.6   *ProcessFile procedure from our COM Add-In.*

```
Private Sub ProcessFile(sFileName As String)
Dim objWord As Word.Application
Dim objNewDoc As Word.Document
Dim objContact As Outlook.ContactItem
Dim sEntryID As String

    Set objWord = OpenWord
    Set objNewDoc = objWord.Documents.Open(sFileName)
    sEntryID = objNewDoc.CustomDocumentProperties("EntryID")
    Set objContact = OLNamespace.GetItemFromID(sEntryID)

    With objContact
        .FirstName = objNewDoc.FormFields("FirstName").Result
        .LastName = objNewDoc.FormFields("LastName").Result
        .HomeAddressStreet = objNewDoc.FormFields("HomeStreet").Result
        .HomeAddressCity = objNewDoc.FormFields("HomeCity").Result
        .HomeAddressState = objNewDoc.FormFields("HomeProvince").Result
        .HomeAddressPostalCode = objNewDoc.FormFields("HomePostal").Result
        .HomeTelephoneNumber = objNewDoc.FormFields("HomePhone").Result
        .MobileTelephoneNumber = objNewDoc.FormFields("MobilePhone").Result

        .Close olSave
    End With

    Set objContact = Nothing
    objNewDoc.Close wdDoNotSaveChanges
    Set objNewDoc = Nothing
    Set objWord = Nothing

End Sub
```

Office as a Report Generator

The previous section demonstrated the power of using Office documents to allow rich data entry and submission, but Microsoft Office is really designed for output. Most people use Office to create documents, so it is not surprising that the most common use of Office from your code and as part of your solutions is also to create documents.

Throughout the history of application development, the generation of reports has been a key requirement. This requirement has usually been met with a report generator tool, such as Crystal Reports; the use of the development tool's built-in report features, such as VB's Data Reports or Fox Pro's reporting tools; or (usually as a last resort, when you can't accomplish what you need using one of the previous choices) by writing directly to the printer (or at least to the printer's device context, through the OS). It seems that no matter what tool you used, you were always fighting against the limitations of that particular choice, trying to produce formatting that was as close as possible to your users' requests.

For the most part, then and now, these tools do a fine job of producing simple reports, especially data listings. More advanced (but commonly used) features, such as multiple grouping levels and so on, are quite simple to produce as well. However, these tools fall short in the following areas:

- Producing sales report style output, documents that commonly incorporate a relatively unstructured format with multiple distinct tables a wide variety of graphic and positional work.

- Creating reports that can be archived or transferred without an on going connection to their source data.

- Creating reports that can be manipulated, allowing the information to be grouped or totaled in a variety of ways.

> ### Possible Is Different From Easily Done
>
> *Certainly there are options for archive reports after generation, such as the Access Snapshot viewer and the Crystal Reports viewer software, but in general this is not as simple a process as the use of Office documents.* ◆

To provide these, and other useful functions, more and more programmers are turning to Microsoft Office as a report creation tool. With these applications, primarily Word or Excel, you can programmatically use all the same formatting options as a user who creates documents manually. This functionality means that there is almost no limitation of the appearance of your output, and by using templates you can provide your users with the ability to customize your reports in a variety of ways without any involvement by the development group. The other desired features described earlier, such as being able to work with the document without a connection to the data or manipulating the information after the report has been produced, are all available because these are Office documents.

This is valuable if you consider large financial or statistical reports. By outputting that information into Excel, the end user can easily sort, group, and perform calculations on the data without ever regenerating the report from your system. This doesn't remove the need for your reports to be worthwhile from the start; you still need to format and summarize the data in the most useful way you can. However, it does remove the need for a large number of different versions of a single report by giving the users the ability to manipulate the data as desired.

This section will cover how to generate these documents, focusing on the general techniques that you use to produce almost any report along with a number of code snippets demonstrating those same techniques. First, the focus will be on the available options and the general process that you will follow to create these documents, then we will move on to specific examples.

> ### The Address Updating System
>
> *This section of the chapter will continue to use the Address Updating System described earlier in the chapter for many of its examples. The code for these examples is provided on the book's Web site at* `http://www.newriders.com/exch_prog.` ◆

General Information About MS Office Automation

Office automation is a topic worthy of a book of its own. This book does not provide a complete reference to this topic, simply some basic examples of how it works and some tips for using it as part of your collaborative solutions. Check the end of this chapter for some other resources on Office automation.

Setup and Initialization

Before you can work with any of the Office applications, you need to create an instance of it in your program. This generally involves two steps: setting a reference to it in your project (which is done through the References dialog box) and creating the instance in code. The first step is relatively easy, using the References menu item, which is found under the Project menu in VB and under the Tools menu in the VBA editor. It brings up a dialog box (shown in Figure 9.6) in which you can find and check off the Office applications you are planning to use.

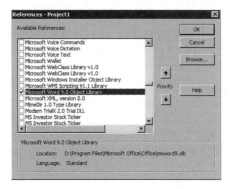

Figure 9.6 *The References dialog box allows you to select which object libraries you are going to use in this project. By having a reference set, you can use object types from that object library.*

With that reference set, you can declare objects using the various classes from the referenced library. This means that you can use code, such as "Dim objWord as Word.Application," if you have set a reference to the Word object library. That reference is what allows VB or VBA to understand the variable type Word.Application, which is actually the class Application within the object library named Word.

After you have this link between your program and the appropriate Office application, the next step is to create an instance of one of the application's exposed objects. Which one you create depends on what you are doing, but as we will discuss further in the next section on the object model, you generally start with the Application object when dealing with any of the Office products.

VBA-Capable Office Components

While we are talking about general techniques for working with any part of the Office suite of applications, it might be useful to point out exactly which applications we are talking about. With the release of Office 2000, the following applications are available for control from your VB or VBA programs (actually, from any COM-capable programming language, including Java or PowerBuilder, but we are focusing on the Visual Basic dialects in this discussion): Word, Excel, Outlook, PowerPoint, Access, Front Page, Project (98), and several utility programs (such as Graph). ◆

The key to creating an instance is understanding what your options are and building a simple procedure that you can always use to create the appropriate object. When creating an instance, you have a few different options: the VB New keyword, the GetObject function, and the CreateObject function.

Both New and CreateObject accomplish the same task; they create a new instance of the object type (specified as a parameter) and return that instance back to the calling program to be assigned into a variable. GetObject is a little different; it can be used to obtain an already running instance of the desired object, which can be handy in the case of the Microsoft Office products because you might not want to start up a new copy of Microsoft Word 2000 if one is already running.

The problem is that GetObject only works if there is already an instance; otherwise, it fails, and CreateObject always creates a new instance, regardless of the existence of a running copy of the object. You need to use GetObject if it is running and CreateObject if it is not. Although it is possible to check if a copy is running and then choose the method accordingly, it is simpler to try GetObject and see if an error occurs. This can be done by using the statement On Error Resume Next, which tells VB to continue on to the next line if an error occurs. On the next line, you can check to see if an error occurred by checking if the desired object has been retrieved, and if the GetObject call failed, you can then call CreateObject and create a new instance. The finished code should help to make this process a bit clearer. The procedure listed in Example 9.7 can be used any time you want to obtain an instance of Word and to use one that is already running if possible.

Example 9.7   *This procedure can be used anytime you want to get an instance of Word and want to use one that is already running.*

```
Private Function OpenWord() As Word.Application
On Error Resume Next
Dim objWord As Word.Application

    Set objWord = GetObject(Class:="Word.Application")
    If objWord Is Nothing Then

        Set objWord = CreateObject("Word.Application")
    End If

    Set OpenWord = objWord
    Set objWord = Nothing

End Function
```

This function, or a variation on it, can be reused in any application where you want to create an instance of Word or—by modifying the specified class name from Word.Application—to create an instance of any application in the Office suite. Given this instance, you move on to working with the desired application.

Understanding the Application's Object Model

Within each of the Office applications, an object model has been created. This means that all of the objects within a particular application's object library are related in some form of hierarchy, and in some cases, you can only get to some objects by working your way down through that hierarchy. This is certainly the case in Word, where the top-level object is Application; it contains a collection of Document objects; each Document object has a collection of paragraphs within it; each Paragraph object contains a collection of words within it; and so on. This type of relationship between the objects simply means that you need to understand the relative position of each object that you want to work with, and understand what is needed to work with that particular object. In most cases, you start with the top-level object in the model; in the Office suite, that top-level object is the Application object. From that object, you can move down into the individual document level (through the Documents collection in Word, the Workbooks collection in Excel, and the Presentations collection in PowerPoint), and finally into the individual components of those documents, such as lines, paragraphs, cells, slides, and so on. The code shown in Example 9.8 demonstrates this type of multi-level object hierarchy through a little demo in Microsoft Word. Notice the use of the OpenWord function discussed in the previous section for creating an instance of Word.

Example 9.8   *Using the various sub-object collections of an object, you can navigate your way down to the lowest level of the object model.*

```
Public Sub TestObjectRelations()
Dim objWord As Word.Application
Dim objDoc As Word.Document
Dim objParagraph1 As Word.Paragraph
Dim objParagraph2 As Word.Paragraph

    Set objWord = OpenWord
    Set objDoc = objWord.Documents.Add

    objDoc.Range.Text = "The Quick Brown Fox Jumped" & _
                        vbCrLf & _
                        "Over The Lazy Sheep Dog!"

    Set objParagraph1 = objDoc.Paragraphs(1)
    Set objParagraph2 = objDoc.Paragraphs(2)

    objParagraph1.Range.Words(2).Text = "Slow "
    objParagraph1.Range.Words(2).Bold = True

    objParagraph2.Range.Words(3).Text = "Happy "
    objParagraph2.Range.Words(3).Font.Color = wdColorBlue

End Sub
```

A great place to learn about the various objects that make up any of the Office object models is the Object Browser (shortcut key F2) inside the VB or VBA environment. This window, which allows you to browse the object model of anything you have referenced, shows you all the properties, methods, and events of the selected object. This tool is not designed to explain an object model to you; it shows you only the objects and doesn't illustrate the relationships between those objects. This doesn't make the browser useless; you simply have to understand which object is the starting point (topmost object) of the model and then follows its properties down through the rest of the objects. As mentioned before, in the Office suite, this usually means starting with the Application object. Full details on the available object models are provided in the help files that come with Microsoft Office 2000 Developer Edition and are also available from the MSDN Web site at http://msdn.microsoft.com.

Using the Macro Recorder

There are hundreds of objects available in the various Office 2000 object libraries, and it can be difficult to determine exactly which object, property, or method is required to accomplish a task. As mentioned earlier, full documentation is available on all of these objects, but documentation doesn't always help when you don't have at least an idea of the object(s) you need to look at. Often, the task you want to accomplish is easily done using the application's user interface, and it is only programmatically that you cannot determine how it is done. This is where the Macro Recorder comes in. This feature, which is present in most of the Office applications (Outlook being the notable exception), generates VBA code for actions you carry out using the application's regular interface. The resulting code is often overly complex and sometimes contains completely unnecessary actions, but does detail the correct objects and object attributes that are needed for your task. Using this type of generated code as a head start can help you quickly determine the proper code for a task and can greatly speed up the overall development time of your solution. For example, if I want to determine the code required to spell check a document, I could start recording (using the Tools | Macro | Record New Macro menu option), carry out the desired actions using Word's user interface, and then stop recording. The recorded code looks something like the code shown in Example 9.9.

Example 9.9   *Macro Recorder code.*

```
Sub Macro2()
'
' Macro2 Macro
' Macro recorded 11/7/1999 by Duncan Mackenzie
'
    If Options.CheckGrammarWithSpelling = True Then
        ActiveDocument.CheckGrammar
    Else
        ActiveDocument.CheckSpelling
    End If

End Sub
```

What I actually take away from this generated code is the single method call CheckSpelling. I will likely not use the ActiveDocument portion, because this is used to indicate whichever document is currently in the front position in Word, and I will have my own Document object to work with instead. Keep this feature (the Macro Recorder) in mind, not as a method for generating your finished code, but as a great learning tool for understanding the object model of an Office application.

Creating Word Documents from VB/VBA/VBS

The basics of creating a Word document from your code are very simple: Create an instance of the Word.Application object and then create the document by using the Add method of the Documents collection (a property of the Application object). That's it. That creates a new, blank document. From there, your most commonly used object is the Range object, exposed as a property of the document and representing the actual contents of the document. Through it, you can add text, set formatting options, and perform many other useful features. The code required to create an entire document is enormous though, so you will want to find a way to accomplish this task with less work.

My general goal when creating documents from a program is that I shouldn't have to have code for any part of the document that is static (unchanging from one running of the program to the next or from one item being processed to another). To provide that static portion of the document, which is likely the majority of the document content, you can use document templates. There are many advantages to using templates, not the least of which is the greatly simplified code, and I suggest this method for any real project in which Word document creation is going to occur. Templates allow you to manually (through the regular Word interface) create as detailed and fancy a document as you want, without any code. They also have another very important benefit: They allow the template to be modified in the future without changing the code. This means that the appearance of the document (such as company logos, fonts, and so on) can be modified independently of the application itself. In the long run, this frees the application developer(s) from the hundreds of small changes to these templates over the life of the application.

To accomplish all the wonderful benefits of these templates, they need to be created carefully. If the users can modify the template after your program has been written, you need a consistent way to determine a location for inserting of the dynamic parts of the document. This need is met by placing bookmarks with predetermined names into the document; the code can be designed to simply replace that bookmarked content as needed. If the template is changed, it doesn't affect the code as long as the appropriate bookmarks still exist (even if they have been moved). Another important point for any document creation, not just when programming, is to use styles. Styles allow you to enforce consistency throughout a document. This pays off when a user wants to modify your template; if he does it by changing the styles, his modifications carry throughout any part of the document that uses those styles. In your code, you should also use the corresponding styles when formatting text that you have inserted, which means that even formatting applied by your program will be consistent with the user's customizations.

After you have created your template, you need to create new documents based on that template, and access the various bookmarks that exist within that document to produce the finished product. The first task, creating a document based on a template, involves only an additional parameter in the Documents.Add method call; simply specify the file path of the template, and the document will be based on it.

```
Set objDoc = objWord.Documents.Add("MyTemplate.dot")
```

Where Does Office Look for Templates?

You have to supply a full file path (such as C:\MyTemplate.dot*) if the template is not in one of Word's default locations for templates. Select Tools | Options to bring up the Options dialog box, and then select the File Locations tab to check where the templates are located on your system.* ◆

The second task is to find and work with the various bookmarks that have been set up in your template, which is also relatively simple. The Document object possesses a Bookmarks collection, which can be indexed by name, and returns an individual Bookmark object if the name supplied can be found. The following shows the code to accomplish this for a bookmark named InvoiceTotal.

```
objDoc.Bookmarks("InvoiceTotal").Range.Text = currFinalAmount
```

If the specified bookmark name is not found, an error occurs, but you can avoid this by checking for the name before trying to use it. The Bookmarks collection has a method, Exists, built in just for this purpose; an example of using this method is shown here:

```
If objDoc.Bookmarks.Exists("InvoiceTotal") Then
    objDoc.Bookmarks("InvoiceTotal").Range.Text = currFinalAmount
End If
```

Whether or not you check for the existence of a bookmark depends on how you want to handle the possibility of the bookmark not being there. In the applications I create, I like to give the user the ability to selectively remove or add bookmarks into his templates, allowing him to choose not to include a particular piece of information (like a customer phone number) on his report. To do this, I was checking the Exists method for each and every bookmark I used, which lead to a lot of duplicated code. This has turned into a simple procedure that I use to wrap the setting of bookmark values, allowing that single procedure to contain the Exists check and the setting of its contents in one location. That procedure is listed here for use in your own programs:

```
Public Sub SetBookmark(objDoc As Word.Document, sBookmarkName As String, Value)

    If objDoc.Bookmarks.Exists(sBookmarkName) Then
        objDoc.Bookmarks(sBookmarkName).Range.Text = Value
    End If

End Sub
```

The use of bookmarks and templates provides you with the most flexibility in creating and using Word documents through code. In this particular example, we built a data entry form, so the techniques required were a little different.

Creating Other Office Documents

Word is a great candidate for document creation, but it is not the only Office application you will want to use. Luckily, most of the applications work in a very similar fashion. The most common types of documents you'll want to create, in addition to Word documents, are Excel workbooks. With that in mind, the next section details some of the code required to work successfully with Excel, followed by some information on PowerPoint to round out your Office automation knowledge.

MS Excel

The first thing to learn about Excel is the application itself. This holds true for any application you are planning to automate, but is essential for Excel. If you do not understand the efficient methods for working within Excel, you will have a great deal of trouble creating quick and simple code to automate it. The basics of working with Excel are rather simple; it is just a matter of understanding the available object model.

Starting with the top-level object of its object model, the Application object, you are presented with an equivalent to Word's Documents collection called the Workbooks collection. Through this collection, you can easily create a new workbook using the Add method or open an existing one using the Open method. Each workbook contains a collection of Worksheets, which can be indexed by position or name (Sheet1 and so forth). After you have the individual worksheet, you are dealing with the contents of that sheet and can use several different mechanisms to get at that information. There are several key collections that are exposed by the Worksheet object, including the Cells, Columns, and Rows (among others). Using these and the Range property that almost every object exposes, it is a simple matter to place values onto your page. Example 9.10 quickly creates an Excel workbook, adds some values to the worksheet, and adds a formula that uses those values in a computation. The OpenExcel function called in this code is an exact duplicate of the OpenWord function covered in the previous section, with the Word.Application elements switched for Excel.Application.

Example 9.10   *Creating an Excel workbook.*

```
Public Function CreateXLWorkbook()
Dim objExcel As Excel.Application
Dim objWorkbook As Excel.Workbook
Dim objWorksheet As Excel.Worksheet
Dim objCell As Excel.Range

    Set objExcel = OpenExcel
    Set objWorkbook = objExcel.Workbooks.Add
    Set objWorksheet = objWorkbook.Worksheets("Sheet1")

    objWorksheet.Cells.Item(1, 1) = "3"
    objWorksheet.Cells.Item(1, 2) = "3"
    Set objCell = objWorksheet.Cells.Item(1, 3)
    objCell.Formula = "=R1C1 + R1C2"

    objExcel.Visible = True

End Function
```

There is such an enormous amount of potential for automation in Excel that it is difficult to determine what to show you. As a final example of working within Excel, Example 9.11 illustrates one of the more exotic (and useful) functions you can find inside the Excel object libraries. The code demonstrates one of the methods of the Range object, CopyfromRecordset, which takes the contents of a Recordset object and places it directly into the worksheet. This means that it is a one-step process to insert the contents of an ADO or DAO Recordset, which is an object that represents a group of selected records returned from a database query, into an Excel document.

Example 9.11   *Using CopyfromRecordset.*

```
Private Sub MakeXLData()
Dim objExcel As Excel.Application
Dim objWorkbook As Excel.Workbook
Dim objWorksheet As Excel.Worksheet
Dim objRange As Excel.Range
Dim objConnection As ADODB.Connection
Dim rsProducts As ADODB.Recordset
Dim sProducts As String

    Set objExcel = OpenExcel
    Set objWorkbook = objExcel.Workbooks.Add
    Set objWorksheet = objWorkbook.Worksheets("Sheet1")

    Set objConnection = New ADODB.Connection
    Set rsCategories = New ADODB.Recordset
    Set rsProducts = New ADODB.Recordset

    objConnection.Open "Provider=Microsoft.Jet.OLEDB.4.0;" & _
    "Data Source=D:\Program Files\Microsoft Visual Studio\VB98\NWIND.MDB;" & _
    "Persist Security Info=False"

    rsProducts.Open "Select * From Products", _
                    objConnection, adOpenStatic, adLockReadOnly

    Set objRange = objWorksheet.Range("$A$1")

    objRange.CopyFromRecordset rsProducts

    objExcel.Visible = True

End Sub
```

With all the useful features of this object model, you should dig through it in detail before using it to build a full application.

Generating a PowerPoint Presentation

The most common response to seeing this heading is "Why?" Why would you want to create PowerPoint presentations using code? Despite the fact that it sounds unlikely, it is not as pointless as you might think. The most common use of PowerPoint is for presentations—which are generally created for a single event or purpose and do not lend themselves well to automation—but this is not the only way this product is used, and some of the other uses of PowerPoint are better suited for code-based document generation. Interactive kiosks are often built with PowerPoint, and many of those kiosks are used for showing multi-layer, menu-based selection of information. An application like this, showing a catalog of products for instance, is a great candidate for automation. In many cases, the information itself is already available in another location, like a database, and is being manually transferred to the kiosk's PowerPoint document, a task that could be carried out (at least in part) through code. Given the ease with which a database can be brought into a VB or VBA solution, it isn't hard to imagine how a VB program could be used to automatically generate a new PowerPoint presentation whenever the underlying catalog information changes. As an example of that type of process, the code shown in Example 9.12 opens up a database connection, selects back a recordset of all the Northwind categories, and proceeds to create one slide of products for each category.

Example 9.12   *Creating a PowerPoint presentation and adding multiple slides.*

```
Private Sub MakePPT()
Dim objPPT As PowerPoint.Application
Dim objDoc As PowerPoint.Presentation
Dim objProductSlide As PowerPoint.Slide
Dim objConnection As ADODB.Connection
Dim rsCategories As ADODB.Recordset
Dim rsProducts As ADODB.Recordset
Dim sProducts As String

Set objPPT = CreateObject("PowerPoint.Application")
Set objDoc = objPPT.Presentations.Add

Set objConnection = New ADODB.Connection
Set rsCategories = New ADODB.Recordset
Set rsProducts = New ADODB.Recordset

objConnection.Open "Provider=Microsoft.Jet.OLEDB.4.0;" & _
                "Data Source=D:\Program Files\Microsoft Visual Studio\VB98\NWIND.MDB;" & _
                "Persist Security Info=False"

rsCategories.Open "Select CategoryID, CategoryName From Categories", _
                objConnection, adOpenStatic, adLockReadOnly
```

```
Do While Not rsCategories.EOF

    Set objProductSlide = objDoc.Slides.Add(1, ppLayoutText)
    objProductSlide.Shapes(1).TextFrame.TextRange.Text = rsCategories("CategoryName")

    rsProducts.Open "Select ProductName From Products Where CategoryID = " _
                & rsCategories("CategoryID"), _
                objConnection, adOpenStatic, adLockReadOnly

    sProducts = ""
    Do While Not rsProducts.EOF
        sProducts = sProducts & rsProducts("ProductName") & vbCrLf
        rsProducts.MoveNext
    Loop

    objProductSlide.Shapes(2).TextFrame.TextRange.Text = sProducts
    rsProducts.Close
    rsCategories.MoveNext

Loop

objPPT.Visible = msoTrue

End Sub
```

The results of this code might not be pretty, but it gives you a good starting point for making your own slides from code. Always remember to use the Macro Recorder as a quick way to learn how to accomplish a task in code.

Creating Your Data Entry Form

The placement of this section might seem a little odd—covering how to build a document after we have covered the code required to retrieve information out of it. This is, however, intentional. Understanding how to get information out of a document is very important when deciding how to construct it. The knowledge of all of your requirements, from the beginning to the end of the process, is instrumental in determining what techniques should be used in this document. In this case, because you are creating a data entry form, you use Word's form field features in the creation of your templates (see the "Creating the Templates" section earlier in this chapter). Then, all you need to do in your application is create new documents based on that template, pre-populate the form fields with the contact's current address info, and send it off to the correct address. The full COM add-in source code and the template are both available on the ImagiNET Web site at http://www.imaginets.com, but the actual document generation code is given in Example 9.13 for your perusal.

Example 9.13   *As the code loops through a set of contact items in Outlook, this procedure is called for each one, generating a copy of our document and emailing it out.*

```
Private Sub MakeAndSendDocument(objContact As Outlook.ContactItem)
Dim objNewDoc As Word.Document
Dim objNewMessage As Outlook.MailItem
Dim objWord As Word.Application
Dim sSavePath As String
Dim objRecipient As Outlook.Recipient
Dim objRecipients As Outlook.Recipients
Dim objAttachments As Outlook.Attachments
    sSavePath = SAVE_PATH

    On Error Resume Next
        MkDir sSavePath
    On Error GoTo 0

    sSavePath = sSavePath & objContact.Subject & ".doc"

    Set objWord = OpenWord

    Set objNewDoc = objWord.Documents.Add("HRAddressVerification.dot")

    objNewDoc.CustomDocumentProperties("EntryID") = objContact.EntryID

    With objContact

        On Error Resume Next

        objNewDoc.FormFields("FirstName").TextInput.Default = .FirstName
        objNewDoc.FormFields("LastName").TextInput.Default = .LastName
        objNewDoc.FormFields("HomeStreet").TextInput.Default = .HomeAddressStreet
        objNewDoc.FormFields("HomeCity").TextInput.Default = .HomeAddressCity
        objNewDoc.FormFields("HomeProvince").TextInput.Default = .HomeAddressState
        objNewDoc.FormFields("HomePostal").TextInput.Default = .HomeAddressPostalCode
        objNewDoc.FormFields("HomePhone").TextInput.Default = .HomeTelephoneNumber
        objNewDoc.FormFields("MobilePhone").TextInput.Default = .MobileTelephoneNumber

        On Error GoTo 0

    End With
    objNewDoc.Protect wdAllowOnlyFormFields, , "password"
    objNewDoc.SaveAs sSavePath

    objNewDoc.Close wdDoNotSaveChanges
    Set objNewDoc = Nothing

    objWord.Quit wdDoNotSaveChanges
    Set objWord = Nothing
```

```
Set objNewMessage = OLApplication.CreateItem(olMailItem)

With objNewMessage

    .Subject = "HR Address Verification"
     .Body = "Please review and update the attached document," & _
    " then send it back to us at hr@Imaginets.com"
    .Save
    Set objAttachments = .Attachments
    objAttachments.Add Source:=sSavePath

    Set objRecipients = .Recipients

    Set objRecipient = objRecipients.Add(objContact.Subject)
     'Assumes that contact folder is one of your address books.

    objRecipient.Resolve
    .Save

    If objRecipient.Resolved Then

        .Send

    Else

        MsgBox "Recipient Resolution Failed. Check your Drafts Folder"
        .Close olSave

    End If

End With

End Sub
```

For this listing to work, it needs to be part of the complete COM add-in, because the Outlook Application and Namespace objects used in it are module-level variables from that project.

Chapter Summary

Most collaborative solutions created with Outlook and Exchange have a hidden benefit in common: Their users all have Office on their machines. The code and information in this chapter have prepared you to take advantage of that fact by using the power of those applications to accomplish tasks that would otherwise take many hours of additional coding on your part. You should always try to leverage the available technology, and never lose sight of all the functionality given to you and your users through the Office suite.

For More Information

As stated earlier in this chapter, this topic could be (and is) a book in itself, and this chapter can only provide an introduction into Office 2000 programming. With that in mind, here is a list of other resources on this topic to help you find out whatever level of detail you need to build a complete solution:

- **Web links.**

  Office Development Home at Microsoft:
  `http://msdn.microsoft.com/officedev/`.

  Web site for the *Microsoft Office and VBA Developer* magazine:
  `http://www.officevba.com/`.

- **Books.**

  Visual Basic Applications for Office 2000 Unleashed by Paul McFedries, SAMS Publishing.

  Word 2000 VBA Programmer's Reference by Duncan Mackenzie, Wrox.

10

Outlook Web Access

Exchange and its client Outlook are often treated as a single product, but there is another potential client interface into this mail and collaboration system. This other interface, known as Outlook Web Access (OWA), provides a view of Exchange that is completely Web based. This Web view, the benefits of which are discussed throughout this chapter, can play a role in the use and development of your company's collaborative systems. This chapter discusses that role and how you can take advantage of it with the following topics:

- Overview of OWA
- Converting Outlook forms for use in OWA
- Customizing and adding to OWA

Overview of Outlook Web Access

Outlook Web Access is an alternative Exchange client, similar to Outlook in its purpose—to provide the user with an interface into the storage and transport functionality of Exchange Server. Not everyone has access to a full desktop at all times, but the availability of the Web and a Web browser is almost universal among workers. Its interface has a similar look and feel to the regular Outlook application (see Figure 10.1), but is somewhat limited in appearance and interactivity by its Web nature. In addition, the Web interface does not support the full feature set of its rich client relative, although it does support the most common and most needed features.

One of the key differences between Outlook and OWA is that OWA does not support offline use. This is not surprising, due to its Web nature, but that feature is critical to many employees who need to work in a completely disconnected environment. There are other differences as well—no Journal folder, missing options that can only be accessed through the regular Outlook client, and other items of various significance. For many companies, the missing features are such that OWA cannot be their only mail client, but it can still serve as a supplementary system.

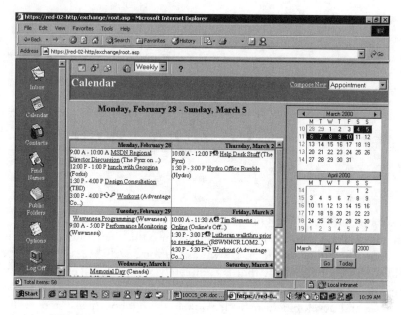

Figure 10.1 *Outlook Web Access is designed to resemble the desktop Exchange client Microsoft Outlook.*

In the critical function areas, such as reading and sending email, the Web interface works very well, so it is a good alternative to the full client in situations where a browser-based solution is most suitable. The situations that often call for this solution are those where the users have hardware issues (they can't run Microsoft Office or computers are too slow), bandwidth issues (OWA works well over a dial-up line), or platform issues (no Outlook version for UNIX, but the Web version works fine). In a large enterprise, the likelihood of encountering at least one of these situations is very high, so the implementation of Outlook Web Access must be considered as a current or future fact. As developers of collaborative solutions, you must consider how your system(s) works (if at all) for users of the Web interface and what changes are required to fix any issues.

What You Can Do with OWA

One of the first steps in evaluating how OWA can work within your Exchange infrastructure is to understand exactly what can be done with the technology. The features provided by OWA in its out-of-the-box state are already pretty impressive: Users can access all their email (new and old, shown in Figure 10.2), send mail, view and edit their contacts, work with their calendars, access public folders, and browse the Global Address List (see Figure 10.3), all through a Web browser.

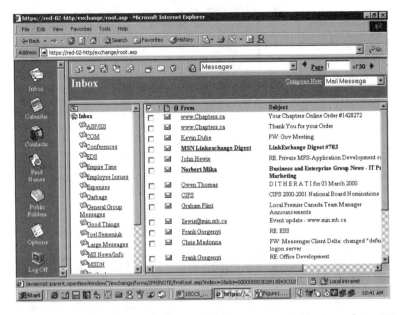

Figure 10.2 *The Inbox and all its sub-folders are available through OWA's interface. Your complete set of messages is broken up into separate pages to make it easy to work with in a Web interface and to speed loading times.*

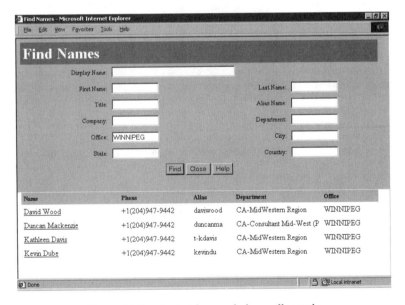

Figure 10.3 *A simple search form allows the user to query the Global Address List.*

Browser Dependence

Not every browser is supported with the shipping version of OWA. Because JavaScript and frames are both used, it is necessary to have a browser that supports them. These are not very advanced features, so this level of browser support is easy to find, but if lower-level browsers must be supported, a completely plain HTML version that uses no scripting or frames (developed for use with Windows CE devices, which have limited browser functionality) is downloadable from the Web. This version of OWA (see Figure 10.4) is not as easy to use, but does provide an almost complete set of functionality. You can download the Active Server Pages (ASP) files for this version from http://www.microsoft.com/windowsce/prod-ucts/download/mail.asp. *It is important to note that the CE version can be installed onto your Exchange server and co-exist with the existing OWA version without any difficulty.* ◆

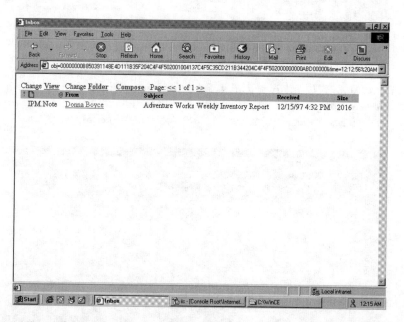

Figure 10.4   *The CE version of OWA doesn't use frames or client-side script, which makes it appropriate for a variety of situations outside of Windows CE.*

Overall, OWA provides most of the functionality required by Exchange users and is a good solution in situations where the full Outlook client isn't suitable. This type of system is often used to provide email to non-Windows users and remote or traveling users where bandwidth is the issue. The few features that are not provided, such as control over folder security and exporting of vCards from contacts, are not commonly used; but they can be added if required. The details on how you go about adding to the functionality of Outlook Web Access are discussed in the section "Customizing and Adding to OWA." The section provides a walk-through of the code needed to add a new feature to the Contact form, a vCard exporter.

How OWA Works

OWA is known as server-side code; the pages you see are generated by code on the Web server. The data they contain is therefore retrieved from Exchange at that end and then formatted into the final Web page that is returned to the browser. The specific technology used is a combination of Active Server Pages (ASP), Collaborative Data Objects (CDO), and a special library known as the CDO rendering library. These technologies together create the final solution; ASP runs the code to generate each page, using VBScript to create the CDO objects that make the actual Exchange connection and pull back the data for display. The CDO rendering library exists completely for this purpose. It works behind the scenes of OWA, taking CDO objects (like a Folder object representing the user's Inbox) and creating HTML representations of those objects. This is how OWA displays folders, individual messages, and calendar information, all of which are CDO objects rendered into HTML. To create an efficient application, the act of logging in to OWA creates several key objects that are saved for the duration of that user's session with the Web server. Session is an ASP term that means the time from the user's first request until a certain number of minutes (a timeout value) have passed since the user's last request. While a session is active, variables and objects can be stored in memory and kept associated with the user. OWA uses this capability to keep a large amount of the information that is determined at logon time (such as font sizes, feature support of the browser, and authentication information) around and to hold onto a large number of objects (including several CDO Rendering objects and the user's CDO Session object). This framework greatly simplifies the code required in each of the pages past the initial logon. They just use the already created objects, and if those objects are not present (due to a Session timeout, for instance), they just call the initial page again to force a reload. This keeps the entire user authentication and the bulk of the object creation in a single set of pages, simplifying maintenance.

Flow of Outlook Web Access

The functionality of CDO rendering objects is all wrapped together with a set of related ASP files to produce a complete interface. As mentioned earlier, these pages use frames extensively, so it can take a bit of work to understand which file corresponds to which part of the OWA interface.

To make it a bit easier for you to follow, here is a rough flowchart of the system, detailing the key pages you need to be aware of. All these files are available under the ExchSrvr\WebData\USA directory (usually installed onto your boot drive, such as c:\ExchSrvr) and are broken into a variety of sub-folders based on function.

LOGON.ASP is the first page the user sees (shown in Figure 10.5), and it is where the user needs to type in his Exchange alias to log in. At this point, there is a branch: the user can choose to log in or connect anonymously. The possibilities available with anonymous connection are quite interesting, but for the purposes of this book, we are most interested in how an Exchange user logs in. Upon submission of this form, which is handled by LOGONFRM.ASP, the user is required to log in using basic authentication (see Figure 10.6). After that authentication is achieved, the code attempts to determine the correct Exchange profile information and log on to that mailbox. If the authentication provided has sufficient rights to connect to the specified mailbox, the logon process succeeds and a variety of initialization tasks occur. These tasks set up the CDO objects (Session, Rendering, and so on) needed for the rest of the system to function and store most of the settings and objects into the ASP Session object.

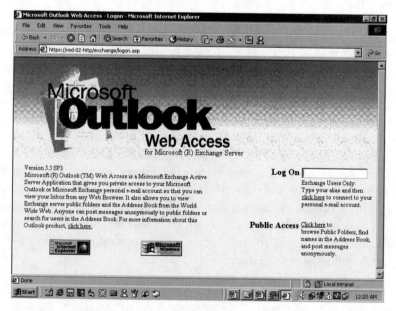

Figure 10.5   *The logon page is a prime candidate for customization because it is seen by every user.*

Figure 10.6 *Code in the LOGONFRM.ASP page forces the browser to authenticate the user, and those authentication details are sent on to the server-side pages.*

From this point on, the interface consists of a single main page (frameset) that contains the folder lists, message views, and other necessary files. This main page, ROOT.ASP, and its contents are laid out as shown in Figure 10.7.

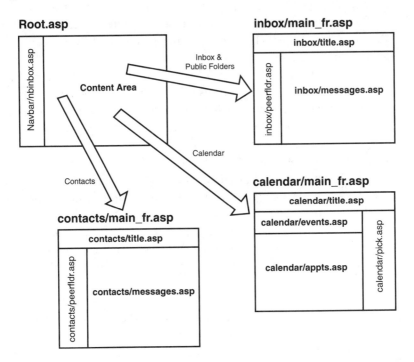

Figure 10.7 *Each navigation option loads up another set of frames within the main framework.*

The Navigation bar options Find Names and Options each load up into a new floating window, but their functionality is almost completely contained with their pages, FindUser\Root.asp and Options\Set.asp, respectively. If you decide to modify any part of the OWA system, this information about system flow should prove useful to track down exactly which file contains the code you need to modify.

After you get into the code of these pages, you will find that a large amount of the important functionality is contained in a set of include files (*.INC), one or more of which are linked into almost every other page. These include files act as code libraries, supplying common functions across the entire OWA system and common constants to make the rest of the code cleaner and easier to read.

Converting Outlook Forms for Use in OWA

A very useful feature of OWA is that in addition to the standard forms (Email, Contact), you can make your custom Outlook forms available on the Web. This is very useful because you can easily port the same functionality from your Outlook based application to an application on the Web. The actual conversion occurs using a tool called Microsoft Outlook HTML Form Converter. This tool can take an installed form (from the Outlook form libraries) or a form that has been saved to disk as a template (an .OFT file) and turn it into a set of ASP files that are used by OWA to display items intended to use the original Outlook form. The conversion process is fairly straightforward, but you must have the Form Converter installed for it to work. This tool can be installed from your Exchange Service Pack CD (SP 1, 2, or 3), where it can be found as FCSETUP.EXE under \ENG\FORMSCNV.

With the Form Converter installed, you need the appropriate access to the Exchange Server running OWA, because you will upload the converted files to that location. You also need access to the original form that you are converting, of course, and an exchange profile available that connects to the corresponding Exchange Server as the OWA server. If all these things are in place, you can run through the Forms Converter without many hassles.

The Conversion Wizard

The details of exactly what the Conversion Wizard can handle in terms of form features will be covered in a few moments, but for now, just know that it is intended to transfer simple forms without requiring change. For this example, we'll start with a fairly simple form (shown in Figure 10.8) that was created in Outlook as a variation on the IPM.POST form and was designed to allow the submission of software issues (like bugs) to a public folder. The focus of this exercise is the conversion process, not the form itself, but if you want more information on Outlook forms development, check out Chapter 6, "Microsoft Outlook 2000 Forms Development."

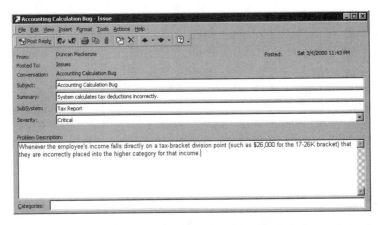

Figure 10.8   *This simple IPM.Post.Issue form, which adds little beyond the three additional fields, is an example of a very simple Outlook form.*

The Form Converter Wizard walks you through three steps to convert your form, a very simple process if you have the correct credentials for your Exchange Server. The first step (technically the second, but the first is simply a splash screen) is to pick between converting an OFT file (Outlook Form Template) and a form from the Outlook Form libraries. Also in this step, shown in Figure 10.9, regardless of the choice you make, you need to enter the name of your Outlook Web Access server. On that server, the Webdata folder (from under the Exchsrvr directory) must be shared (as Webdata), and you must have sufficient permissions to connect to it or the conversion process will be unable to continue.

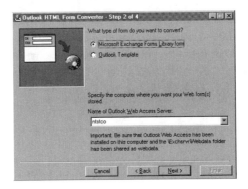

Figure 10.9   *In the first step of the Form Converter Wizard, you must supply the name of your OWA server and have the form available.*

If you choose a template, you are prompted to select the OFT file you want to use. Then you skip right to the last step, where you click Finish to generate the converted form. If, as we did for the Issue form, you choose a form from the Forms library, you must go through an additional step. In this step (see Figure 10.10), you browse the available form locations (including your personal and public folders, the Exchange organizational forms library, and your personal forms library) to find the particular form you want to convert. After that, the process is pretty straightforward; just click Next and Finish, and you are done. A form comes up displaying some information on possible errors and other notes about the conversion, but the form is created regardless.

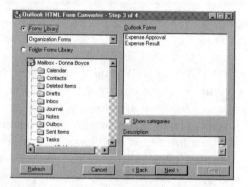

Figure 10.10   *Before you can locate a form in the Exchange forms library, a MAPI session must be established on your machine. This might require you to select a profile and/or enter a password.*

The files that make up the new form are located under the USA\Forms directory of the Webdata share, under a path that corresponds with the form's message class. For instance, all the files corresponding to a form of type IPM.Post.Issue are located at \\<OWA Server>\Webdata\USA\Forms\IPM\Post\Issue. After the form is converted, any time you attempt to open a message of that class (IPM.Post.Issue) from within OWA, the new HTML version is opened.

What Works and What Doesn't

The Forms Converter is quite powerful, but it doesn't always produce HTML forms that work or are formatted correctly. Even the simple form discussed in the previous section converts with a few issues (see Figure 10.11).

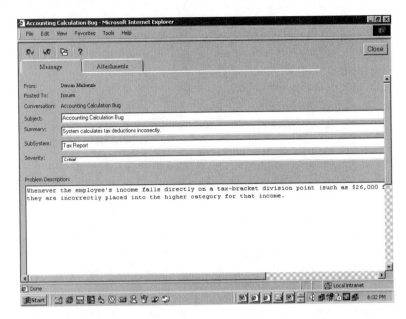

Figure 10.11   *Even simple Outlook forms require*
a bit of touching up after they are converted.

The more complex the form, the more issues you are likely to encounter. An example of the conversion of a form with more formatting is shown in Figures 10.12 and 10.13, showing the original Outlook form and the HTML result.

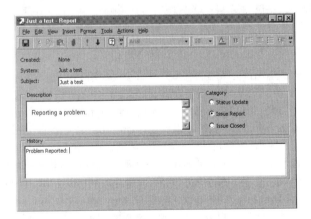

Figure 10.12   *This specialized version of the IPM.Post form contains*
several controls that overlap and extensive use of containers.

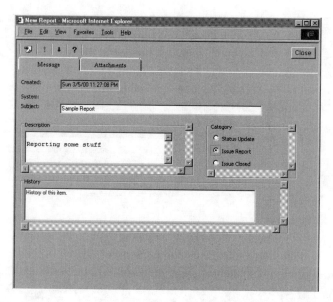

Figure 10.13   *Converted to HTML, the handling of the containers (frames) has produced some undesirable interface items.*

These problems usually occur because of a few particular things the converter cannot handle—namely, ActiveX controls, VBScript behind the form, and controls that are in containers (frames) or overlap on the form. The level of difficulty this causes depends completely on the situation. Most formatting issues require some careful work with a Web page editor like Front Page or Visual InterDev to arrange the various form fields, graphics, and text in an appealing manner—even forms that convert well can often benefit from tweaking their Web appearance. The simple form example in this case, the Issue form, can be corrected by modifying the width attribute of a few controls (the converter set it to a specific width when it should be 100 percent) and making a few other small formatting changes. The code and control issues are more complicated, though; the code might transfer with only small changes, but it depends on what it is designed to do. You must decide between client- and server-side code; if you choose client side, you might have to do a bit of work to convert your VBScript code from the Outlook form to JavaScript for the Web page. Finally, the functionality provided by any ActiveX controls on your form(s) usually has to be provided in a different way, such as client- or server-side script. Although ActiveX controls can be placed onto Web pages, using them could limit your form to use in Internet Explorer on Windows, which could be contrary to the point of having OWA in the first place. Overall, you are limited in what you can automatically do with OWA and custom Outlook forms. If these forms are even a little complex, you must do some work to create HTML versions. In addition to the technical limitations of the Form Converter, it has a more basic restriction—it can only convert forms that are based on IPM.Contact, IPM.Note, or IPM.Post. This means that some custom forms, such as appointment forms, cannot be converted by this program at all.

Customizing and Adding to OWA

Outlook Web Access does its job admirably, but if you want to distribute it to users across a corporation, you might want to make some changes. You can easily customize OWA to fit the look of your organization, with certain colors, fonts, and logos, but it is also possible to modify the actual workings of the system. The flexibility gained by having the source code of all the pages is enough to let you add almost anything. If you plan on making any modifications, it is important that you understand the different files involved and how to move through them, which is covered earlier in this chapter in the section "Flow of Outlook Web Access."

Backup Warning

If you customize any of the OWA files (contained in the WebData folder), you should be aware that these files are often overwritten by the installation of service packs and feature upgrades. Always keep a backup of your changes. ◆

Customizing the Visual Appearance

Looking at these Web pages, it is difficult to believe that OWA was created by the same organization that created the Outlook Today and Team Folder pages (described in Chapters 11, "Team Folders," and 12, "The Digital Dashboard"), not because of any problem with its appearance but due to the methods used. These pages make almost no use of cascading style sheets to handle formatting. This makes it very difficult to make wide sweeping changes to the appearance, but was required to make the Web interface as browser independent as possible. Because of this, it is in some ways simpler to change the look of this system; you just have to edit many pages. There can be some great value in making your own version of the LOGON.ASP page (see Figure 10.14).

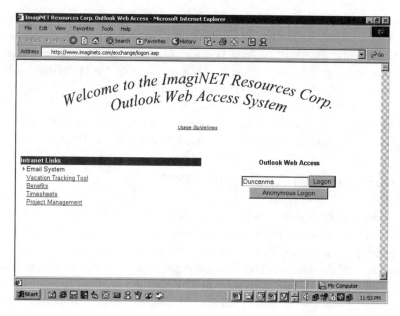

Figure 10.14 *ImagiNET provides its employees with a custom logon page that, in addition to the important feature of logging into Exchange, provides some additional related links to tie into its intranet servers.*

If you plan to make this type of change yourself, your best bet is to create a simplified version of the page first, changing the text of the ASP file so that the actual functional bits of code are clearly separated from the cosmetic aspects of the page. Then, after you have separated out the important parts of the page, remove everything you can and still have a functional page. The goal is to start your development with the simplest possible version of the page. If possible, you should even strip any large blocks of code out into an include (*.INC) file. Example 10.1 shows the LOGON.ASP file modified in this fashion (the output of this ASP code is shown in Figure 10.15); refer to the original LOGON.ASP on your system for comparison.

Example 10.1   *Modifying the LOGON.ASP file.*

```
<% @ LANGUAGE=VBSCRIPT CODEPAGE = 1252 %>
<!— #include file='constant.inc' —>
<!— #include file='lib/session.inc'—>
<!— #include file='simplecode.inc'—>
<% SendHeader 0, 1 %>
<%
'Microsoft Outlook Web Access
'Logon.asp
'Copyright  Microsoft Corporation 1993-1997. All rights reserved.
'Modified by Duncan Mackenzie, March 2000
%>
```

```
<HTML>
<HEAD>
<TITLE>Microsoft Outlook Web Access - Logon</TITLE>
<!— #include file='simpleclientcode.inc' —>
</HEAD>

<BODY>
<% if isSupportedBrowser() then %>
<form name="logonForm" action="LogonFrm.asp" method="GET"
onSubmit="sendForm(false);return(false);">
<% If urlNewWindow<>"" Then %>
<input type="hidden" name="isnewwindow" value="1">
<% Else %>
<input type="hidden" name="isnewwindow" value="0">
<% End If %>

<INPUT TYPE=text NAME=mailbox VALUE="" MAXLENGTH=60 SIZE=20>

    <br><font <%=bstrFace%> size=2>
    Exchange Users Only:<br> Type your alias and then <a
href="JavaScript:sendForm(false)">
    click here</a> to connect to your personal e-mail account.<br>
    </font>

<p> </p>

    <font <%=bstrFace%> size=4>
    <b>Public Access </b>
    </font>
    <br>
    <font size=2><a href="JavaScript:sendForm(true)">Click here</a> to:<br>
        browse Public Folders,
        find names in the Address Book,
        and post messages anonymously. </font>

    <script language="JavaScript">
        document.logonForm.mailbox.focus()
    </script>

</form>
<% Else %>
<table width=100%>
<tr>
<td>
    <font <%=bstrFace%> size=2>Sorry, you must have a 3.0 browser or better to use this
web site.</font>
</td>
</tr>
</table>
<% End If %>
<%Set objRenderApp = Nothing%>
</body>
</html>
```

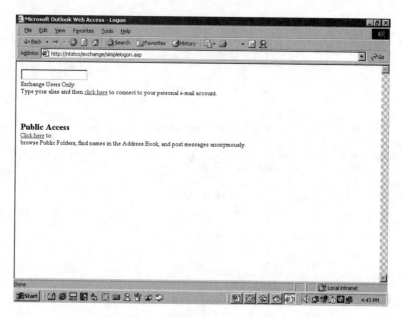

Figure 10.15   *This simple version of the logon page is 100 percent functionally equivalent to the regular page.*

To go beyond a visual change, the framework of OWA makes it easy to tweak the interface in more functional ways. Consider the navigation bar along the side of the page. It is intended to have the same look and feel as the Outlook bar, but the Outlook bar shows the number of unread messages in the Inbox; the OWA version does not. To create a version that does this involves only a few lines of new code to obtain the already created CDO Session object, get the Inbox object from it, get the number of unread messages, and then insert that value into the page. The relevant portions of the page's code are shown in Example 10.2, a modified version of NBINBOX.ASP, and Figure 10.16 shows an overlapped screenshot containing the Outlook bar from Outlook 2000, the regular OWA appearance and the modified version.

Example 10.2   *Modifying OWA to obtain number of unread messages in the Inbox.*

```
<% @ LANGUAGE=VBSCRIPT CODEPAGE = 1252 %>
<!—#include file="../lib/jsutil.inc"—>
<!DOCTYPE HTML PUBLIC "-//IETF//DTD HTML 3.2//EN">
<!—Microsoft Outlook Web Access—>
```

```
<!-Nbinbox.asp : Navbar for the Mailbox window->
<!-Copyright  Microsoft Corporation 1993-1997. All rights reserved.->
<!-#include file="../constant.inc"->
<%
Dim objInbox
Dim objSession
Dim iUnreadMessages

Set objSession = Session(bstrOMSession)
Set objInbox = objSession.Inbox
Dim objMessages

Set objMessages = objInbox.Messages

objMessages.Filter.Unread = TRUE
iUnreadMessages = objMessages.Count
%>
<HTML>
<HEAD>
<STYLE TYPE="text/css">
<!-
A:link     { color: white;text-decoration: none}
A:visited      { color: white;text-decoration: none}
A:active     { color: white; text-decoration: none}
->
</STYLE>
</HEAD>
<BODY BGCOLOR=gray LINK=333300 VLINK=333300 ALINK=333300 TEXT=000000>
<table border=0 cellpadding=3 cellspacing=5 width=100% bordercolor=666633 bgcolor=gray>
<!- Inbox ->
<tr align=center>
    <td>
        <A HREF="JavaScript:parent.RefreshNavbar(0);">
        <img src="inbox.gif" width=32 height=32 alt="Inbox" vspace=5 border=0><br>
        <div align=center><font <%=bstrFace%> size=2 color=White>Inbox <%="(" &
iUnreadMessages & ")"%></font></div></a>
    </td>
</tr>
(remainder of file unchanged)
```

If you are willing to get deeper into the various pages of OWA, your customization possibilities are almost endless. As long as output produced by the CDO Rendering objects has a place to go and doesn't clash with your design, almost anything else can be changed.

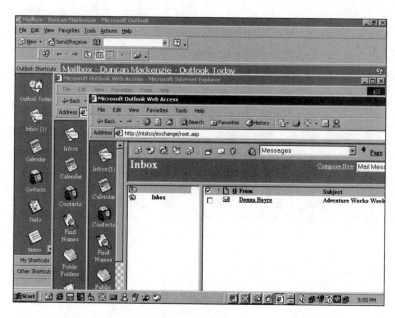

Figure 10.16 *A few lines of code can bring OWA*
even closer to the interface of Outlook 2000.

Adding Your Own Code

The addition of an unread message indicator to the Navigation bar, men-
tioned earlier in this chapter, is a simple example of adding your own
Exchange based code to OWA. You have all the source code of the Web
interface now; there is no technical barrier preventing you from adding to
OWA's functionality. In addition to the very small things, like the Inbox
unread messages count, you can build complete add-ons to OWA, like a
Web based Digital Dashboard (see Chapter 12 for details on this topic),
Account Management tools, or even a search engine feature. To illustrate
again how this type of work is done, we will add a feature to the Contact
form that creates a vCard on demand from an individual contact. These
vCard files are one of the few truly cross-product methods for exchanging
person-style data, and they are supported by the full Outlook client, which
allows you to export one from any Contact item. Adding this type of function to the Web based Contact form makes these vCards much easier to use
for your Web interface users.

For this particular feature, you want to add a special hyperlink onto the
title portion of the Contact form (Forms/IPM/Contact/postTitl.asp). The
modification to this page is very minor; a link is simply added to the toolbar

right after the Help icon. To accomplish this change (shown in Figure 10.17), and pass in the object ID so that our vCard generator can get at the appropriate Contact item, add the following line of code immediately after the link to the Help files:

```
<A href="vCard.asp?obj=<%=bstrObj%>"><font face="arial" size=1>Export to
vCard</font></a>
```

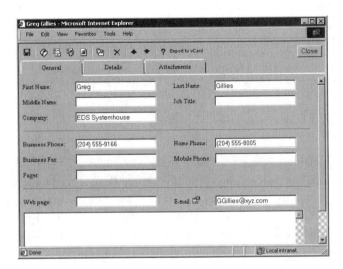

Figure 10.17   *An additional toolbar button has been added so the new feature looks like part of the original system.*

Upon clicking this link, you redirect the user to another page that uses the already created CDO objects to load up the appropriate Contact item and then output a vCard from that information. With the CDO session already created and the object ID passed in as the obj parameter, all the details are taken care of except the creation of the output.

vCards

A vCard is a relatively new protocol for the exchange of contact-style data and is supported by almost every PIM currently on the market. This includes the regular Outlook client, along with Lotus Notes, Act!, Netscape, and many others. If you want to know more about vCards, including all the details of their structure, check out the Web site at http://www.imc.org/pdi. ◆

Creating a complete vCard for all the properties of a Contact item would involve a large amount of code, so this example sticks to a selection of the most common properties: Name, Phone, Fax, and Email Address. The complete vCard for the Contact item shown in Figure 10.17 consists of the code in Example 10.3.

Example 10.3   *Creating a vCard for common Contact item properties.*

```
BEGIN:VCARD
VERSION:2.1
N:Gillies;Greg
FN:Greg Gillies
ORG:EDS Systemhouse
TEL;WORK;VOICE:(204) 555-9166
TEL;HOME;VOICE:(204) 555-8005
ADR;WORK:;;2200 One Lombard Place;Winnipeg;Manitoba;R3B 0X7;Canada
LABEL;WORK;ENCODING=QUOTED-PRINTABLE:2200 One Lombard Place=0D=0AWinnipeg, Manitoba R3B
0X7=0D=0ACanada
EMAIL;PREF;INTERNET:GGillies@xyz.com
EMAIL;INTERNET:greg.gillies@xyz.com
REV:20000306T073446Z
END:VCARD
```

To produce the proper output involves three things: retrieving the appropriate Contact item, creating the vCard text, and convincing the browser that this output is a vCard and not just text. The first task, obtaining the correct Contact item, is based around the obj parameter sent into this ASP page, a value that represents the EntryID of your contact and therefore allows for its quick retrieval:

```
On Error Resume Next
sContactID = Request.QueryString("obj")
Set objSession = Session("AMAuthSession")
Set objContact = objSession.GetMessage(sContactID)
```

With that done, you can retrieve each of the important properties to create your vCard. There are many properties available, but we will create a simple vCard with only the contact's name, title, company, phone numbers, and email:

```
sEmailAddress = objContact.Fields(OutlookEmailAddress1).Value
sFullName = objContact.Fields(CdoPR_Display_Name).Value
sLastName = objContact.Fields(CdoPR_SURNAME).Value
sFirstName = objContact.Fields(CdoPR_GIVEN_NAME).Value
sMiddleName = objContact.Fields(CdoPR_Middle_Name).Value
sBusinessTelephoneNumber = objContact.Fields(CdoPR_Business_Telephone_Number).Value
sBusinessFaxNumber = objContact.Fields(CdoPR_Business_Fax_Number).Value
sHomeTelephoneNumber = objContact.Fields(CdoPR_Home_Telephone_Number).Value
sMobileTelephoneNumber = objContact.Fields(CdoPR_Cellular_Telephone_Number).Value
sTitle = objContact.Fields(CdoPR_Title).Value
sCompanyName = objContact.Fields(CdoPR_COMPANY_NAME).Value
```

All these values can then be output into the proper locations to create a vCard, but if you don't do one final step, the browser simply displays the output as if it were text and not a vCard. To tell the browser that this text is a vCard, set the HTTP header, Content Type, to a value of "text/x-vcard". In ASP, this value can be easily set through the Response.ContentType property. The full ASP page, including the Response.ContentType line, is listed in Example 10.4 to show you the defined constants and output code.

Example 10.4   *ASP page listing for a vCard.*

```
<% Response.ContentType = "text/x-vcard" %>
<%
Const CdoPR_DISPLAY_NAME = 805371934              '(&H3001001E)
Const CdoPR_GIVEN_NAME = 973471774               '(&H3A06001E)
Const CdoPR_MIDDLE_NAME = 977535006              '(&H3A44001E)
Const CdoPR_SURNAME = 974192670                '(&H3A11001E)
Const CdoPR_BUSINESS_FAX_NUMBER = 975437854          '(&H3A24001E)
Const CdoPR_BUSINESS_TELEPHONE_NUMBER = 973602846      '(&H3A08001E)
Const CdoPR_CELLULAR_TELEPHONE_NUMBER = 974913566        '(&H3A1C001E)
Const CdoPR_HOME_TELEPHONE_NUMBER = 973668382        '(&H3A09001E)
Const CdoPR_TITLE = 974585886              '(&H3A17001E)
Const CdoPR_COMPANY_NAME = 974520350            '(&H3A16001E)

'To get the email address requires
'a multi-part string id, as it is
'an Outlook property and not one of
'the built-in CDO properties.

Const OutlookEmailAddress1 = "{0420060000000000C000000000000046}0x8083"

Dim objSession
Dim sContactID
Dim objContact
Dim sFullName
Dim sLastName
Dim sFirstName
Dim sMiddleName
Dim sBusinessTelephoneNumber
Dim sBusinessFaxNumber
Dim sMobileTelephoneNumber
Dim sHomeTelephoneNumber
Dim sEmailAddress
Dim sCompanyName
Dim sTitle

On Error Resume Next
sContactID = Request.QueryString("obj")
Set objSession = Session("AMAuthSession")
Set objContact = objSession.GetMessage(sContactID)

sEmailAddress = objContact.Fields(OutlookEmailAddress1).Value
sFullName = objContact.Fields(CdoPR_Display_Name).Value
```

continues ▶

Example 10.4   *continued*

```
sLastName = objContact.Fields(CdoPR_SURNAME).Value
sFirstName = objContact.Fields(CdoPR_GIVEN_NAME).Value
sMiddleName = objContact.Fields(CdoPR_Middle_Name).Value
sBusinessTelephoneNumber = objContact.Fields(CdoPR_Business_Telephone_Number).Value
sBusinessFaxNumber = objContact.Fields(CdoPR_Business_Fax_Number).Value
sHomeTelephoneNumber = objContact.Fields(CdoPR_Home_Telephone_Number).Value
sMobileTelephoneNumber = objContact.Fields(CdoPR_Cellular_Telephone_Number).Value
sTitle = objContact.Fields(CdoPR_Title).Value
sCompanyName = objContact.Fields(CdoPR_COMPANY_NAME).Value

%>
BEGIN:VCARD
VERSION:2.1
<%
'FN, Formatted Name property
If sFullName <> "" Then
%>
FN:<%=sFullName%>
<%
End If
'N, Last Name; Given Name; Middle Name; Prefix; Suffix
%>
N:<%=sLastName%>;<%=sFirstName%>;<%=sMiddleName%>;;
<%
If sBusinessTelephoneNumber <> "" Then
%>
TEL;PREF;WORK;VOICE:<%=sBusinessTelephoneNumber%>
<% End If %>
<%
If sBusinessFaxNumber <> "" Then
%>
TEL;WORK;FAX:<%=sBusinessFaxNumber%>
<% End If %>
<%
If sHomeTelephoneNumber <> "" Then
%>
TEL;HOME;VOICE:<%=sHomeTelephoneNumber%>

<%
End If
If sMobileTelephoneNumber <> "" Then
%>
TEL;CELL;VOICE:<%=sMobileTelephoneNumber%>
<%
End If
If sTitle <> "" Then
%>
TITLE:<%=sTitle%>
<%
End If
If sCompanyName <> "" Then
%>
ORG:<%=sCompanyName%>
```

```
<%
End If
If sEmailAddress <> "" Then
%>
EMAIL:<%=sEmailAddress%>
<% End If %>
END:VCARD
```

The final result of this addition is that you can easily download or open a vCard that corresponds to any of your Contact items. This vCard provides easy import into another PIM or can function as an attachment to your email.

Adding Non-Exchange Content to OWA

Outlook Web Access is based around CDO, but it is still just a regular Web application, using Active Server Pages to do the server-side scripting. ASP applications are commonly used for other purposes, such as database based Web sites. Anything that can be built with ASP can be combined with the OWA interface. In this way, you can integrate a non-Exchange business application right into the framework, building something like a product price list and linking it in as another icon on the Outlook bar frame (see Figure 10.18).

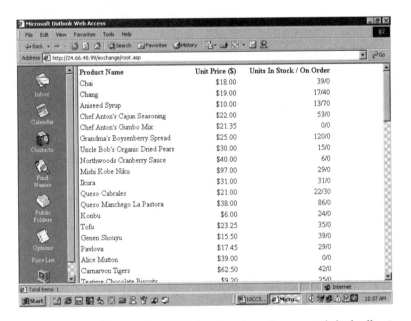

Figure 10.18 *Adding to the OWA interface is easily accomplished, allowing you to integrate additional systems directly into this common framework.*

The code required to add this icon to the framework is quite simple because it is just a static link, but this is just an example. You can create a more powerful and expandable solution in which a series of icons are added based on the results of a database query. The code that produces the database report simply consists of ADO objects called from ASP. It is listed in Example 10.5, but it requires that an ODBC DSN named NWIND exist on the OWA server and point at the sample Access Northwind database.

Example 10.5 *Using a database report to add icons.*

```
<html>
<head>
<title>Product Listing</title>
</head>
<%
Dim Conn
Dim rsProducts
Dim objField

Set Conn = Server.CreateObject("ADODB.Connection")
Conn.Open "NWIND"
Set rsProducts = Server.CreateObject("ADODB.Recordset")
rsProducts.Open "Select * From Products",Conn
%>
<body>
<table>
  <tr>
    <td><b>Product Name</b></td>
    <td width="20"> </td>
    <td><b>Unit Price ($)</b></td>
    <td width="20"> </td>
    <td><b>Units In Stock / On Order</b></td>
  </tr>
  <%
Do While Not rsProducts.EOF
  %>
  <tr>
    <td>
        <%=rsProducts("ProductName")%>
    </td>
    <td> </td>
    <td align="right">
        <%=FormatCurrency(rsProducts("UnitPrice"))%>
    </td>
    <td> </td>
    <td align="right">
        <%=rsProducts("UnitsInStock") & "/" & rsProducts("UnitsOnOrder")%>
    </td>
  </tr>
  <%
    rsProducts.MoveNext
```

```
Loop
%>
</table>
</body>
</html>
```

Almost anything is possible, as long as you do not alter the parts of these files that implement the OWA features. To make the customization as painless as possible, follow the example of the LOGON.ASP file given earlier in this chapter, break the page down into only the required portions, and build up slowly from there. You also can take advantage of the underlying ASP technology to tie databases into main parts of the framework, such as providing a database lookup within a Contact form.

Chapter Summary

Outlook Web Access is intended for use when the regular Windows version of Outlook is not available, but it has many features that make it a good interface choice even when the regular Outlook is a possibility. No deployment is a critical feature that could have a major effect on the overall cost of maintaining an Exchange system, and Web based applications have much lower hardware requirements than their rich client counterparts. Moving beyond deployment benefits, the Web-based interface also permits an almost unlimited amount of customization. Regardless of the improvements in Microsoft Outlook, there are still (and likely will be for quite some time) some things you cannot change about the interface's behavior or appearance. However, given the complete source code, you can make a Web-based system do anything you want.

11

Team Folders

Starting with Outlook 98, Microsoft began to incorporate some interesting Web technologies directly into Outlook, going beyond the inclusion of HTML as an email format. The most noticeable result from this integration is Outlook Today, a Web-style view of your calendar, messages, and tasks in an at-a-glance format. This new feature actually involves two distinct characteristics: viewing a Web page from within Outlook, and viewing your Outlook information in a Web page format. These two characteristics combine to produce the useful Outlook Today feature, but it is the extension and reapplication of these Web technologies that interests us the most, as we will discuss in this chapter and the next.

In this chapter, we will cover the following:

- **Outlook Today.** What it is and how can you customize it
- **Folder home pages.** Extending the Web-view to any folder
- **Team folders.** An easy but powerful application of Outlook Today

The applications of Outlook Today are explored further in Chapter 12, "The Digital Dashboard," detailing the concept and construction of a Digital Dashboard.

Outlook Today

As mentioned earlier, Outlook Today is new to Outlook (as of version 98) and is likely one of the most underutilized features of the product. Figure 11.1 shows my Outlook Today page, detailing some overdue tasks, my upcoming seven days of calendar events, and the number of unread messages I have in several key folders.

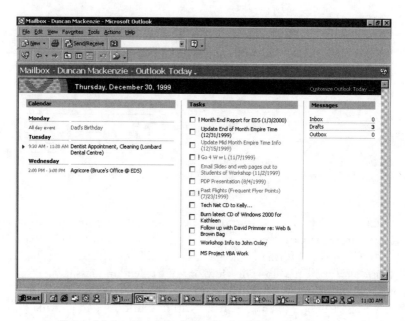

Figure 11.1 *The default Outlook Today page, showing a variety of useful information in a single location.*

This page is an HTML file that is stored locally on your machine and displayed by Outlook using browser technology. This Web page could be any HTML page and does not have to be related to Outlook in any way. It is logical, though, that this page be related to Outlook in some fashion, and the default page Outlook supplies provides a useful view. This view is still just a regular HTML page, however, and it provides the connection to your Outlook information through a set of ActiveX controls that exist on the page and allows access to your calendar, task, and message information. The default page allows a certain amount of customization (accessed by clicking the Customize Outlook Today link, and shown in Figure 11.2), such as the number of days of calendar information that is displayed, the layout of the page, the folders that are listed, and the type of tasks that are

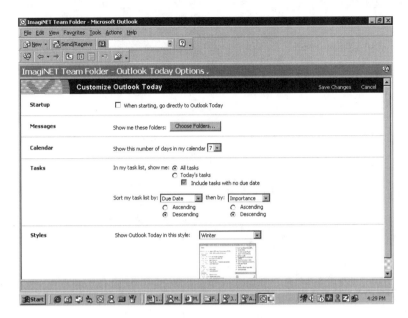

shown.

Figure 11.2 *The default settings for Outlook Today include a special page where you can perform some limited customization.*

Changing the URL of the Outlook Today Page

To perform further customization, beyond what is available in the screen shown in Figure 11.2, you can replace the default Outlook Today page with your own. The default page is located within a resource DLL (a special kind of library file that has a .DLL extension and can hold graphics, text, and other media for use by a program) and is referenced with the URL `res:F:\Program Files\Microsoft Office\Office\1033\outlwvw.dll/outlook.htm` (the exact path is based on the location of your Outlook installation and can differ from machine to machine; in my case, it is installed on the F drive). You can see this location by selecting File, Folder, Properties from the menu when you have the Outlook Today page displayed. The dialog box shown in Figure 11.3 is displayed.

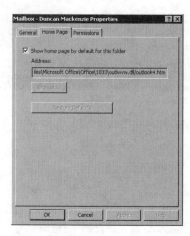

Figure 11.3   *The properties dialog for the Outlook Today folder*
displays the current address (URL) of the folder's Web view.

On the Home Page tab of this dialog box, there is a text box labeled
Address, in which you can see the address of the current Outlook Today
page. This might seem like the perfect place from which to change this
address, but notice that the Address text box is not enabled, meaning you
cannot edit its contents. You will see later, in the section "Folder Home
Pages" that this text box is not always disabled. For now, we must find
another way to change the URL of our Outlook Today page, and that way
is through the Registry. Because the Registry is the primary storage location
of all your system's software and hardware settings, you should try to avoid
working with the Registry, but sometimes it cannot be helped. Using
Regedit (the Registry editing software installed on your machine by default;
you run it by typing regedit into the Run command dialog box), navigate to
the HKEY_CURRENT_USER\Software\Microsoft\Office\9.0\Outlook\Today
key in the Registry. If you've never used Regedit before, simply use each
part of the preceding path in sequence to get to this particular location,
expanding HKEY_CURRENT_USER first, followed by Software, Microsoft,
and so on. After you have selected the appropriate key, you will see at least
one icon in the left pane—"(Default)." You might see others, depending on
whether you have used any of the customization options from the
Customize Outlook Today page. You can see in Figure 11.4 that my
Registry contains several key values.

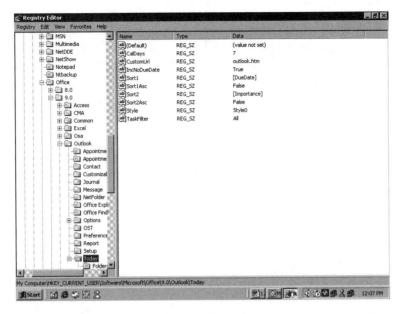

Figure 11.4   *The Registry, which is used by many programs to store preference information, is shown here with the various Outlook Today settings for a specific user.*

You might notice that none of the keys contain the default URL for our Outlook Today page, but the CustomUrl key should be set to Outlook.htm or Outlook4.htm. This is similar to what we are looking for, but it only allows us to change the last part of the Outlook Today URL, which means that we would still be pointing at a page contained with the outlwww.dll. That is too limiting for our purposes, but there is another option. By adding a new Registry entry called URL and setting its value to a complete URL, you can manipulate the address of Outlook Today. Add a string value named URL and set its value to the address of a Web page or site that is accessible to you, such as `http://www.microsoft.com`. Now, switch back to Outlook and reload the Outlook Today page by switching to your Inbox and then back to Outlook Today. The Web page you entered should be displayed in place of the regular Outlook Today page, as shown in Figure 11.5. Entering Microsoft's home page might not be the most useful thing for your company, but you can choose instead to point at your own intranet site or a custom Outlook Today page that you have created and made available to users.

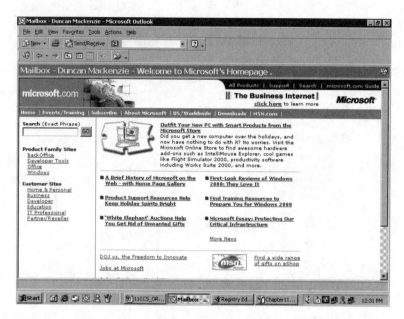

Figure 11.5   *Whatever address you enter into the new URL value is what appears when you select the Outlook Today folder.*

Restoring the Default Outlook Today Page

When you radically change something, such as your Outlook Today page, you should also know how to undo your changes. In this case, the restoration process is easy: Delete the URL string value from the Registry, and the previous settings are restored. If you want, you can also set the URL value to blank, which accomplishes the same result, but the URL value stays in the Registry to simplify future changes. Either way is fine; both methods produce the same result.

Creating Your Own Outlook Today Page

Setting the URL value to some Web site is not the same as making your own Outlook Today page; the Web site is not likely to incorporate any of your personal Outlook information into it. To build your own version of this page, you need to understand what the default pages look like. The five versions of Outlook Today that come with Outlook 2000 are simply layout variations on the same information, changing the colors and changing the number of columns used. There are two key aspects to each page: style sheets and the location of the three ActiveX controls on the page. You can create your own custom page to contain any content you want, but it is through manipulation of style sheets and the ActiveX controls that you can control the appearance of the regular Outlook Today items.

Style Sheets

Style sheets, or cascading style sheets (CSS) as they are officially known, are a feature of HTML that allows you to create names that represent specific formatting and apply those names to a section of your page. This allows you to place all of your font and other formatting information into one location and have the rest of the page or pages base their appearance on that information. There are very few production Web sites that do not take advantage of this technology, as it makes formatting changes extremely simple. If you decide, for example, to change all your headings from blue to green, you simply change the style defined for that heading in one location and every page that references that style automatically displays the new color.

In your page, these style sheets consist of two elements: the style definition and the application of those styles. The definition is the first thing you do, specifying the name and the associated formatting information. This information is put into the page as a series of individual style definitions contained within a set of <STYLE></STYLE> tags and located within the header section of the HTML page. Each style definition simply includes the style's name followed by its formatting information (contained within { and }), as shown in the following example:

```
<style>
a              { color: windowtext }
body           { margin-left: 0px; margin-right: 0px; margin-top: 0px }
.options       { color: white; font-family: Tahoma; font-size: 8pt; text-decoration:
➥none }
.date          { color: white; font-family: Arial; font-size: 11pt; font-weight: bold;
               margin-bottom: 4px }
</style>
```

Within the style definitions here, four styles are defined, two of which refer to existing HTML tags (the ones without a starting period) and two of which are user-defined style names. Within the page itself, any a or body section automatically takes on the styles defined using their names; but for the user-defined styles, you have to explicitly indicate the style name. An example of this is shown next, specifying that the contents of this tag use the .date style:

```
<div id="dateScript" class="date">
```

Notice that the leading period is not required when specifying the style name. This specification can occur on any tag and is not limited to the <DIV> tag. The syntax for specifying formatting within a style sheet and advanced functions, such as using a separate file for your style sheet, are beyond the scope of this chapter, but following are a few good references regarding that type of information:

- *HTML 4 Unleashed,* by Rick Darnell, Sams Publishing (ISBN: 0672313472).

- *Cascading Style Sheets: Designing for the Web, Second Edition,* by Hakon Wium Lie, Bert Bos, and Robert Cailliau, Addison-Wesley Publishing Company (ISBN: 0201596253).

- On the Web, check out
  `http://msdn.microsoft.com/workshop/author/css/css.asp`

If you want to quickly customize the look of one of the existing Outlook Today pages (a sample page that you can quickly use as a starting point is included on the Web site for this book), such as its fonts and colors, the fastest method is to alter the style information and change nothing else on the page.

Using the ActiveX Controls

As detailed earlier, the style sheet of the Web page provides the formatting, but the data or information on the page comes from Outlook and is provided through a set of three ActiveX controls. These controls contain the code required to connect to Outlook and retrieve the appropriate data. In order to work properly, the Outlook Today page must simply contain the controls. The HTML text required is rather complicated, and the simplest method for using any of these controls is to copy the appropriate content from an existing Outlook Today page. Despite this, it is always beneficial to understand the HTML you are using, even if you do not need to enter it yourself. The three controls are the following:

- Messages
- Calendar
- Tasks

The workings of these controls are covered briefly in the sections that follow.

Overview of Data Binding

The Outlook Today ActiveX controls function through the use of data binding. This is done on a per table basis in your HTML page, and for each table that you want to bind data to, you must specify a special attribute on that table called datasrc. This attribute is set equal to the name (id) of the item on the page that contains the data you want to bind to—in the case of an Outlook Today page, that is the ActiveX control. Inside the table, you provide a single sample row that indicates (using the datafld attribute) where in that row the various data elements should be placed. After the page is being displayed in a browser (such as in Outlook), that single sample row is duplicated as needed to display all the available data items.

In the specific case of the Outlook Today ActiveX control, you need to place the control onto the page and give it a name (using the ID attribute); then, create a table at the location in your page where you want to display the data. Within the table, you specify the datasrc attribute and set up a sample row using the datafld attribute. Sample code is given for each of the three possible types of data: Calendar control, Task control, and Messages control. These samples assume that you do not have any styles defined.

The Outlook Today ActiveX Control

All three types of Outlook data (calendar, task, and message) are provided by the same ActiveX control, so a parameter (module) must be supplied to tell the control what data is desired. The appropriate parameter values are shown in each of the three examples. ♦

The Calendar Control

The output provided by the Calendar control is a concise, Web-style view of up to seven days ahead in the user's schedule. The code to place this onto your Outlook Today page is given in Example 11.1 and is also contained in the sample Outlook Today pages available from this book's Web site.

Example 11.1   *Calendar section of a sample Outlook Today page.*

```
<object id="CalList" classid="CLSID:0468C085-CA5B-11D0-AF08-00609797F0E0">
  <param name="Module" value="Calendar">
</object>
<table id="CalendarLiveTable" border="0" cellspacing="1" cellpadding="2" valign="top"
width="100%" name="ItemCol" datasrc="#CalList">
  <tr>
    <td nowrap valign="top" width="10px" align="left">
      <div datafld="Next" dataformatas="html">
      </div>
    </td>
    <td valign="top" nowrap>
      <div datafld="StartEnd" dataformatas="html" class="CalendarStartEnd">
         
      </div>
    </td>
    <td valign="top" width="100%">
      <div datafld="SubjectLocation" dataformatas="html" class="CalendarSubjectLocation">
         
      </div>
    </td>
  </tr>
</table>
```

The result of Example 11.1 is a table containing the HTML representation of your Outlook calendar. Note that if you haven't defined certain styles in your HTML page, the formatting leaves much to be desired. The output of the ActiveX control makes use of several specific styles, the names of which are fixed and cannot be changed by the developer. The styles specific to the Calendar module are listed in Example 11.2, and (when put into the page) greatly enhance its appearance.

Example 11.2   *Entering Calendar-related style information to properly format the ActiveX control's output.*

```
<style>
a               { color: windowtext }
.CalendarSubjectLocation {  }
.CalendarStartEnd {  }
.itemNormal  { font-size: 8pt; font-family: Tahoma; text-decoration: none; color:
➥windowtext }
.times          { font-size: 7pt; line-height: 11pt; font-family: Tahoma; text-decoration:
➥none;
                cursor: hand; color: buttonshadow }
.PastTimes   { color: buttonface; line-height: 11pt; font-size: 7pt; text-decoration:none;
                cursor: hand }
.SplitDayTimes { color: teal; font-size: 7pt; line-height: 11pt; text-decoration: none;
                cursor: hand }
.allDayEventTimes { color: teal; line-height: 11pt; font-size: 7pt; text-decoration: none;
                cursor: hand }
.itemImportant { color: red }
.dayHeaders { font-family: Tahoma; font-size: 8pt; font-weight: bold; width: 100%; height:
                100%; color: windowtext; cursor: default;
                border-left: .1em none #CCCCCC; border-right: .1em none #CCCCCC;
                border-top: .1em none #CCCCCC;
                border-bottom: .1em solid #CCCCCC }
.SplitDay    { font-size: 8pt; font-family: Tahoma; text-decoration: none; color: teal }
.allDayEvent { font-size: 8pt; font-family: Tahoma; text-decoration: none; color: teal }
.ApptPast    { color: buttonface }
.NextAppt    { font-family: Marlett; font-size: 10pt; line-height: 12pt; font-weight: bold;
                text-decoration: none; color: darkred }
td              { font-family: tahoma; font-size: 8pt }
</style>
```

The Task Control

The data produced by Example 11.3 data binding is a listing of tasks from your Outlook's default Task folder, and is not properly formatted unless certain style sheet entries are added to the style sheet of this page.

Example 11.3   *Using a module to cause ActiveX control to provide a listing of tasks from your Tasks folder.*

```
<object id="TaskList" classid="CLSID:0468C085-CA5B-11D0-AF08-00609797F0E0">
  <param name="Module" value="Tasks">
</object>
<table border="0" name="TaskCol" cellspacing="0" id="TasksLiveTable" datasrc="#TaskList"
width="100%">
  <tr>
    <td width="1px"><input type="checkbox" dataformatas="Text" datafld="Complete"
height="20px" value="ON"></td>
    <td width="1px">
      <div datafld="Importance" dataformatas="html" class="TaskImportance">
      </div>
    </td>
    <td>
      <div datafld="Subject" dataformatas="html" class="TaskSubject">
      </div>
    </td>
  </tr>
</table>
```

The following code adds three styles to our sample page to provide proper formatting:

```
.OnGoing      { font-family: Marlett; font-size: 10pt; line-height: 12pt; font-
➥weight:bold;
               text-decoration: none; color: darkred }
.ImportanceIcon { font-family: Symbol; font-size: 11pt; font-weight: bold; text-
➥decoration: none;
               color: red }
.TskDone      { font-size: 8pt; color: gray; text-decoration: line-through }
```

The Messages Control

You might think that the name Messages implies that this module produces a view of your Inbox or other message folder, but instead it provides a list of the current unread count for a set of folders (see Example 11.4). The actual folders shown is determined by the values in the Registry key HKEY_CURRENT_USER\Software\Microsoft\Office\9.0\Outlook\Today\Folders.

Example 11.4   *Setting the Outlook Today ActiveX control to the newtoday.htm module outputs a list of folders, displaying the number of unread messages next to each.*

```
<object id="MailList" classid="CLSID:0468C085-CA5B-11D0-AF08-00609797F0E0">
  <param name="Module" value="Inbox">
</object>
```

continues ▶

Example 11.4 *continued*

```
<table border="0" name="MailCol" id="InboxLiveTable" datasrc="#MailList" cellspacing="0"
➥width="100%">
  <tr>
    <td align="left" valign="top" class="borderBottom">
      <div datafld="Name" dataformatas="html" class="Folder">
         
      </div>
    </td>
    <td nowrap valign="top" class="borderBottom" align="right">
      <div datafld="Count" dataformatas="html" class="InboxCount">
         
      </div>
    </td>
  </tr>
</table>
```

As per the previous data types, the formatting is not complete without the addition of several styles, listed here:

```
.borderBottom {      border-left: .1em none #CCCCCC;
                     border-right: .1em none #CCCCCC;
                     border-top: .1em none #CCCCCC;
                     border-bottom: .1em solid #CCCCCC }

.InboxCount   { font-weight: bold }
.InboxCountZero { font-weight: normal }
```

To complete this page, you might also want to add some headers above each section. Placing the three individual ActiveX controls' code snippets onto a page along with the combination of all the various styles that have been listed produces a functional Outlook Today page. The complete code, along with simple headers, is shown in Example 11.5 and is also available on this book's Web site at http://www.newriders.com/exch_prog.

Example 11.5 *Sample page illustrating a starting point for an Outlook Today page of your own.*

```
<html>

<head>
<title>Outlook Today Sample</title>
<style>h2           { font-family: Tahoma; font-size: 14pt; font-weight: bold }
a            { color: windowtext }
.CalendarSubjectLocation { }
.CalendarStartEnd { }
.itemNormal { font-size: 8pt; font-family: Tahoma; text-decoration: none; color:
windowtext }
.times       { font-size: 7pt; line-height: 11pt; font-family: Tahoma; text-decoration:
➥none;
             cursor: hand; color: buttonshadow }
```

```
.PastTimes    { color: buttonface; line-height: 11pt; font-size: 7pt; text-decoration: none;
                cursor: hand }
.SplitDayTimes { color: teal; font-size: 7pt; line-height: 11pt; text-decoration: none;
                cursor: hand }
.allDayEventTimes { color: teal; line-height: 11pt; font-size: 7pt; text-decoration: none;
                cursor: hand }
.itemImportant { color: red }
.dayHeaders   { font-family: Tahoma; font-size: 8pt; font-weight: bold; width: 100%;
➥height:
                100%; color: windowtext; cursor: default;
                border-left: .1em none #CCCCCC; border-right: .1em none #CCCCCC;
                border-top: .1em none #CCCCCC;
                border-bottom: .1em solid #CCCCCC }
.SplitDay     { font-size: 8pt; font-family: Tahoma; text-decoration: none; color: teal }
.allDayEvent  { font-size: 8pt; font-family: Tahoma; text-decoration: none; color: teal }
.ApptPast     { color: buttonface }
.NextAppt     { font-family: Marlett; font-size: 10pt; line-height: 12pt; font-weight:
➥bold;
                text-decoration: none; color: darkred }
td            { font-family: tahoma; font-size: 8pt }
.TskDone      { font-size: 8pt; color: gray; text-decoration: line-through }
.OnGoing      { font-family: Marlett; font-size: 10pt; line-height: 12pt; font-weight:
➥bold;
                text-decoration: none; color: darkred }
.ImportanceIcon { font-family: Symbol; font-size: 11pt; font-weight: bold; text-
➥decoration: none;
                color: red }
.borderBottom { border-left: .1em none #CCCCCC; border-right: .1em none #CCCCCC;
                border-top: .1em none #CCCCCC;
                border-bottom: .1em solid #CCCCCC }
.InboxCount   { font-weight: bold }
.InboxCountZero { font-weight: normal }
</style>
<meta name="GENERATOR" content="Microsoft FrontPage 4.0">
<meta name="ProgId" content="FrontPage.Editor.Document">
</head>

<body>

<h1 align="left">Sample Outlook Today Page</h1>
<object id="CalList" classid="CLSID:0468C085-CA5B-11D0-AF08-00609797F0E0">
  <param name="Module" value="Calendar">
</object>
<h2><a href="outlook:calendar">Calendar</a></h2>
<table id="CalendarLiveTable" border="0" cellspacing="1" cellpadding="2" valign="top"
➥width="100%" name="ItemCol" datasrc="#CalList">
  <tr>
    <td nowrap valign="top" width="10px" align="left">
      <div datafld="Next" dataformatas="html">
      </div>
    </td>
    <td valign="top" nowrap>
      <div datafld="StartEnd" dataformatas="html" class="CalendarStartEnd">
```

continues ▶

Example 11.5   *continued*

```
       
     </div>
    </td>
    <td valign="top" width="100%">
      <div datafld="SubjectLocation" dataformatas="html" class="CalendarSubjectLocation">
       
      </div>
    </td>
  </tr>
</table>
<object id="TaskList" classid="CLSID:0468C085-CA5B-11D0-AF08-00609797F0E0">
  <param name="Module" value="Tasks">
</object>
<h2><a href="outlook:tasks">Tasks</a></h2>
<table border="0" name="TaskCol" cellspacing="0" id="TasksLiveTable" datasrc="#TaskList"
➥width="100%">
  <tr>
    <td nowrap valign="top" width="14px" align="left"> </td>
    <td width="1px"><input type="checkbox" dataformatas="Text" datafld="Complete"
➥height="20px" value="ON"></td>
    <td width="1px">
      <div datafld="Importance" dataformatas="html" class="TaskImportance">
      </div>
    </td>
    <td>
      <div datafld="Subject" dataformatas="html" class="TaskSubject">
      </div>
    </td>
  </tr>
</table>
<object id="MailList" classid="CLSID:0468C085-CA5B-11D0-AF08-00609797F0E0">
  <param name="Module" value="Inbox">
</object>
<h2>Messages</h2>
<table border="0" name="MailCol" id="InboxLiveTable" datasrc="#MailList" cellspacing="0"
➥width="100%">
  <tr>
    <td align="left" valign="top" class="borderBottom">
      <div datafld="Name" dataformatas="html" class="Folder">
       
      </div>
    </td>
    <td nowrap valign="top" class="borderBottom" align="right">
      <div datafld="Count" dataformatas="html" class="InboxCount">
       
      </div>
    </td>
  </tr>
</table>

</body>

</html>
```

To make this your Outlook Today page, place this file onto your local machine and put its path into the URL Registry entry. This page is not a good replacement for the attractive pages that come with Outlook 2000, but it does provide a good starting point for your own development.

Folder Home Pages

Outlook 2000 takes the concept of Outlook 98, and the technology it provided, a step further with its folder home pages. This new feature allows any folder to be assigned a Web page URL, allowing you to use these folders to link to external Web sites or create customized Web views for individual folders. Like the Outlook Today page, these pages can contain anything that you can place onto the Web, which means that ActiveX controls, VBScript, Java, and many other technologies are available to the Outlook developer

The true value of this technology will be explained later in this chapter and Chapter 12, but for now only the basics will be covered.

Setting the URL for a Folder Home Page

Back in the "Outlook Today" section, we discussed how the current URL for that special folder was displayed on the Home Page tab of the folder's property dialog box. Unfortunately, the displayed value was read-only; we had to go to the Registry to edit the URL as needed. With folder home pages, luckily, the same dialog box is available, and you can do your editing directly in that dialog box. To try this out, simply right-click on a folder in Outlook (make sure the Folder List is visible, if it isn't already; to make it visible, select View, Folder List). From the menu that appears, select Properties. From the dialog box that appears, select the Home Page tab (see Figure 11.6).

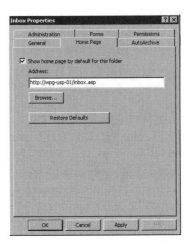

Figure 11.6   *For any folder except the Outlook Today folder, the Home Page tab can be used to set or change the URL for that folder's Web view.*

On this page, you can set or change the URL for the folder home page and also choose whether that home page should appear by default when a user selects this folder (using the check box above the URL). You can either enter the URL manually or use the Browse button to search for the desired page. The final, extremely convenient, button on this page is Restore Defaults, which sets everything back to the standard Outlook setting.

There are a few important things to note about these settings. First, they are stored in or with the folder itself, not in the Registry as with Outlook Today. Next, they are not limited to HTML files; you can set them to any file or Web path. Finally, keep in mind that these folder home pages are not limited to your own personal folders; they can be set for any folder, including those in PSTs and in the Public Folders store. If you set a home page URL for a public folder, because it is stored with the folder instead of just on your machine, anyone who views that public folder can see the same home page. Experiment a little with this technology, set home pages for some of your personal folders, and if you have rights to edit a public folder, try setting some of this information on a folder that is accessible to multiple people.

Building a Folder Home Page

With regard to technical issues, building a page for use as a folder home page is identical to building one for use as an Outlook Today page. You can even use the same ActiveX controls on both types of pages. However, from a design standpoint, there are more differences between the two items. Outlook Today is a single location designed to summarize all of a person's Outlook information, but every individual folder can have a distinct folder home page, and those pages should be designed to reflect the distinct content of that specific location. This is difficult to do using the controls provided with Outlook Today, but a new control that comes with the Team Folder Kit (discussed in the section "Setting Up a Team Folders Solution") makes it much easier. For the purposes of experimentation, stick with the same ActiveX controls and example HTML as shown in the Outlook Today section and use the same page as your sample folder home page.

Browser Technology Differences

When the Outlook developers integrated Web browser technology into their product, they didn't have to work from scratch. They took advantage of the existing Internet Explorer product; because of this, your pages can include script, Dynamic HTML, and all the other features supported by this browser. Interestingly though, they did not use Internet Explorer directly; they performed certain customizations and built the result directly into Outlook. This means that (in Outlook Today) there are a few minor differences between how it and IE work. One key example of this is security settings. Security is ignored for the Outlook Today page set in the Registry, although it is in effect for any page visited after that initial URL. This security problem is a legitimate worry and causes a great deal of stress to most network professionals, but it is not a problem with folder home pages other than Outlook Today. These other home pages use IE directly, simply hosting that browser within the Outlook window, and therefore behave exactly like that browser and obey all of its security settings. It is possible to make Outlook Today behave this way, but it involves changing another Registry setting, which might not be a simple matter in every situation. The Registry changes required are detailed in the following list:

- Add a new subkey to your Registry at HKEY_CURRENT_USER\ Software\ Policies\Microsoft\Office\9.0\Outlook\Webview\mailbox
- Under this key, mailbox, add the following string values: "url" and "navigation"
- Set "url" to the path to your new Outlook Today page and "navigation" to "yes"

In addition to making Outlook Today use the full Internet Explorer security functionality, this overrides any value specifying in the URL key under HKEY_CURRENT_USER\Software\Policies\Microsoft\Office\9.0\Outlook\ Today. As mentioned earlier, making a Registry change on each and every user's machine is often not desired, and such a change is required to set Outlook Today and fix this security hole. For this reason and others, setting a folder home page on a public folder is a much simpler method of providing a customized Web view to your users. More information on this and other deployment suggestions will be provided in the next chapter.

Team Folders

The concept of folder home pages is quite powerful, but it is hard to know where to start with this new technology. Microsoft makes it a little easier by providing one ready-made solution that is built around Exchange public folders and these folder home pages. This solution, team folders, provides a set of features that are designed to be useful to any workgroup or project team. The specific elements provided by the Team Folder Wizard in its canned form are as follows:

- Team Contacts
- Team Calendar
- Team Tasks
- Discussion Folder
- Shared Document Folder

In essence, the wizard creates a public folder with five subfolders (actually six—there is one for administering the set of folders), but the real value is in the fact that the wizard provides a Web view into this information in the form of a folder home page (see Figure 11.7).

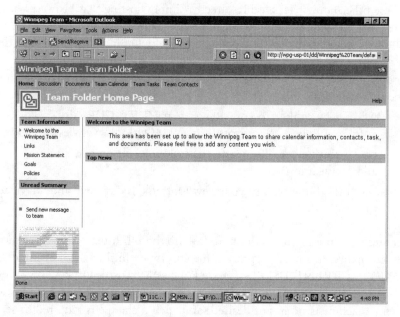

Figure 11.7 *The home page of a team folder solution shows various team messages along with an introduction to this particular set of folders.*

Setting Up a Team Folders Solution

To set up team folders, you must have the Team Folder Kit installed, although you do not need the kit to use the resulting solution. This kit is available for free download from Microsoft at `http://www.microsoft.com/exchange/Collaboration/TFWizard.htm` and is also available on the Digital Dashboard Starter Kit CD (discussed further in Chapter 12). In addition to this kit, you must also have sufficient permissions to create the main team folder and the required subfolders in your public folder tree, because those folders are created as a part of running the wizard. As the wizard runs, you need to make the following choices, so have this information ready:

- A name for your team folder (for example, Winnipeg Team).

- A public folder to create your solution under, in which you have sufficient permissions to create new folders.

- A Web-server of some sort to place the associated Web pages onto; you must have sufficient rights in this location also.

You also have to choose what type of team folder to create—either a complete team folder with all the features described earlier in this chapter or any one of those features on their own. This means you can either create a Team folder, a Team Tasks folder, a Team Calendar folder, a Team Contacts folder, a Discussion folder, or a Documents folder. It is possible to add choices to this wizard, as part of customizing it for your company or group, as discussed a later in this chapter in the section, "Customizing Team Folders."

The Outlook View Control

The biggest difference between the Web views of your team folder and the Outlook Today pages is that the team folder Web pages include a regular Outlook view (of contacts, messages, calendar info, or tasks) as a part of the page itself (see Figure 11.8 for an example of this control displaying one of the many possible views).

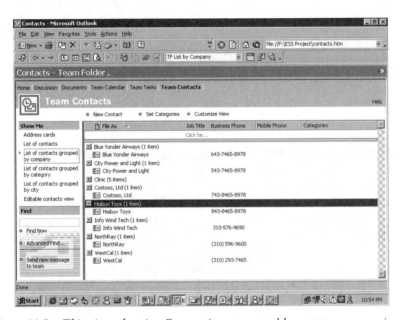

Figure 11.8   *This view, showing Contact items grouped by company name, is one of hundreds of possible views that can be shown in the Outlook View Control.*

This feature, provided by an ActiveX control called the Outlook View Control, allows you to have the full functionality of the regular Outlook interface right in your Web page. This includes the visual appearance, capability to select columns, support for all the built-in and user-defined views, drag-and-drop repositioning of columns, grouping features, and all the other impressive user interface features present in Outlook. When you realize that this includes not only the columnar style views but also the specialized views for Contacts (see Figure 11.9), Task, and Calendar (see Figure 11.10) folders, you can really see the power of this control.

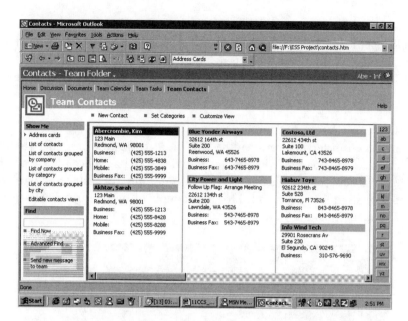

Figure 11.9 *Even non-columnar views, like this address card view of a Contacts folder, are available in this ActiveX control.*

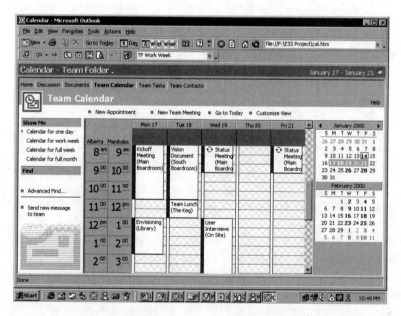

Figure 11.10 *The Calendar views are available as well; this control is the same functionality as in the rest of Outlook, simply moved into a control you can use in a Web page.*

This ActiveX control opens up many possibilities for custom Outlook Today and team folder pages, as it provides a way to display the actual contents of any personal or public folder. The code required to use this control in your page is, as for any ActiveX control, made complex by the inclusion of the control's class id. But after you have used it in one page, you can simply cut and paste it as needed. The basic HTML required to place the control on a page and have it display the contents of your Inbox is shown in Example 11.6.

Example 11.6   *Tells the browser which control to load, and various property settings for initializing it after it is loaded.*

```
<object classid="CLSID:0006F063-0000-0000-C000-000000000046"
   id="InboxView" width="100%" height="430">
  <param name="View" value="Messages">
  <param name="Folder" value="Inbox">
  <param name="Namespace" value="MAPI">
  <param name="Restriction" value="[Importance]=HIGH">
</object>
```

Save Time With the Front Page 2000 Add-ins for Digital Dashboards

Although retyping the preceding code into your own page isn't that complicated, it is easier if you install the Digital Dashboard Starter Kit (detailed further in Chapter 12). Placing this control onto your page is as easy as clicking a menu option in Front Page 2000. The Starter Kit installs this and several other useful features into both Outlook and Front Page, making your Web page development as simple as possible. ◆

This code sets the required properties of the control, Folder and Namespace. These properties tell it which particular folder to display and what messaging system is providing that folder (always MAPI), respectively. It also demonstrates several of the additional properties that can be set—View tells the control which built-in or user-defined view to use, and Restriction specifies a filter to control which items are shown in the control. These properties can also be modified dynamically at run time through the use of VBScript or Jscript as a part of your Web page. This type of flexibility, especially with the View and Restriction properties, allows you to provide a variety of links on your page that change the view settings or apply a particular filter to the folder contents. This type of manipulation is accomplished through the name given to the control by its ID attribute (InboxView in the previous example) and the use of some client side code. Example 11.7 shows an example of this type of functionality. Four buttons have been created above the control using text strings, and each of those four buttons, when clicked, manipulates the settings of the control in some way. This page, set as the Web view for an Outlook folder, is shown in Figure 11.11.

Example 11.7   *Creating four control buttons to demonstrate setting manipulation.*

```
<p>
<font face="arial" size="2">
<span id="button1" onclick="InboxView.View='Messages';InboxView.Restriction='';">
Messages</span>¦ <span id="button2" onclick="InboxView.View='Unread Messages';">
Unread </span>¦ <span id="button3" onclick="InboxView.View='By Sender';">
By Sender </span>¦ <span id="button4"
onclick="InboxView.Restriction='[Importance]=HIGH';">
Important Messages Only</span></font><br>

<object classid="CLSID:0006F063-0000-0000-C000-000000000046"
 id="InboxView" width="100%" height="430">
  <param name="Folder" value="Inbox">
  <param name="Namespace" value="MAPI">
</object>
</p>
```

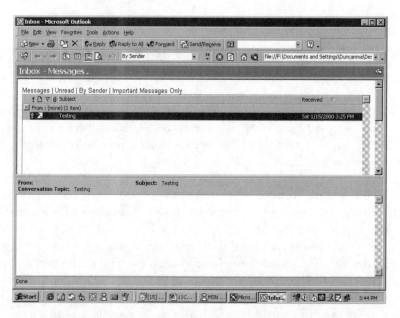

Figure 11.11   *The Outlook View Control provides a perfect set of functionality for use on a folder home page.*

The control itself exposes many more properties and methods, all accessible from script on the same Web page, making it a single method to access almost any Outlook functionality you need on your page. This includes the capability to create new mail messages, calendar entries, and more, but this chapter does not provide full documentation on this control. Everything you need to know about the Outlook View Control is provided in the help files that are installed as part of the Team Folder Kit.

This control, combined with the folder home page technology we have been discussing, makes it possible to create the team folders. This leads us to the concept we will cover in the next chapter: the Digital Dashboard.

Customizing Team Folders

Although the appearance and functionality of the Team Folder Kit is excellent right out of the box, you might get more out of it if you can perform a little customization. You can do this either after the wizard has run or by using the wizard's templates to design a modified version of these folders to be used every time the wizard is run. The best type of customization for you depends on your purpose—Are team folders going to be established as needed by each department or team, are you going to be setting up just one, or is every project going to have one? If you are setting up just one, or if the customization is different for each one you set up, you can work with the existing files; however, if you intend to produce more than one team folder, all with the same customization (your company colors and logo, for example), you should to customize the wizard itself.

To customize the finished product, all you need to do is open up the HTML files and edit them as you see fit. This is suitable for making minor modifications without having to worry about the intricate details of how these pages work. All you need to do is be careful to confine your editing to the formatting of the page, most of which can be edited by modifying the style sheets (*.CSS files) that the wizard copies along with the HTML files and that those HTML files refer to. Of course, edits to the page are often necessary, but be careful to edit only the text. The page is quite complex internally, so unless you feel up to it, restrain your edits. This type of modification can produce fairly nice results, such as the custom appearance (see Figure 11.12) for an ImagiNET style team folder.

To create a custom team folder type, the process is more involved. You need to create a special PST file containing the folders that will be copied (such as the Contacts, Calendar, Task, Discussion, and Documents folders created by the default wizard), a set of HTML pages that will be used as the Web view(s), and a special INI file (TEMPLATE.INI) that defines the various settings and parts of your custom team folder type. More details on how you do this are provided by the documentation installed with the Team Folders Kit, along with a sample PST file, Web pages, and INI file to speed you along in creating your custom team folder type. After you have created and registered (see the help file for more information) your custom creation, it appears in the wizard as a type of team folder that can be created, as in Figure 11.13.

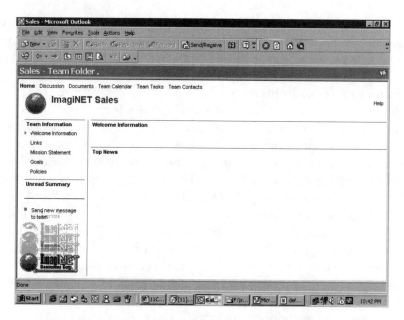

Figure 11.12 *This is the result of several small modifications to the DEFAULT.HTM and CSS.CSS files created by the Team Folder Wizard.*

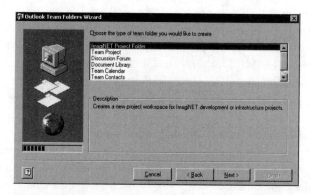

Figure 11.13 *By creating your own custom team folder types and allowing anyone to quickly create their own instance of a team folder personalized to your company, you can increase the value of the Team Folders Kit.*

The most complicated type of customization you can accomplish with this kit is usually done in conjunction with the custom team folder type, adding your own step or steps to the Team Folder Wizard. This, a customization that requires writing your own COM DLL (usually in VB), allows you to obtain any special information from the user that your custom type of team folder needs. This can range from something as simple as displaying a code name for your team when someone views the folder's home page to entering a project code that allows your team folders to pull information from a corporate database system. Figure 11.14 shows an example of such an extension, which appears just before the final confirmation page of the regular Team Folder Wizard, that has pulled a list of project codes from a central database and allows the user to pick one of those codes or create a new project code altogether.

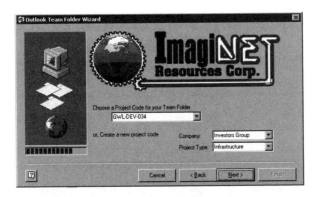

Figure 11.14   *The Team Folder Wizard can be extended, allowing you to insert one or more steps into the existing flow.*

The Team Folder Kit is a perfect example of a quick-fix type of solution that you can customize to a variety of levels, depending on the effort you are willing to put forth for the task. You should install this kit, if only for the documentation it provides to you about the Outlook View Control, but you or your company will likely find a use for the default team folders or, better yet, for a customized version of them.

Chapter Summary

The integration of the Web into Outlook 2000 might seem like a small feature—a bit of flashy Web stuff added into the interface—but it is a whole lot more. With the combined power of the Outlook Today and Outlook View ActiveX controls, along with whatever else you can do using regular Web technology (Java, VBScript, DHTML, ASP!), it is possible to add spectacular functionality to this product. You have already seen some of what is possible through the provided (and custom) Outlook Today pages and in the form of team folders, but the best is yet to come. A new technology (okay, it's just a new application of existing technology, but why be picky?) called the Digital Dashboard is being showcased by Microsoft, and the next chapter will cover that in detail. Continue along and we will teach you everything you need to know to start building your own version of this exciting new application of Outlook 2000's Web integration.

12

The Digital Dashboard

The previous chapter introduced the Web integration features in Outlook 2000, folder home pages, and Outlook Today. When combined with the two different ActiveX controls that are available, the Outlook Today data binding control and the Outlook View Control that comes with the Team Folder Kit, it becomes possible to create powerful Web views into your Outlook information. This Web view has been dubbed the digital dashboard by Microsoft, a term that seems quite appropriate after you have interacted with a finished version of such a system.

In this chapter, we will cover the following:

- The digital dashboard, what it is and why you want to have one
- Building a dashboard, from the basics to advanced concepts
- Deploying a dashboard to your users, what options you have and which one you should choose

By the end of this chapter, you will walk through the creation of your first dashboard and see many advanced possibilities to get you started on a full dashboard for yourself.

Overview of Digital Dashboards

The purpose of a digital dashboard is to provide an at-a-glance view of information to users, like a driver gets from an automobile dashboard or a pilot receives from an airplane's instrument panel in the cockpit. The Web view technology in Outlook 2000 is perfect for that purpose, allowing you to expand on the concept of Outlook Today to provide even more information in a single view. A screenshot of a sample dashboard is shown in Figure 12.1; this one is part of the Digital Dashboard Starter Kit.

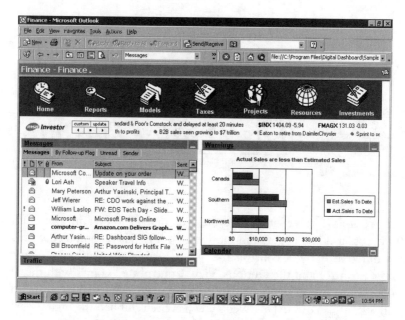

Figure 12.1   *A digital dashboard, like this one, includes
a variety of information on a single page.*

The Digital Dashboard Starter Kit

*In addition to several sample dashboards, the starter kit includes documentation
and tools that are essential to building your own dashboard. You can order or
download this kit by visiting* http://www.microsoft.com/DigitalNervousSystem/
km/DDSK.htm, *a site that also includes additional information on the dashboard
concept. The rest of this chapter assumes that you have downloaded and installed
this starter kit, if you plan on following along with the sample code and procedures presented.* ◆

Dashboard Content

A dashboard is ideally made up of the following types of information:

- Personal data, like the user's calendar, email, and tasks

- Corporate information, company news, and resources, as in online
  Human Resources and vacation functions

- Workgroup or team collaboration, data tailored to the individual and
  his department or project, such as project status or shared contacts

- External information, taking advantage of the Web to bring in information on competitors, news feeds, stock data, and links to related
  Web content

Of course, you do not need to include everything, and you might have some additional ideas for content, but these preceding four areas are the targets of most dashboards. It is the integration of the first item, personal data (from Outlook), that differentiates a dashboard from just another Web portal (like msn.com, or my.yahoo.com) by providing the user with his own email and other data. If you stop at that point though, you aren't exceeding the basic functionality of Outlook Today by much, and so you build in the other content to increase the usefulness of your dashboard to the user. The following sections go into more detail on each of the four key information types in a dashboard.

Personal Data

This is the first thing you usually put into a dashboard, because it is readily available from Outlook and all of the tools needed to get at and display that data are provided to you. The two key tools for this work are the ActiveX controls that were discussed in the previous chapter, the Outlook Today Control and the Outlook View Control. There is a certain amount of overlap in these two controls, giving you the choice of displaying the user's task and calendar information using either one. The proper choice depends on the effect you want, the fully featured Outlook view or the more aesthetically pleasing HTML view provided by the Outlook Today controls. There is no right answer, but I personally prefer the HTML view and use it whenever I can. With these two controls, you can provide the user's inbox, contacts, calendar, tasks, and a listing of unread messages in a variety of folders, as shown by the Inbox listing in Figure 12.1.

A combination of these will likely be used; keep in mind that the goal of the dashboard is to provide a single location for the user to work and that should guide your decision on what information to include.

Corporate Information

This is where it starts to get interesting, bringing company-wide data right into Outlook for the user, removing the need to go into six different locations just to find current information. This can take many different forms, depending on the company's existing systems. If there is already an intranet set up, that is likely your first place to look. As a dashboard is Web based, anything that is up and running on a company's internal Web site(s) should be easily brought into your system.

Linking to existing corporate applications, data warehouses, and shared documents also falls under this category and can take a variety of forms in your dashboard. You could provide a Pivot Table view into a data warehouse (refer back to Figure 12.1 for an example of using the Office Web Components for linking to corporate data), use the Outlook View Control to display the contents of an Exchange public folder holding shared documents, or perhaps build a Web interface into the company's service access point (SAP) system. The possibilities are really limitless, but they are dependent on the infrastructure of the company. The difficulty is usually not in getting the data from the corporate systems into your dashboard, but in those systems themselves.

Start small and pick your components based on the return on investment you will receive by incorporating them into the dashboard. If you pick the system that there is the most demand for, you can come back and work on integrating the lower priority systems at a later date. Do not hold back on rolling out something simply because you want to build everything or nothing. What you are trying to achieve is momentum; make the dashboard useful and there will be support to add features to it.

Workgroup or Team Collaboration

In many ways, this type of data is related to the previous item, but it is tailored to a single department, project, or role of employee. This could take many forms, such as shared public folders for each group or filtered data from corporate information systems (sales information for the group's region or product). The common element is that the data should be specific to the user and his job in the company, which involves knowing exactly who the user is (see the "Personalization" section later in this chapter). Within the Winnipeg team of Microsoft, we have chosen to use the Team Folder Kit to provide this type of functionality in our dashboard (see Figure 12.2).

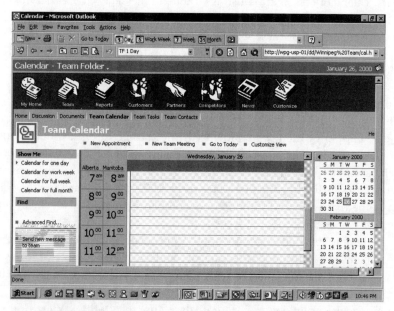

Figure 12.2   *Although team folders can exist on their own, they also can make up part of a digital dashboard.*

Other useful functions could focus on the collaboration between members of a team. This could include quick links to send email, schedule appointments, or for real-time communication methods like MSN Messenger (http://messenger.msn.com) or Microsoft NetMeeting.

External Information

The final type of content that is usually found in a dashboard is information from the Web or other external sources. This can include competitive information (see Figure 12.3), news (on the company, its competitors, or the industry in general; see Figure 12.4 for an example), stock quotes, and/or links to any useful information on the Web.

Figure 12.3   *Providing direct access to competitors' Web sites makes it easy for the user to stay on top of the industry.*

Incorporating this information into a dashboard page is very easy. You can use a link or take advantage of an interesting HTML tag (<IFRAME>) that allows you to embed a Web page as a scrollable frame anywhere within another page. The dashboard pages in Figures 12.3 and 12.4 both use this technology to incorporate other Web content.

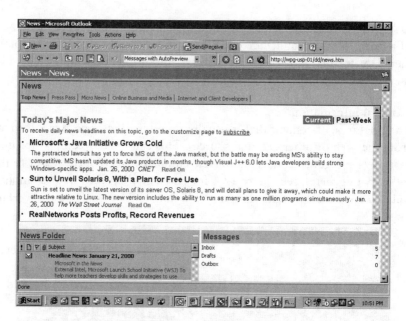

Figure 12.4 *News is available from a wide variety of sources, and bringing that information into a single location makes it much more useful.*

Dashboard Structure

After you have determined the content of your dashboard, the next decision is how to present it. Remember that dashboards are Web pages; they can be laid out in any way that Internet Explorer allows (including use of Dynamic HTML and scripting). The point of a dashboard is to provide a single view into a large set of useful information, so keep simplicity in mind as you design your interface.

Multiple Pages Versus One Page

Dashboards are designed to provide an at-a-glance view, which implies a single page, but the screenshots shown throughout this chapter all show dashboards with a navigation bar across the top allowing movement between a set of pages. This is not required, but it is often necessary to avoid cluttering a single page beyond the point of usability. Ideally, you want all the information presented in a single page, easily read with minimum scrolling (nuggets are designed to help accomplish this ideal and are described in the next section), but it is difficult to meet those goals. Splitting the content across multiple pages and providing a navigation bar to move from one to another allows you to have simpler individual pages at the cost of overall simplicity. The way you build your dashboard depends on your content choices, but keep usability in mind at all times.

Nuggets

To avoid clutter and keep the page(s) simple, developers created a common interface across the sample dashboards. Individual sections of content, such as a user's calendar or a chart view of this year's sales, are identified using common headers (refer to Figure 12.3 to see this concept in use). These pieces of content, or nuggets as they are referred to in the dashboard documentation, are designed to be independent of the rest of the page. This independence allows them to be treated like components. They can be developed, tested, used, and reused without concern for the rest of the page. Content is divided at the page level and then again at an individual nugget level. Finally, the nuggets help to simplify the interface by each having a minimize button, allowing individual nuggets to be independently shown or hidden (leaving only the header visible). In Figure 12.1, for example, the chart and the Inbox are the only nuggets visible, but there are several more on that page, all minimized. In the section "Basics of Building a Dashboard" you will learn how to build these nuggets for yourself, including the Dynamic HTML required to show and hide the nuggets' content.

Common Dashboard Components

There are no rules about what you put into a dashboard—your content should be whatever is useful for you—but many dashboards are based on the samples in the starter kit and contain certain common elements. Consider these to be canned nuggets (no, it's not a new type of snack food) that you can quickly use in your dashboard without much customization (if any). Some of the sample nuggets include the following:

- Calendar
- Inbox
- Tasks
- Traffic cams (not very useful in Winnipeg, we don't even have a freeway)
- The MSN Investor Stock Ticker (shown in Figure 12.1)
- Embedded Web pages, like MSNBC
- A weather map or current weather conditions
- Custom views into a folder of Office documents (see Figure 12.5 for an example from the Healthcare sample dashboard)

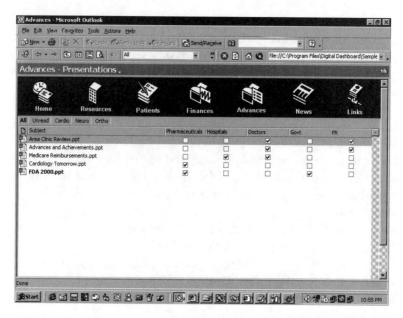

Figure 12.5   *You can use Outlook's built-in features combined with the Outlook View Control to create a useful nugget that shows shared Office documents.*

The power of the nugget style interface is very apparent when you need to reuse some content. Each nugget can (if designed correctly) be used independently of the rest of the page. You likely can even find some complete nuggets available from outside your organization, either given away by helpful developers or for sale.

Basics of Building a Dashboard

Now that we have covered the concept and purpose of a dashboard, it is time to learn how to build one. This dashboard starts off as a single page, with very basic functionality to illustrate the techniques involved. This sample dashboard shows you how to make nuggets, use the COM add-ins provided by the Digital Dashboard Starter Kit, and how to use some Dynamic HTML to implement the show/hide functionality of the sample dashboards (see Figure 12.6).

The four elements of creating a dashboard that will be covered in this section are creating the layout, inserting the proper controls (using the COM add-ins supplied by the starter kit), structuring the nuggets for ease of use and reuse, and using a combination of script and the features of Dynamic HTML (DHTML) to implement the show/hide functionality for your nuggets. At this stage in learning how to build a dashboard, we won't use a

Web server; we will simply use FrontPage 2000 to create pages in a regular file location (on your hard drive, for instance). Before you can follow all the parts of this section, make sure that you have downloaded or ordered the Digital Dashboard Starter Kit and that it is installed on your machine.

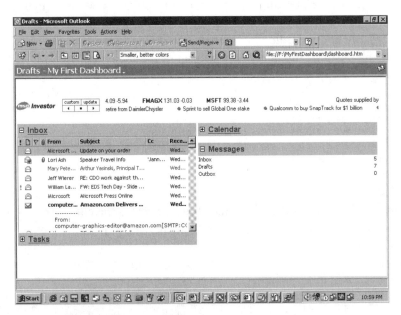

Figure 12.6   *If you follow along with this chapter, you will produce a dashboard like the one shown here.*

Layout

The most consistent element in most dashboards being created these days is the layout—a navigation bar across the top followed by a stock ticker and two columns of nuggets on the page. This is not required, but it is a nice layout, so I will show you how to duplicate it. Please remember though, that you can arrange your dashboard any way you like, making it perfect for your information and your users.

To achieve the layout just described, you need to use a large table with two columns (each set to occupy 50 percent of the page width) to hold the various nuggets, and anything you want to stretch across the entire page is placed outside and above that table. Making this layout starts your page off, so you should open FrontPage 2000 and make sure that a new blank HTML page is open. (This is the default when you open FrontPage; an empty page called new_page_1.htm is created.) If you don't get a new page, click the New Page icon on the toolbar to make one. Before you go ahead with any work on this page, save it to your hard drive with an easy-to-remember path (such as C:\dashboard.htm). First, you need to put something across the top of this page. Because you are building a single page, you will not be using a navigation bar, so you can go right to the next element from all your samples, the MSN Investor Stock Ticker.

It is possible to install this ticker using FrontPage's menu options, but the resulting code would not be as complete as you might desire. Instead, you can simply add the following HTML into the page (using the HTML view, available through the tabs at the bottom of the page), between the <BODY> and </BODY> tags:

```
<p>
<object id="TickerObj"
 type="application/x-oleobject"
 classid="clsid:52ADE293-85E8-11D2-BB22-00104B0EA281"
 codebase="http://fdl.msn.com/public/investor/v7/ticker.cab#version=7,1999,0803,1"
 width="100%" height="34">
</object>
</p>
```

This produces a ticker control that stretches across the entire page (width="100%") and is 34 pixels high (height="34"). At this point, switch back to the normal view and your new control should be on the page and working (it might need to be installed first). Step one of building your digital dashboard is complete.

Intranet Considerations

When using a public ActiveX control like the stock ticker and Internet access is not, or will not be, available to your users, you should download the .cab file indicated in the preceding HTML to some local path. Please note that this is the method you should use whenever you are referencing the file location for an ActiveX control and Internet access is not available; but in this case, the ticker does not work without the Internet. The control installs successfully (if you move the .cab file and change the codebase attribute) but does not download any information. ◆

Now, you need to create the table to hold your two columns of nuggets. Creating a table can be done in many ways, but for now let's stay directly in the HTML. You can, of course, use the various tools of FrontPage 2000 to do many of these things; feel free to experiment with them as you want.

Below the ending </P> tag that you added for the ticker control, you create a table that takes up the full page width and has one row and two columns (which each take 50 percent of the table's width):

```
<table width="100%">
  <tr>
    <td width="50%">Column 1</td>
    <td width="50%">Column 2</td>
  </tr>
</table>
```

Now, the dashboard is almost complete (Figure 12.7 shows what the page should look like), except for the nuggets you need to add, which are simple to add using the Component Object Model (COM) add-ins that the Digital Dashboard Starter Kit has installed into FrontPage 2000.

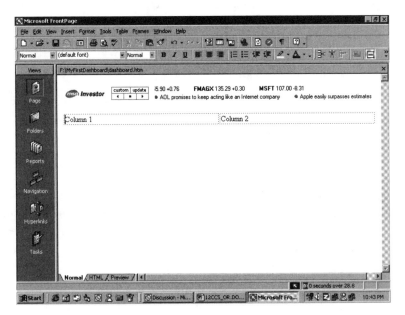

Figure 12.7   *With your ticker in place and the table created, the dashboard is almost ready to go.*

Using FrontPage 2000 to Add the Outlook Controls

Adding the standard Outlook-orientated nuggets to your dashboard page couldn't be easier; simply insert them using the nice menu options in FrontPage 2000. The Digital Dashboard Starter Kit has added a new menu item to the Insert menu—Outlook Controls. Under this menu item, you have four options, all three of the possible uses of the Outlook Today Control and the versatile Outlook View Control. Adding any of these items is as simple as selecting the area of the page where you want the nugget to be added and then clicking the menu option. The effect of all of these new menu options is to insert the appropriate HTML text at the current cursor position into the document. In addition, the Outlook View Control menu item also brings up a dialog box (see Figure 12.8) prompting you to choose at which Outlook folder the control should be pointed.

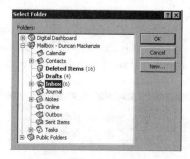

Figure 12.8   *When inserting the Outlook View Control onto your dashboard page, you have to pick an Outlook folder for the control to view.*

This helpful bit of functionality sets up the parameters of the control appropriately for that folder. For all four options, you will experience better results if you already have Outlook running in the background, which avoids it having to be loaded by the control itself.

For your sample dashboard, we will use these commands to add four nuggets to the page, the Outlook View control pointing at the user's inbox, and then all three types of HTML controls (calendar, tasks, and unread messages). The two nuggets that you should be most interested in are the Inbox and the Calendar, so they each go at the top of a column. For this example, follow along and do the steps, but in your dashboards, you can make your own decisions about where to place each nugget.

To get started, place the cursor in front of the C in Column 1. Now, select Insert, Outlook Controls, Outlook View Control from the menu. The folder selection dialog box appears (it might be hidden underneath FrontPage, in which case the taskbar button for Microsoft Outlook blinks and clicking it brings up the dialog box). Select your Inbox folder and then click OK. This adds the Inbox nugget to your page. We will look at the code it has added a little bit later, but for now simply notice that (in addition to the control itself) it has added a header bar. The nugget might seem too wide, but this is because it is set to a percentage; it appears correctly when it is viewed. On the other hand, its height is set to a static value (430 by default) and appears the same in Outlook as in FrontPage, so adjust the height as you see fit. To change it to a value (200, for example), you can right-click on the control in the Normal view of FrontPage and select the ActiveX Control Properties menu item, or you can look within the <OBJECT> tag in the HTML view. In either case, you see an attribute called Height with a value of 430; change this to 200 (if you are using the dialog box, click the OK button to finish).

To insert your second nugget for this column, carefully select the text Column 1 and then select Insert, Outlook Controls, My Tasks from the menu to add the Outlook Today style Task listing to the page. Moving on to the second column, place your cursor before the Column 2 text and select Calendar from the Insert, Outlook Controls menu. Finally, select the Column 2 text and insert the New Messages nugget. At this point, you have a functional digital dashboard page (see Figure 12.9), but it needs a bit of work to tidy up what the controls inserted and add the fancy hide and show functionality for each nugget. If you want to view your page in action, make sure you save the file, switch to Outlook, and set some folder's home page to your new page.

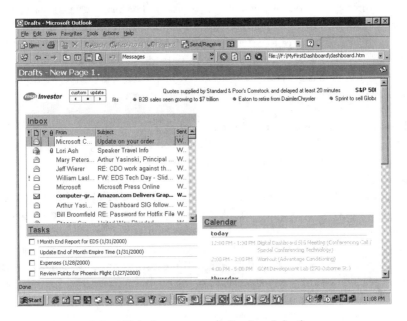

Figure 12.9 *With the structure defined and the four nuggets added, your dashboard page is up and running.*

Proper Nugget Structure

As you can see on your own machine, or later in Figure 12.11, the dashboard needs a bit of work. First, there are the obvious problems: the page title is still New Page 1, and the top two nuggets are not lined up (they don't both start at the top of the column). These problems are easily fixed: the title attribute can be changed through the File, Properties menu option, and the alignment issue is because the columns are set to center align vertically (the default), which can be fixed by adding valign=top within the <TD> tag for each column. These are the easy problems; however, there are a couple more that require you to go into the HTML of the page.

Relative Folder Paths

When the Outlook View Control nugget is added to the page, you select your Inbox as the folder that it should display. This selection is used in two ways: to create the link used in the nugget's header and as the folder parameter for the object itself. If you look at the HTML that is inserted into your dashboard, you will find one reference to \\Mailbox - <your name>\ Inbox in the header and no folder path in the control's parameters at all. The first reference is a problem. It refers specifically to your Inbox and does not work for any other user that uses this dashboard; the lack of a reference in the control is due to the fact that the default value for that parameter is the user's Inbox, and so it is deemed unnecessary. The proper value for each location should be a simple reference to Inbox (outlook:Inbox for the URL in the header), which indicates the default Inbox of the current user and works for anyone. The control ends up with these path issues whenever you select a folder within your own mailbox, but it has the correct settings if you are selecting a folder in the Public Folders store.

Duplicate and Missing Style Entries

For proper display of the three Outlook Today controls, certain styles have to be defined in your page. Without them, the controls produce very unappealing results. The COM add-in handles this issue when inserting a control by adding all the required styles into a <STYLE></STYLE> block at the top of your page. This is quite useful, because you can edit these styles to control the appearance of the Outlook Today controls. The problem is that the COM add-in inserts them every time you add another control, which means that by the time you finish your page, three copies of the style entries have been placed within your page. To fix this problem, switch to HTML view, scroll up to the top of the page, and remove all but one <STYLE></STYLE> block. The other problem with the style entries added by these COM add-ins is that they miss a few important styles in the process. This can result in an incorrect display of some items, such as overdue tasks. Fixing this requires the addition of the missing styles, all of which can be found in the sample Outlook Today pages included on this Book's Web site. The simplest method for adding in all the styles, if you haven't customized the styles yourself yet, is to copy the entire <STYLE> block from the Outlook Today page and replace your dashboard's style block with it.

Picky Details

Looking at the HTML, there are few more things I would change, even though they do not affect the functionality of the page in any way. I won't cover all of these items, but here is one good example: whenever the Outlook View Control is inserted onto a page, it is placed within a table that starts off with a tag of <table table table>, which can be shorted down to just one table. Most of the other items I would change are designed to make it easier to access the nugget when doing script and are therefore covered in the next section (where you will learn how to use script to show and hide your nuggets).

Implementing the Show and Hide Functionality

A very distinctive interface feature of the digital dashboard concept is the capability to minimize or roll up each individual nugget so that only the header information is visible. This is designed to allow more information to be placed on the page without causing clutter and overwhelming the user, and it works quite well. The sample dashboard created in the preceding sections doesn't have this feature, so we will add it to complete the job. Adding this feature, and the associated graphics, to your page seems like a complex and daunting task, but it can be made much easier by breaking it down into several smaller and simpler tasks.

Break That Big Project Down!

The technique we are using to build this dashboard, re-describing a task in terms of the many smaller tasks that make it up, is not a new idea (divide and conquer), but we often forget to do it even when we know it makes the work easier. Computer programming tasks often seem daunting, which can make it hard to know where to start, so I always approach a new problem in this way and then work on each item as if it is a task of its own. ◆

For this particular problem, we will follow the divide and conquer approach and work on the problem one step at a time. There are several different stages that make up this task, as listed here:

- Run code as a result of clicking an area of the dashboard
- Hide an area of the dashboard from code and show that same area again
- Be able to consistently identify the header and content areas of a nugget
- Make the code generic so that it can be used for all your nuggets on all your dashboards
- Use an image to indicate the action desired (show/hide) and change that image when you change the nugget's state

It is not necessary to follow through the steps in order, simply work on them one at a time.

Making Your Nugget Clickable

First, you need to make something to click on in the header of the nugget, eventually a minimize picture, but text will do for now. Before you do too much within your page, I'll let you in on a little hint: Turn on the automatic HTML formatting in FrontPage 2000 (Tools, Page Options, HTML Source tab) and you'll find the HTML much easier to understand and work with. Let's work with the first nugget, the Inbox nugget, and add some text into the header so that you can click on it, as follows.

```
    <table border="0" width="98%" cellspacing="0" cellpadding="0" align="center">
      <tr>
        <td width="100%" valign="top" bgcolor="#B5C7DE" style="padding: 4"><b>
<a href="outlook:Inbox"><font face="Arial" size="3" color="#4A3C8C">Inbox</font></a></b>
        </td>
        <td width="20%" align="right" valign="top" bgcolor="#B5C7DE" style="padding: 4">
          Show/Hide
        </td>
      </tr>
      <tr>
        <td width="100%" colspan=2>
          <object classid="CLSID:0006F063-0000-0000-C000-000000000046"
id="ViewCtlFolder" width="100%" height="200">
            <param name="View" value="Smaller, better colors">
            <param name="Folder" value="Inbox">
            <param name="Namespace" value="MAPI">
            <param name="Restriction" value>
            <param name="DeferUpdate" value="0">
          </object>
        </td>
      </tr>
    </table>
```

The modifications made to this nugget have added a Show/Hide bit of text to the header bar. To make this work, notice the colspan=2 on the <TD> tag that contains the control. Due to the fact that there are now two columns in this table, you must specify when you want a single column to span across the entire table. Now, with your new text in place, you need to specify some code to run when it is clicked, which you do with an onclick event attribute added to the <TD> tag that surrounds your new Show/Hide text. When scripting Web pages, any tag on the page can have a name (using the ID attribute) and can have code associated with it (using event attributes like onclick). In this case, you start by adding a call to a simple JavaScript function called alert, which simply displays a message. A snippet of HTML follows, showing the modification:

```
<td width="20%" align="right" valign="top" bgcolor="#B5C7DE" style="padding: 4"
onclick="alert('Hello!');">
Show/Hide
</td>
```

Save the file and switch to viewing it in Outlook to try out this modification. Whenever you click the Show/Hide text, a message appears saying Hello! Although you haven't achieved your end result, you are a lot closer; you have an area of the dashboard that you can click and run some JavaScript code in response to that click. To take this a little further, you need to replace your simple Hello! code with JavaScript that hides the Inbox nugget, which leads you to the next task, naming areas of your page.

Referencing Sections of a Web Page by Name

As mentioned a little earlier, any area of a Web page can have a name (specified by an ID attribute on the tag). This name is especially useful when you want to manipulate the corresponding area of the page, because it gives you a way to refer to that section in your code. A name can be assigned to any tag, but there is not always a set of tags that surround the exact section of the page that you need to refer to, which is why HTML provides the <DIV></DIV> tags. These special tags can have an ID attribute, and therefore can be referenced in code, but they do not have any effect on the text they are placed around. This behavior means that you use these tags throughout your page to simply identify key areas of the page's content without worrying about its effect on the page's appearance. In the case of the Inbox nugget, you can place a <DIV></DIV> set of tags around it and give the entire nugget a name. The HTML for the nugget, with these new tags in place, is shown here:

```
<div id="InboxNugget">
    <table border="0" width="98%" cellspacing="0" cellpadding="0" align="center">
        <tr>
(Rest of Inbox Nugget goes here!)
        </tr>
    </table>
</div>
```

Now, you can refer to this particular section of the page in your code by using the name InboxNugget.

The Style Attribute, Dynamic Formatting Changes

With the nugget's name in place, it is possible to use a script to hide this nugget when the user clicks the Show/Hide text. All elements in a Web page, including the block of text represented by a set of <DIV></DIV> tags, have a style attribute that has a set of its own attributes controlling various aspects of its formatting. One of those style attributes is called display, and it can be used to hide the entire element through a setting of none. To hide the InboxNugget, you could replace the onclick code (the "alert('Hello!');" text) with the JavaScript shown here:

```
"document.all.InboxNugget.style.display='none';"
```

Save your dashboard page and refresh the view in Outlook to see the result this produces—it is close, but not quite perfect. As it is, this code hides the entire nugget, including the header bar. You need to identify the area to be hidden as a subset of the entire nugget. This can be accomplished by another set of <DIV></DIV> tags—this time around only the <OBJECT> tag for the Outlook View Control and with an ID of Contents. Now, you can modify the JavaScript to refer to document.all.InboxNugget.all.Contents and you get the result you want—the nugget's contents are hidden and the header bar is left visible. The next thing to worry about is the fact that the nugget can be hidden, but it can't be shown. Fixing this requires a bit more code than you have been dealing with, which means that you should probably switch to calling a procedure from your onclick event and having that procedure defined elsewhere on the page. The new procedure you create consists of an IF statement that is used to toggle the nugget's visibility when called. The procedure itself, which can be placed anywhere on the page but is usually placed at the very bottom or the top of the page, is listed here:

```
<SCRIPT language=VBScript>
Sub ToggleNugget()
Dim oNug
Dim oContents
    Set oNug = document.all.InboxNugget
    Set oContents = oNug.all.Contents

    If oContents.style.display = "none" Then
        oContents.style.display = ""
    Else
        oContents.style.display = "none"
    End if
End Sub
</SCRIPT>
```

Replace the onclick code with ToggleNugget() and then save and reload in Outlook. You will find that it functions properly. However, the appearance could be improved with some extra work, such as the following:

- Change the Show/Hide text to Hide and assign an ID of MinimizeButton to the <TD> that surrounds it.
- In the ToggleNugget procedure, add code that sets the innerHTML of the MinimizeButton object to Show when you are hiding and Hide when you are displaying.

Now, when clicked, the code sets the text to the appropriate value. It displays Hide when the nugget is visible and Show when it has been hidden.

Turning Nugget-Specific Code into a General Use Routine

Your code is becoming more and more functional, but it is not very generic, because the InboxNugget is named in the ToggleNugget procedure. You can make it very generic with one modification: Pass the nugget into the procedure instead of specifying it in the procedure. The modified ToggleNugget code is shown here:

```
<SCRIPT language=VBScript>
Sub ToggleNugget(oNug)
Dim oContents

    Set oContents = oNug.all.Contents

    If oContents.style.display = "none" Then
        oContents.style.display = ""
    Else
        oContents.style.display = "none"
    End if
End Sub
</SCRIPT>
```

Now, with the onclick code changed to ToggleNugget(InboxNugget), you have truly generic code. You can use that same routine for every nugget on the page. To complete this code, all you really need to do is replace your text minimize button with an image. To accomplish this final step, replace the text with a picture, such as one of the GIF files that comes with the sample digital dashboards. Next, give the new <IMAGE> tag a name, like ButtonPic, so that it can be referred to in your code. Finally, modify the ToggleNugget routine to change the SRC attribute of this element between two images (one for minimize and one for show) in place of the lines that currently switch between Show and Hide. A completed version of this routine is in Example 12.1 as a part of the sample layout.

A Consistent Nugget Structure

The previous sections have slowly converted the nuggets from their default state into something that allows for easy management and has the added functionality you need. All of the changes are spread throughout the section, but Example 12.1 illustrates the key elements that you need to create for each of your nuggets.

Example 12.1   *Nugget templates illustrating a very consistent and structured way to create your dashboard code.*

```
<!--- Begin <Nugget Name> --->
<div id="<Nugget Name>">
    <table border="0" width="98%" cellspacing="0" cellpadding="0" align="center">
```

continues ▶

Example 12.1 *continued*

```
      <tr>
          <td width="100%" valign="top" bgcolor="#B5C7DE" style="padding: 4">
          <b><a href="<URL for Nugget>">
          <font face="Arial" size="3" color="#4A3C8C">Nugget Display Name</font>
          </a></b>
          </td>

          <td id="MinimizeButton" align="right" valign="top" bgcolor="#B5C7DE"
          style="padding: 4" onclick="ToggleNugget(<Nugget Name>)">
          <img id=ButtonPic border="0" src="images/close.gif" width="17" height="13">
          </td>
      </tr>

      <tr>
          <td width="100%" colspan="2">
              <div id="Contents">

                  <!--- Section of Nugget to be hidden when minimized --->

                              </div>
          </td>
      </tr>

  </table>
</div>
<!--- End <Nugget Name> --->

<SCRIPT language=VBScript>
Sub ToggleNugget(oNug)
Dim oContents
Dim oButton
Dim oPic

    Set oContents = oNug.all.Contents
    Set oButton = oNug.all.MinimizeButton
    Set oPic = oButton.all.ButtonPic

    If oContents.style.display = "none" Then
        oContents.style.display = ""
        oPic.src = "images/close.gif"
    Else
        oContents.style.display = "none"
        oPic.src = "images/open.gif"
    End if
End Sub
</SCRIPT>
```

The ToggleNugget procedure only appears once per page, but the nugget structure outlined by this listing is used for each nugget on the page. The comments in the preceding template serve a very useful purpose. Beyond simply increasing the readability of your final page, they clearly define the start and finish of each individual nugget. This clear delineation of content makes it simple to copy a single nugget out of one page and place it into another.

To complete your sample dashboard, you must modify all the other nuggets on your page to include the minimize image in the header and the appropriate code in the nuggets' onclick events.

Originality in a Dashboard

The capability to show and hide each individual nugget is a key element of a dashboard. It is one of the things that differentiates a dashboard from the regular Outlook Today pages. Although that is certainly true, it doesn't mean that you need to always use this feature, or that you have to implement it in the same way. Always keep in mind the purpose of this feature, to reduce clutter and to keep the critical information viewable in a single page. If you have a better way to accomplish this, or perhaps your page isn't cluttered (even with all the nuggets visible), use your own judgment on what features to include. In addition to choosing if you are going to include this minimize feature, you can also choose to implement it in different ways, such as using a different picture for the minimize button. The dashboard shown in Figure 12.6 uses plus and negative signs (like in a tree view) to indicate that the nugget is being expanded or collapsed; this is different from the starter kit dashboards like the one shown in Figure 12.1. You can produce a unique look with minor modifications, and that takes your dashboard one step farther away from the canned demo version.

Advanced Dashboard Work

The previous sections walked you through the creation of a simple digital dashboard, but that is not the limit of this technology. In fact, due to the way in which this technology is provided, there are few limits to what you can do. Building on the features of Web browsers, Outlook, and the power of scripting languages (like VBScript) that can call COM objects, you can make a digital dashboard do almost anything. This section will guide you through some bits of information that will allow you to start customizing and expanding on your dashboard(s).

Linking to Outlook Folders and Items

A common element on your dashboard is hyperlinks from the dashboard to Outlook folders or a specific Outlook item (like an appointment, email message, or a task), functionality that is already part of the HTML generated by the Outlook Today Control. If you want to add this type of hyperlink yourself, you need to know how to format it so that the correct item is opened.

When linking to a folder, the syntax is simple: outlook://<folderpath>. Certain special folders can be referenced using just a name, such as the user's default inbox (outlook:inbox), calendar, tasks, and other pre-defined items, but you must supply a full path to all other folders. Linking to items is a little more complex. You have two different options for referring to a specific Outlook item—by using a path or the item's Entry ID. The preferred method is to use the Entry ID, but it is not very easily done when making a link by hand. Referring to an item by path means that you have to specify the path to the folder that contains the item, followed by the item's display name (which is the subject for an email message, task, or calendar entry, but is the display name for a Contact item)—for example, outlook:inbox/~Hello. This link opens up the first message in the Inbox with a subject line of Hello. This method of referring to items is simple to understand but not very precise. You don't really know which item it is going to open (another message could come in with that subject line at any time). The other method of referring to an item is, as mentioned earlier, difficult to work with when creating links manually because it consists of nothing humanly readable in the link. This type of reference uses the item's Entry ID (which every Outlook item has) to form the URL, as in the following link:

```
outlook:EF000000198262C0AA6611CD9BC800AA002FC45A060000000100000003BF89DFA00100000
➥C030C04
```

This link is precise. It refers to one and only one item. To create links of this sort, you need to programmatically work with the item so that you can simply write out the value of the item's Entry ID as the link. If you are generating a page from code, this is the method you should use for producing links, just like the Outlook Today controls do.

Accessing CDO and Outlook from Within Your Dashboard

Sometimes being able to link to items and display the various Outlook controls is not enough. You want to be able to get deeper. The key to a large amount of advanced functionality in your dashboard is to get access to the complete Outlook object model from script code running on your page. The Outlook object model, covered in MSDN and in the help files that ship with Office 2000 Developer Edition, gives you access to a wide variety of information including all the folders, items, and address lists, everything you need to build some advanced features into your page. Using this object model from your script is quite simple, because you can get at the object model's topmost object (Outlook.Application) through the window.external. OutlookApplication property. After you have this object, you can get at any other information you need by working your way through the object hierarchy. One use of this access to the Outlook object model is to obtain the user's name, which is available through the Namespace object's CurrentUser property. Example 12.2, which requires a <DIV> block on your page called UserName and another one called dateScript to work properly, uses this property to get the user's name and display it on your dashboard page.

Example 12.2   *The CurrentUser property returns a Recipient object representing the user's information.*

```
Sub UpdateName
 Dim objOutlook
 Dim sName

 Set objOutlook = window.external.OutlookApplication
 sName = objOutlook.GetNamespace("MAPI").CurrentUser.Name
 document.all.UserName.innerText = sName

End Sub

Sub UpdateDate

 document.all.dateScript.innerText = FormatDateTime(Now(),1)

End Sub
```

Although the Outlook object model provides a great deal of functionality, you might want to use CDO instead for some of your dashboard features. CDO, which is covered in Chapter 8, "Visual Basic, CDO, and MAPI," and Appendix A, "The CDO Object Model," provides an alternative method for many of the Outlook object model's capabilities along with a number of unique features. CDO is implemented as a COM library, which means that you can access it from VBScript just like any COM object, using the CreateObject function. This function works the same in your script as it does in a VBA or VB program and returns a reference to the specified COM library. The code shown in Example 12.3 demonstrates how to obtain an instance of the CDO library, log in (specifying NewSession:=False so that the MAPI session that has been created by Outlook is reused by CDO), and access some CDO properties.

Example 12.3   *Using the CDO library from your dashboard page.*

```
Set objSession = CreateObject("MAPI.Session")

objSession.Logon ,,,False

sName = objSession.CurrentUser.Manager.Name
document.all.ManagerName.innerText = sName
```

With CDO, Outlook, or some combination of the two object models, you can build complex connections between your dashboard and the user's Outlook/Exchange data.

Saving/Retrieving User Preferences

A required feature of most user interfaces, at least those that are well designed, is the capability to remember the user's preferences from one use to the next. In the case of most applications, this covers things from option settings to the position of windows. In the case of a digital dashboard, the first thing a user expects to be remembered is the state of the nuggets, which ones are visible and which ones are hidden. All the sample dashboards that come with the starter kit provide this functionality, but the one we have been building in this chapter does not. You need some way to store this information (the state of the nuggets and any thing else you need to keep track of) on a per user basis. Regular Windows applications that need to accomplish this task use the Registry to store their settings, because it is a per-user location designed for just that purpose. Fortunately, the people designing the Web view interface into Microsoft Outlook took this need into account and have provided two useful functions, GetPref and SetPref, which are methods of window.external. GetPref takes a setting name (not a full path to a Registry entry, just the value as all settings get stored into the same location HKEY_CURRENT_USER\Software\Microsoft\Office\9.0\ Outlook\ Today\<setting name>) as a parameter and returns that key's contents; SetPref takes two parameters, the value name and the value itself, and saves the setting into the Registry.

To use these commands to save and restore the state of the nuggets on your dashboard, you need to add code to two places. First, you need to add code to save a nugget's state to the ToggleNugget procedure you placed at the end of your dashboard. Then, you must create a procedure that runs when the page is loaded, goes through each nugget on your page, and sets the visibility of that nugget based on the previously saved setting. The modified ToggleNugget procedure and the appropriate page setup code are listed in Example 12.4. These procedures create dynamic names for the state of each nugget using the nugget's name and the page title. As long as you use unique page names, you can keep track of the state of any number of nuggets on many different pages. Before the new code will work, though, you need to modify the main <DIV> tag of each of your nuggets to look like <div id=InboxNugget class="Nugget">. By adding a class attribute to a nugget's surrounding <DIV> tag, you can use that value to identify each individual nugget on your page (as shown in Example 12.4).

Example 12.4 *Initializing the state of the page so that your dashboard remembers how the user left it.*

```
<SCRIPT language=VBScript>

RestoreState

Sub RestoreState()
On Error Resume Next
Dim oTag
Dim sValueName
Dim sValue

  For Each oTag in document.all
    if oTag.tagname="DIV" then
     if oTag.classname="Nugget" then

      sValueName = "DD_CONTENT_" & document.title & "_" & oTag.id
      sValue=window.external.GetPref(sValueName)

      select case sValue

        case "show"
         oTag.all.Contents.style.display=""
         oTag.all.MinimizeButton.all.buttonpic.src = "close.gif"

        case "hide"
         oTag.all.Contents.style.display="none"
         oTag.all.MinimizeButton.all.buttonpic.src = "open.gif"

      end select

     end if
    end if
  next

End Sub


Sub ToggleNugget(oNug)
Dim oContents
Dim oButton
Dim sValueName

      Set oContents = oNug.all.Contents
      Set oButton = oNug.all.MinimizeButton
      sValueName = "DD_CONTENT_" & document.title & "_" & oNug.id

     If oContents.style.display = "none" Then
         oContents.style.display = ""
         oButton.all.buttonpic.src = "open.gif"
         window.external.SetPref sValueName, "show"
```

continues ▶

Example 12.4   *continued*

```
    Else
            oContents.style.display = "none"
            oButton.all.buttonpic.src = "close.gif"
            window.external.SetPref sValueName, "hide"
    End if

End Sub
</SCRIPT>
```

Saving the state of your nuggets is not the only thing that you can use the Registry for. There are many settings in a dashboard that you will want to persist between views of your page, and these functions make that easy.

Personalization

Dashboards are automatically more personalized than most Web pages. They show the user's email, personal calendar, task list, and more. However, that isn't the limit of the personalization you can do, and the more you can tailor your page to a specific person (or his department, role, city, or other distinguishing piece of information), the more useful your dashboard is likely to be for him. How do you personalize content? Well, the first step is figuring out what information you want to use to do your customization, whether that is the user's name, department, title, location, or even employee ID. After you have made that decision, you need to get at that piece of data from your page. The simplest place for you to find the information is from within the Outlook object model, if it is available. This involves getting the information from the Global Address List (GAL), assuming that information has been entered into that system, and relying on the accuracy of that entry. If the data is there, retrieving information from the fields of the GAL is not complicated. Example 12.5 shows how to pull the user's name, department, office location, and title from his address entry.

Example 12.5   *Using CDO to obtain personal information for use in your page(s).*

```
Sub Personalization()
Dim objSession
Dim objAddressEntry
Dim sDepartment
Dim sOfficeLocation
Dim sTitle

Set objSession = CreateObject("MAPI.Session")

objSession.Logon , , , False
```

continues ▶

```
Set objAddressEntry = objSession.CurrentUser

sDepartment = objAddressEntry.Fields(974651422).Value
sOfficeLocation = objAddressEntry.Fields(974716958).Value
sTitle = objAddressEntry.Fields(974585886).Value

document.all.userinfo.innerHTML = "<p>" _
        & sDepartment & "<br>" _
        & sOfficeLocation & "<br>" _
        & sTitle & "</p>"
End Sub
```

If, for whatever reason, the information you want is not in the GAL, you might have to do more work before you can start modifying the data to fit the user. This other work can involve connecting to a company database or other back-end system, but I promise it won't be as simple as using the built-in feature of Outlook/Exchange.

Regardless of how you get the piece of information you need, after you have it, you can start customizing the dashboard appropriately. The possibilities for personalization are as varied as the number of different companies that might use this technology. Some of the simpler ways to personalize the data are as follows:

- Place the user's name or other information onto the page (like the earlier example that put up the date and the user's name).
- Provide a nugget filled with links to external Web sites, the links displayed depending on department or role. (Managers have different needs and interests than programmers; Sales have different needs and interests than Accounting.)
- Completely remove or add a nugget (or nuggets) based on title or department (show the Microsoft Developers Network search nugget on the programmer's dashboard but hide the Sales Forecasting nugget).
- In a multi-page dashboard, selectively build the navigation bar to provide access to pages that are tailored to the user.

Exactly what you do to personalize your pages is dependent on your company, but if you like the concept and want to take it further, take a look at the example of advanced personalization (using ASP and a back-end database) that is discussed in the "Back-End Databases" section.

Creating More Nuggets

To get the most out of your digital dashboard, you need to bring more information into this single location. This is referred to, by some people who feel a strong need to name things, as "nuggetizing" another system or data source. The specifics of doing this depend on the information, but a large amount of the corporate systems you want to integrate fall into one of several key categories (described individually in the following sections) and therefore match up with one of several suggested nuggetizing methods.

Back-End Databases

The data you want is often stored in some corporate database—for example, Oracle, SQL Server, or Sybase. To bring this information into your dashboard, you have to choose between one of four common choices:

- Link the database (using OLE DB) into an Office Web component (like a chart or pivot table; see Figure 12.10 for an example).

- Create an ASP interface into the data and view that ASP page in an IFRAME on your dashboard.

- Using JDBC, or similar technology, create a Java applet that links to the database.

- Create a custom ActiveX control that uses ADO/OLE DB to link to the database.

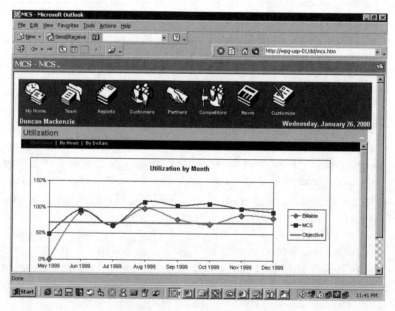

Figure 12.10   *This Office Web component is used in conjunction with an Active Server Page (ASP) to display information from a SQL Server database.*

Whatever method you choose to connect to the data, your goal is simple—if you can get the data onto a Web page, you can get it into a dashboard with minimal difficulty.

Legacy Applications

Legacy is a term with a wide variety of meanings (I have even seen it applied to mean Windows 95). But in this section, I use it to indicate applications that run on a company's mainframe or older UNIX systems and are, therefore, accessible only through certain restricted interfaces. In such situations, the choices are usually more limited than for databases (discussed earlier)—either use terminal emulation (that is, 3270 software) or build an alternative interface (for example, COM or Java) that links up with the mainframe system using Systems Network Architecture (SNA) or other connectivity software. Again, if you can somehow get the information/ interface you need onto a Web page, you are 99 percent of the way to getting it into a dashboard.

COM Applications

If the application or data that you need is available through a COM interface, you are in a great position to bring it into your dashboard. VBScript on your page is capable of creating and using COM objects directly, meaning that you can connect to the appropriate object(s), use properties and methods to get the specific data you want, and then display in a nugget environment. My own personal digital dashboard does just what I am describing. It uses the exposed COM interface of MSN Messenger (http://messenger.msn.com) to retrieve all sorts of information. The resulting nugget, as shown in Figure 12.11, uses the information available through the COM interface to display a listing of my contacts, including who is online and their status (idle, busy, out to lunch, and so on).

Code on my page also takes advantage of the COM interface to do more than just get data; it also uses methods of the Messenger object to make things happen. If I click the name of someone who is online, it starts up a Messenger chat session with that person; or if that someone is offline, it opens up a new email message pre-addressed to that person. In your case, Messenger might be a good choice, but any application that exposes COM objects will do. You might think that this type of link is limited to Microsoft applications (which almost all expose a COM interface), but many companies see COM as a good linking tool. A good example of this is SAP. SAP's system, which might be running on a large UNIX server in your company, provides a tool (the DCOM Connector) that exposes a COM interface into its business information. You can link to that information and create nuggets that provide a view into SAP or perhaps allow the user to interact with the system. Of course, because SAP has a database engine, you can also use OLE DB (or any one of the many possible database related tools) to connect it to your dashboard.

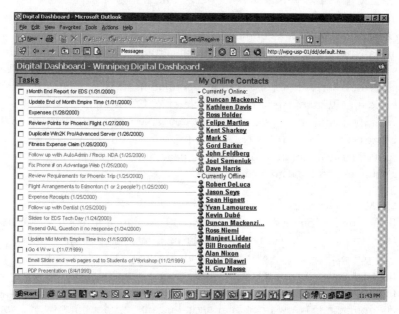

Figure 12.11   *Using COM, many applications can be integrated directly into your dashboard, increasing the usefulness of this single interface.*

Integration with Team Folders

Team folders and digital dashboards are two implementations of the same concept using the same technologies, identical except for the exact template of appearances and their intended purposes (one serves as the focus point for a team, the other is a portal page for an individual user). It is not surprising that the two can be easily integrated. Figure 12.2 shows a portion of the Microsoft Winnipeg's digital dashboard. One of the links on the navigational toolbar is labeled Team, and this is where it takes you. The team folder you see on the page is, aside from the addition of the navigation bar along the top, no different than any other such folder created by the Team Folder Wizard. All that is required to accomplish this integration is to create the team folder as normal and place a link to that public folder in your dashboard's navigation bar. Usually, you create the team folder in a sub-folder of a main dashboard folder and place the Web pages onto the same Web server as the pages used by the rest of the dashboard, but none of that is required; it is merely common practice.

Using ASP with a Digital Dashboard

Dashboards consist of two main parts—the Outlook folder they are attached to and the Web pages that form their interface. Those Web pages can be files on your hard drive, files on a Web server, or ASPs. ASPs are server-side scripts that, when requested by Outlook or another browser, are executed by the Web server and the results returned. To the browser, this looks like any other Web page, but it provides you with the ability to write code into the page that runs at the server, not at the client. In the world outside of digital dashboards, a major advantage of this technology is that (although it is producing dynamic content that can be different every time the page is refreshed) the pages it returns can be browser independent. In the context of building your dashboard with ASP, the advantage is having the page do all sorts of complex things (querying databases, using COM objects, talking to Exchange, or connecting to SAP), without being dependent in any way on the user's machine. All the work is done at the server.

The ways in which you can use this technology together with the digital dashboard concept are so many and varied that there is no point trying to cover them all. Instead, I will detail a single possible use for the convergence of the two technologies—a user based, dynamic, database generated digital dashboard. In this system, each individual nugget is stored as a record in a database table. A relationship is set up in the database linking groups of nuggets to a specific NT user ID. Every single person's dashboard folder (public folder or local) is pointed to the same ASP file on your Web server. That ASP file grabs the user's ID (easily done in ASP using the header information that browsers pass when they request a page) and uses that ID to query the database. Then, the retrieved data (consisting of all the nuggets that have been associated with the current user) is used to build a complete digital dashboard page. The completed page is returned to the user and displayed, with absolutely no connection between the user's machine and the database required.

This system might sound complicated, but it consists of only one Web page and a simple database with two or three tables (a table of nuggets and a table that links user IDs with nuggets while also specifying the desired position of the nugget on the user's page). The execution of the server-side code is much faster than you might expect, but consider that it is running in close proximity to the database server and on a machine that is likely dedicated to the task of serving out Web pages. This is a theoretical system at the moment, but you could take this concept, refine it, add to it, and then build it for your company's use.

Deployment

After you have designed your dashboard, a critical issue is determining how you will get it out to the users. This isn't really an issue if you are working on a dashboard for yourself, so this section is aimed at corporate or work-group development.

When deploying a digital dashboard, you need to worry about the following three things:

- Setting the required Folder Home Page/Outlook Today options for each user.
- Making the HTML files available to every user.
- Making the Exchange content available (folders for shared contacts, documents, and so on).
- Ensuring that the entire dashboard can go offline and be used by a roaming user.

The first problem comes into play with the Outlook Today settings. These settings, including URL, are stored on a per-user basis on each user's machine. To set everyone's Outlook Today to point at your custom page requires making that change on all of those computers. In a system you are deploying out to your entire company, this is much more complex and high maintenance than you want. The Web view settings for a public folder, on the other hand, are stored with the folder. This means that if you set the Web view of a public folder to http://myserver/dashboard.htm, every single user who can see that folder will be shown that same page.

This brings us to the second issue, making those Web files available to every user. The Digital Dashboard Starter Kit stores all of its HTML files into a directory on your hard drive, then points folders to that path. But that location is not suitable when working with a multiple-user dashboard. You need to place the files somewhere where they are accessible to everyone, and the perfect place is an internal Web server. Web servers are designed for this purpose—to give access to HTML documents—and they are very good at it. Placing the files onto a Web server has many side benefits, including the availability of ASPs (which cannot be used without some form of Web server). Create a sub-directory of your company's internal Web server, or set up a server just for this purpose, and then place the pages themselves along with any supporting files (script files, images, and so on) onto the server using FrontPage 2000 or through FTP.

Now you have a public folder set up with a home page setting that points to an accessible internal Web server. The next item of concern is easily solved—where do you put any Exchange data that is required by the dashboard, like shared contacts? Following the example of the Team Folder Wizard, you can create a set of sub-folders underneath the single main Digital Dashboard folder and use them to store all the information you need. You could have these folders scattered all over and still use them from your dashboard, but keeping them all under a single main folder makes the solution to the final issue, accessibility to offline users, much easier.

Offline use is a big feature of Microsoft Outlook, and it wouldn't be right to build a beautiful dashboard as a feature of Outlook and not make it available to disconnected users. Fortunately, the same features that allow Outlook to take your email and calendar offline also work for digital dashboards. The first thing you have to do is add the main Digital Dashboard public folder to your Favorites folder. This can be accomplished manually by selecting the folder and then the File, Folder, Add to Public Folder Favorites menu option. This brings up a dialog box that specifies how you want this folder to be added (see Figure 12.12), makes sure you expand the options section, and makes your choices as shown in the figure. When you do this, all the current and future sub-folders of this folder are automatically part of your Favorites. Adding the folder to your Favorites means that you can sync those folders down for use in Offline mode, but it has to be done for each user individually. (This is not really controllable from the back end.) It makes everything simpler if you can automate it, which we will cover a little later. After you have done that, you can set offline settings for these folders that control how and when they are synchronized for disconnected use.

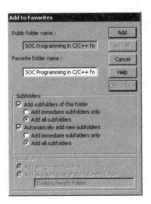

Figure 12.12   *After you select the Add to Public Folder Favorites menu option, you are presented with a dialog box that allows you to specify a different name for the folder in your Favorites and various options regarding sub-folders.*

With a multi-page digital dashboard, there are links from each page to others. In such a case, there are two things for you to remember. The first thing is to refer to each folder using its Public Folder Favorites path, which allows a single path to work when you are offline or online. The second thing is to always link to the other folders of your dashboard, not the other pages (that is, outlook://Public Folders/Favorites/Dashboard/Contacts instead of `http://myserver/dashboard/contacts.htm`). The reason behind the second requirement is difficult to explain; suffice it to say that if you link directly to the page, Outlook can treat the page as if it is a regular page and not a folder home page. This potential issue, which is due to the way in which the embedded browser functions, can cause the Outlook View Control and certain scripting functions not to work.

Finally, you will find that the preceding issues are not the only deployment problems you run into when trying to roll out a dashboard to a large number of users. Assuming that you do not limit yourself to the provided Outlook controls only, your page can have a variety of setup/installation requirements. Those requirements, along with the need to add your dashboard into the Public Folder Favorites folder, lead to the creation of a special Setup page for your system. This page, which is usually set as the home page of a sub-folder of your main dashboard folder, consists of mostly script, and when it is viewed, it uses that code to carry out its required installation requirements. The sample setup page in Example 12.6 adds the dashboard folder to the user's Public Folder Favorites, removing the need for the user to perform that task.

Example 12.6   *A setup page is the installation program of your dashboard, it is responsible for setting up all the individual Registry entries and other settings required by your system.*

```
<h1>Welcome to the Prairie's BSG Digital Dashboard Setup Page</h1>
<p>This page is currently performing all of the required setup for you to use
the Prairies BSG Digital Dashboard. Specifically, it is:
<ul>
  <li>adding the entire BSG Public Folder hierarchy to your Favorites
</ul>
When the phrase &quot;Complete!&quot; shows up at the bottom of this page, the
operations have completed...
<p>To use the Digital Dashboard, simply click on the <b>BSG</b> folder in your
&quot;Public Folder Favorites&quot;.
<p>Good luck!<br>
<a href="mailto:arthurya">Arthur</a>
<div id="pageStatus">
</div>
<br>
```

```vbscript
<script language="vbscript">
  Dim oApplication
  Dim myNS 'As NameSpace
  Dim myFolder 'As MAPIFolder

  document.all.pageStatus.innerHTML = "<center><b>Please wait...</b></center>"

  set oApplication=window.external.OutlookApplication
  Set myNS = oApplication.GetNamespace("MAPI")
  Set myFolder = myNS.Folders("Public Folders")
  Set myFolder = myFolder.Folders("All Public Folders")
  Set myFolder = myFolder.Folders("Arthur").Folders("Dashboards")

  myFolder.Folders("BSG").AddToPFFavorites

  document.all.pageStatus.innerHTML = "<center><i>Complete!</i></center>"

</script>
```

This particular code snippet comes from a fellow named Arthur Yasinski, but similar code has been written for a variety of dashboards. The code on this page is the minimum required to set up your particular folder, but you might need to add more setup tasks depending on the contents of your dashboard. You can even use a setup page to force the pre-install of any ActiveX controls that exist on your page, simply by placing those controls onto this setup page.

Chapter Summary

Digital dashboards are not new ideas, they are an evolution of the Web portal and corporate portal concepts—a single interface that empowers users by giving them all the information and tools they need in one location. Regardless of the history, this is a good idea, and the digital dashboard is a powerful implementation of the concept. By combining the personal information of Outlook along with team, corporate, and/or external features you can make users more efficient and effective in their work. Build yourself a beginning dashboard right away and start planning a production dashboard. This is a high profile, high-value project, and you don't want to miss the opportunity.

13

Designing and Building Tracking Solutions

In this last part of the book, Part III, "Putting the Pieces Together—Developing Collaborative Solutions," I will present the evolution of a collaborative solution that will encompass most of what has been presented up to this point in the book. In this chapter, I will focus on building the first release of this solution, which is responsible for tracking a corporation's client contacts.

The following scenario outlines what you will build in this chapter. ImagiNET Resources Corp. employs a number of sales people responsible for the acquisition of new business and the maintenance of existing clients. ImagiNET has grown considerably over the last three years and is now in dire need of a new Sales Contact Management and Order Entry System. ImagiNET Resources has a number of extremely talented developers on staff who are currently between projects, so ImagiNET has decided to build its own solution to best match its current needs. By developing an in-house solution, ImagiNET can utilize staged releases, adding new functionality at each release while maximizing the usage of each component as it is released.

The first release of the Sales Contact Management and Order Entry System (SCOES for short) will focus primarily on a contact management solution tailored to the ImagiNET's sales staff. Additionally, the order entry component's design is well underway and will be built upon a SQL Server 7.0 database.

To determine the needs of the resulting contact management solution, the developers staged a number of design meetings with ImagiNET's sales team. The developers quickly arrived at the following design goals:

- The sales staff wants a way to specify which sales person is assigned to which client.

- The sales staff wants to use Microsoft Outlook and Microsoft Word exclusively to manage and send correspondence to their many assigned clients. The sales staff wants to use Outlook for the following reasons:

  All members of the sales staff are proficient users of Outlook and do not want to relearn how to use another contact management application.

  The sales staff appreciates the tight integration that Outlook has with the rest of the Microsoft Office suite of products. The sales staff finds it extremely easy to right-click a contact from a Contacts folder to create a message, task assignment, appointment, or journal item associated with that contact.

  Everyone in Sales uses folder views to organize, sort, and filter contact information, and they do not want to switch to other methods.

- All of the sales people have mobile computers and must have the ability to work with their client information offline. They want to have the ability to add, delete, and modify client information offline and, when online, have their changes automatically propagated to everyone else in the organization.

These goals weren't quite what the developers were expecting because the order entry component had already been designed around a SQL Server database for efficiency and performance reasons. To accommodate both ImagiNET's sales force's requirements and the order entry design, the developers decided to take the following steps to arrive at a solution for Release 1 of SCOES:

1. Create a Client Contacts public folder to house the client contact information required by ImagiNET's sales force. Additionally, a Client Activity Journal public folder will be created to maintain client journal entries.

2. Customize the built-in Contacts form to capture and display client information in a format that would best suit the sales staff. This new form, called Client Contact, would then be the default post form for the new Client Contacts public folder.

3. Create an event scripting agent to handle one-way synchronization of contact information from the Client Contacts public folder to a SQL Server database.

4. Finalize the Microsoft Outlook client components, such as creating the appropriate views and configuring the new folders for offline use.

So get comfortable, sit back, put up your feet, and let me explain how to build SCOES.

Review the Design

Let me take a few minutes to formalize the design to make sure that we are all on the same playground. The entire premise of this solution revolves around the reuse and customization of the built-in Outlook Contacts form to meet the needs of ImagiNET's sales staff. The Outlook Contacts form will be modified to remove the fields that are not needed while adding fields and controls to capture additional information required by the sales staff.

Just to make things more interesting, the new Client Contact folder will have an additional tab that allows users to view all of the orders for that client. This information will come directly from a SQL Server. Of course, this functionality only works if the sales person is connected to the same network as the SQL Server, either directly or through a VPN connection. In addition to this new public folder, a corresponding folder that holds all of the contact activity for the new Contacts public folder will also be created.

If ImagiNET wants to store order and product information in a SQL Server, client information must also be accessible from the SQL Server to ensure that the appropriate relationships and references are established. Because Exchange 5.5 does not support OLEDB, you must replicate the information that resides in the new Contacts public folder to the SQL Server using an event scripting agent. Every time a new contact is added to the associated public folder, an Add event fires. Code is written behind this event to add a new entry to a Clients table in a SQL Server database. The same is true when Contact items are modified or deleted. Their counterpart records in SQL Server are correspondingly modified or deleted. To make life a little simpler, replication only happens in one direction, from the Exchange public folder to the SQL Server.

Pictures make more sense than words, so take a look at Figure 13.1 for an overview of this solution.

Would You Do the Same Thing with Exchange 2000?

If you are using Exchange 2000, is it necessary to create a synchronization routine between an Exchange public folder and a SQL Server database? Probably not. Remember that Exchange 2000 now supports OLE DB, even though this is server side only. Smart developers can use this feature to create a linked server in SQL Server (assuming that the SQL Server resides on the same server as the Exchange Server) allowing the use of distributed queries. This allows you to store all contacts, for example, in Exchange exclusively, which is much nicer than solutions that require synchronization. ◆

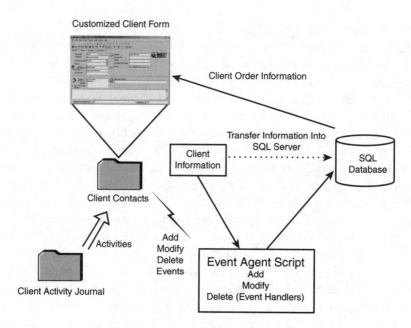

Figure 13.1 *The SCOES solution architecture.*

Creating the Folders and Fields for the Sample

Now that you have a better understanding of what you build, let's get on with it. As I already stated, the first step you should take in this process is to create the appropriate public folders where you will house the information about ImagiNET's clients.

Development, Testing, and Production Environments

If this scenario was in the real world, you wouldn't create a production public folder right off the bat. Many organizations have either a staging, testing, or development environment that is completely separate from anything related to a production system. All development and testing is performed in the staging and testing environments before being released to the production system. Transferring forms and folders typically entails the creation of a personal folder (PST file) to temporarily house your folder and form designs. You can then copy the folders and forms from the personal folder file to the production Exchange Servers manually, provided you have the appropriate Exchange administrative rights.

Another method that some organizations use to stage forms and folder collaborative development is to section off the Exchange public folders into two groups: production public folders, which everyone in the organization has access to, and development public folders, which collaborative developers have exclusive rights

continues ▶

to. Sectioning off public folders is accomplished by simply creating a separate top level folder, the exchange development folder, and assigning appropriate security and access permissions to testers and developers. The transition from development and testing to production is a bit easier with this method because you don't require a physical transfer of information as you do using a PST file to transfer forms and folders into a production system. I always get a little uneasy when development environments mix, in any way, with stable production environments, so I do not recommend this method. ◆

Use Microsoft Outlook to create the folder hierarchy depicted in Figure 13.2. Use Table 13.1 to determine the folder types that you will assign to each new public folder.

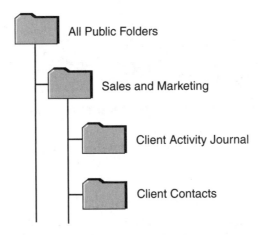

Figure 13.2   *The SCOES public folder structure.*

Table 13.1   *SCOES Folder Types*

Folder Name	Folder Type
Sales and Marketing	Mail items folder
Client Activity Journal	Journal items folder
Client Contacts	Contact items folder

Step two is to configure the Client Contacts Activities property page to ensure that this folder is referencing the Client Activity Journal public folder to display client recorded activities. Do this by right-clicking the Client Contacts public folder from within Outlook and selecting Properties. Select the Activities tab and then click the New button. From the resulting dialog box, place a check mark beside the Client Activity

Journal Public Folder and type **Client Activity** in the name field. When you're done, click the OK button. This ensures that any journal entry added to the Client Activity Journal will be reflected in the appropriate client contact's Activity page.

Public Journal Folders

Remember that Outlook does not use the Client Activity Journal public folder to automatically create Journal items created for contacts in the Client Contacts public folder. Unfortunately, any Journal item that is added to the Client Activity Journal must be done manually by either dragging the appropriate Client Contact item into the Client Activity Journal folder or by creating a blank Journal item that references a particular client contact or group of contacts in the Client Contacts folder.

Additionally, the Client Activity Journal folder is not restricted to maintaining journal entries related to the client contacts stored in the Client Contacts public folder. However, I'm sure with some ingenuity this could be arranged (Hint: Component Object Model (COM) add-ins). ◆

Later in this chapter, after the new Client Contact form has been built and event scripts have been written, I will revisit some of the other folder configuration issues, such as view creation and default post form for the new folder.

Customizing the Outlook Contact Form

Now that you have created the folder that will contain the client contacts for ImagiNET, I will focus on the Contact form customization that must be performed to capture and present the appropriate contact information in the way that best suits the sales team. Let me quickly remind you that the new Client Contact form is based on the default Contact form that is provided with Outlook. Remember that this is one of the built-in Outlook forms that is completely customizable, meaning that you can customize the built-in fields and controls that are displayed on the General tab of the Contact form. This makes your job even simpler.

Reviewing the Client Contact Form

Before I describe how to create it, let's see what the new Client Contact form will look like. Figure 13.3 displays the new Client Contact form.

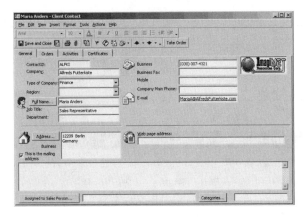

Figure 13.3   *The Client Contact form.*

Generally, here are the steps taken to build this form:

1. Put a default Contact form in design mode.

2. Remove the controls and pages that are not needed on the form. Modify existing control properties, such as the controls caption, to meet design specifications.

3. Create new fields that will be used to capture new information on the form. Add these fields, assigned to the appropriate form control, to the form. Arrange all of the controls on the form to the design specifications.

4. Disable all of the existing actions and create a new action that allows a user to take an order from a customer. Order information is stored in a SQL Server.

5. Place VBScript behind the form that displays a list of orders taken by the client directly in the form, in the Orders tab.

6. Set the remaining properties of the form.

7. Name and publish the new form to the Client Contacts public folder.

Creating a New Contact

Let's begin by creating a new contact in the new Client Contacts public folder. I will use this as the template for the new Client Contact form. Next, place the form in design mode by selecting Tools, Forms, Design This Form from the menu bar.

The next step is to create new fields that will capture some ImagiNET specific information types. Create the new fields according to the specifications in Table 13.2.

Table 13.2   New Fields Required by the Client Contacts Form

Field Name	Field Type
ContactID	Text
Region	Text
Type of Company	Text

Reusing Built-In Fields

ImagiNET's sales people also want the ability to assign clients to a particular sales person. Instead of creating a new field to capture this relationship, I have decided to reuse the Contacts field for this purpose. This provides a great deal more flexibility in the long run, because selecting a contact for a form brings up the Select Contacts dialog box, allowing the user to select just about any contact in any Contact folder he has access to. Unfortunately, this does not allow the user to assign people from the Global Address Book. ◆

Adding New Controls

The next task is to create a couple of new controls on the form for the fields you just created. For the ContactID field, simply use your mouse to drag the field from the Field Chooser dialog box. For convenience, I will assign the Region and Type of Company fields to combo boxes so that users can choose from possible valid values when entering data. This, unfortunately, is a two-step process. For each field, create a new combo box on the form. You must then assign each combo box to the appropriate field by going into the properties of the combo box and selecting the appropriate field in the Value tab of the properties window.

After you have assigned the fields to the new combo boxes, make the form pretty by rearranging and removing unnecessary controls. At this point, you can do just about anything you want to make it look and feel better, such as add graphics and rename controls. Notice that in Figure 13.3, I renamed the Contacts button Assigned to Sales Person, removed a number of unnecessary controls, such as the Address drop-down box, and drastically rearranged the controls on the form to make better sense for the business needs.

Tab Order Maintenance

Just remember that when you add or rearrange controls on the form, you should always modify their tab order on the form as well. You can do this by selecting Tab Order from the Layout menu. ◆

Always make sure that you publish or save your form frequently. There is no Auto Save feature when developing Outlook forms, and the longer you go without saving or publishing your form, the greater amount of lost work you will have if something goes wrong. You can publish the Client Contacts form by selecting Publish Form from the Tools, Form menu. Outlook confirms the location to which you want to publish the form. In this case, choose the Client Contacts folder by clicking the Browse button. You must also provide a Display Name and the Form name. Type **Client Contact** in each field.

The Client Contact Message Class

Notice the message class that appears at the bottom of the Publish Form dialog box. It should look something like IPM.Contact.Client Contact. This forms message class is comprised of the name of the form that was just provided and the base form that the Client Contacts form was constructed from, Contact. ◆

The previous set of steps was pretty darn easy. Let's leave the General tab of the Client Contacts form and move on to some of the other tabs that need modification.

Adding a Tab

As I mentioned earlier, I am going to add a tab to the form that allows sales people to view all of the orders placed for the selected customer. Figure 13.4 should give you a pretty good picture of what I mean.

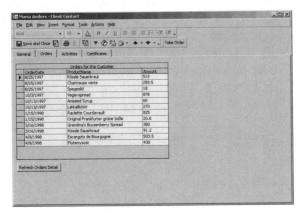

Figure 13.4   *The Orders tab of the Client Contact form.*

All you need for this is two controls: a button and a grid of your choice. In this case, I chose to use the Microsoft's DataGrid for no other reason than the fact that you can assign it a recordset and it handles the rest (and the fact that I'm quite lazy).

Let me take a moment to tell you why I chose to put a Refresh Orders Detail button on the form instead of having the DataGrid populated on form open. First, this form will be accessed when not connected to the SQL Server, so any attempt to automatically retrieve data would fail at that time. Second, if all the sales person needs is the contact's phone number, he would probably get annoyed waiting the extra second it takes to fill the DataGrid control.

The first step is to enable one of the unused tabs that appears in design mode. Select the (P.2) tab, enable it, and rename it to Orders using the appropriate options in the Form menu of the Forms Design window. Because I decided to use the Microsoft DataGrid control, the control reference must be added to the control toolbox by displaying the control toolbox and selecting Custom Control after right-clicking some free space in the control toolbox window. This displays the Additional Controls window where you can select the check box beside the Microsoft DataGrid control to add it to the control toolbox.

Using Custom Controls on Forms

Remember that for the Client Contact form to work properly, the controls you use on your forms must be present on every computer that launches the form prior to users using the form. ◆

The controls that appear on this page of the form are not bound to any data field, which makes your next step pretty straightforward. Simply draw the button and DataGrid controls on the screen. In the properties dialog box of the DataGrid, type **dgOrders** in the Name field and **Orders for this Customer** in the Caption field. Similarly, give the button the name **cmdRefreshOrders** and **Refresh Orders Detail** as a caption. Additionally, I use script to ensure the position of the DataGrid control on the screen, which executes when the form opens. Example 13.1 illustrates the code that accomplishes this.

Example 13.1   *Setting up the form.*

```
Function Item_Open()

' Set the size of the DBGrid control
    Dim dgOrders

    Set dgOrders = Item.GetInspector.ModifiedFormPages("Orders").Controls("dgOrders")

    dgOrders.Top = 12
    dgOrders.Width = 312
    dgOrders.Left = 6
    dgOrders.Height = 192

End Function
```

The next step is to place additional VBScript code in the click event of the cmdRefreshOrders button. When the user clicks this button, the VBScript should attach to SQL Server using ActiveX Data Object (ADO) and retrieve the orders placed by the currently viewed client contact. Take a look at the VBScript code in Example 13.2 that refreshes order information within the form.

Example 13.2   *Refreshing order data.*

```
Function cmdRefreshOrders_Click()

' Connect to SQL Server and get all of the orders from this client

    dim adoConnection
    dim sCommand
    dim dgOrders
    dim sCustomerID

    On Error Resume Next

    if not (Item.UserProperties.Find("ContactID").Value = "") then
        sCustomerID = chr(39)& Item.UserProperties.Find("ContactID").Value & chr(39)
        sCommand = "Select OrderDate, ProductName,Amount from CustomerOrders where
CustomerID = " & sCustomerID & " order by OrderDate"

        Set adoConnection = CreateObject("ADODB.Connection")
            Set adoRecordset = CreateObject("ADODB.Recordset")

            adoConnection.ConnectionString = "driver={SQL
Server};server=Joelhome;uid=sa;pwd=;database=collabmtp"
        adoConnection.Open

            adoRecordSet.Open sCommand, adoConnection, 1, 3, 1

        if adoRecordSet.RecordCount > 0 then
            set dgOrders = Item.GetInspector.ModifiedFormPages("Orders").Controls("dgOrders")
            set dgOrders.Datasource = adoRecordSet
        else
            msgbox "There are no orders for this customer"
        end if
    else
        msgbox "The ContactID field is blank.  No orders returned."
    end if

End Function
```

As you can see from the preceding code, this is fairly simple. I wanted to demonstrate two things in this example. First, you have the ability to instantiate and use any COM object registered on your computer, including objects that run in a middle tier solution, such as Microsoft Transaction Server. Second, you can integrate with other services, such as Microsoft SQL

Server, to give your forms quite a bit of added functionality. Of course, generating really funky code isn't a lot of fun to do in the Outlook Forms Script Editor due to its Notepad-like qualities, but it gets the job done in the long run. I'm hoping that future releases of Outlook provide something better. Sometimes I feel like I'm programming with VI all over again.

Let's take a quick look at this code again. First, take a look at the name of the function:

```
Function cmdRefreshOrders_Click()
```

This is the Click event handler for the cmdRefreshOrders button.

Button Event

Remember that a button in an Outlook form has only one event—the Click event. ◆

Good Coding Practices

One of the things I like to do is make VBScript code as readable as possible, because more than likely you or someone else will have to revisit the code to debug, extend, or modify it. So be nice to others and make sure that your code is properly formatted and commented. ◆

Because orders that are stored in the SQL Server database are tied to a client identifier, the code checks to ensure that this contact has this field set. If it does, the code goes on to dynamically construct a SQL query that will be used to obtain the orders from SQL Server. The resulting SQL query should look something like this:

```
Select OrderDate, ProductName,Amount from CustomerOrders where CustomerID = "ALFKI"
order by OrderDate
```

After the SQL Query has been constructed, the following code connects to the SQL Server and executes the SQL Query to fill a recordset:

```
Set adoConnection = CreateObject("ADODB.Connection")
Set adoRecordset = CreateObject("ADODB.Recordset")

adoConnection.ConnectionString = "driver={SQL Server};server=Joelhome;uid=sa;
➥pwd=;database=collabmtp"
adoConnection.Open
adoRecordSet.Open sCommand, adoConnection, 1, 3, 1
```

Late Binding COM Objects

Late binding is used to make reference to COM objects. ◆

After the recordset is populated, the DataGrid's DataSource property can be set using the following lines of code:

```
set dgOrders = Item.GetInspector.ModifiedFormPages("Orders").Controls("dgOrders")
set dgOrders.Datasource = adoRecordSet
```

Notice how you had to use the implicit Item object to get a reference to the control on the form.

Using Literals

When writing in VBScript, there is a tendency to use a lot of literals throughout your code. In practice, you should try to minimize this or at least format your code so that these literals stand out and easy to change. ♦

All you need now is some cleanup work and the form should be complete. Let's start by configuring the built-in actions on this form. When the form is in design mode, select the Actions tab and configure the listed actions according to Table 13.3.

Table 13.3   The Form's Action Properties

Action	Property
Reply	Disable
Reply to All	Disable
Forward	Disable
Reply to Folder	Disable

You might have noticed that the form depicted in Figures 13.3 and 13.4 has an extra action called Take Order. This new action simply launches another Outlook form that is responsible for gathering and submitting order information. The Take Order form does not create any new Outlook items; it simply gathers order information and stores it directly into the SQL Server database that maintains order and product information. I will cover the creation of the Take Order form in Chapter 14, "Designing and Building Workflow Solutions," because a bit of workflow will be added to this portion of the solution.

The final task that must be completed is to set the forms properties using the Properties tab found on the form at design time, according to Table 13.4.

Table 13.4   Properties of the Client Contact Form

Property	Value
Category	Sales and Marketing.
Sub-Category ManagementContact	Client Contact Provide a valid contact name.
Version	1.0.
Form Number	Provide a form number that helps you locate or identify this form.
Password	Enter a password for this form to prevent users in a production environment from placing the form in design mode.

Finally, publish the Client Contact form in the Client Contacts public folder, if you haven't already done this, and you are done.

Building the Folder Event Agent

For the client contacts to exist in SQL Server, some synchronization mechanism is required. In this case, synchronization is handled by a server-side folder event agent. Basically, any time a client contact is added, modified, or deleted from the Client Contacts folder, an event agent script ensures that the appropriate action is performed on the SQL Server Clients table.

Understanding How the Exchange Event Service Works

Let me take a moment to reflect on how the Exchange Event Service works. The Exchange Event Service is a Windows NT service. Functionally, however, the Event Service is responsible for querying an information store, stored on the Exchange Server, for information about all of the events that occurred, including additions, deletions, or modifications to items in a folder, since the last time the Event Service checked for changes. Interestingly, the Event Service uses the same technology Outlook does when it performs synchronization between the client OST file and the Exchange folders, called Incremental Change Synchronization (ICS). Every change is caught by the Event Service—even if the Event Service is not running—and forwarded to an installed event handler. Not only changes cause actions to be taken by the Event Service. Scheduled events can be configured to cause some action to be taken without any changes being made to messages in the associated folder.

The default event handler, and the entire focus for this section, is the Exchange Event Script Agent. This event handler allows developers to write custom event handlers in either VBScript or Jscript. As you will see, these scripts have the capability to manipulate the message and folder that caused the event to occur. You can even make calls to other COM components, such as ADO or Active Directory Services Interface (ADSI), in your scripts. In fact, your scripts will probably use a great deal of CDO because all event handlers are passed a pre-logged-on CDO session, the message ID of the message that caused the event, and the folder ID of the folder the event occurred in. You can use CDO to manipulate or reference these objects to perform required tasks such as message routing or tracking. The remainder of this chapter focuses on the creation of scripts that are executed by the Exchange Event Script Agent whenever events fire within a particular public folder. I will also discuss how to use the intrinsic objects I mentioned earlier to do some really fun things.

Preparing to Write the Script

Before you write any folder event agent, it is important to understand the requirements of the Microsoft Exchange Event Service and Outlook. In this section, I will discuss what must be done before you can create agents and expect them to run.

Event Service Account

Agents are pieces of code that are executed by the Microsoft Exchange Event Service. Remember that the Event Service is actually just a Windows NT service running in the background, and the Windows NT account under which the Microsoft Exchange Event Service is logged in is one of the most important configuration parameters that needs to be set to ensure proper function and execution of the agents you write as emphasized in Figure 13.5.

By default, the Exchange Event Service logs on using the same Exchange service account that all of the other Exchange services use. This provides adequate permissions to access Exchange resources but very limited access to other resources that the agents may be interacting with, such as SQL Server and NTFS files and folders. Depending on your requirements, you might want to change the Windows NT account that is used by the Event Service to an account that has a bit more, or a bit less, security than the default.

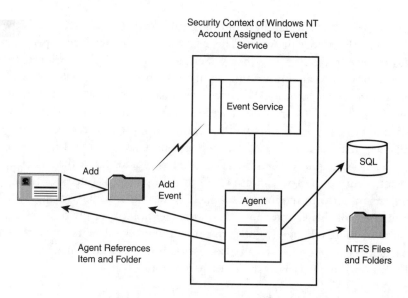

Figure 13.5 *The Event Service must have adequate permissions to access resources in and outside of Exchange.*

Granting Permissions to Create Agents

Helping the Debugging Process

The Event Service relies on values stored in the System Registry to control how events are fired and how much is logged in the Windows event log. Table 13.5 summarizes the Registry values that exist in the following Registry key:

HKEY_LOCAL_MACHINE\System\CurrentControlSet\Services\MSExchangeES\ Parameters ◆

Table 13.5   *Event Service Registry Values*

Name	Description	Valid Range	Recommended Value
Logging Level	Amount of information written to Windows event log.	0–5 (0 is default.)	5—Development. 1—Production.
Maximum execution time for scripts in seconds	Number of seconds that a script is allowed to run in seconds.	Positive integer values (900 is default).	As required by functionality in the script.
Maximum size for agent log in KB	Sets the maximum size for logs created by agents.	Positive integer values (32 is default).	As required. Logs are overwritten as necessary.

Note

Additionally, the ICS notification interval in HKEY_LOCAL_MACHINE\System\ CurrentControlSet\Services\MSExchangeIS\ ParametersSystem specifies how often Exchange checks public folders to see if changes have been made. The default value is 5 minutes (300 seconds). You can decrease this value, but you might not want to because this will negatively impact the performance of the Exchange Server. ◆

The next step you must take to create folder agents is to assign the appropriate permissions to users who require this ability. To do this, you must set permissions on a special system folder called EventConfig_<ServerName> where <ServerName> is the name of the Exchange Server the Event Service is running on. This folder is located in the following location in the Exchange Administrator program:

```
..\Folders\System Folders\Event Root\
```

Simply display the properties of this folder and click the Client Permissions button located on the General tab of the properties dialog box. Add the users that will be creating agents and ensure that they hold the Author, or higher, role.

The Agents Tab Does Not Display?

You have set up the Exchange Event Service and are ready to write some cool scripts in a public folder, but you don't see the Agents tab in the properties window of the folder. To create agents for a public folder using Outlook, two conditions must be satisfied. First, you must own the public folder. Second, the Server Scripting Outlook add-in must be installed and enabled.

You can enable the Server Scripting add-on by opening the Outlook Options window from the Tools menu, selecting the Other tab, and clicking the Advanced Options button. From the Advanced Options dialog box, click the Add-In Manager button and ensure that the Server Scripting add-in has a check mark beside it. ◆

Other Ways of Running the Event Agents

Some organizations might want the event scripting agent to run within MTS to run it in a different security context or to isolate it in a different middle tier process. Well, because the event scripting agent is a DLL, SCRIPTO.DLL, this is indeed possible. Microsoft makes this even simpler by providing a pre-built MTS package for this purpose. The package is called Scripto.pak and is located on the Exchange 5.5 CD in the Server\Support\Collab\ Sampler\Scripts folder.

continues ▶

For load purposes, you might also want to have the agents run on computers other than the server where the public folder is located. Exchange fully supports this because agents can be quite I/O and processor intensive. ✦

Creating the Script

Before I describe how to write the agent that synchronizes changes from the Client Contacts public folder to the SQL Server database, it is beneficial to discuss the implicit objects that need to be manipulated to accomplish this task. The following is a list and description of each of these objects:

- **EventDetails.Session**. A pre-logged on CDO session. The session is logged on under the user of the last person to save the agent.
- **EventDetails.FolderID**. The entry ID of the folder from where the event occurred.
- **EventDetails.MessageID**. The entry ID of the message that caused the event.

GetFolder and GetMessage

You can use the GetFolder and GetMessage CDO functions in your script to gain an object reference to the folder and message that the EventDetails.FolderID and EventDetails.MessageID refer to. ✦

In SCOES, this chapter's sample application, the event scripting agent needs to respond to the OnMessageCreated, OnChange, and OnMessageDeleted events. In the OnMessageCreated, the agent must connect the SQL Server and execute an Insert statement to add a record to the appropriate table. The OnChange and OnMessageDeleted events similarly execute Update and Delete SQL statements, respectively.

You can begin creating your scripts by displaying the properties dialog box for your public folder and selecting the Agents tab, as shown in Figure 13.6. Next, click the New button to create a new event script for your folder. You are required to specify what events you would like to have monitored as well as the name of the agent. In case of client contact, I only want events to fire whenever new items are added to the folder, items are updated, or when items are deleted from the folder.

Out-of-Sync Data

The method I use to synchronize contact information between Exchange and SQL leaves room for the SQL Server to become out-of-sync with the Client Contacts public folder. Future considerations could use the scheduled event to perform consistency checks and backfills against the SQL data store to ensure that both data locations are completely synchronized all the time. ✦

When you are ready to start coding the script, click the Edit Script button, as shown in Figure 13.7.

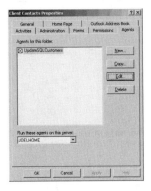

Figure 13.6   *The Agents tab in the properties dialog box of a public folder.*

Figure 13.7   *The Event Script dialog box that allows you to view schedule details such as the schedule, event logs and the event script.*

Before you start writing the agent, let's take a look at what there is to start with. Example 13.3 is what you would see if you created a new agent using the Outlook interface.

Example 13.3   *Default agent VBScript.*

```
<SCRIPT RunAt=Server Language=VBScript>

'_____

'FILE DESCRIPTION: Exchange Server Event Script
'_____

Option Explicit

'_____
```

continues ▶

Example 13.3   *continued.*

```
' Global Variables
'_ _ _ _ _ _ _ _ _ _ _ _ _ _ _ _ _ _ _ _ _ _ _ _ _ _ _ _ _ _ _ _ _ _ _ _ _ _ _


'_ _ _ _ _ _ _ _ _ _ _ _ _ _ _ _ _ _ _ _ _ _ _ _ _ _ _ _ _ _ _ _ _ _ _ _ _ _ _
' Event Handlers
'_ _ _ _ _ _ _ _ _ _ _ _ _ _ _ _ _ _ _ _ _ _ _ _ _ _ _ _ _ _ _ _ _ _ _ _ _ _ _

' DESCRIPTION: This event is fired when a new message is added to the folder
Public Sub Folder_OnMessageCreated
End Sub

' DESCRIPTION: This event is fired when a message in the folder is changed
Public Sub Message_OnChange
End Sub

' DESCRIPTION: This event is fired when a message is deleted from the folder
Public Sub Folder_OnMessageDeleted
End Sub

' DESCRIPTION: This event is fired when the timer on the folder expires
Public Sub Folder_OnTimer
End Sub

</SCRIPT>
```

As you can see, the default script provides a place for you to stick global variables and placeholders for the four folder events OnMessageCreated, OnChange, OnMessageDeleted, and OnTimer.

MAPI Session

The Event Service is passed a logged on MAPI session, so there is no need to write any code in your script that establishes a MAPI session. Exchange uses the identifier of the person who last saved the agent as CDO logon credentials. ◆

Using a Script Recipient

It is a good idea to create a separate recipient for creating and managing scripts. This ensures that the CDO session your agents use is logged on using the same credentials every time instead of using the credentials of whoever saved the script last. Additionally, if your scripts create and send mail messages to other users, the message is addressed from this new user and not the developer of the script. ◆

When you start to build folder agents, you quickly see the importance of logging. The Event Service provides an implicit object called Script.Response that can be used to save string responses that are later saved into the event handler's corresponding log file. You can see the contents of this log file by clicking the Logs button as displayed in Figure 13.7. The contents of the

Script.Response object are not written to the log file until the end of the script and is not written at all if unhandled errors occur from within the script. This means that you have to concatenate all of your error and logging strings as you go, while assigning the result Script.Response. To make this job a little cleaner and to make my code a little easier to read, I use a homemade function called Log. Here's the code:

```
Public Sub Log(sMessage)
' Collect the Logged Messages in Script.Response Object
' Adding the correct formatting

    Script.Response = Script.Response & vbNewLine & Now & vbTab & sMessage
End Sub
```

That's it. You simply pass Log a parameter, sMessage, and it concatenates it onto the existing Script.Response value, adding time stamps and line formatting as well.

I will focus exclusively on the OnMessageCreated event handler in the agent because all of the other events are extremely similar. The code is shown in Example 13.4.

Example 13.4 *Using the OnMessageCreated event to store data into SQL Server.*

```
Public Sub Folder_OnMessageCreated
'===========================================================================
' DESCRIPTION: This event is fired when a new message is added to the folder
' NOTE: Extensive Logging is enabled for demonstration purposes only
'===========================================================================
' Local Variables
    dim iFolder
    dim iMessage
    dim cdoSession
        dim oContactItem
    dim oContactsFolder
    dim adoConnection
    dim sConnectionString
    dim sSQL
    dim sValues

    Log "The OnMessageCreated Event Fired"

    on error resume next

    ' Load the Intrinsic objects into local vars
    '=========================================
    iFolder = EventDetails.FolderID
    iMessage = EventDetails.MessageID
    Set cdoSession = EventDetails.Session

    err.Clear
```

continues ▶

Example 13.4 *continued*.

```
' Get the Message that Caused the Event
'======================================
Set oContactItem = cdoSession.GetMessage(iMessage, Null)
if Err.Number <> 0 then
    log "Error getting oContactItem"
else
    'For Logging Purposes
    '=========================================================
    Log "Processing Contact"
    Log "Customer ID: " & CStr(oContactItem.Fields.Item("ContactID"))
    Log "Company Name: " & CStr(oContactItem.Fields.Item(974520350))
    Log "Contact Name: " & CStr(oContactItem.Fields.Item(3604510))
    Log "Contact Title: " & CStr(oContactItem.Fields.Item(974585886))
    Log "Address: " & CStr(oContactItem.Fields.Item(975765534))
    Log "City: " & CStr(oContactItem.Fields.Item(975634462))
    Log "Region: " & CStr(oContactItem.Fields.Item(("Region"))
    Log "Postal Code: " & CStr(oContactItem.Fields.Item(975831070))
    Log "Country: " & CStr(oContactItem.Fields.Item(975568926))
    Log "Phone: " & CStr(oContactItem.Fields.Item(973602846))
    Log "Fax: " & CStr(oContactItem.Fields.Item(974913566))

    'Construct SQL
    '=========================================================
    Log "Constructing Values String..."
    sValues = ConstructValueString(oContactItem)
    Log sValues

    if sValues <> "" then
        sSQL = "Insert Into Customers"
        sSQL = sSQL & "(CustomerID, CompanyName, ContactName, Contacttitle,"
        sSQL = sSQL & " Address, City, Region, PostalCode, Country, Phone, Fax)"
        sSQL = sSQL & " Values (" & sValues & ")"
    End if

    log sSQL

    'Connect to SQL Server
    '=========================================================
    Set adoConnection = CreateObject("ADODB.Connection")
    if Err.Number = 0 then

        Log "Connecting to SQL Server"
        sConnectionString = "driver={SQL
Server};server=Joelhome;uid=sa;pwd=;database=collabmtp"

        log "Opening SQL Connection"
        adoConnection.ConnectionString = sConnectionString
        adoConnection.Open

        if Err.Number = 0 then
            adoConnection.Execute sSQL,,128
            if Err.Number <> 0 then
```

```
            Log "There were Problems executing SQL"
            Log "Error" & Err.Description
         end if
      else
         Log "Error opening: " & sConnectionString
         Log Err.Description
      end if
   else
      Log "Error Referencing ADO" & Err.Description
   end if
   'Execute the Script
end if


End Sub
```

This probably looks a lot more complex than what you thought it would, huh? It only looks complicated because of the extra inline error checking and handling, and all of the extra logging I do for debugging purposes.

The first thing that this event handler does is assign the implicit variables into local variables:

```
' Load the Intrinsic objects into local vars
'=========================================
iFolder = EventDetails.FolderID
iMessage = EventDetails.MessageID
Set cdoSession = EventDetails.Session
```

After these values have been obtained, they can be used to get an object reference to the new client contact message that fired the event. To get this message, the CDO session object's GetMessage function is used. Notice that the cdoSession object is used for this purpose because it is obtained from an implicit pre-logged on CDO session passed by the Event Service. The GetMessage function accepts the unique identifier of the message—in this case, the iMessage variable that was copied from EventDetails.MessageID— and an optional reference to a CDO Information store—in this case, Null:

```
' Get the Message that Caused the Event
   '========================================
   Set oContactItem = cdoSession.GetMessage(iMessage, Null)
```

After the message is obtained, the script proceeds to build the appropriate SQL string that is passed to the SQL Server through the ADO Connection object. The SQL string that is built in this event is an Insert SQL statement that must be built dynamically from the field values of the oContactItem message that was just obtained (see Example 13.5).

Example 13.5   *Constructing the SQL string.*

```
sValues = ConstructValueString(oContactItem)

    ...

    if sValues <> "" then
        sSQL = "Insert Into Customers"
        sSQL = sSQL & "(CustomerID, CompanyName, ContactName, Contacttitle,"
        sSQL = sSQL & " Address, City, Region, PostalCode, Country, Phone, Fax)"
        sSQL = sSQL & " Values (" & sValues & ")"
    End if
```

To make the job of extracting the field values from the OcontactItem
message object easier, I constructed a function called ConstructValueString
that accepts the OContactItem message object and returns the appropriate
string of comma delimited values that will be used in the Insert statement.
Example 13.6 lists the code for this function.

Example 13.6   *Extracting item values to be used in a SQL Insert command.*

```
Public Function ConstructValueString(oContactItem)
' This function will collect the fields from the ContactItem
' and build the appropriate Value String used in Insert and Update
' SQL Statements
'
' Note:  Chr(39) = ' (single quote)
'        Chr(44) = , (comma)

    dim sTemp

    on Error Resume Next
    ' Get Value for ContactID
    sTemp = chr(39) & CStr(oContactItem.Fields.Item("ContactID")) & Chr(39) & chr(44)

    ' Checked to see if we died on reference to the oContactItem
    if Err.Number = 0 then
        ' Get Value for Company Name
        sTemp = sTemp & chr(39) & CStr(oContactItem.Fields.Item(974520350)) & Chr(39) &
chr(44)

        ' Get Value for Contact Name
        sTemp = sTemp & chr(39) & CStr(oContactItem.Fields.Item(3604510)) & Chr(39) &
chr(44)

        ' Get Value for Contact Title
        sTemp = sTemp & chr(39) & CStr(oContactItem.Fields.Item(974585886)) & Chr(39) &
chr(44)

        ' Get Value for Address
        sTemp = sTemp & chr(39) & CStr(oContactItem.Fields.Item(975765534)) & Chr(39) &
chr(44)
```

```
        ' Get Value for City
        sTemp = sTemp & chr(39) & CStr(oContactItem.Fields.Item(975634462)) & Chr(39) &
chr(44)

        ' Get Value for Region
        sTemp = sTemp & chr(39) & CStr(oContactItem.Fields.Item("Region")) & Chr(39) &
chr(44)

        ' Get Value for Postal Code
        sTemp = sTemp & chr(39) & CStr(oContactItem.Fields.Item(975831070)) & Chr(39) &
chr(44)

        ' Get Value for Country
        sTemp = sTemp & chr(39) & CStr(oContactItem.Fields.Item(975568926)) & Chr(39) &
chr(44)

        ' Get Value for Phone
        sTemp = sTemp & chr(39) & CStr(oContactItem.Fields.Item(973602846)) & Chr(39) &
chr(44)

        ' Get Value for Fax
        sTemp = sTemp & chr(39) & CStr(oContactItem.Fields.Item(974913566)) & Chr(39)

        ConstructValueString = sTemp
    else
        ConstructValueString = ""
    End If

End Function
```

The method used here is not as obvious as you might imagine. First of all, to gain access to the values that are stored in the fields of the message, I'm using functions that look like the following:

```
oContactItem.Fields.Item(974520350)
```

Why don't I just reference the fields by their names? In CDO, all of the default field names, such as Address and City, do not have named fields, thus forcing us to reference them using their IDs. I could have made the code more readable by using constant values, but I wanted to emphasize the underlying field identification values. Notice that I do reference some of the fields using their corresponding field name, such as oContactItem.Fields. Item("Region"). I do this because these fields correspond to custom fields that I created when I created the Client Contact form. These fields have IDs, but they will not be the same in your implementation of this script. Don't worry, this really bugs me too.

CDO Constants

Unfortunately, CDO's built-in constants don't work in the event script to reference the fields. Typically, you simply use the field ID constant instead of the actual number. For example, you can use CdoPR_COMPANY_NAME instead of the number that it represents (974520350) to reference the field. If you are wondering how I found the values for these fields, I just use Visual Basic's object browser to look for CDO constants that meet my field requirements and pull the value for the constant into VBScript. Again, I could just recreate the constants in the script to make the code more readable. ◆

After the SQL statement has been created, the next step is to connect to the SQL Server and execute the script. I first create a reference to ADO using late binding, as in the following:

```
Set adoConnection = CreateObject("ADODB.Connection")
```

Then I simply connect to the appropriate database using the following code:

```
sConnectionString = "driver={SQL Server};server=Joelhome;uid=sa;pwd=;database=collabmtp"
adoConnection.ConnectionString = sConnectionString
adoConnection.Open
```

If no connection errors occur, I go ahead and execute the SQL Statement using the following line of code:

```
adoConnection.Execute sSQL,,128
```

If errors occur during the execute, I log them; otherwise, the client contact synchronization is successful. You can always double-check the results by looking at the resulting log file shown in Figure 13.8.

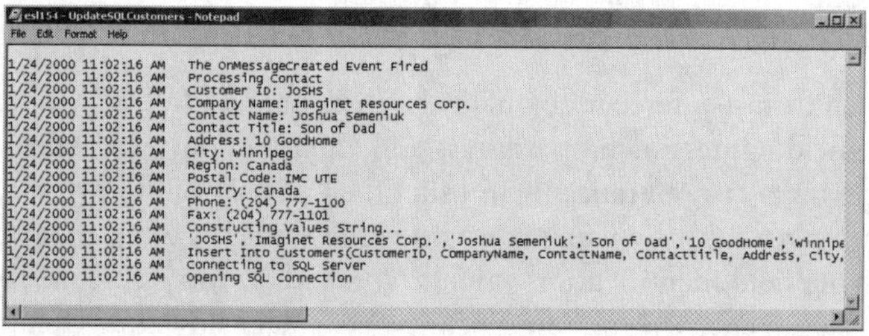

Figure 13.8   *The log file generated after the OnMessageCreated event fires.*

The code that needs to be created for the other two events, the OnChange and OnMessageDeleted events, looks similar to the preceding code we discussed, so I will refrain from that discussion and assume you can take it from here. Just remember that in the OnChange event handler, you build an UPDATE SQL string, and in the OnMessageDeleted, you create a DELETE SQL string.

Other Ways of Managing Server Scripts

There are other ways you can create and bind agents to a folder. In fact, you can do this without any user interface programmatically. The Microsoft Exchange Event Service provides an object library that allows you to create and remove agents programmatically. I will not go into detail on how this is done; however, I will give you some direction on where to get started. The best place to start is with the Microsoft Exchange Event Service Config 1.0 Type Library object that you can reference from a Visual Basic application. After you reference this object in Visual Basic, you can spend some time examining the object hierarchy. The Microsoft Exchange Event Service Config 1.0 object library is stored in ESCONF.DLL, which is usually installed in the c:\ExchSrvr\bin directory. ♦

The OnTimer Event

The one event that has not been discussed much in this chapter is the OnTimer event. As you might have guessed, this event is fired according to some schedule that you determine.

To configure the OnTimer event to fire and to set its firing schedule, open the Agent and make sure the A Schedule Event Occurs check box is selected. Next, to configure the frequency that this event fires, click the Schedule button to display the Scheduled Event dialog box, as shown in Figure 13.9. ♦

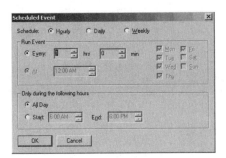

Figure 13.9   *The Scheduled Event dialog box that allows a schedule to be set for the OnTimer event to occur.*

Completing Outlook Client Configurations

The last process involved in configuring SCOES is the creation of folder views that will commonly be used by all of ImagiNET's sales staff. Additionally, the Client Contacts form must also be assigned as the default Post form for the Client Contacts public folder. Sales people will also be required to have access to these contacts when offline, so the final step in this process is to configure the folder for offline access.

Modifying the Default Post Form

Start by setting the Client Contacts form as the default Post form for the Client Contacts public folder. To do this, view the property dialog box for the folder and select the General tab. From the When Posting to This Folder, Use: pull-down box, select the Client Contact form. Click OK when you're done. Now, whenever you double-click in the Client Contacts folder or choose to create a new contact when the Client Contacts folder is selected, the Client Contact form will appear.

Creating the Outlook Folder Views

Creating views is the final stage, and at this point, I'm going to assume that you remember how to create and customize views without needing to go through every detail. Tables 13.6, 13.7, 13.8, and 13.9 illustrate the specifications for the views that are required for this folder. See Figure 13.10 for additional information on the views required for SCOES.

Table 13.6   View Definition for Client by Sales Person and Region

View Name	Clients by Sales Person and Region
Fields	ContactID
	Full Name
	Type of Company
	Company
	Business Phone
	Business Fax
Group By	Contacts (Renamed to Display Sales Person)
	Region
Other Properties	Allow In cell editing: No
	Show New Item Row: No
	Filters: None
	AutoPreview: No
	Show Preview Pane: No

Table 13.7   View Definition for Clients by Region and Sales Person

View Name	Clients by Region and Sales Person
Fields	ContactID
	Full Name
	Type of Company
	Company
	Business Phone
	Business Fax

View Name	Clients by Region and Sales Person
Group By	Region then by Contacts
Other Properties	Allow In cell editing: No
	Show New Item Row: No
	Filters: None
	AutoPreview: No
	Show Preview Pane: No

Table 13.8   View Definition for Clients by Region

View Name	Clients by Region
Fields	ContactID
	Full Name
	Type of Company
	Company
	Business Phone
	Business Fax
Group By	Region
Other Properties	Allow In cell editing: No
	Show New Item Row: No
	Filters: None
	AutoPreview: No
	Show Preview Pane: No

Table 13.9   View Definition for Client by Sales Person

View Name	Clients by Sales Person
Fields	ContactID
	Full Name
	Type of Company
	Company
	Business Phone
	Business Fax
Group By	Contacts
Other Properties	Allow In cell editing: No
	Show New Item Row: No
	Filters: None
	AutoPreview: No
	Show Preview Pane: No

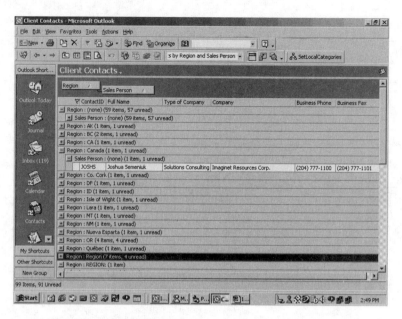

Figure 13.10   *An example of one of the views required for*
SCOES: Clients by Region and Sales Person.

Configuring the Client Contacts Folder for Offline Access

As I mentioned earlier in this chapter, all of the sales people have laptops
and require access to their assigned clients when offline. Here are the steps
required to accomplish this:

1. Make a reference to the Client Contacts folder in the Favorites public
   folder. Simply drag the public folder into the Favorites folder.

2. Ensure that the contents of this folder are available offline by viewing
   the properties of the Client Contacts folder that resides in Favorites
   and selecting the Synchronization tab. Select the When offline or
   Online option.

3. When offline, the sales staff only wants to view the contacts that have
   been assigned to them. To accomplish this, you can use a synchronization filter. Click the Filter button on the Synchronization tab to set a
   filter. The resulting filter criteria should look something like the filter
   displayed in Figure 13.11.

After this last step, SCOES should be complete.

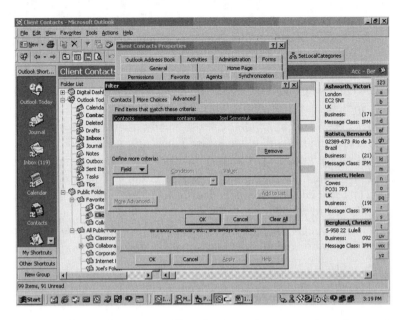

Figure 13.11   *The Synchronization filter that is used to ensure that sales people only view clients that they are assigned to when accessing the Client Contacts folder offline.*

Creating Contacts Offline

What happens if the sales staff creates new client contacts when they are not connected to the SQL Server? Remember that the OnMessageCreated event fires when new messages are created in the public folder stored on the Exchange Server. If sales people create client contacts when offline, the new entry is added to the OST file first. When the sales person returns to the office and synchronizes his offline store with Exchange, the appropriate events fire. ◆

Chapter Summary

In this chapter, we focused all effort on the creation of an Outlook based client management system that was geared to providing added and customized functionality required by ImagiNET's sales force. We began by looking at some of the overall requirements of this solution, and then we built it. This solution, SCOES as we called it, is comprised of two distinct stages. The first stage encompassed the design and publishing of a new

Client Contacts form. The process of creating this form involved adding a few more fields, removing some built-in graphic elements on the form, and adding a new form tab that had the capability to connect to a SQL Server and retrieve client order information.

The second stage of this process involved creating a set of customized event handlers that were responsible for transferring all client contact changes or additions to a SQL Server. Actually, we only covered how to build the event handler that was called when new items were posted to the folder; however, you can use all of the information and examples provided here to build the rest of the solution simply enough. The result of this is that every client contact that is added to the Client Contacts public folder is also replicated to the SQL Server.

In the next chapter, Chapter 14, we will further extend the functionality of this solution by adding a certain degree of workflow.

14

Designing and Building Workflow Solutions

In this chapter, we will focus on building various routing solutions based on technology we have already discussed. As always, these solutions must meet business requirements, which are expressed in the following narrative.

The members of the ImagiNET sales department are quite happy with their new client contacts solution and are realizing that some of what they wish for really is possible. As it happens, the members of the sales department have two additional wishes that they believe would help them do their jobs.

Their first new wish centers around the time that it takes to create, edit, and revise sales proposals. The sales team wants to ensure that all proposals are reviewed and edited by all senior sales employees before being delivered to any of ImagiNET's clients. They want to make this process easier and more standard for all sales employees by requiring that all such documents be sequentially routed via email to a predefined group of senior sales staff, then sent back to the creator of the document for final revisions and edit integrations.

Enhancing the travel approval process is ImagiNET's sales team's second wish. Currently, all travel requests are submitted and approved using paper forms. The sales staff must fill out a Travel Request form that summarizes the time, date, and expected expense of a business related trip and submit it to the sales manager. Unfortunately, the sales manager maintains an extremely cluttered and messy desk and sometimes misplaces or forgets about many of the requests, causing great frustration among the rest of the sales staff. Additionally, whenever the sales manager goes on holidays or is out of town on business, these travel requests get ignored completely. The sales staff has called upon the creators of the client contacts solution to see if this process could be enforced electronically. Additionally, because ImagiNET is a fast growing company, the sales staff is concerned that any solution be robust enough to model any new travel approval process.

On another note, ImagiNET's CIO has been reading *Byte* magazine and has learned about the great many enhancements that are to come with Exchange 2000. She has seen all that has been done for the sales department and is interested to see whether Exchange 2000 provides any benefits over Exchange 5.5 with regard to workflow and business process modeling.

As you can gather by the narrative, I am going to address the following points in this chapter:

- How to build fairly simple workflow solutions with Office
- How to construct simple approval solutions with Outlook 2000 and Exchange 5.5
- How to build more complex routing and workflow solutions with Outlook 2000 and Exchange 5.5
- The impact that Exchange 2000 will have on collaborative solutions that require routing and workflow

Review the Design

Let's take a step back and try to understand what these sales people want. First, they want to ensure that all client proposals get routed to senior sales employees before being delivered to the clients. Second, the sales team would like to have an automated travel request solution to help expedite travel requests that must be approved before travel plans can be made.

For quick and easy Office document routing, the document routing features provided by almost all of the Microsoft Office products is a good place to start. For Sales' second request, which deals with travel request approvals, I think Exchange routing fits the bill. However, before I get into the Exchange Routing Engine, let me discuss the document routing problem in a bit more detail.

More Than One Way to Route a Cat

Either of the services requested by ImagiNET's sales staff could be implemented differently. For example, instead of using Office document routing to facilitate a proposal review process, you could solve this problem using full-blown Exchange

continues ▶

routing. I will demonstrate both routing solutions, office based and Exchange routing, to emphasize that simple routing does not need to be enforced by the Exchange Server, but in fact, by products, such as Microsoft Word and Excel. These products provide excellent routing capabilities for simple requirements such as content review and modifications. Additionally, using Office Document routing works well in environments that do not have the messaging capabilities of Microsoft Exchange. ◆

The problem of sequentially routing a proposal from one person to another for review does not mean that you have to pull out the big guns and start writing VBScript. The quickest, and probably most effective, way to route in a dynamically changing organization is to use the built-in document routing functionality of the Microsoft Office Suite of products. In this case, you can create a new Proposals template with a preset route that ensures all routing destination points are reached, as depicted in Figure 14.1.

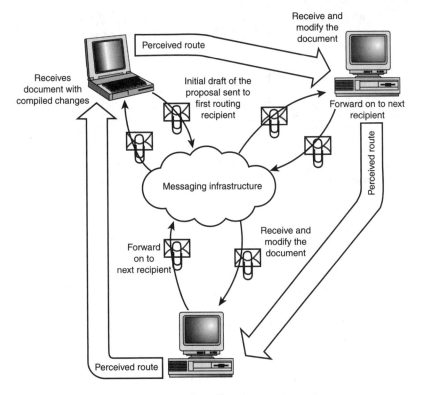

Figure 14.1 *Simple Office document routing.*

The travel request problem needs more thought and implementation than the document routing problem. When it comes to travel requests, it would be nice if the requests were automatically sent to the requestor's manager. More importantly, if the travel request has not been accepted or denied after a given number of days, the request should be automatically routed to some other manager or department head who has travel request approval authority. This entire process should be handled automatically by the solution to minimize the number of mistakes and help unify the process for the entire organization, as shown in Figure 14.2.

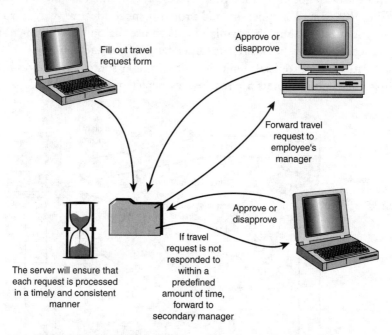

Figure 14.2   *The logical view of the travel request solution.*

With this in mind, it seems that Exchange routing is the perfect solution. Sales staff can submit travel requests to a public folder. The Microsoft Exchange Routing Engine Agent is responsible for forwarding the request to the requestor's manager. If the manager does not respond in a timely manner, the Routing Event Agent forwards the travel request to some other authority for acceptance review. In any event, the sales person who submitted the request is notified at each leg of the routing process as well as with the final travel request decision.

Implementing Simple Workflow

Let's get started with the creation of our simple workflow solutions, starting with the document workflow solution, as described previously, and moving on to the more complex travel request workflow solution.

Implementing Simple Document Workflow

As you can probably guess, this section will not kill too many trees (or too many brain cells for that matter). This process is extremely straightforward and should be used whenever possible to implement this *ad hoc* form of routing. The best thing to do is to create an Office template that has all formatting and, more importantly, all routing information built into it. This is the best approach if you want to enforce some sort of routing standard. Of course, you can never really enforce Office document routing, but you can make it as painless as possible for all users.

Routing Office Documents

I will describe how to route an Office document in Microsoft Word; however, you can use the same concepts (and same menu items) to do the same thing using Excel or PowerPoint. ◆

The process is simple. Follow these instructions to enable document routing:

1. Complete your document template and save it into the appropriate template folder (preferably somewhere on the network where everyone can gain access to it).

2. From the File menu, select Send To, then Routing Recipient.

3. Click the Addresses button to add destination recipients. When finished, you can reorder the recipients in the Routing Slip dialog box using the up and down arrows directly to the right of the recipient list box, as shown in Figure 14.3.

4. Provide a message subject and message body you want users to see in the email message they receive along with the attached document.

5. Choose the type of routing: One After Another or All at Once. In this case, select One After Another for the routing type.

6. Specify if you want the document to be routed back to the originator when the route has been completed and whether the status should be tracked. In this case, ensure that this option is selected.

7. Specify if you want to have status information tracked. This ensures that the originator of the document gets notified at every step of the routing process. For this example, ensure that this option is selected.

8. Specify how the original document will be protected throughout the route. The options are None, allowing all people on the route to make any change to the original document; Comments, allowing routing recipients to add only comments; Tracked Changes, to enable Office's reviewing functionality; or Form, if the document contains a form that must be filled out without allowing users to enable the form itself. In this case, select Tracked Changes.

9. Click the Add Slip button to save the routing parameters to the document. Clicking the Route button causes the document to be routed according to the routing slip just defined.

10. Save the template again to permanently save all changes regarding routing.

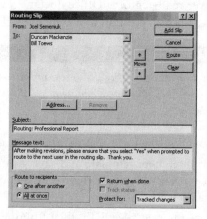

Figure 14.3   *An Office document's routing slip.*

Any user can create a new document based on this template. When the user chooses to close the document, Word prompts the user to see if he wants to route the document to the next user at that time, as shown in Figure 14.4.

As you can see from Figure 14.4, you cannot force the document to take this route because the option to route to the next user is ultimately in the hands of the current user. Using Office document routing does, however, strongly promote document routing to a predefined set of users.

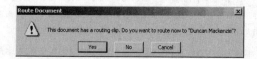

Figure 14.4   *The message that Microsoft Word displays when you attempt to close a document containing a routing slip.*

Implementing Travel Request Workflow

As I promised, let's take a look at how to build the travel request workflow solution using Exchange routing. I always like to start off with a simple solution and work from there, so let's begin with the Routing Wizard, which I briefly described in Chapter 3, "Overview of Collaborative Tools and Techniques."

The Travel Requests Public Folder

I will not cover the creation of the Travel Requests public folder or the folder's default form that will be used to capture travel requests submitted by ImagiNET's employees. The previous chapter, Chapter 13, "Designing and Building Tracking Solutions," gives you enough information to do this on your own. ◆

I will begin by demonstrating the steps required to establish routing using the Routing Wizard. Let's try to implement the more complicated travel request routing solution that I described earlier in the chapter using the Routing Wizard. Start off by launching the wizard and progressing past the initial startup screens that prompt you to log on and select the folder for which you want to place a route. Select the appropriate folder—in my case, the Travel Requests public folder.

Where to Find the Routing Wizard

You can find the Routing Wizard in one of the following locations:

- *The latest Exchange 5.5 Service pack under:*

  `Eng\Server\Support\Collab\Sampler\Routing\WINNT\i386`

- *From the Microsoft Web site at:*

  `http://www.microsoft.com/TechNet/exchange/tools/`
  `AppFarm/MiscTool/rwsample.asp ◆`

The first screen prompts for the type of route you want to establish for new messages that are entered into the folder. Figure 14.5 depicts this form, and as you can see, it only allows the selection of either a Sequential Route or a Parallel Route. If you specify that you want the approval route to be sequential, you must also specify the number of recipients that will appear in this route.

Sequential Versus Parallel Route

There are some differences between setting up a sequential route versus a parallel route using the Routing Wizard.

continues ▶

The first major difference is that a sequential route can use roles. The Routing Wizard only lets you select individual recipients or distribution lists when setting up a parallel route. Additionally, after a serial route is complete, the results are sent to the original sender. When setting up a parallel route, the Routing Wizard allows the final status message to be sent to one or more pre-assigned recipients or distribution lists. ◆

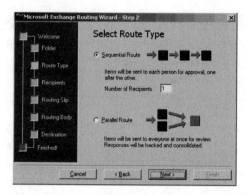

Figure 14.5   *Selecting a route type using a Routing Wizard.*

If you refer to the scenario shown in Figure 14.2, you will see that the route between an employee and his manager is linear, so when you try to implement the required scenario using the Routing Wizard, the sequential option is best. After you have selected the sequential option, specify that two recipients will be included in the route and click the Next button. On the resulting screen, you can select the appropriate recipients by clicking the First Recipient and Second Recipient buttons. For each recipient in the sequential route, you can configure the parameters shown in Table 14.1 (Figure 14.6 also shows these parameters).

Table 14.1   *Sequential Recipient Options*

Parameter	Description
Send to	Specify the recipient by his name or respective role.
If Rejected	Specify what the routing engine should do with the request if the selected recipient rejects the request. Options are:
	Return to the previous recipient (blank if the first recipient is selected)
	Return to the original sender

Parameter	Description
Time limit for this recipient	Specify a limit of time that the request must be accepted or rejected within (measured in hours or days).
If time limit exceeded	Specify what the routing engine should do if the request has not been accepted or rejected for the time specified in the time limit box. Options are:
	Return to Previous Recipient
	Return to Original Sender
	Automatically Approve
	Automatically Reject

Figure 14.6   *The Sequential Recipient Options dialog box.*

Other Roles

Manager is the only role that the Routing Wizard recognizes automatically. New roles can be created using the Roles Administrator program, which is shipped as part of a service pack for Exchange, or with some fun Active Directory Services Interfaces (ADSI) programming, which I will describe a little bit later in this section. ◆

To implement a route that is much like the scenario depicted at the beginning of this chapter, configure the recipients according to Table 14.2.

Table 14.2   Parameters for the Sample Routing Application in this Chapter

Recipient	Parameters
First Recipient	Send to Role (Manager).
	If rejected, return to the original sender.
	Recipient time limit = 4 hours.
	If time exceeded, return to the original sender.
Second Recipient	Send to a specific recipient, not a role. This person is the head of some department such as human resources.
	If rejected, return to the previous recipient.
	Time limit for this recipient = 4 hours.
	If time exceeded, return the request to the original sender.

You can configure other options, such as the following:

- Whether to attach the original request to the routed items sent to recipients along the route or send a link to the original item, which requires Outlook Web Access (OWA) to be installed because the link is an HTML link.
- The text of the message that will be sent to each recipient.
- Final destination of the route, which could be a folder or a recipient. You also have the option of choosing to send summary information along with the original request.

These parameters do not affect the functionality of the route as much as the selection of the route type and the selection of the recipients that the request is routed to. Simply fill out the rest of the requested information and complete the wizard.

Adding Roles Other Than Manager for the Routing Wizard

As you know, the Routing Wizard only recognizes one role by default, Manager. What if you want to use other roles? Luckily, to do this, you can use a utility called the Roles Administrator, which ships with the latest Exchange 5.5 service pack. You can find the installation for the Roles Administrator application, which is Web based, in Eng\Server\Support\Collab\Sampler\Routing\WINNT\i386 on the Exchange 5.5 service pack CD.

So what does the Routing Wizard consider to be a role? Interestingly, the Routing Wizard recognizes distribution lists that have the property PR_GIVEN_NAME equal to ROLEPERFORMER as a role. Any recipient or distribution list that is a member of a ROLEPERFORMER distribution list assumes that role.

continues ▶

You don't need the Roles Administrator to create new roles; in fact, you can do it yourself programmatically using ADSI, because that is exactly what the Roles Administrator does (it requires ADSI 2.0). The Roles Administrator uses ADSI to create, edit, and delete distribution lists that have the ROLEPERFORMER for their PR_GIVEN_NAME property. If you want to write this yourself, you can easily look at the ASP code that does this in the Roles Administrator Web application. For example, the chunk of code listed in Example 14.1 is all you need to create a new distribution list using ADSI. ◆

Example 14.1   *Creating a new distribution list using ADSI.*

```
' — — Server, Org and Site information
server = "JOELHOME"
org = "ImagiNET"
Site = "JUNGLE"


' —· Distribution List — —·
strDisplayname = "Project Managers"
strAlias = "pm"
strSMTPAddr = "ProjectManager@ImagiNETS.com"


' —· Build Recipient container's adsPath that looks like this:
' LDAP://myserver/CN=Recipients, OU=Site, O=Org

ADsPath = "LDAP://" + server
ADsPath = ADsPath + "/cn=Recipients,OU="
ADsPath = ADsPath + Site
ADsPath = ADsPath + ",O="
ADsPath = ADsPath + org


Set objCont = GetObject(ADsPath)

'Create a new DL
Set objNewDL = objCont.Create("groupOfNames", "cn=" & strAlias)

'Set the DL props
objNewDL.Put "cn", CStr(strDisplayname)
objNewDL.Put "uid", CStr(strAlias)
objNewDL.Put "mail", CStr(strSMTPAddr)
objNewDL.SetInfo


' _ _ _ _ _ _ _ _ _ _ _ _ _ _ _ _ _ _ _ _ _ _ _ _ _ _ _ _ _ ·
' —· ADDING MEMBERS TO A DISTRIBUTION LIST
' _ _ _ _ _ _ _ _ _ _ _ _ _ _ _ _ _ _ _ _ _ _ _ _ _ _ _ _ _ ·
Set dl = GetObject("LDAP://excsrv11/cn=dpm,cn=Recipients,ou=REDMOND,o=Microsoft")
dl.Add "LDAP://excsrv11/cn=jsmith,cn=Recipients,ou=REDMOND,o=Microsoft"
dl.Add "LDAP://excsrv11/cn=andyhar,cn=Recipients,ou=REDMOND,o=Microsoft"
```

Roles Created by the Roles Administrator

Don't get confused with how these applications, the Routing Wizard and the Roles Administrator, create and manipulate roles. The Roles Administrator is meant to work with the Rule Administrator or anyone else who wants to implement roles in this manner. Not all applications or developers may choose this method to implement this functionality. ◆

Let's take a look at what was actually built using this quick and easy Routing Wizard. Figure 14.7 shows the resulting route.

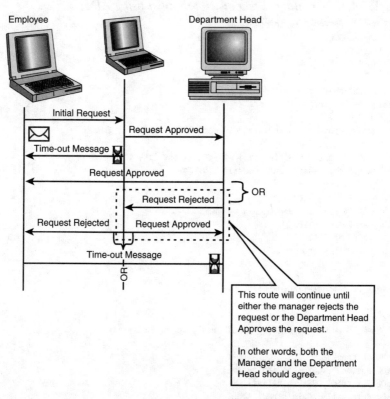

Figure 14.7 *The route created using the Routing Wizard.*

Interestingly enough, the sender can also determine who approved what along the route by looking at the Tracking tab of the final message he receives after the routing process completes, as shown in Figure 14.8.

You might notice that the routing scenario depicted in Figure 14.8 is a little different from that presented in Figure 14.2. The primary difference between the desired route and the one built using the Routing Wizard is that actions are taken when routing requests time out. Instead of forwarding the message to the head of the department, the request simply gets sent back to the original requestor with neither an acceptance nor a rejection. Additionally, the original scenario doesn't intend to have the department head part of every travel request approval process, only at times when the sales manager hasn't approved or rejected the request in an appropriate amount of time.

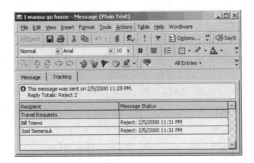

Figure 14.8   *The results of the routed request can be viewed in the Tracking tab of the final message sent to the employee who originally created the request.*

So how do you accomplish this using the Routing Wizard? You might notice that when a route times out, the only available option is to return the request to the original sender. It only gave you the opportunity to send to another folder, where a separate route could be defined that would send the request to the department head. So, as you can see, there are many routes that would be difficult, if not impossible, to implement using the Routing Wizard. So what can be done to work around this issue? Simple, build your routes manually and programmatically. Before you can do this, you must first have an understanding of what's involved.

How the Routing Wizard Works

In Chapter 2, "Typical Collaborative Development Examples," I described the pieces of any typical workflow solution: roles, routes, rules, and data. As you can see, all of these components come together in the solution that is created using the Routing Wizard. In this case, roles are managers. The route is defined sequentially from the employee to the employee's manager to the head of the department. Rules are placed on the route to ensure that if the manager does not address the request in a specific amount of time, some other action needs to be taken. And finally, the data is simply the details of the request itself.

So how does Microsoft Exchange represent routes and rules? How does it manage the routes and the rules? Basically, Exchange implements routing using the following three components:

- **The Routing Engine.** This is a custom event handler for the event scripting agent. The Routing Engine tracks all messages along with its routing map for a particular folder in Exchange. A map is basically the definition of a route that a message must take. The message along with its map is called a process instance.

- **Routing objects.** These are a set of Component Object Model (COM) objects that allow developers to define and modify maps and process instances in public folders. In essence, these objects let you programmatically define and install routing maps into a folder.

- **Actions.** Actions are simply functions defined by the route map that are called by the Routing Engine. There are two types of actions: Intrinsic and Custom. Intrinsic actions are those that are built into the Routing Engine. Custom actions are ones that developers create using VBScript, very much like the script that was discussed in Chapter 13.

To summarize, the Routing Engine executes actions defined by the routing map, which is installed into a public folder, for every message that is posted to that folder.

In fact, Exchange routing is just a simple extension to event scripting, discussed in the previous chapter. All of the requirements for event scripting, such as the use of server-side folders, are also required for Exchange routing. If the Microsoft Exchange Event Service isn't running for some reason, routing is temporarily paused. However, just like message event handling, messages are not missed if the Event Service is unavailable. All new messages and route updates are processed when the Event Service comes back online.

Routing is based off of a hub and spoke architecture. For example, even though we set up a sequential route using the Routing Wizard, how do you think the Routing Engine knows what steps to take next? After every leg in the route, the message must be returned to the original folder where it can be analyzed so that the Routing Engine can determine what it should do with the message next, which is determined by the routing map. Figure 14.9 shows this architecture.

Multiple Route Maps

Not only can a folder have a route map associated with it, it can have many. To further complicate the matter, individual messages can have their own route maps. ♦

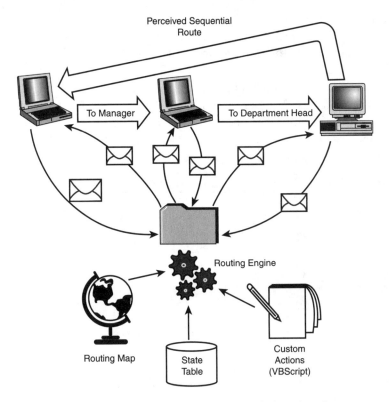

Figure 14.9   *All Exchange routing is hub and spoke even if perceived as sequential or parallel.*

I mentioned earlier that a process instance is a combination of a message and a route map. I also mentioned that Exchange has the capability to route and keep track of many messages at the same time. If the public folder that acts as the hub in a particular routing solution continually receives messages from all legs of a route, how does it know which message is associated with which process instance? This problem is simply solved by a Route Unique Identifier (RUI), that is assigned to every process instance. Every message that has been generated by the process instance is stamped with the RUI of that process instance. If a message is received that has no RUI, Exchange assumes that a new process instance needs to be created. When a message arrives that does not have a route map as part of the message, the folder's default route, which is stored as a hidden message in the folder, is copied into the message and a new process instance begins.

Maps and Actions

Let's take a closer look at maps and actions. As I have already stated, the routing map defines the routing process. It provides all the routing logic to the Routing Engine very much like a set of instructions in a function or procedure. In fact, the routing map tells which functions the Routing Engine should execute based on the conditions of the message. The functions that the map specifies are called actions, which come in two flavors—intrinsic (built-in functions) or custom (functions written in VBScript). Table 14.3 is an example of a very simple routing map.

Table 14.3   Routing Map Rows Created Using the Routing Wizard

ActivityID	Action	Flags	Parm1	Parm2
100	OrSplit	0	IsNDR	
110	Goto	0	30000	
200	ORSplit	0	IsReceipt	
210	Goto		30000	
300	ORSplit	0	IsPost	
310	Goto	0	30100	
500	PreProcessing	2	False	
1000	Send	2	Manager	+ 6 other parameters
1010	Wait	0	240	
1020	ORSplit	0	IsTimeout	
1030	Goto	0	5000	
1040	ORSplit	0	IsNDR	
1050	Goto	0	5000	
1060	ORSplit	0	IsReceipt	
1070	Goto	0	1010	
1080	ORSplit	0	IsOOF	
1097	Goto	0	1010	
1100	Receive	2	False	
1110	Consolidate	2	False	
...				

You probably didn't think such a complex looking map would produce such a simple route, did you? As you can see, a routing map is divided into a number of columns: ActivityId, Action, Flags, and parameter columns. Only the first three are required. The activity ID designates an action number, much like a line number in a programming language such as Basic. The Action column holds the name of the action that is to be executed by the

Routing Engine. The flag tells the Routing Engine if the specified action is intrinsic or custom, where 0 signifies an intrinsic action and 2 denotes a custom action.

Naming Actions

The action name must exactly match the name of an intrinsic action or a custom action, implemented as a function in VBScript in the associated event script. The function names in VBScript must be prefixed with the word ROUTE_. For example, when activity 1100 is reached, the Event Engine is told to execute a custom action called Receive. The Routing Engine looks for a function called ROUTE_Receive in the map's associated event script. ◆

Intrinsic Actions

Let's take a quick look at some of the intrinsic actions before we go on to create custom actions. The Routing Engine comes with the following six built-in actions:

- AndSplit
- Goto
- New
- OrSplit
- Terminate
- Wait

Let me describe each of these independently to give you a better understanding of how the map depicted in Table 14.3 works.

AndSplit

The AndSplit action severs the map into two independently running processes, where the parent process is blocked until the return of each child process. Each new process ends when it hits a Terminate action. The AndSplit takes two parameters—the ActionID's of the sub processes that are launched. Basically, the current map is copied into each of the new sub processes, and execution is started on the activity ID that is specified in the appropriate parameter. Figure 14.10 represents the processing involved in an AndSplit.

Ending a Sub Process with a Terminate

It is extremely important that the Terminate action exists in each of the sub processes to designate when the sub process is to return to its parent. ◆

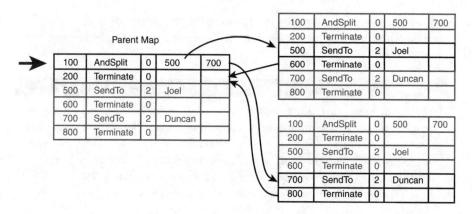

Figure 14.10   *The AndSplit action.*

GoTo

Goto is an extremely easy action to explain. As you have probably already guessed, the Goto action instructs the Routing Engine to go to a specific action ID, identified in the parameter of the Goto activity.

New

The New action spawns a new process that begins executing at the activity ID specified in the action's parameter. The routing engine copies the currently executing map into the new process to create the new process instance, ending with a Terminate action. Unlike the AndSplit action, the existing process continues to execute at the same time as the new process. Figure 14.11 demonstrates how the New action works.

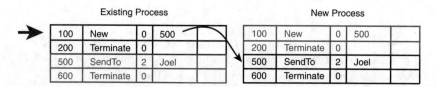

Figure 14.11   *The New action.*

OrSplit

The parameter that is passed to the OrSplit function is the name of a VBScript function that returns True or False. When the Routing Engine encounters an OrSplit action, it executes this function. If it returns True, the action that immediately follows the OrSplit action is executed. If the function returns False, the Routing Engine skips the action immediately after the OrSplit, and the row following is executed. Figure 14.12 demonstrates how the OrSplit action works.

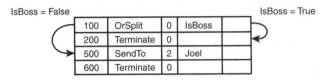

IsBoss = False

IsBoss = True

100	OrSplit	0	IsBoss	
200	Terminate	0		
500	SendTo	2	Joel	
600	Terminate	0		

Figure 14.12   *The OrSplit action.*

Terminate
I don't need to explain the Terminate action. Simply put, the Terminate action ends the current process instance.

Wait
The Wait action simply instructs the Routing Engine to wait a given amount of time, provided to the Wait action using the first parameter in minutes. The Wait action is commonly used to implement timeouts, such as with the simple travel request solution that was built in the beginning of this chapter using the Routing Wizard. In fact, if you refer to action 1010 in Table 14.3, you can see that the Wait action instructs the Routing Engine to wait 240 minutes (4 hours) before continuing on with the map. The action that follows the Wait action checks to see if a timeout has occurred to decide what action should be taken next.

Custom Actions
Custom actions are simply actions that you provide to the Routing Engine by creating functions in VBScript. There are some rules that you should be aware of before going off and creating your own custom actions. First, you must make sure that you name your functions properly. All routing functions that implement custom actions must begin with Route_. Second, be very aware of what the return values of the function are. Normally, many custom actions return either a True or a False. Example 14.2 was taken from the Routing Wizard to demonstrate how the IsTerminate custom action was implemented.

Important Note!

All the code presented in this chapter has been snipped from samples provided in the Microsoft Product software development kit (SDK). ◆

Example 14.2   *The IsTerminate custom action.*

```
'+++++++++++++++++++++++++++++++++++++++++++++++++++++++++++++++++++++++
'   Name: Route_IsTimeout
'   Area: Core Routing
'   Desc: This function checks to see if the timeout has occurred
'         and returns this value is true for yes, false for no.
'         No would normally proceed to receive in the map.
'   Parm: byRef boolSuccess
'   Retn: None
'+++++++++++++++++++++++++++++++++++++++++++++++++++++++++++++++++++++++

Sub Route_IsTimeout(boolSuccess)

  On Error Resume Next

  Dim boolRes              'Boolean Result

  Call TraceHeader("IsTimeout")

  boolRes = InitializeBaseObjects
  If Not boolRes Then
      Call TraceAppend("InitializeBaseObjects Failed")
      'Initialize Objects Failure
  Else
    'Since InitializeBaseobjects is used get the
    'procinstance here.
    Set g_oProcInstance = RouteDetails.ProcInstance
    boolSuccess = g_oProcInstance.Timeout
    If Err Then
      Call ErrorCheck("g_oProcInstance.Timeout")
    End If
    Set g_oProcInstance = Nothing
  End If

  Call TraceAppend("IsTimeout returns " & boolSuccess)
  Call traceOutput("IsTimeout", 2)

  Call ReleaseBaseObjects

End Sub
```

How Do the Pieces Fit Together?

Let's try to put these pieces together to see if more sense can be made of them. First of all, remember that the Routing Engine is a custom event handler for event scripting, and this requires the creation of an agent in the folder, typically a public folder, where you want the Routing Engine to run. Remember also that the script used by event scripting is stored in a hidden message that resides in the public folder. You can programmatically manipulate this hidden message using a set of COM objects provided to you from the Exchange Event SERVICE and Collaborative Data Object (CDO). Additionally, I mentioned that there exists a set of COM objects, called routing objects, that allow developers to programmatically manipulate the routing map and the process instances in your routing solution. All of these together give you routing and workflow in Exchange 5.5. Just to give you a taste of what is required to accomplish all of this programmatically, take a look at Example 14.3, taken from the Routing Wizard, which binds your map and event script to a folder using Exchange routing objects.

Example 14.3   *Programmatically binding routing maps.*

```
Private Function SaveDefinition() As Boolean

On Error GoTo SaveDefinitionErr

Dim oRow As Variant
Dim bExrtobjErrorFlag As Boolean
Dim ofolder As Object
Dim oTemp As Object
Dim oEvents As Object          'Events Object
Dim oBoundFolder As Object     'Bound folder Object
Dim oBindings As Object        'Bindings Collection
Dim oBinding As Object         'Binding Object
Dim oMsg As Object             'Message Object
Dim oSchedule As Object        'Schedule object
Dim strid As String            'String Id


'Note: Attempt to create the row first so if exrtobj.dll
' is not registered properly or doesn't exist the function exits
' before an unfinished agent is created.
bExrtobjErrorFlag = True
Set oRow = Nothing
Set oRow = CreateObject("exrt.row") 'Creating Rows
Set oRow = Nothing

bExrtobjErrorFlag = False
'Get events Com Object (ESCONF.DLL)
Set oEvents = CreateObject("MSExchange.Events")
oEvents.Session = CDOClass.Session

'Get CDO folder, then bound folder, then bindings
'associated with the folder.
Set ofolder = CDOClass.GetFolderByID(WizClass.FolderID)

'If EventPermissions are valid then write agent with
'latest script.
If WizClass.EventPermissions Then
```

continues ▶

Example 14.3   *continued*

```
'Failure here mean no permissions
Set oBoundFolder = oEvents.BoundFolder(ofolder, 1)
Set oBindings = oBoundFolder.Bindings

'Verify proper binding agent conditions are met.
If bAssignRoutingAgent(oBindings, oBinding, oMsg) Then
    If oBinding Is Nothing Then
        'Must add new agent
        'Create New Binding Message
        Set oBinding = oBindings.Add
        oBinding.Name = "Routing Agent"
        oBinding.Active = True
        oBinding.EventMask = 1 + 2 + 4 + 8
        'This is the class ID of the exrteng.dll which is located on the server
        oBinding.HandlerClassID = mstrHANDLER_CLASS_ID_ROUTING_AGENT
        oBinding.savechanges
        Set oSchedule = oBinding.Schedule
        oSchedule.Interval = 60
        oSchedule.Type = 1
        oSchedule.Days = 127
        oSchedule.Starttime = 0
        oSchedule.EndTime = 0.99999
        oBinding.savechanges
    Else
        'Always update Binding name because route may have changed type.
        oBinding.Name = "Routing Agent"
        oBinding.savechanges
    End If


    'Get binding entry id to use in get message call to get
    'message object so properties and can added or read.
    strid = oBinding.EntryID
    Set oMsg = CDOClass.Session.Getmessage(strid, Null)

    'Write RoutingAgent Property
    oMsg.Fields.Add "RouteAgent", VT_BOOL, True   'Boolean

'Update Script
'   If the agent already existed the currently stored script
'   will be used, otherwise a new default script will be
'   used.

If Not oMsg Is Nothing Then
    oMsg.Fields.item(PR_EVENT_SCRIPT) = WizClass.EventScript
Else
    MsgBox "No Agent Available (Shouldn't get this message)."
End If

oMsg.Subject = oBinding.Name
oMsg.Update
```

```
        oBinding.SaveCustomChanges oMsg
        oBinding.savechanges
        oBoundFolder.savechanges


    End If


    '
    ' Validations for adding a routing agent failed
    ' We just don't write anything to the Routing Agent.
  End If


  If bWriteRoutingMap(ofolder) Then
      'Success
      If WizClass.EventPermissions Then
          MsgBox "The Route Map and Route Agent was successfully installed.", vbInformation
➡+ vbMsgBoxSetForeground, App.Title
      Else
          If WizClass.AgentExist Then
              MsgBox "The Route Map was successfully installed.", vbInformation +
➡vbMsgBoxSetForeground, App.Title
          Else
              MsgBox "The Route Map was successfully installed but won't run until a Route
➡Agent is installed.", vbInformation + vbMsgBoxSetForeground, App.Title
          End If
      End If
      SaveDefinition = True
  Else
      If WizClass.EventPermissions Then
          MsgBox "The Route Agent was installed but the Route Map installation failed.",
➡vbExclamation + vbMsgBoxSetForeground, App.Title
      Else
          MsgBox "Unable to successfully install map.", vbCritical + vbMsgBoxSetForeground,
➡App.Title
      End If
      SaveDefinition = False

      frmWizard.MousePointer = vbNormal

  End If


ReleaseStuff:


  Set oTemp = Nothing
  Set oBinding = Nothing
  Set oBindings = Nothing
  Set oBoundFolder = Nothing
  Set oEvents = Nothing

  Exit Function
```

continues ▶

Example 14.3   *continued*

```
SaveDefinitionErr:

  If Err = 429 Then
    If bExrtobjErrorFlag Then
      Call CDOClass.MapiErrorHandler("EXRTOBJ.DLL Error." & vbCrLf & "Verify that this
➥DLL exists and is registered.")
    Else
      Call CDOClass.MapiErrorHandler("ESCONF.DLL Error. " & vbCrLf & "Verify that it
➥exists and is registered.")
    End If
    Err.Clear
  Else
    Call CDOClass.MapiErrorHandler("SaveDefinition in FrmWizard")
  End If

  If WizClass.EventPermissions Then
    MsgBox "Unable to complete installation due to a detected error.", vbCritical,
➥App.Title
  End If

  GoTo ReleaseStuff

End Function
```

As you can see, most of this code manipulates the Exchange Event objects that are originally declared using the following:

```
Set oEvents = CreateObject("MSExchange.Events")
```

After a reference to the Events object is made, you can eventually get a reference to that hidden message that stores the script and, eventually, the routing map. The following snippet of code references this message:

```
strid = oBinding.EntryID
Set oMsg = CDOClass.Session.Getmessage(strid, Null)
```

Finally, the script, which is just a string of text, gets saved into the message using the following code:

```
oMsg.Fields.item(PR_EVENT_SCRIPT) = WizClass.EventScript
```

The next major hurdle is to save the routing map into the appropriate hidden message. The lines of code shown in Example 14.4 save one line of the map to the hidden message, taken from the Routing Wizard application.

Example 14.4   *Saving the map into the hidden message.*

```
If Not bGetMapMessage(ofolder, oMsg, bMapFound, bstrRouteType) Then
  'An error condition occurred.
  bWriteRoutingMap = False
  Exit Function
End If
```

continues ▶

```
'Create Map FAI Message if not exist.
If Not bMapFound Then
    Set oMsg = ofolder.HiddenMessages.Add("Routing Map Message", "", "IPM.Note", 1)
    oMsg.Fields.Add "RouteMap", VT_BOOL, True
    oMsg.Update
End If

If frmWizard.optAttach.Value Then
  bLinkNotEnabled = True
Else
  bLinkNotEnabled = False
End If

'Create the exrt map object.
Set oMap = CreateObject("exrt.map")
oMap.DeleteMap    'Clears out map
oMap.Message = oMsg
oMap.SaveMap
oMap.OpenMap TBL_OPEN_READWRITE

' _ _ _ _ _ _ _ _ _ _ _ _ _ _ _ _ _
'       MAP ROWS
'
'   Rows that affect all
' _ _ _ _ _ _ _ _ _ _ _ _ _ _ _ _ _

' (ALL) — IsNDR — NDR HANDLING
' _ _ _ _ _ _ _ _ _ _ _ _ _ _ _
Set oRow = Nothing
Set oRow = CreateObject("exrt.row") 'Creating Rows

lParamcols = 1
ReDim vntField(lParamcols - 1)

vntField(0) = "IsNDR"

oRow.SetArgs lParamcols, vntField
oRow.ActivityID = WIZ_NDR
oRow.Action = "ORSplit"
oRow.Flags = WF_Flag_Intrinsic
oMap.insertactivity -1, oRow
```

As you can see, this ends up being quite a bit of work.

I will not go into any more detail on this process of programmatically binding maps and scripts to a folder, because it is outside the scope of this book. If you are interested in more information on this topic, download the source code for both the Routing Wizard and the Agent Editor applications, which are both written in Visual Basic, and step through the code.

Building More Complex Workflow Solutions

So, how do you build more complex routing solutions that better model your business? Do you really sit back, bring out Visual Basic, and code like hell for a week? Possibly. I've known people who have done it—myself included. However, there is another possibility, for those smart enough to install and search Microsoft's Platform Software Development Kit. This kit provides an overwhelming amount of information and samples. One of the samples provided in the SDK is called AgentEd (short for Agent Editor). AgentEd is a VB program that provides a GUI for the creation of standard event scripts, as described in Chapter 13, as well as the creation of complex routing maps. If you need to implement routing in your organization under Exchange 5.5, AgentEd is a good place to start. First of all, you can download and use the code from the Platform SDK. This allows you to dive into working code to give you a better understanding of how maps and scripts are installed into a folder. Second, AgentEd works really well for most routing processes. You can easily use it to create both normal event scripts, as described in the previous chapter, and full fledged routing solutions. It's too bad that this application, or a version of it, didn't ship with Exchange 5.5 to begin with.

Where to Find AgentEd

AgentEd is found on the Platform SDK, which you can download and install right off of Microsoft's Web page. After you have installed the Platform SDK, you can find AgentEd in all of its glory in the following location:

```
C:\Program Files\Microsoft Platform SDK\Samples\DbMSG\Exchange\Aeditor ◆
```

Using AgentEd

Let's take a quick look at what AgentEd can do.

When you run AgentEd, it automatically logs you on. Before you can do anything further, you must select a folder using the Select Folder option from the Agent menu. After you have selected a folder, AgentEd allows you to create a new agent, or edit or delete existing agents in the selected folder. If you choose to create a new agent, AgentEd prompts you for the type of agent you want to create, allowing you to choose from a routing agent or a script handling agent, as shown in Figure 14.13.

After you have specified the type of agent you want to create for the selected folder, you are presented with a default script, shown in Figure 14.14 (which happens to be the same script that the Routing Wizard provides, so all of those cool custom actions are already implemented for you), a blank map, and an area to set up some of the properties of the agent. When you're done creating your agent, choose Save Changed from the Agent menu and everything else is done for you.

Figure 14.13   *The New Agent properties dialog box.*

Source Code for the Routing Wizard

Microsoft has provided the source code for the Routing Wizard and AgentEd only as a learning tool. You should not use any part of that code to produce a production routing solution. ◆

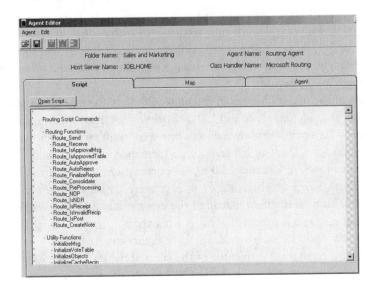

Figure 14.14   *The default script provided by AgentEd.*

Using Off-the-Shelf Solutions

Before you go off and start building complex routing solutions, you should take a look at the many products you can buy that do a great job of implementing routing solutions with little to no effort. If you think about the extreme amount of effort it would take to implement event the simplest route, an off-the-shelf Exchange Routing product soon becomes very attractive.

Where to Find Third-Party Software

To get a fairly current list of third-party software that you can use to implement workflow, check out the following site:

`http://www.microsoft.com/isapi/industry/directory/default.asp` ◆

Unfortunately, Exchange 5.5 does not provide a very robust user interface for creating and managing routes. As a result, I tell many of my clients to evaluate and purchase an off-the-shelf routing solution, because the relative cost of purchasing such a solution is probably much less than implementing and maintaining a similar solution from scratch.

The Exchange 2000 Solution

Exchange 2000 has really matured with regard to its routing capabilities. Exchange 2000 should have everything you need to effectively build and maintain simple and complex workflow solutions. For those of you who have invested a great deal of time and money into routing solutions under Exchange 5.5, those solutions will still work correctly, but you should consider redeveloping your solutions to take advantage of the new features Exchange 2000 provides.

Some of the major changes in Exchange 2000, with respect to event handling and routing, circle around CDO Workflow objects, which is an enhanced library of workflow services based on simultaneous and synchronous events, providing a high level of performance, reliability, and security. The event model, in Exchange 2000, supports synchronous events. This means that when a synchronous event is triggered, Exchange performs no further processing on the item that fired the event until all of the event's associated business logic is executed. This is a big change from the model that you have to rely upon in Exchange 5.5, where events can be fired asynchronously, making you constantly suspicious of the state of the underlying item.

Some of the underlying goals that Microsoft attempts to achieve in Exchange 2000 include the following:

- To make it extremely easy to add simple workflow to server applications.
- To allow the same workflow solution to work with either Office or Web applications at the same time. For example, the same events would be fired and handled from either a File.Save, a Web app, or a Post from Outlook.
- Focus workflow development to ease the most common scenarios that include approval solutions, document review solutions, data routing, and tracking solutions.

- The development environment and tools should be targeted to a typical Office developer skill set.

- To provide better tools and interfaces for creating and managing workflow.

In fact, Exchange 2000 comes with a really cool component called the Exchange Workflow designer (which is kind of like AgentEd on steroids). With the Exchange Workflow Designer, you can view your workflow design graphically instead of looking at a cryptic map of actions conditions. The most important change the Workflow Designer makes to the development of workflow solutions is that complex business models, which you would typically stay away from in Exchange 5.5, can be more easily modeled, built, and maintained. More and more complex business processes and information flow scenarios can be built with even less effort—taking us one step closer to that ever-distant digital universe I dream about before I fall asleep every night.

Additional preliminary documentation on Exchange 2000 workflow solutions can be obtained in the \Support\CDO\exchserv2k.chm file. This book was written when Exchange 2000 was in Beta 3, so much of the technical details are subject to change.

Chapter Summary

In this chapter, I described how to build two types of workflow samples. The first used Office document routing to get the job done. This turned out to be extremely easy to implement, but equally limiting in terms of control and functionality. However, if you ever need to accomplish simple document routing, this should be the first thing you evaluate.

I switched gears considerably to discuss Exchange routing. I discussed the following:

- The Routing Wizard ships with the latest service pack for Exchange and can be used to create simple sequential or parallel routing solutions.

- The components of Exchange routing were examined to gain a better understanding of how the Routing Wizard works.

- More advanced routing tools exist in the Microsoft Product SDK, such as AgentEd, that allow you to build more complex routing solutions in Exchange 5.5 much easier.

- Writing routing solutions from the ground up might not be practical for many organizations. Third-party workflow applications should be considered when many complex routing solutions are required.

- Exchange 2000 redefines how workflow solutions are built in Exchange by adding enhancements to CDO and the Exchange event model, as well as providing a more intuitive administrative interface when defining the desired workflow or business model.

15

Designing and Building Knowledge Management Solutions

As promised, in this final chapter, I am going to discuss how to build knowledge management solutions. Let me stress the word *discuss*. Knowledge management solutions are not as clear-cut as Visual Basic for Applications (VBA) solutions because they exist at a much higher level. In fact, I have already covered almost everything you need to build an effective knowledge management solution using Microsoft Exchange, Outlook, and the Web. The problem with knowledge management solutions revolves around what kind of solutions can be created with the tools I have discussed so far. With this in mind, I am going to focus more on examples and theory rather than hard core programming.

Even though knowledge management solutions do not necessarily involve Microsoft Exchange and Outlook, these products can enhance the processes of gathering, storing, and presenting knowledge in ways that appear almost seamless to the end user. In fact, the word seamless is what makes the creation of an effective knowledge management solution so difficult. For those project managers out there who have ever struggled to get simple status reports out of your workers, you will agree that the typical knowledge worker is generally lazy when it comes to reporting and communicating, even though this is the lifeblood of any corporation. Effective knowledge management solutions really only accomplish two goals. The first is to make it extremely easy to acquire new knowledge. The second is the capability to present all gathered knowledge in a meaningful and structured way. As you can see, these are two very broad goals, and I truly believe that as the evolution of knowledge management solutions continues, these goals will be met with greater ease than what developers are faced with today, because creating really good knowledge management solutions is quite difficult.

When you look at Microsoft BackOffice and Microsoft Office, you can see that these packages contain all of the software required to build almost any knowledge management solution you can think of. The primary Office products are excellent at knowledge acquisition. Microsoft Exchange provides the capability to store and route this knowledge in an extremely intuitive and efficient manner. If you look to some of the additional products that are part of the Microsoft BackOffice suite of products, such as Microsoft SQL Server and Microsoft Site Server, you will find that you can take this one step further. As you already know, SQL Server provides one of the best means of storing and retrieving structured, relational data. Site Server provides a mechanism to easily index content stored on almost any supported data storage facility, such as a file system or Microsoft Exchange public folders. In fact, this is such an important concept that Exchange 2000 has a mini-Site Server built in that is primarily used to index content stored within the Web Store managed by Microsoft Exchange. This means that you can find just about anything you need regardless of where it is stored or who created it.

In this chapter, I will do the following:

- Explain how to use Microsoft Exchange public folders to store knowledge

- Describe techniques that will make assimilating knowledge as seamless as possible by using Exchange distribution lists

- Illustrate how to effectively present the organization's knowledge

Storing Knowledge—Team Folders Revisited

What is knowledge? Where is it? Where can you keep it? How can you get it? In an organization, knowledge is typically stored in documents that are maintained somewhere on corporate file systems or within public folders. Knowledge can also be stored in databases that collect statistics on sales, products, contacts, or virtually anything else. However, some really important knowledge is contained within email messages sent between people in the organization. Typically, the communication that takes place between the people in an organization is full of status, updates, quick fixes, insight, direction, late breaking news, and opinion. If only some form of structure could be placed on this type of knowledge, while still providing facilities to store, retrieve, and search this information to produce some meaningful result. Here is where public folders play an important role when it comes to the massive amounts of knowledge imbedded into the messages and documents that are exchanged between people in a corporation. They are the perfect medium for storing and managing this sort of information effectively and easily.

This book already covers a great deal of information relating to team folders—what they are, how they work, what their potential is. But really, what are team folders? They are nothing but organized public folders with a fancy, yet complicated, Web front end. You already knew this was possible—big deal. Hold on a second, it is a big deal if you look at team folders at a much higher level—a knowledge management level, that is. Let's look at what we know about team folders. First, there is a Team Folder Wizard that can be used to set up different, predefined team folder types, such as Projects, Discussions, Contacts, and Documents. The wizard sets up all of these team folders in the same structured way. Additionally, customization and administration is left primarily in the hands of the user. This is wonderful! Team folders, and especially the Team Folder Wizard, enforce the use of public folders in a very structured and standardized way. More importantly, team folders and the Team Folder Wizard are extremely easy to use, so they can be used by an organization's knowledge workers (to coin a phrase) with little to no effort or learning curve.

Not only do team folders provide structure to public folders and their contents, but the Web pages that help provide access to the contents of their underlying public folders demonstrate an effective means of presenting and organizing information within.

Those of you who have used team folders right out-of-the-box might have thought that they do not really fit your organization's needs. Take heart. Remember that team folders are completely customizable. You can add underlying folders, completely customize each team folder's Web page, and add business logic processing of public folder content. You can even customize the Team Folder Wizard application used to create new team folders within your environment to fit your needs exactly.

Let me use an example to clarify how you can effectively use team folders to help gather and store knowledge on Microsoft Exchange Server.

ImagiNET Resources is involved with many different clients. For any given client, many projects exist. Projects must have a project manager who is responsible for the health of a project plus one or more team members. Additionally, it is not uncommon for a single project manager to be assigned to more than one project, depending on the size of the projects he is working on. ImagiNET realizes that every project manager—and in fact, almost every team member—consistently gathers, sorts, and categorizes emails sent and received regarding specific projects, to the point where every team member's mailbox becomes hundreds of megabytes large. They do this because they want to ensure that they can refer to conversations, conducted electronically over email of course, that reflect decisions, comments, suggestions, status, and direction.

Why can't all of this accumulative information be available to everyone on the team, accessed from a centralized location? Better yet, why can't this practice be extended to reflect one point of reference for all electronic communications, documentation, assigned tasks, status reports, issues, build reports, and bug reports regarding certain projects? ImagiNET realizes that structuring and gathering information of this sort is made easier with team folders. However, the default set of team folders, and the Team Folder Wizard, requires modification to allow ImagiNET's employees to store additional information about each project, as well as to make it more intuitive to use and operate. In fact, ImagiNET requires the following information to be stored and maintained in Exchange public folders (as shown in Figure 15.1):

- **Discussion.** This repository acts much like a default team folder discussion forum. Every team member is urged to maintain all project-related communication in this folder. Distribution lists, as I will discuss later in the section "Using Distribution Lists for Knowledge Management," make this task extremely easy.

- **Documents.** All related project documents are stored in this library. All documents are categorized as they are inserted into the folder. Views are used to group documents by their assigned category types and document types.

- **Calendar.** Important project-related events, such as major milestones and meetings, are recorded in this repository. All client interaction is also clearly entered into this folder, such as meetings, client upgrades, and updates. Additionally, any scheduled vacations of team members of key client contacts are recorded.

- **Contacts.** This folder stores all of the project's related contacts. Responsibilities and reporting relationship can clearly be defined at the Contact item level.

- **Tasks.** All major and minor tasks (for example, Fix Bug 1203B—Assigned to Joel Semeniuk) are maintained here. This folder, and associated views, turns out to be extremely important for the project manager because this provides the project manager the ability to quickly get task level status on any given project he manages. Team members are not overly burdened with weekly status reports because they simply update task information as it happens (for example, Fix Bug 1203B—Completed). Filters can be used to show tasks that have been completed for the previous weeks or month. Tasks can also be grouped by priority and assigned team member.

- **Issues.** Every project has issues and everyone knows that issues must be tracked. It is essential that issues are tracked electronically and are available for reference at any time. The Project Issues folder holds all issues related to a given project, using custom forms and fields.

- **Change Requests.** Like issues, projects can change, and all changes must be recorded and authorized. The Project Change Requests folder maintains all change requests for a given project, implemented using custom forms and fields.

- **Bug Reports.** Another necessity is bug tracking. Every reported software bug, related to the project, is entered into the Bug Reports folder. A flag that signifies status (resolved, unresolved) is maintained in this folder as well. With views, users can view only unresolved bugs, view bugs that have highest priority, and sort bug reports by the date that they were entered.

- **Status Reports.** Status reports must also be tracked. The folder is configured so that only project managers can view all submitted status reports; other team members can submit reports and view only the reports that they have submitted. Of course, status reports can be grouped by the team member who submitted the report or filtered by date (for example, All Status Reports for Last Week).

- **Best Practices.** Every project can be considered a learning experience. Simply stated, if you learn something that relates to technology, project management, client relationships, or presentations, submit it into the Project Best Practices folder. The Project Best Practices folder allows any team member to enter any lessons learned throughout the life of the project. All lessons are categorized and views exist to better organize this information.

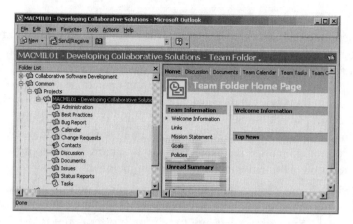

Figure 15.1   *Enhanced team folders.*

To help enforce the usage of these team folder types, ImagiNET also has to create a new team folder template, as well as make modifications to the Team Folder Wizard, by creating Team Folder extensions in Visual Basic. Generally, users need to be able to launch the Team Folder Wizard to create a new set of ImagiNET project folders without having to provide Web site or public folder information. The Team Folder Wizard is also modified to prompt for project specific information, such as associated project codes, project type, and client (see Figure 15.3). After this information is entered, the wizard automatically creates the new set of team folders under the appropriate public folder root. Users also do not have to specify any Web server information; appropriate Web server installation locations are retrieved from a special message located in the root of all ImagiNET project folders and are thus controlled centrally. Figure 15.2 demonstrates the ability for users to select a new template of team folder, the ImagiNET Project Team Folder; Figure 15.3 depicts an added step taken by the Team Folder Wizard during the creation of a new ImagiNET project team folder.

Team Folders and Distribution Lists

During the setup of a new ImagiNET project team folder, the Team Folder Wizard creates new associated distribution lists in Exchange. These new distribution lists make it easier to send and receive correspondence to the individuals or groups of individuals working on a specific project. I will discuss this later in the section "Using Distribution Lists for Knowledge Management." ◆

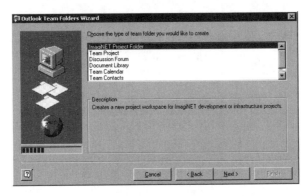

Figure 15.2   *Users can select the ImagiNET project folder while executing the Team Folder Wizard.*

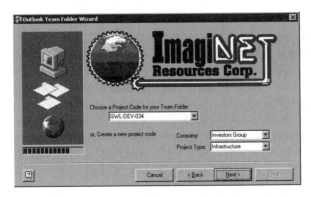

Figure 15.3   *Defining a new ImagiNET project using the Team Folder Wizard.*

What you are left with is a set of very organized and useful knowledge repositories that is used to store business critical information that is easy to access and reference anywhere in the organization.

After downloading the Team Folders Kit from http://www.microsoft.com/ exchange/Collaboration.htm, you should have everything you need to accomplish this task. When installed, the Team Folders Kit provides samples, templates, and some very good documentation created as Windows Help files. To build a solution similar to the one I just talked about, you have to do two things: Create a new team folder template and customize it.

Create a New Team Folder Template

Creating a new team folder template involves the following steps:

1. Create and customize all the folders, forms, and views that will be used by the new template.

2. Store these new folders, along with their associated forms and views, into a personal folder store (PST) file that is used by the Team Folder Wizard to create the structure of the team folders into the designated sub-folder.

3. Create folder home pages. You can create one big folder home page, which results in extremely complicated underlying HTML code, or a separate folder home page for each underlying folder. Using a single Web page obviously results in faster load performance, but it is more difficult to maintain.

4. Create an Administration page for your new team folder template.

5. Create a Template Initialization file. This file is used by the Team Folder Wizard to publish message classes for the underlying team folders, replace strings in HTML files for customization, map team folders to folder home pages, and control localization.

6. Copy the template to the machines that will be used to run the Team Folder Wizard to install a new team folder based on your new template. This location is usually in its own folder in C:\Program Files\Microsoft Office\Office\TFWizard\1033\. Each folder contains the template's TEMPLATE.INI, the corresponding PST file, and any associated Web pages that must be copied to a Web server during the installation process.

7. Register the new template with the Team Folder Wizard. This requires adding a Registry key to HKEY_CURRENT_USER\Software\ Microsoft\ Office\Outlook\Addins\Microsoft.OLTeamFolderWizard\1033. Each new template has its own Registry key, as shown in Figure 15.4, containing information on the template, such as the location of the PST file, the path to the template, the name of the PST, and so on.

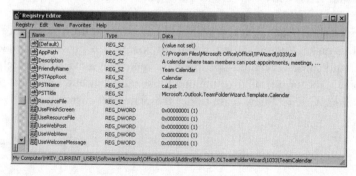

Figure 15.4 *A Registry key that corresponds to a team folder template.*

Customize the Team Folder Wizard

Customizing the Team Folder Wizard involves creating a Team Folder Wizard extension. The following steps outline this process:

1. Create an ActiveX DLL that implements a certain Component Object Model (COM) interface, IteamFoldersExtension, which can be referenced from the Tfexten.dll type library. This ActiveX DLL should contain all of the wizard forms and logic required to use your new team folder template. The ActiveX DLL must implement three functions that the wizard calls: ExtExec, which is called by the Team Folder Wizard when entering the extension for the first time; ExtUndo, called by the Team Folder Wizard when the extension is entered again; and ExtCancel, which is called when a user clicks Cancel somewhere in the wizard.

2. You must ensure that your new Team Folder Wizard extension is registered as part of the template that it was designed to work with. Specifically, the Registry key that contains your new team folder template's parameters must also contain two additional values: Execution Class, which specifies program ID of the ActiveX DLL that you just created, and ExtensionSteps, which specifies how many extra steps the Team Folder Wizard extension adds to the wizard process.

Word From the Wise

If you want to save yourself hours of precious time, don't start from scratch. The Team Folder Kit provides many samples, and you can always use the built-in team folders to get you going. The sample Team Folder Wizard extension, written in Visual Basic (VB), is extremely easy to follow. I recommend that you make a copy of this sample and use as the basis for your new extension. ✦

Using Distribution Lists for Knowledge Management

I described how you can use team folders and the Team Folder Wizard to build public folders that act as knowledge repositories. You can make the process of using these repositories of knowledge even easier by using distribution lists. You're probably asking yourself, "What do distribution lists have to do with knowledge management?" To answer that question, take a moment to review what distribution lists provide to your work environment. At their base form, they are used to represent a virtual end point of information. This virtual end point can be comprised of many other recipients, folders, and distribution lists, something that the sender of the message does not need to concern himself with. For example, suppose a user sends an email message to the Project Managers' distribution list. The sender does not need to understand who exactly the Project Managers' list is comprised of, he just assumes that the distribution list represents all project managers in the organization. The recipients included in the Project Managers' distribution list could contain other distribution lists, such as Project Managers for Client A, individual recipients, custom recipient, and public folders.

In Chapter 14, "Designing and Building Workflow Solutions," I described how you can use distribution lists to represent roles that can be used in the routing process. I think it is important to note that you can use distribution lists to represent roles in your organization regardless of the workflow solution you implement. For example, suppose you are working on a project. In that project, several distinct roles exist: Project Manager, Project Sponsor, Query Analyzer (QA), Testing, Developers, and so on. Each of these roles can be represented with a distribution list. For example, if you want to create a distribution list that represents the team of developers for the Sales Force Automation project, you could create a distribution list called SFA Developers. Now, anyone in the organization who wants to communicate with this group can be completely ignorant as to who these people are. They are simply sending email to a certain role in the organization.

Archiving Information

Using distribution lists as a way of representing roles in an organization also makes some additional niceties possible, such as email archival. Suppose that you want to track all communication sent to the project manager for a project. An easy way to accomplish this is to create a distribution list called PM for Project Alpha. In this distribution list, place the recipient that corresponds to this role and also place a reference to a public folder (using the Distribution List tab located in the properties dialog box of a public folder in the Exchange Administration program). Now, every piece of email sent to the project manager using the PM for Project Alpha distribution list is also stored in the assigned public folder; thus, a history of communication and discussions can easily be created and maintained without writing a single line of code, as depicted in Figure 15.5.

Turning Electrons into Knowledge

In a way, having a system track and store email exchanges between roles of a project or organization in a central location where they can be referenced and analyzed by everyone is like taking simple email traffic and turning it into usable knowledge for the entire organization. ◆

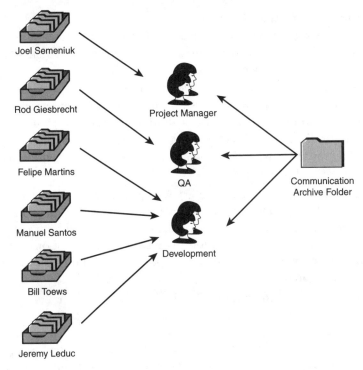

Figure 15.5   *Using distribution lists and public folders.*

Distribution List Best Practices

Here is a brief list of some of the things you can do to make the most out of distribution lists in your environment:

- Use distribution lists. This should be a given, but you would be surprised at how many organization misuse or don't use distribution lists.

- Create distribution lists to represent job roles within your organization. This allows for the position to change without having to notify anyone.

- If you want to track discussions or correspondence for a defined role in your organization, place a reference to a public folder in the distribution list you create for that role.

- Create automated procedures to allow users to create their own distribution lists and add or remove themselves from existing distribution lists. This saves administrators time and money managing the many distribution lists required by an organization.

Managing Distribution Lists

As I mentioned in the preceding section, "Distribution List Best Practices," you should always try to create some automated procedure that allows users to create and manage their own distribution lists, as well as provide the ability for users to add or remove themselves from existing distribution lists. This serves two purposes. First, it minimizes the administrative duties required for complex and robust distribution list usage. Second, it promotes the usage of distribution lists throughout the organization. There are, of course, a number of ways that you can make the management of distribution lists easier. For example:

- You can create a distribution list Web page that allows users to view a list of all distribution lists. Users also have the ability to add and remove themselves from existing distribution lists within the organization. If you really get ambitious, you can create a solution that requires the owner of a distribution list to approve any additions or deletions using routing.

- You can create an Outlook COM add-in that allows users to create new distribution lists and add or remove themselves from existing distribution lists. Routing and approval can be used to control access to existing distribution lists. The drawback with this option is that the COM add-in needs to be installed on everyone's computer. Routing and approval can be used to control access to existing distribution lists.

- The Team Folder Wizard can also be modified to automatically create the appropriate distribution lists whenever a new set of team folders is created. Of course, you also have to modify the Administration page of the team folder templates to allow assigned team folder administrators to modify these distribution lists after they are created. For example, if you want to create a new set of team folders that help to manage software development projects, you can modify the Team Folder Wizard to have users specify all of the roles that exist within the project, as well as who is currently assigned to each role. The Team Folder Wizard then can create distribution lists that correspond to each of the roles, placing the appropriate recipients in each new list. Additionally, Discussion folders, which are created as sub-folders of the Software Development Project team folder, are added to each new distribution list to ensure that all project-related communication is effectively tracked.

Whatever you choose to do, you will probably use Active Directory Services Interface (ADSI) to implement the actual process of creating or modifying distribution lists within Exchange. For your convenience, Examples 15.1 through 15.4 show some examples of common Lightweight Directory Access Protocol (LDAP) functions using VB code.

ADSI VB Code

This ADSI code, which is used to create, modify, and delete distribution lists, is written in VB. To write the same functions in VBScript for use in the Web or Outlook forms requires little to no effort. ◆

Example 15.1   *Creating a distribution list.*

```
sExchangeServer = "EXCH01"
sExchangeOrg = "Imaginet"
sExchangeSite = "WINNIPEG"

sDisplayname = "Project Managers"
sAlias = "PM"
sSMTPAddress = "ProjectManagers@Imaginets.com"

' Build the appropriate LDAP Path
sLDAPPath = "LDAP://" + sExchangeServer
sLDAPPath = sLDAPPath + "/cn=Recipients,OU="
sLDAPPath = sLDAPPath + sExchangeSite
sLDAPPath = sLDAPPath + ",O="
sLDAPPath = sLDAPPath + sExchangeOrg

' Create the object based on the string we just created
Set adLDAPContainer = GetObject(sLDAPPath)

' Create a new distribution list in
Set adDistributionList = adLDAPContainer.Create("groupOfNames", "cn=" & sAlias)

'Set the Properties of the Distribution List
adDistributionList.Put "cn", CStr(sDisplayname)
adDistributionList.Put "uid", CStr(sAlias)
adDistributionList.Put "mail", CStr(sSMTPAddress)
adDistributionList.SetInfo
```

Example 15.2   *Setting the owner of a distribution list.*

```
adDistributionList.Put "Owner", "cn=JoelS,cn=Recipients,ou=" & sExchangeSite & ",o=" &
↪sExchangeOrg
adDistributionList.SetInfo
```

Example 15.3   *Adding members to a distribution list.*

```
sLDAPPath = "LDAP://EXCH01/cn=JoelS,cn=Recipients,ou="
sLDAPPath = sLDAPPath & sExchangeSite & ",o=" & sExchangeOrg
adDistributionList.Add sLDAPPath

sLDAPPath = "LDAP://EXCH01/cn=DuncanM,cn=Recipients,ou="
sLDAPPath = sLDAPPath & sExchangeSite & ",o=" & sExchangeOrg
adDistributionList.Add sLDAPPath
```

Example 15.4 *Removing members from a distribution list.*

```
sLDAPPath = "LDAP://EXCH01/cn=JoelS,cn=Recipients,ou="
sLDAPPath = sLDAPPath & sExchangeSite & ",o=" & sExchangeOrg
adDistributionList.Remove sLDAPPath
```

Indexing Your Knowledge—Using Site Server

As the information contained within your knowledge management solution grows, the problem of referencing this information grows. Of course, if you store all of your information within Microsoft Outlook, you can use the product's Advanced Find capabilities to search for messages based on various aspects of the message, including subject content, size of the message, the dates the message was sent, and the content of custom fields. However, this method typically does not lend itself to large knowledge management solutions, where information is distributed not only across many different Exchange public folders, but across different mediums, such as SQL Server database and Office documents stored on corporate file servers.

To help solve these problems, you can employ the power and diversity of Microsoft Site Server. Microsoft Site Server is part of the Microsoft BackOffice line of products, and it provides full-text indexing and searching of Exchange public folders, Web sites, file share, and databases, as shown in Figure 15.6. Site Server builds indexes and stores them in constructs called catalogs, which are file based resources that are accessed during index population and searches.

Microsoft Site Server crawls through the content of Exchange public folders, stepping through every message of every folder flagged for indexing, indexing every important word and phrase. Generally, when setting up a new index catalog in Site Server, you specify a root of a public folder tree to begin the crawl. For example, if you want to index the content of all public folders in your organization, you would typically set the starting address for the Exchange data source to be exch://Public Folders/All Public Folder.

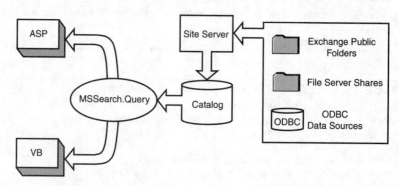

Figure 15.6 *An overview of Site Server catalogs.*

To ease the process of configuring catalogs, Site Server provides you with a Catalog Definition Wizard. You can use this wizard to specify all of the different data sources that will be used to populate the catalog, consisting of public folders, databases, Web sites, Network News Transfer Protocol (NNTP) newsgroups, or file server shares.

Because this is not a Site Server book, I don't want to discuss every feature that the product exposes. Nor do I want to detail exactly how to create indexes and initiate their build. What I do want to discuss is how you can gain access to the information contained within the indexes Site Server builds and maintains. I mentioned earlier that Site Server builds catalogs, which are simply indexes of documents and mail messages. The process of building catalogs is actually quite simple. First, you define what the catalog will index (public folders, NNTP newsgroups, and so on). After the catalog has been defined, Site Server begins to populate the index by traversing documents and messages, extracting and indexing content. Indexing consists of keeping track of which words are used and where they are located in each document. Upon completion, the catalogs are compiled and can then be distributed.

Location of Indexed Documents

Remember that a catalog is simply an index comprised of properties and the content of documents. Site Server's catalogs do not contain the actual documents; however, it does reference the documents that it indexes. ♦

Unwanted Index Content

To prevent the index from becoming congested with words that do not help users find documents, Site Server ignores noise words, such as a, and, the, and so on. Site Server provides noise word lists for nine languages. These noise word lists should be sufficient for most normal operations, but can be modified for specific environments. ♦

To do a search, you must specify what part of the cataloged documents to search. There are many types of columns included in the catalogs, including text columns, numeric columns, and date columns. There are also two special columns: the contents column, which contains a searchable indexed copy of the cataloged documents, and the all column, which contains the contents column as well as all other columns. For performance reasons, catalogs typically contain only the columns that are actually searched or displayed. So for each search catalog, you must know which columns are available.

Text columns include the contents column with the full-text of the document, any column that stores information as a string, such as the DocTitle and DocAuthor columns, and any columns created by META tags.

The basic syntax for searching text columns is the following:

```
@column_name query_term
```

For example, to find all documents that contain the word Collaborate in the DocTitle column, use the following query:

```
@DocTitle collaborate
```

If no column name is specified, the contents column is used.

Complex Searches

Use wildcards and stemming or regular expression pattern matching to help target your search. If you prefer, you can also use free text queries. With free text queries, you can enter any text, including words, phrases, or sentences, as the query term. When submitting a free text query, you do not need to worry about the query syntax because the query engine identifies important words and phrases. Free text queries ignore wildcards and stemming, noise words, Boolean operators (AND, OR, NOT), and the proximity operator (NEAR) and finds documents that contain any of the important words and phrases. This makes free text queries less precise than other query methods, so the results of free text queries should be sorted by rank. ◆

To better illustrate this, Table 15.1 provides some examples of simple catalog searches.

Table 15.1   Examples of Catalog Searches

Example	Results
ImagiNet	Files with the word *ImagiNet*.
"Collaborative Solutions"	Files with the exact phrase *Collaborative Solutions*. Note that phrase searches are not case sensitive.
Imag*	Files with words beginning with the prefix *Imag*.
book**	Files with the stem *book*, such as *book, books, booking*.
@DocAuthor Joel Semeniuk	Files authored by *Joel Semeniuk*, even if there are multiple authors.
@DocTitle "Collaborate"	Files with the phrase *Collaborate* in the title.
@DocTitle Exc*	Files with a title that contains a word with the prefix *Exc*.

Table 15.2 illustrates the use of free text queries.

Table 15.2   Examples of Free Text Queries

Example	Results
Building collaborative solutions	Pages that mention any of the words or phrases in the query.
$DocTitle how to create an Outlook VBA form?	Pages with a DocTitle property that includes any of the words or phrases in the query.

Table 15.3 shows a variety of Boolean queries that work whether or not enumeration is enabled.

Table 15.3   Boolean Queries and Results

Example	Results
ImagiNet and @Size < 1000000	Pages with the word *ImagiNet* that are less than one million bytes.
ImagiNet and not @size = 100	Pages with the word *ImagiNet* that are not equal to 100 bytes.
@DocTitle Collaborate OR #Filename *.asp	Pages with the word *Collaborate*, or with a filename extension of *.asp*.
@FileWrite > 2000/01/01 AND < 2000/01/01	Files modified in January 2000.
@DocTitle newfoundland and not (dogs or puppies)	Files with the word *Newfoundland* in the title, but not the words *dogs* or *puppies*.
VBA and Access - Or- access & basic	Pages with both the words *VBA* and *Access*.
ASP or HTM - Or - ASP | HTM	Pages with the words Active Server Pages (*ASP*) or *HTM*.
VBA and not access - Or- VBA & ! Access	Pages with the word *VBA* but not *access*.
Project near Start - Or- Project ~ Start	Pages with the word *Start* within fifty words of the word *Project*.

Table 15.4 shows a variety of Boolean queries that work only if enumeration is enabled.

Table 15.4   Enumeration-Enabled Boolean Queries

Example	Results
@FileWrite > -1d OR @Create > -1d	Documents modified or created in the last day.
Not @size = 100	Pages that are not equal to 100 bytes.
@DocTitle Dogs OR @DocTitle Puppies	Documents with either *Dogs* or *Puppies* in the title.

Site Server Documentation

Please refer to the Site Server documentation for more information on building search strings:

`http://<Your Web Server>/SiteServer/samples/knowledge/search/` ◆

Integrating this level of search functionality into knowledge management solutions is a must. There are a number of ways you can integrate this level of search into your applications. First, you can simply rely upon the search page that Site Server installs by default. Site Server comes with a default Web page that you can make available to your knowledge management applications. This page presents users with a field to enter a word or phrase to search for and a list of all the catalogs on your search server to choose from. It includes a Tips page to provide users with information on the search query syntax and advanced search options. The page is set up to handle catalogs that include NNTP messages and Microsoft Exchange public folders, as well as HTML and Microsoft Office documents. It requires NTLM or Basic authentication to preserve security of any secure indexed documents.

The default search page is available to your site visitors from the URL `http://<Your_server_name>/Siteserver/Knowledge/Search/`.

Viewing Search Results

Because you use Site Server to index Exchange public folders, you need to understand how users can view the messages returned by the Site Server search engine. You have two options: allow users to view the resulting messages using Outlook or Outlook Web Access (OWA). You should check the value of the ExchangeViewer variable in the Searchright.asp page. By default, it is set to both. This setting is used to specify that users can either view messages using the Microsoft Outlook client on their computers or OWA. If neither of these options is available at your site, you need to change the ExchangeViewer variable to the one that is available. ◆

The source for this page can be found in C:\Microsoft Site Server\SiteServer\
Knowledge\Search by default.

Before you go and customize this search page for your own use, it is
important to understand how this pages works. The heart of any application
that uses Site Server catalogs is the Site Server Query COM object
(MSSearch.Query). The Query object provides all of the properties and methods required for defining and executing a search query. Table 15.5 highlights
the object's properties and Table 15.6 illustrates the object's methods.

Table 15.5   Query Object Properties and Descriptions

Property	Description
AllowEnumeration	Specifies whether enumeration is allowed when resolving queries. Enumeration is the recursive search required by some complex query syntax in which the query is compared to one section of the catalog and then again to another section of the catalog.
	For example: <% Q.AllowEnumeration=TRUE %> *(where Q is the Query Object)*
Catalog	List of one or more catalogs to be searched by a query.
	For example: <% Q.Catalog = "catalog1,catalog2" %>
Columns	List of one or more columns to be returned in the recordset.
	For example: <% Q.Columns = "Title, DocAddress, Description" %>
LocaleID	Specifies the language to be used in the query. This property selects the word breaker and stemmer when executing a query.
	For example: <% Q.LocaleID = 1033 ' EN-US locale code %>
MaxRecords	Maximum number of records to be returned in the recordset. The default setting of this property is 0, which means all the matching records are returned.
	For example: <% Q.MaxRecords = 10 %>

continues ▶

Table 15.5   *continued*

Property	Description
OptimizedFor	Optimization constraints provide control over whether the search is optimized for accuracy or performance, and whether it is possible to calculate the total number of results found. Options are:
	Performance | Recall [,hitcount|nohitcount]
	If the option is set to performance, scope and security trimming are deferred until after the maximum number of hits is collected. If the option is set to recall, result set trimming occurs while the query is being executed, which can result in slower search performance but leads to an accurate total hit count.

	For example:
	`<% Q.OptimizeFor =`
	`"performance, nohitcount" %>`

Query	The query string.

	For example:
	`<% Q.Query = "#DocTitle Exchange*`
	`and collaborate near create"%>`

Starthit	The row in each catalog where the recordset begins.

	For example:
	`<% Q.StartHit =`
	`RS.Properties("NextStartHit") %>`

SortBy	Specifies the sort order of the results of up to four columns. A and D specify ascending or descending order.
	For example: `<% Q.SortBy = "Title, rank[d]" %>`
QueryTimedOut	Read only property that specifies that the query has exceeded its time limit.

	For example:
	`<%`
	`if Q.QueryTimedOut=TRUE then`
	`Response.write "Query Time Out."`
	`end if`
	`%>`

Property	Description
QueryIncomplete	Read only property that specifies that the query could not be resolved. If the AllowEnumeration property is set to TRUE, the QueryIncomplete property always returns FALSE.

Table 15.6   *Query Object Methods*

Method	Description
CreateRecordSet	Execute the query and create a resulting recordset. If no matches are found, both the EOF and BOF properties of the recordset are set to TRUE. For example: <% set RS = Q.CreateRecordSet("sequential") %
DefineColumn	Define a display name for a column to be used in the query. The argument syntax looks like: *displayname* [(*type*)] = *propset-id prop-id*	" *prop-name*) *Displayname* is the display name given to the property. *Type* is an optional parameter containing the DBTYPE of the column (by default, *type* is set for strings: DBTYPE_STR | DBTYPE_BYREF). *Propset-id* is a GUID giving the property set ID for the column, and *prop-id* and *prop-name* give the property ID or property name for the column.
Reset	Clear all properties of the Query object. For example: <% Q.Reset %>
QueryToURL	Produce the query string portion of an URL from the query parameters. This string is used to pass the query to successive pages of results. For example: <a href=(http://server/sample.asp?<% = Q.QueryToURL %>">Next page</a>
SetQueryFromURL	Set the Query object properties based on the query string provided. This method is used when the two-character conventional query string variables are used in the query string. For example: <% Q.SetQueryFromURL(Request.QueryString) %>

Conventional query string variables are two-letter tags designed to make it easy to set the values of the Query property from the information in the query string. The SetQueryFromURL method takes the tags in the query string and sets the appropriate properties of the Query object. QueryToURL does the exact opposite by taking the relevant properties of the Query object and turning them into an URL string using the conventional query string variables.

The tags illustrated in Table 15.7 are associated with specific Query object properties.

Table 15.7   Query Object Properties

Method tag	Description
ae	Allow enumeration. Associated with the AllowEnumeration property. If set to a nonzero digit, enumeration is allowed.
ct	Catalog. Associated with the Catalog property.
mh	Maximum hits. Associated with the MaxRecords property.
op	Optimize for. Associated with the OptimizeFor property. The first character of the value can be x for performance or r for recall. An optional h can be added to specify no hitcount.
qu	The query term. Associated with the Query property.
sh	Start hit. Associated with the StartHit property.
sd	Sort down (in descending order). Associated with the SortBy property.
so	Sort in ascending order. Associated with the SortBy property.

The following tags are used to create multiple-column queries. You set each of the column (c), operator (o), and query (q) tags for each component of a multiple-column search. In each, the n is a number from 0–9. These tags are then concatenated together into the query string using the & operator. Table 15.8 describes these tags.

Table 15.8   Multiple-Column Query Tags

Tag	Description
c*n*	Column for a built-up query. Associated with the Query property. For property value queries, the column name should be preceded with an at sign (@). If blank or not present, the contents column is assumed.

Tag	Description
o*n*	Operator for a built-up query. Associated with the Query property. Should only be used for numeric and date queries and should be left blank for string comparisons. The operators are equals (=), not equals (!=), greater than (>), greater than or equal to (>=), less than (<), and less than or equal to (<=).
q*n*	Query string for a built-up query. Associated with the Query property. When q*n* is used without an associated c*n* and o*n* term, the contents column is searched. The following is an example using query tags:

```
q1=Imaginet&ct=PFCat&c2=@FileWrite&o2=>&q2=-1d&c3=@Size&o3=<&q3=512288
```

Basically, to use the MSSearch.Query object to retrieve information from your catalogs, you must do the following:

1. Instantiate the MSSearch.Query object.
2. Set the appropriate properties of the object.
3. Construct your query string using conventional query string variables.
4. Call the CreateRecordSet method to create a result ADO recordset.
5. Display the recordset to the user.

Because I am talking about knowledge management solutions and have been placing emphasis on team folders and digital dashboards, I suggest that you integrate Site Server's indexing and searching functionality right into your team folder and digital dashboard Web pages. If you do this, these pages should be located on the same server as Site Server, because they need to reference the MSSearch.Query object, implemented as a DLL.

Another way of using this technology is to integrate it directly into Microsoft Outlook by creating a COM add-in. The only problem with creating and using a COM add-in to access Site Server's searching facilities is that you need to use Microsoft Transaction Server to allow you to reference the MSSearch.Query object using DCOM. After you place the MSSearch.Query object into Microsoft Transaction Server (MTS), you can configure MTS to create a client installation program that registers the object on the client computer in such a way that it can be instantiated through MTS. However, after you can gain access to this object from client computers, you can extend Outlook's interface to provide the advanced searching functionality provided by Site Server.

Putting the Pieces Together

Up to this point, we have discussed each piece of the knowledge management puzzle separately, but the pieces can be combined to form a more complete solution. Team folders and the Team Folder Wizard provide a way of ensuring that the structure and content of public folders remain consistent throughout the organization. Distribution lists allow you to effectively represent different roles in an organization or business process to make it easier for people to communicate and track knowledge. Site Server's advanced indexing and searching mechanisms provide you with the ability to perform complex searches on information stored in virtually any location in your organization. Finally, as discussed in Chapter 12, digital dashboards act as the interface that brings all of this information together in a meaningful way.

The best way to describe how to use each of these facilities to build an effective knowledge management solution is to illustrate with an example. And the best example comes from a real-life experience of mine.

Where Is the Code?

I am not going to provide the source code for this example for two reasons. First, everything you need to develop this example has been provided to you in previous chapters. Second, there would be a heck of a lot of code, and who likes to read through 20–30 pages of straight VBScript and HTML? ◆

This example deals with a project management issue that plagues many corporations. As the owner of ImagiNET Resources, I like to have my hands in almost every detail of all ongoing projects. However, I don't like to overburden my project managers with complex weekly status reports and status meetings. In fact, the real goal is to attempt to completely eliminate status reports while providing myself, and anyone else in the organization, with real-time data relating to the status of each current project. What ImagiNET needs is a project management digital dashboard. In a nutshell, here is what it does.

First, team folders and the Team Folder Wizard are put to good use. The first required modification is the customization of the team folder templates to better capture information that is important to a project, such as the following: Project Discussions, Project Documentation, Project Calendars, Project Contacts, Project Tasks, Project Issues, Project Change Requests, Project Bug Reports, Project Status Reports, and Project Best Practices. New views, forms, and folder Web pages are created for each new folder.

One of the most important additions to the new team folder template is a customized Team Folder Administration page. The Team Folder Administration page is customized to focus on the project team and collect information about the project the team folders support. One of its most important new features is the capability to create and maintain Exchange distribution lists that correspond to predefined roles for each project. For example, every project has a project manager, developers, testers, QA, and logistical. The Administration program prompts the user to assign users to each of these roles. After this has been done, it creates distribution lists that contain each person or persons defined for each role. Additionally, the Administration page ensures that the project's Discussion folder is included in all distribution lists.

Site Server is configured to index all project team folders. In fact, all project team folders are located under a central folder, as demonstrated in Figure 15.1. All messages, custom properties, and related documents are indexed and available for search. In addition, the primary search catalog is configured to index locations on the corporate file servers that correspond to project information.

After a new team folder template is created, the Team Folder Wizard is modified. Simply stated, the Team Folder Wizard is modified to plainly request some basic information about a new project, such as the project name, the client name, and start date, before the template folders and Web pages are installed to the appropriate areas.

Next, a digital dashboard is created to help summarize all project information. Of course, the digital dashboard is implemented as a folder Web page that is accessed from the Project folder, which is the parent folder of all project team folders. The most important aspect when designing and developing a digital dashboard is to identify what information you want to see. In this case, I want to have the ability to come to work in the morning and see the following information for each active project (see Figure 15.7):

- The start date of each project
- The project manager of each project
- The number of team members assigned to each project
- The number of outstanding versus total issues for each project
- The number of outstanding versus total bugs for each project
- The number of outstanding versus total change requests for each project
- Milestones for current week for each project
- Milestones for current month for each project
- Number of overdue tasks per team member
- Billing information (amount billed by month, quarter, and year)
- Cost Information (costs by month, quarter, and year)
- Profit projections based on cost and billing data

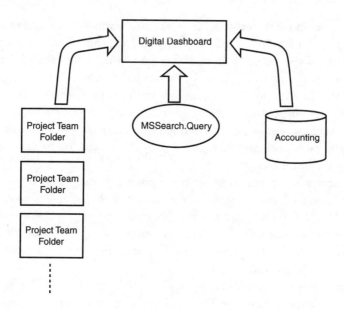

Figure 15.7   *The initial project management digital dashboard.*

Of course, not all of this data comes from the information stored within the customized set of team folders. Much of the billing and cost information needs to come directly from the accounting system. But that is the beauty of the digital dashboard solution. When it is implemented, the user does not need to know where the data is coming from; he sees only the consolidated data. Figure 15.8 displays the resulting digital dashboard.

As you can see, the information presented in the project management digital dashboard is completely dynamic. No one person is responsible for its contents. More importantly, the information presented in the dashboard is collected from every day activities of team members and the accounting staff, not from weekly status reports or lengthy status meetings. Also, if I ever need any more detail on issues, bugs, change requests, and so on, I only need to go to the appropriate project team folder located in one of the sub-folders of the Projects folder, where the digital dashboard is accessed from.

This type of solution allows me, and others within the organization, to stay in tune with how projects are progressing. More importantly, this relieves project managers from the burden of lengthy and monotonous status reports that are a week out-of-date at best. As long as information is being recorded into the appropriate team folders on a regular basis, which you will find becomes second nature, all of this information is readily available to everyone, in real time!

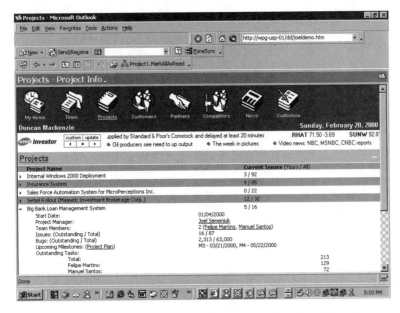

Figure 15.8   *The final project management digital dashboard.*

Chapter Summary

In this chapter, I described how you can take some of the concepts that have already been discussed, such as team folders, views, forms, distribution lists, and digital dashboards, and turn them into a completely dynamic and ever growing reservoir of knowledge and information. Specifically, I described the following:

- How to use team folders to effectively store knowledge

- How to use distribution lists to increase communication and help capture knowledge as it flows from person to person over email

- How to index knowledge collected by a knowledge management system to ensure that all users have the ability to search the wealth of knowledge in an organization

- How to tie all of these concepts and technologies together to create a knowledge management solution directed to the project management process

The CDO Object Model

We have touched on CDO (Collaborative Data Objects) throughout this book because this library is the main method used to programmatically work with Exchange. This appendix will provide a reference to the objects in this library and their properties and methods to make it easier for you to work with in your projects. In addition to the object model, this appendix will discuss the following additional topics:

- Setting up your project (in VB or VBA) to use CDO
- Using the Object Browser to explore the CDO library
- CDO in Exchange 2000 and Windows 2000

We will start with the coverage of the object model itself, including an object-by-object breakdown of the library, followed by the additional topics mentioned in the preceding list.

Session Object

The Session object is the top-level, or main, object of the CDO library. It is the first object you create, and it provides (through its methods and properties) the link to all other objects you need to use. The Session object's position in the object model means that you are likely to use it in every CDO program you create; however, it also means that the code you write with it is likely to perform a similar set of actions every time.

Session Properties

As a top-level object, Session has many properties (see Table A.1) that describe key characteristics of the current MAPI connection.

Table A.1   *Properties of the Session Object*

Name	Returns	Description
Session	Session	Read Only. Returns a reference to itself (common property of many of the CDO library objects; not very useful in this particular case).
Class	Long	Read Only. Another common property, this numeric value indicates what type of CDO object you are working with. The possible values are held inside the CdoObjectClass enumerated type and can be viewed using the Object Browser (see the section "Using the Object Browser to Explore the CDO Library").
Version	String	Read Only. Returns the version of the CDO library you are using (not necessarily the highest available version on the system). Generally a numeric value, but this is not assured for future versions (they might include some alpha characters).
OperatingSystem	String	Read Only. Another informational property, this returns a string displaying the name and version number of the OS. This information is not easily parsed, but there are Windows API calls available to get detailed OS version information, if desired.
Name	String	Read Only. Returns a string containing the name of the profile this session is using. An error occurs if you try to retrieve this property before the Session object has been logged in (using the Logon method).
CurrentUser	Address Entry	Read Only. As with the previous entry, this is only valid after you have logged in and it returns an AddressEntry object representing the MAPI user for this session. An example of using this property to obtain the name of the current user is shown later in the "Session Object" section.
Inbox	Folder	Read Only. A convenient shortcut, this property returns a Folder object corresponding to the user's default Inbox.

Name	Returns	Description
Outbox	Folder	Read Only. As above, this property is a simple shortcut to the default Outbox folder for this profile.
InfoStores	Info Stores	Read Only. Returns an InfoStores object, which represents a collection of all the available stores.
AddressLists	Variant	Read Only. This property has two possible return values, depending on the characteristics of the current MAPI profile. It can return either a single AddressList object (if there is only one AddressList available) or an AddressLists collection (if there is more than one). When working with an Exchange user's profile, there is usually more than one (the Global Address List and the user's personal contacts being the most common combination).
OutOfOffice	Boolean	Read Only. Simply returns a True/False value indicating whether the user has set his OutOfOffice flag.
OutOfOfficeText	String	Read Only. Returns a string containing the OutOfOffice message set by the user. This is the same message that is used for autoreplies while the user has his OutOfOffice flag set.

Too Many Variants

The Returns column is somewhat misleading. Almost every property of this object (and many of the other CDO objects) officially returns a Variant data type, but in the situations where a property consistently returns a specific type of data (like a string or an object type), I placed that type into the Returns column. ♦

Session Methods

The key method of this object is Logon, which you must use before beginning work with this Session. It also provides many other methods that greatly simplify work with these objects (see Table A.2).

Table A.2   *Methods of the Session Object*

Name	Returns	Parameters	Description
Logon		[Profile Name], [Profile Password], [Show Dialog], [New Session], [Parent Window], [NoMail] [Profile Info]	The key method of the Session object, this logs you onto MAPI, determines which MAPI Profile you are using, and must be called before you can really do anything with CDO. One critical parameter is NewSession, which can be set to either True or False and determines whether CDO should attempt to simply Logon to an existing session (such as the one created by a running copy of Outlook) or always create a NewSession.
Logoff			Logs you off your session.
GetInfoStore	InfoStore	[StoreID]	Given the ID of an InfoStore (the Public folders Info Store, for example), returns the appropriate InfoStore object.
GetFolder	Folder	FolderID, [StoreID]	Returns the appropriate Folder object, given a Folder ID. A StoreID can also be supplied to reduce the possibility of ambiguity, but is not necessary.
GetMessage	Message	MessageID, [StoreID]	Returns the appropriate item based on the EntryID supplied (MessageID parameter corresponds to the ID property of a CDO Message object). Remember that (in CDO) messages can be Mail items, Contact items, Task items, and so on. As with the GetFolder call, you do not need to supply the StoreID, but it generally produces better performance.

Name	Returns	Parameters	Description
GetArticle	Variant	ArticleID, FolderID, [StoreID]	This method is an alternative to the GetMessage call, and can sometimes be easier to use. ArticleIDs are not unique across all folders and therefore do not need to be as large as MessageIDs (32 bits instead of more than double that value), but not every message store supports these values. If the value is available for a message, you can retrieve it using the Property ID CdoPR_ INTERNET_ARTICLE_ NUMBER.
GetAddress Entry	Address Entry	EntryID	Given the ID of an AddressEntry object, returns the appropriate entry.
AddressBook	Recipients	[Recipients], [Title], [One Address], [Force Resolution], [Recip Lists], [ToLabel], [CcLabel], [BccLabel] [Parent Window]	Used to display the address selection dialog box (as shown when the To button is clicked on a new email message). The Recipients parameter allows you to supply an existing set of selected addresses so that it can be modified. The Title parameter allows you to place your own message as the caption of this window. RecipLists takes an integer value (1–3) that specifies how many different list boxes and associated buttons should appear in the resulting form, and the ToLabel, CcLabel, and BccLabel parameters take strings that become the captions for the buttons of the first, second, and third lists, respectively. Note that all the selections are returned in a single Recipients collection

continues ▶

Table A.2 *continued*

Name	Returns	Parameters	Description
			(regardless of how many lists there are), which means you need to use the Recipient object's Type property to determine the location of each selected item (CdoTo, CdoCc, or CdoBcc).
DeliverNow			This method initiates delivery of any messages that are still undelivered (in the Outbox).
CompareIDs	Boolean	ID1, ID2	A utility function that compares two CDO objects based on their EntryIDs.
Create Conversation Index	String	[Parent Index]	Either creates a new (string) value that can be assigned to a message's ConversationIndex property to indicate a new conversation (no parameter supplied) or creates an index that indicates a child conversation (parameter supplied from the parent message's Conversation Index property).
SetLocaleIDs		LocaleID, CodePageID	Used to control how MAPI deals with international characters, sorting, and other locale-specific features.
GetDefault Folder	Folder	ObjectType	An extremely useful method, GetDefaultFolder takes a parameter indicating which one of the MAPI default folders it should return (CdoDefaultFolderInbox, CdoDefaultFolderContacts, and so on) and returns the appropriate Folder object.

Name	Returns	Parameters	Description
GetAddress List	Address List	ObjectType	Returns the user's Personal Address Book, the Global Address List, or all entries depending on the parameter passed in (CdoAddressListGAL, CdoAddressListPAB, or CdoAddressListAll).
GetOption	Variant	OptType	This method takes a string parameter corresponding to one of several possible settings and returns the current value of that setting. These settings correspond to various options for calendar rendering using the CDO HTML rendering library.
SetOption		OptType, OptValue	This method sets a value for the setting discussed in GetOption.

InfoStores Collection

The InfoStores collection, returned from the InfoStores property of the Session object, contains all the loaded InfoStore objects available in the current MAPI session. It contains the standard CDO properties of Session and Class and the standard attributes of a collection (a Count property and an Item method) but has no attributes specific to it.

InfoStore Object

Each individual InfoStore available in a MAPI session is represented as an InfoStore object. This can include various types of items, such as PSTs that have been added to the current profile, the current user's Mailbox set of folders, and in the case of an Exchange user, the Public Folders InfoStore. All of the available objects can be accessed through the InfoStores collection.

InfoStore Properties

All CDO objects have the common properties Session (representing the current CDO Session object) and Class (numeric value representing which object you are working with). Properties unique to this object are described in Table A.3 and include such useful attributes as RootFolder.

Table A.3   Properties of the InfoStore Object

Name	Returns	Description
Index	Integer	Read Only. Returns this InfoStore's position within the InfoStores collection.
Name	String	Read Only. Returns a string containing the display name of this InfoStore (such as "Public Folders").
ID	String	Read Only. Returns a string containing the StoreID, a unique identifier for this InfoStore. This identifier can be used in calls like GetMessage to specify which store an object is contained in.
ProviderName	String	Read Only. Returns the name of the provider that corresponds to this InfoStore (such as "Microsoft Exchange Server" for the Public Folders store and the user's Mailbox, and "Personal Folders" for any loaded PSTs).
RootFolder	Folder	Read Only. Returns the topmost Folder object of that InfoStore, useful when you want to traverse the store's collection of folders and/or items.
Fields	Variant	Read Only. Returns a Fields collection containing a variety of settings and other information about this InfoStore (including several other properties from this object, such as the ProviderName and Name values).

InfoStore Methods

The InfoStore object possesses the IsSameAs method (shown in Table A.4), which is common to many CDO objects, but does not have any other methods unique to itself.

Table A.4   Methods of the InfoStore Object

Name	Returns	Parameters	Description
IsSameAs	Boolean	Object	This is a common method across many objects in the CDO library. Given another object of the same type, it checks to see if the objects both refer to the same entity.

AddressLists Collection

The AddressLists collection, returned from the AddressLists property of the Session object, contains all the loaded AddressList objects (such as the Global Address List and the Personal Address Book) available in the current MAPI session. It contains the standard CDO properties of Session and Class and the standard attributes of a collection (a Count property and an Item method), but has no attributes specific to it.

AddressList Object

Each available address list (like the Global Address List from Microsoft Exchange or the Personal Address Book stored locally) is represented by an AddressList object. These objects, in addition to the common properties like Class and Session, contain various attributes describing those underlying address lists.

AddressList Properties

All CDO objects have the common properties Session (representing the current CDO Session object) and Class (numeric value representing which object you are working with). In addition to these common attributes, the AddressList object also provides access to its contents (through the AddressEntries property) and several other useful properties (listed in Table A.5).

Table A.5   Properties of the AddressList Object

Name	Returns	Description
Address Entries	Variant	Read Only. This property can return either a single AddressEntry object or an AddressEntries collection, depending on whether this AddressList contains one or more entries.
ID	String	Read Only. Returns the unique ID for this address list.
Index	Integer	Read Only. Returns this object's positionalindex within the Session's AddressLists collection.
Name	String	Read Only. Returns a string containing the display name of this address list (such as "Global Address List" or whatever name you have given your personal Outlook contacts).
IsReadOnly	Boolean	Read Only. Returns True or False, indicating whether this address list can be modified.
Fields	Variant	Read Only. Similar to the AddressEntries property, this property can return either a single Field object or a Fields collection, depending on the number of fields that exist.

AddressList Methods

This object has only one method, IsSameAs, which is common to many CDO objects. Given another object of the same type, this method returns True or False indicating whether both objects refer to the same entity.

AddressEntries Collection

The AddressEntries collection, returned from the AddressEntries property of an AddressList object, contains all the address entries available in that list. It possesses the standard CDO properties of Session and Class and the standard attributes of a collection (a Count property and an Item method) and a few methods (Add, GetFirst, and so on) that are present in many CDO collections. In addition to the common properties and methods, Table A.6 lists those properties that are either unique to this object or that require some explanation in connection with this object.

Table A.6   Properties of the AddressEntries Collection

Name	Returns	Description
Count	Long	Read Only. Returns the number of address entries in the collection. If you are dealing with a very large collection of entries, this value might not be accurate.
Filter	Address Entry Filter	Read Only. This property returns an AddressEntryFilter object that you can use to set up various filter attributes.
Item	Address Entry	Read Only. Given an index value, this returns a single AddressEntry object.
Delete		Method. Be careful with this one; this method deletes *all* of the address entries in this collection.
Add	Address Entry	Method. Taking three parameters (Emailtype, Name, and Address, with Name and Address both optional), this method creates a new AddressEntry object, adds it to the collection, and returns it to you.
GetFirst	Address Entry	Method. Returns the first object in this collection or Nothing if there are no objects in the collection.
GetNext	Address Entry	Method. Returns the next object in this collection or Nothing if you are already at the last object or there are no objects in the collection.

Name	Returns	Description
GetLast	Address Entry	Method. As with GetFirst, this method returns the last object in the collection or Nothing if there are no objects in the collection.
GetPrevious	Address Entry	Method. Returns the previous object in the collection or Nothing if you are already at the first item or if there are no objects in the collection.
Sort		Method. Taking two parameters, SortOrder and PropID, this method sorts the collection using that property and order specified. SortOrder can be CdoAscending or CdoDescending.

Folder Object

Every folder in an InfoStore is represented by a Folder object, making this a commonly used item. The two key properties of this item are its Folders collection (containing all the folders beneath this one) and its Messages collection (containing all the items from this folder).

Folder Properties

All CDO objects have the common properties Session (representing the current CDO Session object) and Class (numeric value representing which object you are working with). Table A.7 lists those properties of the Folder object that are unique to this specific object or that are worth a special mention in this context.

Table A.7   Properties of the Folder object

Name	Returns	Description
Name	String	Read Only. Returns the name of the Folder ("Inbox," for example).
ID	String	Read Only. Returns the unique ID that identifies this folder.
FolderID	String	Read Only. Returns the ID of the parent folder of this object.
StoreID	String	Read Only. Returns the unique ID of the InfoStore that contains this folder.
Folders	Folders	Read Only. Returns the collection of folders contained with this folder (sub-folders).

continues ▶

Table A.7   *Properties of the Folder object*

Name	Returns	Description
Messages	Messages	Read Only. Returns the collection of Messages within this folder (but not the hidden messages; see the *HiddenMessages* property for more info).
Fields	Variant	Read Only. As before, this property can return either a Field object (if there is only one field for this item) or a Fields collection. This makes coding against this property rather difficult, because you need to determine which object was returned before attempting to work with it.
Hidden Messages	Messages	Read Only. Returns a Messages collection containing special message items that are invisible to the regular interface of Exchange/Outlook.

Folder Methods

As one of the main objects in CDO, the Folder object has many methods (listed in Table A.8) that you will need to use on a regular basis.

Table A.8   *Methods of the Folder Object*

Name	Returns	Parameters	Description
Update		[Make Permanent], [Refresh Object]	Saves changes to this object. The parameters are used to specify if the changes should be saved to persistent storage and whether the properties of the Folder object should be reloaded.
CopyTo	Folder	FolderID, [StoreID], [Name][Copy Subfolders]	This method copies the folder to a new location. The new location is specified by providing the ID of the new parent folder in the FolderID parameter (the folder is then copied to a location under that folder). You can specify a new name using the Name parameter and control whether or

Name	Returns	Parameters	Description
			not sub-folders are copies by providing a value for the CopySubfolders parameter. Returns the new Folder object if the copy action is successful.
MoveTo	Folder	FolderID, [StoreID]	Similar to the preceding method, but this method moves the folder to a new location. Due to the fact that this is a move, you do not get to specify a new name, and sub-folders are always moved with the folder.
Delete			Deletes the Folder object.
IsSameAs	Boolean	Object	This common method returns True if the object passed in as a parameter is the same folder as this object.

Folders Collection

The Folders collection contains the standard CDO properties of Session and Class and a group of methods and properties that are common in most CDO collections. These common items (GetFirst, GetLast, GetNext, GetPrevious, Count, Item, Delete, Add, Session, Class, and Sort) are covered in the AddressEntries collection earlier in this appendix and will only be covered from this point on when they differ from that description. Those methods that have specific functionality related to this object are described in Table A.9.

Table A.9   Methods of the Folders Collection

Name	Returns	Description
Add	Folder	Method. Takes only a single parameter, Name, and adds a new folder with that name into the collection. Returns the new Folder object.
Delete	Variant	Method. This method functions the same as in previous collections, but it is worth noting again that it deletes all the folders in the collection and should be used cautiously.

Messages Collection

The Messages collection contains the standard CDO properties of Session and Class and a group of methods and properties that are common in most CDO collections. In addition to these common items, covered in earlier objects, this collection also has a Filter property. The Filter property provides you with a Filter object that can be used to restrict the Messages collection to only certain items. As with the Folders collection, the Messages collection has certain properties and methods that are unique to this object or have special behavior when used with this object. These properties and methods are listed in Table A.10.

Table A.10   Properties and Methods of the Messages Collection

Name	Returns	Description
Filter	Message Filter	Read Only. Returns a MessageFilter object, which you can modify to restrict the items in this collection.
Add	Message	Method. Although you can use this method without any parameters, it can take any combination of Subject, Text, Type, and Importance. The newly created message is returned from this call.
RawTable	Special	This property exists for internal use by Outlook and other programs and is not something that you will work with.

Message Object

This is a key object in CDO, representing almost every item you can place into a folder in Exchange. This object has the common CDO properties of Session and Class, in addition to those properties described in the following sections.

Message Properties

In addition to the properties common to most CDO objects, the Message object has a large list of attributes unique to itself. These properties are listed and described in Table A.11.

Table A.11   Properties of the Message Object

Name	Returns	Description
FolderID	Variant	Read Only. Returns the ID of the folder that contains this message.
StoreID	String	Read Only. Returns the ID of the InfoStore containing this message.

Name	Returns	Description
ID	String	Read Only. Also known as the EntryID, this property returns the unique identifier for this message.
Type	String	Indicates the message class of the object (such as "IPM.Note").
Size	Variant	Read Only. Returns the size of the object in bytes.
Importance	Variant	Indicates the message's importance setting: CdoHigh, CdoLow, or CdoNormal.
Subject	String	The message's subject line.
Sender	Address Entry	Returns an AddressEntry object describing the sender.
TimeSent	Date	Read Only. Returns the date and time the message was sent.
TimeReceived	Date	Read Only. Returns the date and time when the message was received.
TimeCreated	Date	Read Only. Returns the date and time of the message's creation.
TimeExpired	Date	Read Only. If there is an expiration date set, this property returns it.
TimeLast Modified	Date	Read Only. Returns the date and time of the last change to this item.
Text	String	Returns or sets the body text of the email.
Sent	Boolean	Read Only. Indicates whether the message has been sent.
Unread	Boolean	Indicates whether the message has been read. Note that this is a per-user setting; it only indicates whether the current user has read the message.
Signed	Boolean	Read Only. Indicates if the message has a digital signature.
Encrypted	Boolean	Read Only. Indicates if the message has been encrypted.
ReadReceipt	Boolean	Read Only. Indicates if a Read-receipt has been requested. Can be used to warn a user (such as from a COM add-in) before he reads a message that will send a read-receipt.
Delivery Receipt	Boolean	Read Only. As ReadReceipt, but indicates whether a delivery receipt has been requested for this message.
Conversation Index	Variant	Read Only. Returns the index used to track this conversation thread.

continues ▶

Table A.11   continued

Name	Returns	Description
Conversation Topic	Variant	Read Only. Returns the text describing the conversation to which this message belongs.
Fields	Variant	Read Only. This property returns either a Field object (if there is only one field available) or a Fields collection. This inconsistency makes using this property rather difficult.
Recipients	Variant	Read Only. Similar to the Fields property, this returns either a single Recipients object or a Recipients collection and can be confusing.
Attachments	Variant	Read Only. As with the previous two properties, this returns either a single Attachment object or an Attachments collection. Note that for all of these collections, the property is read only. This indicates that you cannot set this property equal to an Attachments object, but the object exposed by this property is not read only; and it is through that object that you make your changes.
Categories	String	Specifies the categories assigned to this object.
Sensitivity	Variant	Specifies the sensitivity of the message. Can be one of the following values: CdoConfidential, CdoPersonal, CdoPrivate, or CdoNoSensitivity.

Message Methods

The Message object has several important methods (listed in Table A.12) that allow you to examine and manipulate this object.

Table A.12   Methods of the Message Object

Name	Returns	Parameters	Description
IsSameAs	Boolean	Object	This common CDO method takes another object as a parameter and returns True if this object and the parameter are the same item.
Delete			Deletes the message.

Name	Returns	Parameters	Description
Update		[Make Permanent], [Refresh Object]	Saves the message. The two optional parameters specify whether the data should be saved to permanent storage (defaults as true) and whether the object's properties should be reloaded from that same storage (defaults to False).
Options		[Parent Window]	Modal call. Displays a dialog box allowing the user to send various message options.
CopyTo	Message	FolderID, [StoreID]	Copies the message into the folder specified by the FolderID parameter. Returns the new copy of the Message object.
MoveTo	Message	FolderID, [StoreID]	Moves the message into the folder indicated by the FolderID parameter.
Send		[SaveCopy], [Show Dialog], [Parent Window]	Sends the message. Key parameter is ShowDialog, which if set to True, means that MAPI may choose to display a dialog box asking the user to resolve addresses or set other send options.
Reply	Message		Creates a new message object with the sender from the current object placed into the recipient of the new message. This new message can now be edited and sent.
ReplyAll	Message		Similar to Reply, but places the sender and all the recipients from the current object into the Recipients collection of the new message.
Forward	Message		Creates a new message containing a copy of the text and attachments from the current object. No copying of recipients occurs, so you need to set a recipient before you can send this new message.

Field Object

This object is used to represent an individual attribute of many other CDO objects. You only need to use these objects if the information you require is not exposed through one of the other object properties.

Field Properties

The Field object has only a few properties, listed in Table A.13. Value, the last property in the list, is the default property (the one that is used if no property is specified and only the Field object is used), but the other items are worth noting.

Table A.13 *Properties of the Field Object*

Name	Returns	Description
Type	Variant	Specifies the data type of this field. Can be any one of the CdoFieldType values (CdoDate, CdoBoolean, and so on).
Name	String	Returns the name of the field.
ID	Long	Returns a numeric value that uniquely identifies this field.
Value	Variant	The contents of this field. Data type is determined by the value of the Type property.

Field Methods

The Field object has several useful methods that allow you to delete it and load or save its contents from a file. All three of these methods are described in Table A.14.

Table A.14 *Methods of the Field Object*

Name	Returns	Parameters	Description
Delete			Used to remove user-defined fields from an object.
ReadFromFile		FileName	Given a filename and path, this method reads the contents of that file (binary or text) into this field.
WriteToFile		FileName	Writes out the contents of this field to the file specified by FileName.

Recipients Collection

In addition to the common collection attributes, the Recipients collection has many important properties and methods that you need to know. Table A.15 provides a list of these attributes along with a brief description of each.

Table A.15   Properties and Methods of the Recipients Collection

Name	Returns	Description
Resolved	Boolean	Read Only. Indicates whether the recipients contained within this collection have been successfully resolved. Only True if all recipients have been resolved.
Item	Recipient	Read Only. Given an index value, returns a single Recipient object from this collection.
Add	Recipient	Method. Can be called with no parameters, an AddressEntry EntryID, or Name and Address values. The possible parameters include Name (if supplied on its own, MAPI attempts to resolve this name against the available address lists), Address (the email address, such as SMTP:duncanma@microsoft.com), Type (one of CdoTo, CdoCC, or CdoBCC), and EntryID (of an AddressEntry item).
AddMultiple		Method. Adds multiple recipients to the collection by supplying a semi-colon delimited string of names to this method (such as "Duncan Mackenzie; Joel Semeniuk; David Wood"). This is equivalent to typing values into the To field of a new email message, and you can use the Resolve method of this collection to resolve the names you have added.
Delete		Method. Deletes all Recipient objects from this collection.
Resolve		Method. Attempts to resolve all the recipients in the collection. Takes a single parameter, ShowDialog, which can be set to True or False to tell MAPI whether it should put up a dialog box when it cannot resolve a name. Make sure you set this parameter to False when working in a non-interactive situation.
GetFirst Unresolved	Recipient	Method. Similar to the GetFirst method found in other collections, this returns the first item that has not be resolved successfully.
GetNext Unresolved	Recipient	Method. Same as GetFirstUnresolved.
GetFreeBusy	String	This method checks the availability of all recipients in the collection and takes three important parameters: StartTime, EndTime, and Interval. The two time values specify the duration of time to check (Now(), Now()+1, for instance, to specify the next 24 hours), and the Interval parameter takes a value (in minutes) that is used to determine how many individual units the total time duration should be broken into (for

continues ▶

Table A.15   continued

Name	Returns	Description
		instance, a value of 60 indicates that there should be one time unit for every hour in the indicated duration). The string returned from this function contains a single character for every time unit within the duration (24 characters for the example values of Now, Now + 1, and 60). Each character is equal to either 0, 1, 2, or 3 to indicate CdoFree, CdoTentative, CdoBusy, or CdoOutofOffice. Note that these values are for all recipients, so if even one person is marked busy for any part of that particular time unit, this function returns a 2 for that position. The values override each other in increasing order, so if one person is Busy and another is OutOfOffice, the end result will be OutOfOffice.

Recipient Object

This object represents a single address to which a message was sent or to which a message is addressed.

Recipient Properties

In addition to the common CDO properties, Session and Class, this object possesses a number of attributes (listed in Table A.16) unique to itself.

Table A.16   Properties of the Recipient Object

Name	Returns	Description
DisplayType	Variant	Read Only. Returns a value indicating what type of recipient this is. This can be one of several values including CdoUser or CdoDistList.
Name	String	Read Only. Returns the display name of this recipient.
Type	Variant	Read Only. Returns the type of this recipient, one of CdoTo, CdoCc, or CdoBcc.
Address	String	Read Only. Returns the full address of the recipient, including the address type (for example, SMTP:Duncanma@Microsoft.com).
ID	Variant	Read Only. Returns a unique ID that can be used to refer to this object.

Name	Returns	Description
Meeting Response Status	Variant	Read Only. When looping through the recipients of an item that represents a scheduled appointment, this property indicates the response that has been received from this recipient (if any). It can be one of CdoResponseAccepted, CdoResponseDeclined, CdoResponseTenative, CdoResponseOrganized (for the meeting organizer), CdoResponseNotResponded (no response received), or CdoResponseNone (equivalent to a Not Applicable indication).
AddressEntry	Address	Read Only. Returns an AddressEntry object, which provides more detail about the address of this recipient.
Ambiguous Names	Address Entries	Read Only. When a recipient cannot be resolved, this property returns an AddressEntries collection containing all the addresses found in the session's available AddressLists that are considered potential matches. If the recipient cannot be resolved, and this collection is empty, no possible matches were found; otherwise, you could use these possible matches to give the user a choice of which was the correct address (similar to what Outlook already does when a name cannot be resolved).

Recipient Methods

The Recipient object has several key methods (listed in Table A.17) that allow you to work with the automatic address resolution features, free/busy time scheduling, and other important features of Exchange.

Table A.17 Methods of the Recipient Object

Name	Returns	Parameters	Description
Delete			Deletes this object.
Resolve		[Show Dialog]	This method is the same as the corresponding method of the Recipients collection, detailed earlier, but works only on this single recipient.
IsSameAs	Boolean	Object	(The IsSameAs method returns True if the Recipient object is the same as the Recipient object being compared against.)

continues ▶

Table A.17   continued

Name	Returns	Parameters	Description
GetFreeBusy	String	StartTime, EndTime, Interval	This method is the same as the corresponding method of the Recipients collection (see Table A.15), but deals with only the single user.

Attachments Collection

This object represents the collection of attachments for a particular message and is accessed through the Attachments property of the Message object. This object has the common CDO properties of Session and Class and also has all the usual methods and properties of a collection. One of those common collection methods, Add, is described in more detail in Table A.18 due to the fact that it has some object specific parameters.

Table A.18   The Add Method of the Attachments Collection

Name	Returns	Description
Add	Variant	This method has four parameters, all of which are optional. The first parameter, Name, provides a display name for the attachment. Position indicates a character position for the attachment in a Rich Text message. Type specifies what type of attachment it is, one of CdoEmbeddedMessage, CdoFileData, CdoFileLink, or CdoOLE. The meaning of the last parameter, Source, depends on the Type parameter. In the case of an embedded message, Source should be set equal to the ID of the message object you want to add; but in the most common situation, inserting a file (CdoFileData), this should be set equal to the path of the file. Regardless of what parameters you specify, this method returns the new Attachment object.

Attachment Object

Each attachment to a message is represented by an individual Attachment object.

Attachment Properties

All CDO objects have the common properties Session (representing the current CDO Session object) and Class (numeric value representing which object you are working with). The Attachment object also has several other properties, described in Table A.19.

Table A.19   Properties of the Attachment Object

Name	Returns	Description
Name	String	Specifies the display name of the attachment.
Type	Variant	Determines what type of attachment it is, one of CdoEmbeddedMessage, CdoFileData, CdoFileLink, or CdoOLE.
Index	Long	Read Only. Indicates the position of this object within the Attachments collection.
Position	Long	Indicates the character position of this attachment within a Rich Text message.
Source	Variant	The value of this property is interpreted differently depending on the Type property. In the case of a file attachment (CdoFileData or CdoFileLink), this property contains the full path and filename. For an embedded message (CdoEmbeddedMessage), Source is equal to the unique ID of the desired Message object. Finally, in the case of an attached OLE object (CdoOLE), this property contains the OLE class name of the item.
Fields	Variant	Read Only. This property returns either a Field object (if there is only one Field) or a Fields collection (if there are multiple fields available).

Attachment Methods

The Attachment object has several important methods, listed and described in Table A.20, including two that it shares with the Field object. These two methods, ReadFromFile and WriteToFile, allow you to easily move Attachment object data to and from the file system.

Table A.20   Methods of the Attachment Object

Name	Returns	Parameters	Description
Delete			Deletes the object.
ReadFromFile		FileName	Loads the attachment from a file using the supplied filename and path.

continues ▶

Table A.20   continued

Name	Returns	Parameters	Description
WriteToFile		FileName	Writes the attachment out to file using the supplied parameter to determine the name and path.
IsSameAs	Boolean	Object	Given another object as a parameter, this method returns True if both the supplied object and this attachment refer to the same item.

AddressEntry Object

The most detailed object used to represent a person's address is the AddressEntry object, available from an AddressList through the AddressEntries collection and from a Recipient object through its AddressEntry property.

AddressEntry Properties

All CDO objects have the common properties Session (representing the current CDO Session object) and Class (numeric value representing which object you are working with). The AddressEntry object also has several other important properties, all of which are described in Table A.21.

Table A.21   Properties of the AddressEntry Object

Name	Returns	Description
DisplayType	Variant	This property specifies what type of entry this is, such as a distribution list (CdoDistList) or a regular user (CdoUser).
Name	String	This property contains the display name of this entry, such as the user's name.
Address	String	Specifies the address information (without the type, just duncanma@microsoft.com, for example) for this object.
Type	String	Indicates the type portion of the messaging address like "SMTP", "X.400".
ID	Variant	Returns the unique identifier for this object.
Manager	Address Entry	Returns an AddressEntry object corresponding to this person's manager, if one exists.
Members	Address Entries	In the case of a distribution list, this property returns an Address Entries collection of the members of that list.
Fields	Variant	This property returns either a Field object (if there is only one field) or a Fields collection (if there is more than one).

AddressEntry Methods

Several key methods are provided by the AddressEntry object (listed in Table in A.22), in addition to those methods common to all the CDO objects.

Table A.22   Methods of the AddressEntry Object

Name	Returns	Parameters	Description
Details		[Parent Window]	Displays the properties window for this entry as a modal dialog box.
Update		[Make Permanent] [Refresh Object]	Saves changes to the object. The two parameters specify whether the update should be done right to permanent storage and whether the properties of the object should be reloaded from disk.
Delete			Deletes this object.
IsSameAs	Boolean	Object	This common CDO method takes an object as a parameter and returns True if the passed item refers to the same AddressEntry as this object.
GetFreeBusy	String	StartTime, EndTime, Interval	This method is the same as the corresponding method on the Recipients collection, except it is only working against this single AddressEntry object. See Table A.15 for more information.

MessageFilter Object

This object is used to specify a filter for a Messages collection. It is obtained from the Filter property of a Messages collection and takes effect as soon as you attempt to retrieve an item from that collection.

MessageFilter Properties

The MessageFilter object contains the following properties that correspond to Message object properties and are used to indicate that the messages will be filtered based on that property and the specified value:

- Conversation
- Importance
- Recipients
- Sender
- Sent

- Size
- Text
- TimeFirst, TimeLast—Used together to specify a range for filtering based on the message's arrival time
- Type (Message Class, such as IPM.Note)
- Unread

Note that all of the preceding properties are represented as variants, as opposed to a specific data type like a Boolean. This is due to the fact that you have the option of not setting a property at all, not specifying that Unread is equal to True or False, but instead indicating it is nothing and therefore not used as part of the filter.

An example of using this object is to set its Unread property to True, which filters the Messages collection to include only those message whose Unread property is also equal to True. There are two specific properties (described in Table A.23) of this object that are not used for the purpose described earlier and are used to determine how all of the other properties will be interpreted.

Table A.23   *Logical Expression Properties of the MessageFilter Object*

Name	Returns	Description
Not	Boolean	If this property is set to True, all of the restrictions set up using the other object properties (listed in the preceding bulleted list) are treated as if they have a NOT in front of them.
		This means that if this property is True and the Unread property is set to True, the filter would restrict the message collection such that only messages where Unread is NOT True are included.
Or	Boolean	This property, if set to True, indicates that all of the other properties specified should be treated as if they are multiple clauses separated by an OR clause, as opposed to the default interpretation where they are connected by AND clauses. If two other properties are set, such as Unread to True and Importance to CdoHigh, and this property is True, all messages where the message is Unread OR of high importance are included. If this property is set to False (the default), only messages that are both Unread and of high importance are included.

AppointmentItem Object

At one time, in MAPI, there was no distinction between messages and Calendar items; everything was a message. This is still true to a certain extent in the underlying system(s), so this object shares many properties and methods with the Message item. These shared attributes, listed in the following, are detailed in the Message item, and only those properties or methods that are specific to this object are covered in the sections that follow:

- FolderID
- StoreID
- ID
- Type
- Size
- Importance
- Subject
- Sender
- TimeSent
- TimeReceived
- Text
- Sent
- Submitted
- Unread
- Signed
- Encrypted
- ReadReceipt
- DeliveryReceipt
- ConversationIndex
- ConversationTopic
- Fields
- Recipients
- Attachments
- Categories
- TimeCreated
- TimeExpired
- TimeLastModified
- Sensitivity

- (method) Delete
- (method) Update
- (method) Options
- (method) CopyTo
- (method) MoveTo
- (method) Send
- (method) Respond
- (method) Forward

AppointmentItem Properties

Although many of the AppointmentItem properties are common with the Message object, and several others are common with most CDO objects, Table A.24 lists the few unique attributes that this object has.

Table A.24   Properties of the AppointmentItem Object

Name	Returns	Description
AllDayEvent	Boolean	Indicates whether this appointment is an all-day event.
BusyStatus	Variant	Indicates how this appointment should be placed into the calendar of the creating user (CdoBusy, CdoTentative, and so on).
Duration	Long	Returns the duration of this appointment in minutes.
EndTime	Date	Indicates the end date/time of this appointment.
StartTime	Date	Indicates the starting date/time of this appointment.
IsRecurring	Boolean	Specifies whether this appointment is a recurring appointment.
Location	String	This property contains the location of the appointment.
MeetingStatus	Variant	Indicates if this Appointment item is a meeting (an appointment with other people, CdoMeeting, CdoMeetingCanceled, or CdoMeetingReceived) or just an appointment for the current user (CdoNonMeeting).
Organizer	Address Entry	Read Only. Returns an AddressEntry object corresponding to the creator of the Appointment item.

Name	Returns	Description
Reminder Minutes BeforeStart	Long	Indicates how long (in minutes) before this appointment a reminder should be given. Note that the reminder only occurs if ReminderSet is also set to True.
ReminderSet	Boolean	Indicates whether a reminder should occur for this appointment.
ReplyTime	Date	Specifies a date/time by which a meeting request must be replied to. Only applies when this item has had such a date set and when it is in another user's folder other than the organizer's. An attempt to use this property when it has not been set results in an error.
Response Requested	Boolean	This property is only valid for appointment items that are meetings (includes more than the one user). This indicates whether the organizer of the meeting would like a response to the meeting request.
Meeting Response Status	Variant	Read Only. This property only applies when you are dealing with an Appointment item that was retrieved from a MeetingItem object's GetAssociatedAppointment method. In such a case, this property indicates whether the user responded with Accepted (CdoResponseAccepted), Declined (CdoResponseDeclined), or Tentative.

AppointmentItem Methods

As with properties, the AppointmentItem object has only a few methods specific to it. These few methods are listed in Table A.25.

Table A.25   Methods of the AppointmentItem Object

Name	Returns	Parameters	Description
Send		[SaveCopy], [Show Dialog], [Parent Window]	Sends the item. If ShowDialog is set to True, MAPI may put a dialog box up if necessary.
Respond	Meeting Item	RespondType	This method returns a MeetingItem object, which is used to indicate a response to a meeting request. The To field is pre-filled in this case with the sender of the original item.

continues ▶

Table A.25   continued

Name	Returns	Parameters	Description
Forward	Variant		Returns a new object of the same type, without setting up any default recipient.
GetRecurrence Pattern	Recurrence Pattern		Returns a RecurrencePattern object, which describes the appointment's recurrence information.
Clear Recurrence Pattern			Totally removes recurrence settings from an Appointment object.

MeetingItem Object

Responses to meeting requests come in the form of MeetingItem objects, indicating the respondent's attendance at the meeting. As a message that is sent through the regular MAPI system, this object's properties and methods are almost a complete duplicate of the Message object. Only those attributes that are not from that object, or that have some different behavior, will be listed in this section.

MeetingItem Properties

The MeetingItem object has only one property (the MeetingType property, described in Table A.26) beyond those common to most CDO objects.

Table A.26   The MeetingType Property of the MeetingItem Object

Name	Returns	Description
MeetingType	Variant	Returns either CdoMeetingRequest or CdoMeetingResponse, indicating whether this is a request for a meeting or a response to such a request.

MeetingItem Methods

The MeetingItem object has two critical methods (both described in Table A.27): Respond, which allows you to accept or reject a meeting request, and GetAssociatedAppointment, which retrieves the AppointmentItem object that corresponds to this meeting request. This second method is essential because it allows you to get at all the important properties of the AppointmentItem, such as StartDate, which are not available through the MeetingItem object.

Table A.27   Methods of the MeetingItem object

Name	Returns	Parameters	Description
Respond	Meeting Item	Respond Type	As described earlier with the MeetingType property, this object can either be a meeting request or a response. If it is a request, this method allows you to create a response. The parameter, RespondType, takes a value of CdoResponseAccepted, CdoResponseDeclined, or CdoResponseTenative and creates the appropriately configured response message.
GetAssociated Appointment	Appointment Item		Returns the corresponding appointment to this request or response.

RecurrencePattern Object

A property of an AppointmentItem object, this object is used to describe the details of that appointment's recurrence pattern.

RecurrencePattern Properties

The properties of the RecurrencePattern object (described in Table A.28) allow you to specify all the details of when the associated AppointmentItem will occur.

Table A.28   Properties of the RecurrencePattern Object

Name	Returns	Description
DayOfMonth	Integer	Indicates the numeric day of the month on which the appointment should reoccur (1 to 31). If 31 is used, it indicates the last day of the month, regardless of the actual number of days in a specific month.
DayOfWeekMask	Integer	A binary mask indicates on which days of the week the appointment should reoccur. This mask is made up by ORing the values CdoMonday to CdoSunday (each of which has a binary value; 1,2,4,8 . . . 64).
Duration, EndTime, StartTime	Variant	Equivalent to the same properties from the AppointmentItem and default to the values from that underlying object.

continues ▶

Table A.28   continued

Name	Returns	Description
Instance	Variant	Used to indicate on which occurrence (within a year or month) of a certain day the appointment should occur. For instance, the third Tuesday of the month would be indicated by a 3 in this property. The last occurrence of a day in a month is indicated by a 5 in this property.
Interval	Variant	Indicates how many units (defined by the rest of the settings) should occur between appointments. Used for pattern elements, such as "Every other Tuesday."
MonthOfYear	Integer	Used to specify the month in which this pattern is to occur, 1–12 is used with the CdoRecurTypeYearlyNth recurrence type.
NoEndDate	Boolean	Indicates whether this pattern is to occur for an infinite period of time.
Occurrences	Variant	Indicates how many times this pattern should occur; not valid if NoEndDate is True.
PatternEnd Date	Date	Sets the date on or before this pattern ends.
PatternStart Date	Date	Sets the date on or after this recurrence pattern begins.
Recurrence Type	Variant	This property is key in defining the recurrence, because it sets the overall type of recurrence that is being set up. This value can be one of CdoRecurTypeDaily, CdoRecurTypeWeekly, CdoRecurTypeMonthly, CdoRecurTypeYearly, CdoRecurTypeWeeklyNth, or CdoRecurTypeYearlyNth. The difference between the various types is best understood by looking at the Recurrence dialog box provided by Outlook. The two last types, WeeklyNth and YearlyNth indicate the weekly and yearly recurrence types where the appointment is set to occur on the Nth (First, Second) Day, Weekday, and so on, of a month.

Setting Up Your Project to Use CDO

Before you can use CDO in your VB or VBA project, you must make sure it is installed on your machine. There are a variety of ways to do this, but the simplest is to open up the References dialog box in your development tool (under the Project menu in VB, and the Tools menu in VBA). This brings up a dialog box listing all the available COM libraries registered on your system. If the CDO library is available, there will be an entry for Microsoft CDO 1.21 Library. If there is no such entry, you do not have CDO on your machine, and you have to install it. It is an optional installation component in Office 2000 and is also available on the Web at `http://www.microsoft.com/exchange/55/downloads/cdo.htm`.

If it does appear in the list, or is in the list after you install CDO and reopen the References dialog box, the next step to set up your project to use CDO is to check it off in the list. This sets a reference to the CDO library from your project and allows you to declare and use object types from that library. At this point, you are ready to start programming.

Using the Object Browser to Explore the CDO Library

Although this appendix has provided detailed documentation of the CDO library, this is not the only way you can learn about the available objects and their properties and methods. A very useful resource for you as a developer, when working with any object library, is the Object Browser dialog box. This dialog box, available through the View menu or the F2 key in both the VBA editor and VB itself, shows you all the available objects in all the referenced object libraries.

Figure A.1   *The Object Browser allows you to select a library using its drop-down menu and view all the objects exposed by that library. Selecting an individual object displays that object's properties, methods, and events in the right-hand pane.*

Use this tool as a resource for learning more about CDO (which is called the MAPI library inside the Object Browser) and any new object libraries. This includes the new versions of CDO available in Exchange 2000 and Windows 2000, which are discussed in the next section.

CDO in Exchange 2000 and Windows 2000

Both Exchange 2000 and Windows 2000 include new versions of CDO, with some new features and a large number of the existing objects that are detailed in this appendix. Neither of these libraries are replacements for the CDO library discussed here; they can and do coexist on a single machine. These libraries do provide some new functionality over the previous CDO libraries, and some different ways of using existing objects. Full documentation on both of these versions of CDO is available on the MSDN Web site (http://msdn.microsoft.com), so explore them and experiment as you want. Just remember that when you are coding with these libraries, you are creating code that might not run on all your user's machines, because they might not be all running Windows 2000; but CDO 1.21 has been available on all Windows platforms since Outlook 98. In addition, in the case of the Exchange 2000 CDO libraries, they might not work except on the server. Use these new libraries only when and if you are sure of their availability. If you only need to send email from behind a Web page and do not require any advanced Exchange specific features, you might consider using CDO for NT Server (CDONTS) instead. This library is designed to work in conjunction with the SMTP services of IIS or Exchange and handle simple mailing tasks. CDONTS is also documented on http://msdn.microsoft.com.

Summary

The CDO libraries are key to working programmatically with Exchange and Outlook and are often used in addition to, or instead of, the objects exposed by the Outlook application itself. Use the information in this chapter to guide your use of these objects, combined with other available resources such as the MSDN libraries available with VB or on the Web (at http://msdn.microsoft.com). With these libraries, you can accomplish anything that you need to do in a collaborative application.

Additional sources of information include the following:

- http://www.cdolive.com

- http://www.microeye.com

- http://www.slipstick.com

- http://msdn.microsoft.com/library/psdk

B

Handling Common Errors in CDO

For a variety of reasons, errors occur all the time when working within Outlook, but in most cases, Outlook deals with them and does not abort. This is because the programmers who wrote Microsoft Outlook knew what types of errors were likely to occur and planned for them. This appendix will help you do the same when you are working with CDO in your programs. Being prepared for errors involves two key elements, both of which are discussed in this appendix: catching the errors when they happen and knowing what error is likely to occur in what situation. When both are taken care of, your program can trap and properly handle the errors that are almost guaranteed to arise.

Trapping Errors in Your Code

Both VB and VBA provide the same mechanism for you to handle errors—the On Error statement. This line of code sets an option, which is used until the end of the current procedure or until another On Error statement is encountered. The option you set determines exactly what occurs when an error is encountered in your code, and can be one of three different options:

- On Error GoTo *<Label>*
- On Error Resume Next
- On Error GoTo 0

The first option, On Error GoTo *<Label>*, indicates that, from that line on (until the end of the procedure or another On Error statement), if an error occurs, the program should immediately jump to the specified Label and execute the code found in that location. An example of this type of error handling is shown in Example B.1.

Example B.1 *On Error GoTo <Label> error handling*

```
Private Sub ErrorHandling()
On Error GoTo MyErrorHandler

Dim X As Integer

    X = 3 / 0

    Exit Sub

MyErrorHandler:

    MsgBox "Error!! Error!!"
    Resume Next

End Sub
```

The On Error statement at the beginning of the procedure means that when an error occurs, such as a Division By Zero error on the line x = 3/0, the code after the label MyErrorHandler is executed. In your error handler, you can choose to have the code resume execution on the line that caused the error (using the Resume statement), on the line after that line (the Resume Next statement), or you can simply exit the program using Exit Sub or Exit Function. Of course, using the Resume statement indicates that you have dealt with the error, or else it will keep occurring. Inside the error handler, you have access to complete information about the error itself, all through the Err object, including its number (Err.Number) and description (Err.Description).

However, from this object, you do not have access to any information that tells you what line caused the error. In the preceding example, this isn't difficult to determine; in a 100-line procedure, you likely have several lines that could cause an error, and you might want to deal with errors in one line differently than another. This type of situation is why there is the second type of On Error statement, On Error Resume Next.

On Error Resume Next tells the program not to jump anywhere if an error occurs, but to simply continue and execute the next line. This can be used in two situations: when you don't care if an error occurs, in which case you use this statement to ignore them, or when performing a type of error handling called inline error handling. We will not pay much attention to the first case—ignoring errors is easy—but the second is a bit more interesting. Example B.2 shows inline error handling.

Example B.2   *Inline error handling*

```
Private Sub ErrorHandling()
On Error Resume Next

Dim X As Integer
Dim Y As Integer

    X = 3 / 0
    If Err.Number <> 0 Then

        MsgBox "Error calculating X!"
        Err.Clear

    End If

    Y = 3 / 5
    If Err.Number <> 0 Then

        MsgBox "Error calculating Y!"
        Err.Clear

    End If

End Sub
```

You place code after each line where you expect an error might occur; if an error did occur, the code handles it accordingly. This allows you to handle errors based on the context within which they occurred.

The third type of On Error statement, On Error GoTo 0, turns off error handling from that line on, telling the program to handle the error by simply raising it to the next procedure in the calling chain. This is the default method of handling errors. Eventually (if no procedures up the calling chain have an error handling routine), a run-time error is displayed to the user and the program ungracefully ends. Because this is the type of event you are trying to avoid by implementing error handling, this form of the On Error statement is not very common.

Common CDO Errors

If you want your program to do more than just announce the fact that some error has occurred, you need to recognize the most common errors that can occur in different situations. This section details, by activity, the errors that are most commonly raised and what causes them. How you handle the error is dependent on your program, but knowing why it has occurred will help. Many of the errors described under one activity can actually occur in a variety of locations, a fact that is noted as each is covered.

Logging In

At the start of any work with CDO, you log in to your Session object, which establishes the connection between that instance of the CDO library and the underlying MAPI system. Many things can go wrong at this point in the process; performing some error handling here is essential. In most cases, the errors are such that your code cannot fix them (for example, the network is down or there is an invalid user ID), but you can at least attempt to give a message that directs the user to the likely cause of the problem.

What's Up With Those Weird Negative Error Numbers?

Errors from CDO use quite large error numbers, usually around –214722xxxx. This can make your error handlers look quite complex and reduce the readability of your code. For that reason, you might want to trap for these errors in a different way. One alternative is to go by the MAPI error code string that is included in the Err.Description result. This value, such as MAPI_E_LOGON_FAILED, is quite readable and easily checked for using a function like Instr. Another alternative, slightly less clear but still produces more readable code, is to add the value of vbObjectError to all the error numbers before checking them. This has the effect of reducing all the numbers down to simple integers like 273 or 305. Both methods have their benefits, but either is usually easier to use than working with the numbers as they are returned to you.

The most common error you will receive is that the logon failed. This returns an error number of –2147221231 and an error description that includes the string MAPI_E_LOGON_FAILED. This particular error, as vague as it is, can happen for a number of reasons, including the following:

- Specifying a profile name that doesn't exist.
- Specifying an incorrect profile password.
- Specifying NewSession as False when there is no existing session (see the upcoming discussion about the ShowDialog parameter).
- Mailbox specified does not exist.
- User does not have sufficient rights to the mailbox.
- Exchange Server does not exist or is down.
- User is not on the network, or network connection is not functioning. (If this occurs after logon, a different error is caused; see the "Accessing Folders, Items, and Properties" section later in this appendix for more information.)

The errors and effects of these errors can greatly differ depending on the value passed for the ShowDialog parameter. If this parameter is True (or omitted), MAPI pops up a dialog box of its own to deal with many errors.

In such a case, your program might not receive an error at all, or it might receive a different error. One common error when MAPI is allowed to display its own UI occurs when the user presses Cancel on one of those dialog boxes. This event causes an error number of –221229 with a MAPI error message of MAPI_E_USER_CANCE.

A final error that can occur, although it should be infrequent, is when the NT User ID your program is executing under Does Not Have Permissions for the Exchange mailbox you are trying to open. This produces an insufficient permissions error with –221219 as the error number and MAPI_E_FAILONEPROVIDER as the text error message.

The errors listed previously do not provide a complete listing of everything that might occur, so you should always allow for the possibility of an unexpected error in your code. A good way to handle this possibility is through a final clause in your error handler that handles all errors not explicitly caught. A sample Logon routine is shown in Example B.3, complete with detailed error handling.

Example B.3   *Sample Logon routine*

```
Private Function Logon() As MAPI.Session
On Error Resume Next
Dim objSession As MAPI.Session
Dim sErrorMessage As String

    Set objSession = CreateObject("MAPI.Session")

    If Err.Number <> 0 Then
        sErrorMessage = "Error Creating CDO Object." & _
        vbCrLf & "Check to insure that CDO is installed correctly."

        MsgBox "There has been an error." & vbCrLf _
        & sErrorMessage, vbCritical, "Logon Error"

        Err.Clear
        Exit Function
    End If

objSession.Logon

If Err.Number <> 0 Then
    If Err.Source = "Collaboration Data Objects" Then
        'CDO Error
        Select Case Err.Number

            Case -2147221231
                'MAPI_E_LOGON_FAILED
                sErrorMessage = "The logon has failed, please ensure " _
                & "that your mail settings are all correct " _
                & vbCrLf & "and that you are able to logon with Outlook"
```

continues ▶

Example B.3   *continued*

```
            Case -2147221227
                'MAPI_E_NETWORK_ERROR
                sErrorMessage = "The logon has failed, please check to " _
                & "make sure your network connection " _
                & vbCrLf & "is available and functioning correctly. " _
                & "If it is, then your mail server may " _
                & vbCrLf & "be unavailable."

            Case -2147221229
                'MAPI_E_USER_CANCEL
                sErrorMessage = "You have selected Cancel on one of " _
                & "the dialogs that are needed" _
                & vbCrLf & "to establish a mail session. " _
                & vbCrLf & "The logon was aborted."

            Case Else
                sErrorMessage = "An unexpected CDO error has occured," _
                & vbCrLf & "please contact your system administrator." _
                & vbCrLf & vbCrLf & Err.Number & " " & Err.Description

        End Select
    Else 'not a CDO error
        sErrorMessage = "An unexpected error has occured," _
        & "please contact your system administrator." _
        & vbCrLf & vbCrLf & Err.Number & " " & _
        Err.Description & vbCrLf & Err.Source
    End If

    MsgBox sErrorMessage, vbCritical, "Logon Error"

    Exit Function

    End If

    Set Logon = objSession

End Function
```

Of course, your error handling code does not have to be quite as complex, but the general concept is the same; trap the errors you expect and provide some code to handle those errors you do not expect. Finally, to best handle unexpected errors and update your program to deal with those errors in the future, always log errors (to a text file, the event viewer, or even into a custom database) with their number and description if possible. A complete listing of the MAPI error codes is provided in the Microsoft knowledge base article Q238119, which you can find on the Microsoft Product Support Web site at `http://support.microsoft.com`. You will find this a useful reference.

Accessing Folders, Items, and Properties

Many errors can occur when you attempt to access an item, a folder, or even an individual property. Several of these errors are the same regardless of which of those activities you are trying to access. This section will discuss many of the more common errors.

When attempting to access a folder that does not exist, trapping the error generated can be a little tricky. This is due to how CDO handles the folder access. If you are using a numeric index to access the folder, such as objInbox.Folders(3), and that index does not exist, the error is Subscript Out of Range. On the other hand, if you are using the folder's name as an index (a much more common method, because numeric indexes can change, using code like objInbox.Folders(Whatever)), CDO tries to find the closest match. This means that the name you search for could return a completely different folder. For instance, using an index of Whatever could match up to a folder named Writing. In such a case, no error would occur at all. Finally, another possibility is that the folder does not exist and a close match is not available (there are no sub-folders at all, for instance), in which case a MAPI_E_NOT_FOUND error occurs, with an error number of –2147221233.

Invalid permissions is another common problem that happens when accessing almost any type of object. This means that the logged on user does not have the right to view or change that item or one of its properties. This type of error brings up an error string of E_ACCESSDENIED and an error number of –2147024891.

Finally, and this is a potential problem at almost any time, general network problems are a common cause of errors. This type of error occurs when the local CDO code could not talk to the server at that moment, even though a connection had been established at some point. The error message contains the string MAPI_E_NETWORK_ERROR, and the error number is –2147221227. Keep in mind that this error can happen at almost any time (reading a property, working with a collection, saving, sending, and so on), whenever the local CDO code would have to talk to the server.

Working with Recipients

When working with the Recipients collection (such as on a new message), you need to watch out for problems with address resolution (when you call the collection's Resolve method or the same method on a single Recipient object). If ShowDialog is set to False, this error causes a trappable error of –2147221233 (MAPI_E_NOT_FOUND). If ShowDialog is set to True, this same event displays a dialog box asking the user to pick the correct name from the available address lists. (If the user cancels that dialog box, the standard Cancel error MAPI_E_USER_CANCEL occurs.) If, instead, you go ahead and send the message without having resolved your address, you get the very useful E_FAIL error message, error number –2147467259.

Sending, Saving, Copying, and Moving Items

All these actions involve one main thing: They require an update to the underlying storage device, the Information Store in Exchange. This means that any one of these actions can cause some of the same errors.

A common error that can occur during any of these actions is that the user's mailbox quota has been exceeded. If this occurs, the error is not really helpful. The client operation would fail with an error number of –2147467259 and error text containing the code E_FAIL.

When copying almost any item or collection of items, error number –2147219964, MAPI_E_COLLISION, can occur. This indicates that the copy could not complete because another item of the same name already exists in the destination (usually a folder, because two messages with the same name is allowed). Another potential problem when copying is that you cannot copy a folder (and its subfolders) into a position beneath itself. This produces the error text MAPI_W_PARTIAL_COMPLETION and an error number (bucking the trend of large negative numbers) of 263808. In addition to the errors listed previously, any of these actions can cause permission errors, network errors, and even a MAPI_E_NOT_FOUND error (which occurs when attempting to copy into a folder that doesn't exist). For that reason, you should always trap for those types of errors, regardless of what activity is going on.

Appendix Summary

In this appendix, although we have covered a small subset of the huge number of errors that can occur in a collaborative application, we have covered some of the most common ones. Use this information, along with the error handling information at the start of this appendix, to make your applications work in a smooth, robust fashion.

C

Real-Time Collaborative Possibilities with Exchange 2000

By far, one of the most exciting upgrades to Exchange 2000, beyond that of its enhanced base messaging and storage capabilities, is its new capability to support real-time collaboration.

In this appendix, we will explore Exchange 2000's enhanced chat services, instant messaging services, and data conferencing and application sharing. Individually, these features add an extremely enhanced level of collaboration within an organization. Combined, these features completely change how people in an organization communicate.

Enhanced Chat Services

An existing feature of Exchange that has been upgraded to meet the growing demands of corporations is the Microsoft Exchange Chat Service. The Microsoft Exchange Chat Service is now extremely scalable, capable of supporting up to 20,000 users while providing extremely tight integration with Windows 2000 Active Directory.

With the Chat Service, users can join channels, otherwise known as chat rooms, which are organized into virtual communities in a public or private setting. The Microsoft Exchange Chat Service can host many chat communities at the same time and can be used by organizations to provide forums of communication for almost any reason.

Additionally, the Chat Service is fully compatible with many chat clients, including the following:

- Any application that supports the IRC protocol, such as PIRCH or mIRC.
- Microsoft Chat version 2.1 and later, which uses IRCX. IRCX is Microsoft's proposed extension to the standard IRC protocol.

Specifically for collaborative developers, Microsoft has created a Chat SDK, which is basically a collection of ActiveX and Java controls that you can use to imbed chat interfaces in almost any application or Web page. This SDK can be downloaded from http://msdn.Microsoft.com/Downloads.

The Chat SDK also contains information on the Chat Server object model and the Chat Server Extensibility API. Using the Chat Server object model and Extensibility APIs, developers can easily extend the base functionality of the chat service to better fit their environment. Sample Chat Server extensions can be found in the Chat SDK for reference purposes.

Instant Messaging Services

Instant messaging is not new. In fact, any user can download a free instant messaging client, called the MSN Messenger, from the MSN home site. The only requirement of the MSN Messenger is that each user must have a HotMail account. Microsoft Exchange now provides facilities to host more centralized instant messaging activity by providing an Instant Messaging Server. Now, users can use the features of instant messaging without requiring a HotMail account.

Instant messaging allows for the immediate transmission of messages within or across organizations. One of the greatest features of instant messaging is that users can see presence information for those they communicate most frequently with. In fact, you can instantly see whether the person you want to instant message with is online, out of the office, out to lunch, on the phone, or simply not online. In fact, presence detection in Exchange Server 2000 is itself considered a form of collaboration.

You can text conference easily with instant messaging as well by inviting more that one person at a time to join a conversation. The instant messaging client used with Exchange 2000 has the capability to simultaneously support instant messaging on the Exchange Server as well as the MSN network. Used with MSN, the client requires a HotMail account.

Instant messaging can be using in a wide range of applications in almost any collaborative solution. It is important to note that the MSN instant messaging client has a rich object model that can be exploited to add instant messaging to any environment that can utilize COM objects.

Data Conferencing and Application Sharing

If you are familiar with products, such as NetMeeting, you should be familiar with the services that are provided with data conferencing and application sharing. In fact, with this service, users can schedule and hold regular online meetings, providing live audio and video, white boarding, chat, file sharing, and application sharing. Meetings can be held in either a private or public venue with two or more people. Data conferencing and application sharing are based on the T.120 standard, offering an enterprise-ready, client-server solution for real-time multimedia conferencing.

Microsoft Exchange also provides a conferencing service that acts as a centralized conference reservation system. Exchange users have the ability to schedule and join meetings directly from their Outlook calendars. More importantly, all meetings are hosted by an Exchange server, not by another client computer on the network.

The Microsoft Exchange Conferencing Service also allows developers to develop and add their own conferencing technologies that complement existing functionality provided by the service.

What Is T.120?

Simply stated, T.120 is a suite of communication and application protocols developed and published by the International Telecommunication Union (ITU). T.120 allows developers to create real-time products, such as conferencing applications or multipoint data connections.

Specifically, T.120 provides the following:

- *Allows multiple users to send and receive data in real time without errors.*
- *T.120 supports multiple topologies and protocols.*
- *T.120 can be integrated into applications that support other ITU standards, such as those that support audio and video conferencing (H.323).*

Note that you can download the NetMeeting SDK, including documentation and sample applications, which allows you to extend any application to take advantage of these services. The NetMeeting SDK can be downloaded from `http://msdn.Microsoft.com/downloads`.

Summary

Real-time collaborative solutions are gaining an extreme amount of momentum in the world of advanced collaborative computing. Once viewed as an unnecessary use of bandwidth, collaborative computing is now being considered an extremely important tool that helps increase productivity by enhancing the way we communicate, even across great distances. The services provided as part of Microsoft Exchange 2000, such as an enhanced chat service, instant messaging service, and conferencing service helps organizations meet the growing requirements of communication.

Index

Symbols

G

H

I

M

Selected Titles from the
New Riders Professional Library

Sandra Osborne:	*Windows NT Registry* ISBN: 1-56205-941-6
Mark Edmead and Paul Hinsberg:	*Windows NT Performance: Monitoring, Benchmarking, and Tuning* ISBN: 1-56205-942-4
Karanjit Siyan:	*Windows NT TCP/IP* ISBN: 1-56205-887-8
Ted Harwood:	*Windows NT Terminal Server and Citrix MetaFrame* ISBN: 1-56205-944-0
Anil Desai:	*Windows NT Network Management: Reducing Total Cost of Ownership* ISBN: 1-56205-946-7
Eric K. Cone, Jon Boggs, and Sergio Perez:	*Planning for Windows 2000* ISBN: 0-7357-0048-6
Doug Hauger, Marywynne Leon, and William C. Wade III:	*Implementing Exchange Server* ISBN: 1-56205-931-9
Janice Rice Howd:	*Exchange System Administration* ISBN: 0-7357-0081-8
Sean Baird and Chris Miller:	*SQL Server System Administration* ISBN: 1-56205-955-6
Stu Sjouwerman and Ed Tittel:	*Windows NT Power Toolkit* ISBN: 0-7357-0922-X
Roger Abell, Herman Knief, Andrew Daniels, Jeffrey Graham:	*Windows 2000 DNS* ISBN: 0-7357-0973-4
Lori Sanders:	*Windows 2000 User Management* ISBN: 1-56205-886-X
Jeffrey Ferris:	*Windows 2000 Deployment and Desktop Management* ISBN: 0-7357-095-0
Doug and Beth Sheresh:	*Understanding Directory Services* ISBN: 0-7357-0910-6
Michael Martin:	*Understanding the Network* ISBN: 0-7357-0977-7
Gilbert Held:	*Understanding Data Communications* ISBN: 0-7357-0036-2

The Circle Series from MTP

March 2000

Thomas Eck:
Windows NT/2000 ADSI Scripting for System Administration
ISBN: 1-57870-219-4

February 2000

Gary Nebett:
Windows NT/2000 Native API
ISBN: 1-57870-199-6

January 2000

Eric Harmon:
Delphi COM Programming
ISBN: 1-57870-221-6

October 1999

Tim Hill:
Windows Script Host
ISBN: 1-57870-139-2

Paul Hinsberg:
Windows NT Applications: Measuring and Optimizing Performance
ISBN: 1-57870-176-7

William Zack:
Windows 2000 and Mainframe Integration
ISBN: 1-57870-200-3

September 1999

David Iseminger:
Windows 2000 Quality of Service
ISBN: 1-57870-115-5

August 1999

Sean Deuby:
Windows 2000 Server: Planning and Migration
ISBN: 1-57870-023-X

February 1999

Gregg Branham:
Windows NT Domain Architecture
ISBN: 1-57870-112-0

January 1999

David Roth:
Win32 Perl Programming: The Standard Extensions
ISBN: 1-57870-067-1

November 1998

Peter Viscarola/Anthony Mason:
Windows NT Device Driver Development
ISBN: 1-57870-058-2

Steve Thomas:
Windows NT Heterogeneous Networking
ISBN: 1-57870-064-7

Todd Mathers/Shawn Genoway:
Windows NT Thin Client Solutions: Implementing Terminal Server and Citrix MetaFrame
ISBN: 1-57870-065-5